Praise for

Inventing Collateral Damage

We may prefer to act as though the crimes that war inflicts on civilians are too horrible to consider, but – as this book correctly insists – those crimes are too horrible to ignore. Here is a book that challenges us to move beyond the moral fog of war's euphemisms and cover stories.

> – Norman Solomon, author, *War Made Easy: How Presidents and Pundits Keep Spinning Us to Death*

It is often stated that it is only recently that civilians have comprised the majority of casualties in war. This wide-ranging and stimulating collection shows that civilian harm has a long history, especially in colonial wars. The volume explores the many ways in which civilians have been affected, and is a valuable addition to the literature.

> – Martin Shaw, Research Professor of International Relations, University of Sussex

Inventing Collateral Damage

Civilian Casualities, War, and Empire

edited by
Stephen J. Rockel and Rick Halpern

Between the Lines
Toronto

Inventing Collateral Damage: Civilian Casualities, War, and Empire

© 2009 Stephen J. Rockel and Rick Halpern

First published in Canada in 2009 by
Between the Lines
720 Bathurst Street, Suite #404
Toronto, Ontario
M5S 2R4

1-800-718-7201

www.btlbooks.com

Library and Archives Canada Cataloguing in Publication

Inventing collateral damage: civilian casualities, war, and empire / edited by Stephen J. Rockel, Rick Halpern.
Includes index.
ISBN 978-1-897071-12-0

1. Civilian war casualties – History. 2. War victims – History. 3. War and society – History. 4. Military history. I. Rockel, Stephen J., 1956- II. Halpern, Rick
U21.5.I58 2009   303.6'6   C2009-904917-1

Cover design by Jennifer Tiberio
Page design and preparation by Steve Izma
Printed in Canada

Between the Lines gratefully acknowledges assistance for its publishing activities from the Canada Council for the Arts, the Ontario Arts Council, the Government of Ontario through the Ontario Book Publishers Tax Credit program and through the Ontario Book Initiative, and the Government of Canada through the Book Publishing Industry Development Program.

 Canada Council Conseil des Arts
for the Arts du Canada

Canadä

 ONTARIO ARTS COUNCIL
CONSEIL DES ARTS DE L'ONTARIO

Contents

Preface

This book, we believe, will make a significant contribution to an understanding of the notion of "collateral damage" and the politics and experience of civilian casualties in wars of various types, but especially in wars of conquest. The volume is an outcome of our highly successful conference, " 'Collateral Damage': Civilian Casualties from Antiquity through the Gulf Wars," held at the Munk Centre for International Studies, University of Toronto, in May 2004.

The aim of the conference was to interrogate the history of civilian casualties and the euphemism that currently functions to obscure the human costs of armed conflict. We hoped that this would be a real contribution to world history and contemporary debate, with examples from almost every continent, as well as discussions of ideology and discourse within the imperial capitals and colonial systems. In the selection of revised conference papers included here, official views, myth making, justifications, and manipulation of memory are contrasted with accounts of popular memories of abuses by armed forces, reportage of atrocities, reckoning of intended and unintended civilian casualties, and the social and economic consequences of the destruction of civil communities.

"Collateral damage" is a misunderstood, misrepresented, and all too commonly manipulated consequence of armed conflict. It is very much part of our contemporary lexicon, regularly invoked by military strategists, politicians, and pundits. As a practice and a discourse, according unarmed civilians a special status in war is not new, although definitional categories and boundaries have frequently been changed to suit the political interests of both victors and victims. Civilian casualties in warfare and debates over their status have a history stretching back to antiquity.[1] From ancient times to the present, perceptions of destruction and devastation have shaped public debate about the conduct, cost, and aims of military engagement. "The hard hand of war," as General Philip Sheridan termed it, has more often than not affected noncombatants both on the battlefield and in the civic realm.

The essays in this book seek to understand collateral damage by historicizing and analyzing the way in which the concept has evolved in speech and policy formulation. We believe this is a timely and significant topic for two major reasons. First, the debates over civilian casualties in recent conflicts often take place in a vacuum, without the aid of relevant historical and contextualizing information. Second, the topic is compelling precisely because "collateral damage" is typically deployed as a euphemism – and many people understand that it hides far more than it reveals. Moreover, the historical and analytical literature on this topic is surprisingly thin.[2] The question of civilian casualties in warfare needs to be distinguished from the related one of genocide, in which the destruction of civilian populations is a primary political and military objective. Another related, but still distinct, topic is that of massacre, recently the subject of a volume of essays.[3] Indeed, the paucity of scholarly material is evidenced by the fact that a recent collection focused specifically on civilian casualties largely avoids Africa, Asia, or the Americas.[4] Of course there is a monographic literature that takes up the issue of civilian death, particularly within the flourishing sub-field of war and society, and a large body of scholarly and practical legal work dealing with the laws of war as they pertain to non-combatants.[5] Closer to our concern, because it foregrounds issues of imperialism and race, is Sven Lindqvist's extended essay, "*Exterminate All the Brutes.*"[6] However, our perspective of studying collateral damage across time and space is a novel one that will yield significant comparative insight.

The chapters emphasize imperial and colonial conflicts involving the West and non-Western peoples, although non-European empires, particularly the Japanese empire, are not ignored. Europe itself is of special importance, both as the progenitor of modern imperialism and also as the epicentre of many of the best-known examples of extreme civilian suffering, especially during the Second World War. Hitler's conquests to the east were colonial wars as much as anything else. Further, medieval Europe and the Crusades and the seventeenth-century religious wars provide vital contextual material for understanding the modern period, drawing attention to early attempts to both limit and rationalize civilian casualties.[7] Several chapters cover civilians during the conquest and pacification of colonized peoples in the great European empires in the Americas, Asia, and Africa from the eighteenth century to the first half of the twentieth century, as well as wars of expansion in the settler states of North America and South Africa. Here we see that Western empires systematically denied the applicability of the rules of war or international law in conflicts between what were industrialized states and pre-industrial peoples. The violence of the colonial state in its formative years was deliberately rationalized. Indeed, there is no basis to conclude that liberal regimes in the West have not practised genocide in their imperial possessions, even if they no longer do so at home.[8] We also include case studies from the post-1945 period and on sexual violence as a weapon of war, a vital new area of investigation.[9] Finally, cultural and technological aspects of warfare are foregrounded. There are important chapters on the visual culture and media coverage of civilian casualties, and the often-misunderstood implications of the development of modern precision weapons.

The result enables us to present an integrated picture of changing attitudes in the West and elsewhere toward the "other" – civilians of non-Western cultures and societies in periods of conflict – and of how colonized and subject peoples fared during wars fought in and over their homelands. Thus questions related to "race," "civilization," "development," "gender," and "culture" are central. In addition, the book illuminates the recent debates over the rights and wrongs of the use of massive force to resolve conflicts, the consequences of changes in the nature of war, and the impact of the use of high-technology weapon systems on civilians.

The idea for the conference grew out of increasing concern over worldwide events after the September 11, 2001 attacks on the United States. But the germ of the idea was already present in our earlier work, concentrating as it does on issues of race, slavery, and empire in different contexts in Africa and North America. Two recent events in Afghanistan precipitated action. The first was the massacre of hundreds (figures vary from 300 to 1,200) of Pakistani Taliban volunteers and local civilians in Mazar-e-Sherif, northern Afghanistan, by Northern Alliance forces commandeered by General Abdul-Rashid Dostum, in November 2001, and the deliberate suffocation of many hundreds (one estimate is 960) of Taliban prisoners in container trucks en route from Konduz to Sheberghan. All of this took place with the tacit or after-the-fact approval of the United States, reminding observers that little seemed to have changed in terms of the long-standing failure of Western powers to observe or require observance by their proxies of the laws of war in conflicts with non-Western peoples.[10] The second, and an obvious example of "collateral damage," was the deaths of three young Afghan boys, victims of American bombs, on the northern edge of Kabul around the same time. They were watching American planes as they attacked Taliban positions. These boys were relatives of a University of Toronto student.

We would like to acknowledge generous conference support from a variety of sources. The Social Sciences and Humanities Research Council provided an Aid to Occasional Research Conferences Grant, while the Bissell-Heyd Chair of American Studies and the Centre for the Study of the United States equally underwrote many conference expenses. The Munk Centre for International Studies at the University of Toronto provided an excellent venue. The Departments of History, Political Science, Geography, and Fine Arts also chipped in. Thanks also to Joan Golding, who worked so hard on conference arrangements, to our colleagues in the Department of History who helped out as panel chairs, and to the graduate students who assisted in various ways. The Department of Humanities, University of Toronto Scarborough, provided aid at a critical moment. Without the constant support and intellectual engagement of Ansuya Chetty, this project would have been impossible. Finally, we must thank Dmitri Miletskii for his brilliant artwork, a focus of attention at the conference and featured on the back cover of this book and, equally, James Orbinski, for his permission to use it.

Notes

1 Thucydides, *History of the Peloponnesian War*, trans, Rex Warner (Harmondsworth, U.K.: Penguin, 1979).
2 The classic work is Michael Walzer, *Just and Unjust Wars: A Moral Argument with Historical Illustrations*, 3rd ed. (New York: Basic Books, 2000).
3 Mark Levene and Penny Roberts, eds. *The Massacre in History* (Providence: Berghahn, 1999).
4 Mark Grimsley and Clifford J. Rogers, eds. *Civilians in the Path of War* (Lincoln: University of Nebraska Press, 2002).
5 There are numerous treatises on this subject, for example, L.C. Green, *The Contemporary Law of Armed Conflict* (Manchester and New York: Manchester University Press, 1993). Most of the relevant international conventions are printed in Adam Roberts and Richard Guelff, eds., *Documents on the Laws of War*, 3rd ed. (Oxford: Clarendon Press, 2000).
6 Sven Lindqvist, *"Exterminate All the Brutes": One Man's Odyssey into the Heart of Darkness and the Origins of European Genocide*, trans. Joan Hay (New York: The New Press, 1996).
7 David Hay, who made an important contribution to the conference by highlighting debates in medieval Europe, opted to publish his paper elsewhere, but his work is discussed in the introduction.
8 Eric D. Weitz, "The Modernity of Genocides: War, Race, and Revolution in the Twentieth Century," in *The Specter of Genocide: Mass Murder in Historical Perspective*, ed. Robert Gellately and Ben Kiernan (Cambridge: Cambridge University Press, 2003), 56.
9 See the important debates in Lois Ann Lorentzen and Jennifer Turpin, eds., *The Women and War Reader* (New York and London: New York University Press, 1998).
10 For example, Robert Fisk, "We Are the War Criminals Now," *The Independent*, November 29, 2001. For a detailed investigation of "death by container" see Babak Dehghanpisheh, John Barry and Roy Gutman, "The Death Convoy of Afghanistan," *Newsweek*, August 26, 2002.

1 Stephen J. Rockel

Collateral Damage

A Comparative History

> They get in the way of bombs and bullets, stumble over mines,
> flee homes, clog roads, get sick, go hungry and generally out-
> number combatants when it comes to dying.
> — *Guardian Unlimited*, March 19, 2003

In February 2003 veteran Malaysian Prime Minister Mahathir Mohamad hosted two major international summits in Kuala Lumpur: the 116-member Non-Aligned Movement, and the 57-member Organization of the Islamic Conference. Long a strident critic of the West and immensely popular in his home country, Mr. Mahathir used his platforms to full effect. The conflicts of the new millennium, he told the assembled leaders at the Non-Aligned summit, were the consequence of "the old European trait of wanting to dominate the world.... The expression of this trait invariably involves injustice and oppression of people of other ethnic origins and colours." The attack by Al Qaeda on the World Trade Center was a response to the suffering of the dispossessed Palestinians and "injustice" toward and "oppression" of Muslims worldwide:[1]

> If the innocent people who died in the attack on Afghanistan, and those who
> have been dying from lack of food and medical care in Iraq, are considered col-
> laterals, are not the 3,000 who died in New York and the 200 in Bali also just
> collaterals, whose deaths are necessary for the operations to succeed?[2]

Mr. Mahathir was of course referring, if in abbreviated form, to the by then widely used term "collateral damage." Every person who heard him must have known what he meant. If Americans (and by extension other Westerners)

1

could downplay and brush aside through euphemism and spin the devastating impact on civilians of the assaults on Afghanistan and Iraq, then opponents of the wars in the non-Western, Non-Aligned world could feel free to do the same when it came to Western civilian casualties. This was breathtaking. Yet Mr. Mahathir got away with it. He was an indispensable ally in the War on Terror, despite the discomfort that his occasionally disturbing remarks caused.

The Argument

This book, although dealing with wars across space and time, is also about the present. The non-combatant victims of wars have a special place in it. But it is also about us, the peoples of the West along with rich nations of the Pacific Rim, the primary beneficiaries of the highly unequal world order of the beginning of the twenty-first century, and of a long history of imperial and colonial warfare. It contains a historical argument concerning the logic of war and human choice that has a moral dimension. For the latter, I am influenced in part by Michael Walzer, although disagreeing with him on the nature of the current War on Terror.[3]

Not all wars are the same. Conventional wisdom suggests that twentieth-century wars saw a massive increase in civilian casualties, with the Second World War being the epicentre. Yet much has been forgotten. Earlier conflicts associated with expanding empires were lethal for conquered and resisting peoples in the Americas and the Caribbean, Africa, Asia, and the Pacific, as they still are. The vast reservoir of civilian suffering in relatively more recent wars – such as the Maji Maji war of 1905–07 against the Germans in East Africa, who responded with a scorched earth policy; the brutal Italian conquest of Ethiopia in 1935–40 using poison gas, which was outlawed; the Japanese invasion of China from 1937, with its hundreds of massacres; the Korean conflict (1950–53), in which the Americans chose to strafe fleeing refugees in case a few Communist fighters were among them; and the liberation war in Algeria, with the massive French resort to torture – has become an empty wilderness where cries are lost in the wind. Few want to talk, and fewer are listening.

Ideas about just and unjust wars, the behaviour of combatants, the status of non-combatants, and limits on war percolated during two great periods: the high Middle Ages and the late Enlightenment. It is only during the last few decades, stimulated not only by the catastrophe of the Second World War but also by the voices of newly liberated peoples taking their place with their own sovereign states in world affairs after the collapse of the great colonial empires, that once again the rights of non-combatants during armed conflict have become a matter worthy of consideration. The more the postcolonial states of

Asia, Africa, and the Non-Aligned Movement demanded that the laws of war meet wider interests than those of the industrial powers, the less the old imperial centres liked it. Few Western states ratified the 1977 Additional Protocols of the Geneva Conventions. Prior to the 1949 Geneva Conventions, the laws of war applied only to "civilized states," i.e., the West and near neighbours, and generally from the Enlightenment onward it was the rights and obligations of soldiers that were considered a priority, not those of civilians. All states and peoples that did not conform to Western levels of development were deemed to be outside the conventions. Western powers did not apply the laws of war when in conflict with non-Western peoples.[4] This was essentially the same as the justification for African slavery during and after the Enlightenment. Universal ideals were not in fact universal. Europe provincialized itself.

Nor is the current obsession with terrorism very relevant. There is a longer history to investigate. The key difference in the historical emergence of "collateral damage" as an idea is not between "terrorists," who kill civilians on purpose, and conventional Western armies, which – we are told – do their best not to, but between the armies of the imperial West, Russia, and Japan and the peoples of the formerly colonized and underdeveloped world. It is impossible to accept as anything other than propaganda for home consumption the statement by George W. Bush in a speech to the United Nations on November 10, 2001: "Unlike the enemy, we seek to minimize, not maximize, the loss of innocent life."[5] Colonial conquests created their own dividing lines and new hierarchies of domination. Ideas of racial difference and inferiority were invented (as in the Japanese invasion of China) if they did not already exist. American soldiers who on September 10, 2001, would probably have had trouble finding Afghanistan or Iraq on a map very quickly started to use derogatory terms like "ragheads" and "hajis."

Late-nineteenth-century imperialism, along with the First and Second World Wars, is the central legacy of positivism. Much of both wars was fought on colonial territories: there were First World War battlegrounds in Africa and the Middle East; the Second, especially Hitler's conquests in the east and Japanese expansion in the Pacific and Asia, was a series of colonial wars. The French, British, and Dutch fought, among other things (chiefly, of course, survival), to reimpose imperialism in Africa and Asia. Thus the usual separation of the World Wars from imperial and colonial conflicts is in many aspects artificial.

With decolonization, what was formally seen as legitimate in imperial and colonial conflicts was no longer so. The carte blanche of earlier periods gave way to the winds of change. New states demanded a voice. Not only had the formerly "uncivilized" and outcast peoples of the colonial world gained their own states and recognition under international law but certain non-state actors could be seen as having state-like characteristics or special international status and thus could potentially shelter under the same law.[6]

In this context, "collateral damage" as a euphemism was borrowed from the terminology of the nuclear arms race and applied to civilian casualties in continuing anti-colonial liberation wars: Vietnam and then the postcolonial (or, more accurately, new imperial) wars in Kosovo, the Persian Gulf, and Afghanistan. As euphemism, politicians, military spokespeople, and others commonly used it in the media. As euphemism, it served to legitimize what was no longer legitimate or lawful; killing on purpose became killing accidentally on purpose. Black and brown peoples, and the economically marginalized of Eastern Europe and the Caucasus, were still outside universalism. As Marc Herold puts it, their lives were less worthy. Killing could continue as business as usual, but shrouded in the mystique of military jargon. When questioned, it was always denied if unproven; when proven, it was regretted as an accident. The people of Vietnam and Chechnya, of Kenya and Afghanistan, Algeria and Iraq, Mozambique and Angola know better.[7]

The current era is the heyday of collateral damage. Increasing reliance by the militaries of advanced industrial countries on high technology and communications, especially bombing, has made it so. The combination of high technology with racial prejudice and distain for the lives of the poor and the foreign is particularly lethal. Conventional explanations and paradigms have completely failed to explain the massive number of civilian casualties in the current wars of the Middle East and Central Asia. High technology and smart weapons have not diminished civilian suffering – they seem to have added to it. In July and August 2006, the Israeli Defence and Air Forces killed many times more civilians (and U.N. observers) in southern Lebanon than Hizbullah did Israeli civilians, despite having far more accurate weaponry.[8] The United States has presided over perhaps as many as 700,000 deaths and the almost complete destruction of civil life in Iraq.[9] More sophisticated military academic thought blames collateral damage on "concealment warfare" practised by the enemies of the West. Such thinking clearly aims to shift blame from those doing the killing to the opposing forces who deliberately conceal themselves within the civilian population. This tactic apparently was to blame for the deaths of hundreds of thousands of civilians in Vietnam and elsewhere.[10] The argument highlights an astonishing ignorance of the history of guerrilla warfare, for centuries the strategy chosen by the weak when fighting the strong, and of national liberation struggles.[11]

Collateral damage in its recent usage is a euphemism to disguise war against whole peoples and innocent civilians.[12] Although on the surface borrowed from the nuclear arms race, in reality the term comes directly from the colonial experience, repackaged, to infect the postcolonial world. Thus, for example, the decades of suffering of the black and brown people of South Africa might be envisaged as a form of "collateral damage." Segregation and then apartheid targeted them all in a form of continual low-intensity warfare and brutally discriminative administrative practice, yet this was "legal" (indeed it was the basis of almost all major legislation in that country from 1910 to 1990), and its terrible effects were often justified as unintentional. This is the logic of Mr. Mahathir's comments. Their deaths and suffering in a sense were "necessary for the operations to succeed."

Legitimizing the Illegitimate: The Metamorphosis of a Euphemism

"Collateral damage" as euphemism has a relatively short history, although its antecedents are centuries old. Interestingly, Wikipedia has one of the best short discussions of the term.[13] The etymology of "collateral" derives from the medieval Latin *collateralis*, combining *col* (together) with *lateralis* (*latus*, *later-*, meaning "side"). "Collateral" in its non-euphemistic usage occurs in, for example, medical terminology (collateral veins) and in business, where collateral security is additional security pledged to guarantee central contractual obligations. But dictionary definitions also point to a slightly different meaning: "additional but subordinate"; in other words, secondary. Thus in American military contexts we occasionally also hear of "secondary effects," essentially a variant of "collateral damage." In its first military usage, during the first decades of the nuclear arms race, "collateral damage" had a somewhat different ring from that acquired later, in actual armed conflict.[14] Perhaps this was because the catastrophic damage to civilians of a nuclear exchange cannot even euphemistically be said to be "unintentional" or "accidental" damage, the usual meaning in non-nuclear conflicts. As Walzer puts it, the mushroom cloud "symbolizes indiscriminate slaughter, the killing of the innocent (as in Hiroshima) on a massive scale."[15] The means of destruction in the nuclear age go so far beyond the threshold that gives the conventions of war meaning that they become beside the point: "The new technology of war simply doesn't fit." Even a so-called limited nuclear war could not meet the criteria of the laws of war.[16] In 1960, U.S. military planner Thomas Schelling thought that "collateral damage" to American civilians could be minimized if the potential targets of Soviet ICBMS (intercontinental ballistic missiles) were located far from urban centres.[17] In 2003, the U.S. military was still giving some attention to the civilians it might target in a nuclear conflict. In an article entitled "An Analysis of Reduced Collateral Damage Nuclear Weapons," Los Alamos-based nuclear strategists argued that a new generation of low-yield nuclear weapons, combined with more accurate delivery, would reduce collateral damage and provide the U.S. government with more options to pursue in its military objectives of "deterrence, dissuasion and assurance."[18] But all attempts to try to tame and rationalize nuclear weapons technology to manage collateral damage and fit into a concept of limited nuclear war seem bound to fail.[19]

According to Wikipedia, "collateral damage" came into its own as a military euphemism during the Vietnam War and over several decades became entrenched in American armed forces jargon. For example, in the *USAF Intelligence Targeting Guide*,

> collateral damage is unintentional damage or incidental damage affecting facilities, equipment or personnel occurring as a result of military actions directed against targeted enemy forces or facilities. Such damage can occur to friendly, neutral, and even enemy forces. During Linebacker operations over North Vietnam, for example, some incidental damage occurred from bombs falling outside target areas.[20]

Putting aside the extreme understatement in the last sentence, the emphasis in the first sentences is whether or not the damage was intentional. There is no distinction between major or minor incidents, between those that are lawful or those that involve war crimes, or between civilian or military casualties: "If it was targeted, it is not collateral. If it was not targeted, even if it was enemy soldiers, it was collateral."[21] If Vietnam was the crucible, then it was the First Gulf War that saw the phrase enter popular consciousness.[22] By the 1990s, "collateral damage" was understand and utilized well beyond the confines of American military usage.

Central to our argument is that the purpose of the term "collateral damage" as a euphemism is to deceive. In many cases, it is used deliberately in public statements to misinform, to say that damage that was in fact intentional was not intended. Misinformation has always been one of the key tools in propaganda campaigns, both against enemies and on the home front. A wide range of military and political euphemisms is designed to cover up or obscure massacres, war crimes, and military blunders, and the military establishment in the West has become increasingly adept at information management.[23] The grotesque and currently frequently heard "friendly fire" (as Canadians and Afghans know so well) is one such example.[24] Victor Davis Hanson, conservative author of the interesting but fatally flawed *Carnage and Culture*, a book that covers 2,500 years of Western warfare against non-Western peoples, is correct when he writes, "Euphemism in battle narrative or the omission of graphic killing altogether is a near criminal offense of the military historian."[25] There is nothing controversial here, but what is unforgivable is to ignore how such euphemisms taint the wider discourse about war, particularly wars in far-off places, remote from the experience of metropolitan publics, against peoples unfamiliar to the users of such euphemism. In fact, there is no index entry for "civilian casualties" in *Carnage and Culture* (except one buried among dozens of entries for Vietnam), let alone one for "collateral damage." Hanson strangely does not see the glaring contradiction between his emphasis on the lethality of Western armies and his near silence on civilian casualties caused by that lethality.[26]

Not only is misinformation, propaganda, and the use of euphemism part and parcel of the discourse about war, particularly while the fighting continues, but as Walzer notes, hypocrisy is also rife. It is essential for the hypocrite to be seen to be right at the time, to appear to be moral and thus to strike a blow in the propaganda war. The hypocrite "presumes on the moral understanding of the rest of us." "We have no choice," argues Walzer,

> except to take his assertions seriously and put them to the test of moral realism. He pretends to think and act as the rest of us expect him to do. He tells us that he is fighting according to the moral war plan: he does not aim at civilians, he grants quarter to soldiers trying to surrender, he never tortures prisoners, and so on. These claims are true or false, and though it is not easy to judge them . . . it is important to make the effort. Indeed, if we call ourselves moral men and women, we must make the effort, and the evidence is that we regularly do so.[27]

Whenever we hear a politician or military spokesperson talk about collateral damage, we should be on the alert for signs of misinformation, deception, doublespeak, spin, and hypocrisy.

At this point, we need to go further to look at the philosophical underpinnings that seem to support the apparent logic of collateral damage, and more particularly the slippage that occurs beneath the surface, that creates the sense of unease that non-military people (and perhaps some military personnel) feel when collateral damage is conventionally used to explain away civilian casualties. Of particular importance is the doctrine of double effect, a concept developed by Christian theologians during the Middle Ages. But first, we must understand the concept of military necessity because the doctrine of double effect itself assumes that military necessity is part of the calculation when a commanding officer weighs up the risk to civilians resulting from a particular decision. Walzer provides a good introduction to both concepts.[28]

Military necessity at its most basic means that one or another course of action "is necessary to compel the submission of the enemy with the least possible expenditure of time, life, and money."[29] The Germans have a similar concept, that of *kriegraison*, or reason of war. Military necessity, however, is not just about justifying actions in order to win the war. It is about reducing the risk of losing the war and reducing losses during the war. As Walzer observes,

In fact, it is not about necessity at all; it is a way of speaking in code, or a hyper-bolical way of speaking, about probability and risk. Even if one grants the right of states and armies and individual soldiers to reduce their risks, a particular course of action would be *necessary* to that end only if no other course improved the odds of battle at all. But there will always be a range of tactical and strategic options that conceivably could improve the odds. There will be choices to make, and these are moral as well as military choices.

The conventions of war allowed some of these choices but did not permit oth-ers.[30] Military necessity or reason of war justifies the killing of soldiers because soldiers bear arms, fight, and potentially kill their enemies. They are com-manded to do so. Because of this they are also liable to be killed themselves. A soldier is both dangerous and endangered. This is what makes soldiers differ-ent from civilians. A soldier therefore can face the greatest risks without his rights being necessarily threatened.

Civilians stand in a very different category. Certain civilians engaged directly in the production or transportation of war material can be legitimate targets under the conventions of war, but only while they are directly involved in such work. Thus merchant shipping and arms factories, with their civilian workers, can be legitimately attacked according to the conventions of war – but only if justified by military necessity – although civilians producing food, for example, for an army, cannot be.[31] "Once the contribution has been plainly established, only 'military necessity' can determine whether the civil-ians involved are attacked or not. They ought not to be attacked if their activi-ties can be stopped, or their products seized or destroyed, in some other way and without significant risk."[32]

One of the most basic principles of the conventions of war is that non-combatants or civilians cannot be attacked. They are immune from military attack because they are not direct parties to the conflict. In other words, they are innocent bystanders. The categories of civilians mentioned in the previ-ous paragraph are exceptional because they are not innocent bystanders. Nevertheless, the reality of war is that civilians are very frequently close to the fighting.[33]

The doctrine of double effect is a tool of ethics regularly invoked in order to examine the morality of military actions where civilians are at risk. The doctrine has its origins in medieval jurisprudence, particularly the contribu-tion of Thomas Aquinas, but has been subject to some modification in recent times.[34] Although the doctrine is applied to all kinds of situations, such as medical ethics, its theorists frequently use military scenarios when debating its merits. As Walzer writes, "It is one of their purposes to suggest what we ought to think when 'a soldier in firing at the enemy foresees that he will shoot some civilians who are nearby.' "[35] The doctrine thus has very serious applications in the real world of conflict.[36] It is a method by which the contradiction between the absolute prohibition against attacking civilians and the war aims of military forces can be resolved. But too often, as Walzer reminds us, the reconciliation leaves us on the short side of a moral decision.[37]

How does double effect work? The basic principle is that an act likely to have bad consequences is permitted as long as four basic conditions are fulfilled. These are:

1. The act is good in itself or at least indifferent, which means, for our purposes, that it is a legitimate act of war.
2. The direct effect is morally acceptable – the destruction of military supplies, for example, or the killing of enemy soldiers.
3. The intention of the actor is good, that is, he aims only at the acceptable effect; the evil effect is not one of his ends, nor is it a means to his ends.
4. The good effect is sufficiently good to compensate for allowing the evil effect; it must be justifiable under Sidgwick's proportionality rule.[38]

The third condition is key, because although an act may produce bad consequences, it is defensible only when the good and bad results are the result of a single good intention. The intention cannot be to cause bad consequences. But there is a problem. The negative consequences of killing enemy soldiers can be very severe, perhaps thousands of dead civilians. The only protection if the act is judged as good – as a military necessity – is the fourth condition, which rests on proportionality. The proportionality rule worked out by British philosopher Henry Sidgwick aims to balance military utility with justice and to prevent pointless and capricious violence. Thus during armed conflict, it is prohibited to do "any mischief which does not tend materially to the end [of victory], nor any mischief of which the conduciveness to the end is slight in comparison with the amount of the mischief."[39] This is precisely where the doctrine breaks down in very many cases, as we will see below.

Before looking at the doctrine more critically, let's consider examples of how it might work in typical battle situations. The first case – a hypothetical and perhaps not very realistic one as far as conflict between the West and a non-Western enemy is concerned – involves a platoon that has come under enemy fire from the other side of a town, close to the platoon's position.[40] The soldiers in the platoon, when returning fire on their attackers, are quite likely to hit non-combatants in the town in the vicinity of the enemy position. The soldiers have, of course, the right to self-defence. They aim to defeat the opposing force. They do not intend to kill any of the inhabitants of the town, but when shooting at the enemy, it is quite likely that some townspeople will be killed. The soldiers foresee this. According to the doctrine of double effect, the platoon commander has the right to order his men to shoot back at the attackers, even at the risk of killing innocents. However, he should also act with restraint and try to minimize civilian casualties as much as possible. Given the danger to civilians, the soldiers in the platoon should do only what is minimally required to defend themselves.[41]

A real rather than hypothetical example, analyzed by Walzer, comes from the Korean War. The original source is from British correspondent Reginald Thompson, who documents the American approach to war, and describes a "typical" encounter as American troops advanced on Pyongyang:

> A battalion of American troops advanced slowly, without opposition, under the shadow of low hills. "We were well into the valley now, halfway down the straight . . . strung out along the open road, when it came, the harsh stutter of automatic fire sputtering the dust around us." The troops stopped and dove for cover. Three tanks moved up, "pounding their shells into the . . . hillside and shattering the air with their machine guns. It was impossible in this remarkable inferno of sound to detect the enemy, or to assess his fire." Within fifteen minutes, several fighter planes arrived, "diving down upon the hillside with their rockets." This is the new technique of warfare, writes the . . . journalist, "born of immense productive and material might": "the cautious advance, the enemy small arms fire, the halt, the close support air strike, artillery, the cautious advance, and so on." It is designed to save the lives of soldiers, and it may or may not have that effect. "It is certain that it kills civilian men, women, and children, indiscriminately and in great numbers, and destroys all that they have."[42]

What does Walzer say about these events? There was an alternative way to fight under these circumstances. When they were first attacked, the Americans could have sent out a patrol to the flank of the enemy position. But instead from the beginning there was the resort to massive bombardment. The tank fire and rockets nevertheless failed to destroy the North Korean positions. So after an hour a platoon patrol was sent. Of course the Americans aimed to protect their own soldiers, and quite reasonably. But in the process they failed to protect any nearby civilians. The commanding officer must value civilians as well as his own soldiers: "He cannot save them [his soldiers], because they cannot save themselves, by killing innocent people. It is not just that they can't kill a lot of innocent people. Even if the proportions work out favorably . . . we would still want to say, I think, that the patrol must be sent out, the risk accepted, before the big guns are brought to bear."[43] In other words, although soldiers have rights, especially that of self-defence, they have obligations as well. Their major obligation is to look after the rights of civilians, especially the civilians who are threatened by the soldiers' actions.

Walzer then argues that the doctrine of double effect is deficient as it stands and needs to be amended. "Double effect is defensible," he maintains, "only when the two outcomes are the product of a *double intention*: first, that the 'good' be achieved; second, that the foreseeable evil be reduced as far as possible." Thus the third condition, above, should be restated as follows:

3. The intention of the actor is good; that is, he aims narrowly at the acceptable effect; the evil effect is not one of his ends, nor is it a means to his ends, and, aware of the evil involved, he seeks to minimize it, accepting costs to himself.

Soldiers, therefore, should make a "positive commitment" to reduce as far as possible civilian casualties, even beyond the fourth condition of proportionality.[44]

Even more compelling is a case from Beryl Fox's brilliant documentary film, *The Mills of the Gods: Vietnam*. It is well documented because both the attack and the rationale for it are captured live on film in images and words. Its consequences for civilians, although generalized, are clear. It is remarkable both because a Canadian Broadcasting Corporation cameraman was in the rear cockpit of the plane of the commanding officer of the four attacking aircraft and because the United States Air Force seems at that time to have been oblivious to the potential impact on public opinion of giving Canadian journalists permission to film whatever they liked. What follows are extracts from a transcript, along with my notes on the visual images, of a live commentary by American officers to a bombing raid in the Mekong Delta region of South Vietnam in 1965.

[Film images: United States Air Force ground attack aircraft taking off, wings laden with ordnance. The camera then focuses in a close-up of the face of one of the pilots, the mission commander, who turns co-operatively from time to time.]

Pilot 1: Ok, we're inbound to the target now.... We'll be approximately, oh about 35 miles south of Càn Tho, down near Cà Mau in the southern Cà Mau Peninsular.... We'd like to make a strike of four Skyraiders; they are ex-Navy aircraft which are used in the 602nd Air Commando Squadron....

[The camera cuts to a view of the other planes as the pilot continues talking.]

Pilot 1: The Skyraider is an outstanding aircraft. We use it ... because it carries so much ordnance. Each aircraft will carry normally 6,000 pounds of bombs and it's absolutely outstanding. Today you will see bombs and napalm and two of our aircraft, me and number 2, are carrying bombs, 500-pound bombs and 250-pound general-purpose bombs, and 3 and 4 will have napalm, so it should be fairly exciting. We should see a little ground fire and a lot of napalm burning and maybe even some Victor Charlie [Viet Cong]. We hope today we'll find some Victor Charlie but you never know. We're waiting for the forward air controller to check in. He will describe the target for us and we'll tell him what our ordnance is and so forth.

[Shot of air controller's aircraft.]

Air controller: Beaver 23. . . . Over.

Pilot 2: Roger. Go ahead.

Air controller: We've had some reconnaissance about fighting down there. We're asking them to go back in and mark specific positions and lines of positions. They've targeted some bunkers and forty metres south of the river at various places but we will try to get 'em smoked and tell you what it is.

Pilot 1: Oh, we got a good target today.

Air controller: The positionists are trying to find exactly where they are [pilots] 2 to 3, but basically they're right along the southern edge of the heavy mangrove on the south of the river and we want to be sure to concentrate on that strip with all our strikes. Over.

Pilot 2: Oh, roger. Where is the mangrove? By the paddy there or you mean to say the mangrove on the river side of the road?

Pilot 3: Ah, no. He's talking about the edge as it goes into the paddies. Once he gets a little clearer on it I'll be able to mark it out for you. He's talking about the tree-lined edge as it goes out into the rice paddies. This is where these people put all their [inaudible] emplacements.

Pilot 1: Ok, he should be about ready to roll in now.

Pilot 2 or 3: Bye bye, Sam.

Pilot 1: There he goes!

Another pilot: Ok, follow his bomb.

Pilot 1: They should come up. They should hit now. Ok, look out the right now. Ok, right down there. Ok, napalm now, there it goes. Oh [excitedly], look at it burn! Look at it burn!

Air controller: Ok, no that tree-lined [inaudible] is going generally north and south. Down on the southern edge of it and there's another one that runs off perpendicular, generally east and west, and that's the one where I'd like to lay the napalm.

Pilot 1: Ok, we got four napalm coming down here.

[The camera captures the four bombs exploding with huge fireballs. Four explosions are heard on the sound track, then a few seconds of silence.]

Another pilot: That was a little short of the tree line but that hit another tree line so no problem.

[Indistinct conversation among the pilots] ... straight left.... Ok, roger ... straight this time.... Roger, then move on in.

Pilot 1: Ok, Sam, we're going very low now to avoid the gunfire (sound of twenty-millimetre cannon fire from the Skyraider). Now I'll pull up short of the tree line. Up we go. And up we go.

[The image shifts rapidly as the Skyraider dives, strafing the tree lines, and then sharply pulls away.]

Pilot 1 [with great exuberance]: Ok. Good hits! Good hits! Real fun! Real fun! That was an outstanding target all right. We bombed first of all and we could see the people running everywhere was fantastic. It's very, very seldom that we see Victor Charlie run like that. When they do we know we got 'em. If we keep 'em on the run, well, we know we're going to really hose them down.

Ok, we bomb first of all, and then we beat up the area, and that's when they start to run, ok. Then the napalmers come after us and we strike immediately in front of them to keep their heads down. We were receiving heavy ground fire. You could see the tracer bullets coming up. Fantastic! And we really made them run. That's outstanding because when they get out of their trenches, in the open, we can really hit them and that's what we like to do. That's what we're here for and why it's outstanding to really catch them in the open. Oh, we don't do that very often.

Cameraman: You got in on target?

Pilot 1: Oh, absolutely.

Cameraman: You think you got them?

Pilot: Oh, didn't we get them? Couldn't you see 'em run down there? Man, I know we got them. I've got four twenty-millimetre cannons you could see out here and we really hosed them down. By Jove, that's great fun. I really like to do that.

Cameraman: Weren't you flying in, flying a little bit low in the rice paddy?

Pilot 1: Ok, what happens when you hit ground fire like that, if you press right down in 'em you're gonna be more effective. I'll be more effective with my own guns and also I can hit 'em much easier and it scares them, see, when I press right down into 'em. Now then, if I pull off and then up immediately, let's say three to four hundred feet then I'm a number one target. They're gonna shoot my ass off and yours too for that matter. The army will go in this afternoon with helicopters and have a look around. They'll probably have to fight their way in because you can't ever get them all out of the bunkers. Oh, it should be fairly exciting. I really wish I could go in on a clear and search immediately after one of our air strikes just to see, you know, really how effective they are. They [the Army] really praise them for those big bombs and the napalm especially. They really like the napalm because when they get there, the ones that the napalm hasn't burned up, well, the V.C. are just addled because of these big bombs. You see, it breaks their eardrums and makes them kind of senseless. . . .

[Cut to the whirring sound of helicopter blades and the image of helicopters taking off for a clear and search mission. The helicopters, full of American soldiers, fly to the river flood plain, land, and capture a young peasant boy herding water buffalo, taking him off for interrogation. A subsequent scene, in a different, highland, location, shows the aftermath of another bombing raid. Smoke ascends into the air. On the ground, the charred and blackened ruins of simple bamboo structures are shown, within a devastated landscape. The camera shows close-ups of numerous dead Vietnamese, nearly all of whom look like peasant farmers. They include a number of women.][45]

A number of issues are highlighted here. First, there is the excessive pride in technology, a frequent accompaniment to disproportionate military action in the twentieth and twenty-first centuries.[46] Second, there is no apparent attempt by the forward air controller or the pilots to assess the presence of civilians in the area to be attacked. Clearly this was a well-settled farming area, close to the river. Third, all civilians are deemed suspicious or potential enemies. Fourth, the narrator, pilot 1, has lost all sense of proportion or morality and exults in killing. Finally, although the final scene of dead Vietnamese peasants is the result of another bombing raid, this in the end does not matter much. It is absolutely clear in these scenes, and throughout the film, that it is Vietnamese peasants who are bearing the brunt of the war and that the doctrine of double effect was meaningless to the American military in this war.[47]

A more contemporary case is the American attempt to kill Saddam Hussein at the beginning of the current Iraq war.[48] In the afternoon of April 8, 2003, a U.S. B-1 bomber dropped four satellite-guided bunker-buster bombs on the al-Sa'ah restaurant in Baghdad. Intelligence sources had led the American government to believe that Saddam Hussein, his aides, and his sons, Uday and

Qusay, were meeting in a bunker below the restaurant, in the Mansour residential district of the city. The intended target, as it turned out, was not present when the bombs hit. Instead, neighbouring homes were destroyed and fourteen innocent people, including three children, were vaporized. The deaths were justified as collateral damage and no one was deemed accountable. What does the doctrine of double effect have to say about this case? Clearly a justification of military necessity would not apply here. The Iraqis had not attacked the B-1 bomber or the United States as a whole. The civilians in the vicinity of the al-Sa'ah restaurant certainly posed no danger to the B-1 crew or the United States. Thus the issue of self-defence (as in the first two examples) is not a factor. Second, the "good" that was intended in the bombing, the elimination of the leadership of Iraq, was (with hindsight) not realistically achievable, while the "bad," the killing of innocent civilians, was obviously going to be a consequence of the bombing. There is a minimal gap in this case between lack of intent to kill civilians and the very obvious foresight that civilians would die. Finally, there was no attempt to mitigate the damage to civilians – witness the weaponry chosen to attack a target in a residential neighbourhood. In this case, the doctrine of double effect does not justify the actions taken.

The doctrine of double effect does not in fact lead in a straight line to collateral damage in either its philosophical roots or its practice according to the conventions of war, although it is frequently assumed to do so. As we have seen, one of the roots of collateral damage as a concept (as opposed to a euphemism) is from theorizing about the fate of civilians in a nuclear conflict; of course the doctrine of double effect cannot justify nuclear war. Philosophers still debate its exact meaning.[49] Many theorists reject the doctrine in its entirety. What is the difference between intention and "foreseen probable effects," critics ask, when the result is the same: the deaths of innocent civilians? And the dead certainly don't quibble about whether their end was intended or merely foreseen. Shouldn't there be some blame in either case?[50] According to Camillo Bica,

> Where the DDE justification goes wrong, then, is in the moral importance it assigns to the *directing of intent*. That is, it relies exclusively upon the intended effect of the act as proclaimed by the actor as the crucial moral consideration for determining the permissibility and moral value of an act, rather than taking into account the entire set of foreseen probable effects. Consequently, only the intended "good effect" becomes morally relevant, and the foreseen evil effect – now termed "collateral damage" – becomes somehow abrogated and moral responsibility for the innocent deaths somehow diffused. The DDE justification fails because morality requires more than merely a proclamation of good intent.[51]

Moral philosopher David Lefkowitz, after a rigorous analysis of the doctrine's logic, goes further, finding weaknesses both in the concept of intention and in the proportionality rule:

> The DDE does not provide a compelling justification for collateral damage. Even apart from any difficulties there may be in specifying the concepts of intended harm and merely foreseen harm (or harm as a side effect), it remains unclear why we should view the agent's intention as relevant to the rightness or wrongness of his act. Moreover, we do not yet have a convincing account of the proportionality condition: that is, of what sorts of considerations provide a sufficient reason to justify acts of war that it is reasonable to expect will cause collateral damage.[52]

Nevertheless, some military analysts do take the doctrine of double effect very seriously, and at least one instructor at the U.S. Military Academy has attempted to adapt it in order to consider its relevance to collateral damage cases.[53] Yet it is continually deployed as a cover for civilian casualties. We will not blame Aquinas and his successors for the nature of its application to the circumstances of war after the thirteenth century, but rather those who use it loosely in the very different conditions of mechanized and digital warfare at the end of the second millennium and beginning of the third.

Thinking about civilian casualties did not begin with the doctrine of double effect, however. Historians of the Middle Ages remind us that well before Aquinas, theologians of the Peace of God movement of the late tenth and eleventh centuries had started to think about the consequences of violence and moral responsibility.[54] Indeed, one of the movement's great contributions was to create a link with later medieval theologians who posited the "natural immunity" of non-combatants and their property during wars. This fundamental distinction between combatants and non-combatants has survived down to the present. Thus certain sections of society had "safe conducts without asking for it," including the religious from bishops down to pilgrims and hermits, as well as "cowherds and all farmers," labourers and merchants, women and children, and the elderly.[55]

The Peace of God theorists did not imagine that their ideas about religious chivalry were relevant to anything but wars between Christians; they did not apply to wars between Christians and what David Hay calls "out-groups."[56] This was the germ of centuries of exclusionary Christian theorizing and practice, carried on through the period of the Inquisition and the founding of the Spanish empire, despite the profound opposition of the great Bartolomé de las Casas, and the temporary cessation by Charles V of further Spanish conquests in the Americas pending a debate before a court of lawyers, held in

Valladolid from August 1550 into the following year, on their purposes and consequences.[57] When Pope Urban II proclaimed the First Crusade in 1095, he used the language of the Peace and Truce of God and promised that crusaders would gain spiritual merit for fighting in the Lord's name; their battle cry was "*Deus vult*," or God wills it. According to Hay,

> With the harsh military campaigns of the Old Testament glossed with evangelical love, the reforming theologians could safely . . . allow the crusaders much wider latitude in determining how to treat local populations and their property than they would have within Latin Christendom. Indeed, the ideology of religious pollution and purification led some of the Christian chroniclers to depict the execution of non-Christian civilians as necessary rather than collateral damage. Raymond of Aguilers, for example, depicts the "cleansing" of the holy places of Christ with "pagan" blood as the incontestable vindication of the enterprise.[58]

If this was the view of the ideologues, the pragmatic experience of soldiers points to some moderation in the reality of crusader behaviour toward Muslim and other non-Christian civilians. Medieval chroniclers' accounts of crusader massacres of Muslims were sometimes exaggerated for the propaganda effect of purification of sacred places. In other cases, the masculine gender is used. Women and children were not a threat but were seen as booty. The crusaders often needed to support themselves by taking prisoners in order to ransom them or sell them as slaves.[59]

A Failure of Reason: Enlightenment Philosophy and Humanity in War

Why has the doctrine of double effect failed? Why the dubious and immoral resort to the euphemism of collateral damage? The first and clearest reason is that moral and legal doctrines developed in the West and relating to warfare were never meant to apply to conflicts between the so-called civilized world and the "uncivilized," the colonizers and the colonized, or to conflicts involving white nations or people on one side and black, brown, or red peoples on the other. Thus, Geoffrey Best writes,

> Within the last few decades . . . the nature of the argument about the use and value of the law of war has changed. Until the nineteen-forties, it applied solely to international wars between the supposedly more advanced countries. The only exception in this rule was allowed in the cases of a civil war between civilized brothers, as in the USA, 1861–65. No attempt was made to extend it to any other non-international war – the doctrine of sovereignty insisted that how

States dealt with rebellions and civil disturbances was their own affair – and it was taken for granted that those kinds of conflicts would be the nastier . . . while the manners in which the British, the French, the Spaniards, the Portuguese and the Dutch put down rebels in their colonial empires, or the Italians acquired one, were every bit as nasty as those in which Paraguayans fought Bolivians, or Japanese, Chinese.[60]

Of course the relevant categories were constructed, changed, contained exceptions, and often had blurred boundaries.[61] We have seen that the basic distinction goes back at least as far as the First Crusade, when it divided Christians from others. It continues, but now in part camouflaged by euphemism. Best's chronology in the above quotation recognizes that since the 1949 Geneva Conventions were codified, the laws of war have applied to conflicts between the West and its colonies and former colonies, but it is also true that no Western state has ever seen its military or political leadership prosecuted for war crimes against a non-Western nation.

As we did with the medieval doctrine of double effect, we must present the major ideas of the eighteenth-century philosophers and jurists on our subject and offer a critique. Our main source, Best's *Humanity in Warfare*, is rightly regarded with respect.

The rational language of Enlightenment and post-Enlightenment philosophy and the norms of international relations spoke increasingly in cosmopolitan and universal terms.[62] The first point from the Enlightenment consensus is that war is a conflict between political groups, or "a clash of agents of political groups who are able to recognize one another as such."[63] Best sees the origins of international humanitarian law from the sixteenth century onward as the law of "political groups," or nations, in the European conception. *Jus gentium*, for contemporary European jurists, aimed to ascertain what justice necessitated for individuals (meaning men) as well as of men "gathered into peoples or nations." With the eventual establishment of the European state system, the interests of "peoples or nations" became less and less separable from the interests of the state apparatus, with its laws, borders, bureaucracies, executive privileges, and, of course, doctrines of sovereignty.[64] On the edge of this consensus lay Jean-Jacques Rousseau, who theorized that "war . . . is not a relationship between man and man, but between State and State, in which private persons are only enemies accidentally, not as men, nor even as citizens, but simply as soldiers; not as members of their fatherland, but as its defenders."[65] We will briefly mention Best's important criticisms of this still influential view: that it exaggeratedly created a hard distinction between citizens/subjects and the states to which they belonged (against the trend toward greater participation, as in the American Revolution) when in reality, as we have seen, there were and are degrees of citizen and soldier involvement in war; but more importantly that it gave the war makers carte blanche to impose unbearable suffering on civilians according to military (or state) necessity without having to provide any justification. "Rousseau said that wars were between 'States,' not 'people(s)'; therefore (if you swallowed this), people(s) were not objects of military operations. But people(s) nevertheless got hurt, often very badly." Thus followers of Rousseau have little choice but to evade the issue as "some sort of unavoidable accident or incidental feature of war, more or less beyond your own control and responsibility. Since it was by definition not your purpose, it was not among the necessary nasty acts for which you were responsible."[66] This logical conclusion was obviously not what Rousseau meant. Nevertheless, we find ourselves back again in the murk and obfuscation of collateral damage. Further (and a point not noted by Best), Rousseau's extreme emphasis on states as opposed to people(s) denied any thought of responsibility for non-combatants in wars against non-state societies, such as nomadic and pastoralist peoples in North America and Africa, or peoples living in small-scale lineage- or clan-based societies, as in much of Southeast Asia, Africa, and the Americas. This understanding is crucial to our argument.

But many Africans, Asians, and Amerindians did live in states. In the sixteenth century, the kings of Portugal and Kongo had strong diplomatic and military relations and referred to each other with perfect equality, as brothers.[67] This typical recognition of parity or near parity between Europeans and Africans – or Europeans and Asians – was lost over the next 200 to 300 years. By the eighteenth century, the existence of such African states was forgotten, ignored, or denied, as the European powers, particularly Britain and France, made huge profits from the Atlantic slave trade, relegating Africans to a lower rank of humanity in the process. These realities must be distinguished from the relatively more nuanced (although still brutal) approach to civilians in conflicts between European peoples both in Europe itself and in North America, discussed here by Brian Sandberg and Scott Nelson.

States – and, as we have seen, military commanders also – based their reasons for going to war in the first place, as well as its conduct, on the idea of necessity. Best observes time and time again that the Enlightenment thinkers' ideas on necessity were cosmopolitan, indeed universalist, yet were balanced by their realism and lack of sentimentalism. If men were indeed brothers then they might also find themselves enemies due to forces beyond their control: in other words, the demands of state necessity. But necessity was bound by strict criteria:

These criteria, to put them at their simplest, were: the fundamental unity of mankind, and the natural rights of man; the preferability of the state of peace to that of war; and the general principle (to which we might give the recently popularized description of "proportionality") that means were not indiscriminately justified by ends and that the ends at stake (in questions of peace, war and the conduct of war) were general, universal, and historical; not particular, local, and temporary.[68]

Thus, he quotes liberally and approvingly from the eighteenth-century theorist representative of the realist approach to conflict, Emmerich de Vattel:

Let us never forget that our enemies are men. Although we may be under the unfortunate necessity of prosecuting our right by force of arms let us never put aside the ties of charity which bind us to the whole human race. In this way we shall defend courageously the rights of our country, without violating those of humanity. Let us be brave without being cruel, and our victory will not be stained by inhuman and brutal acts.[69]

Such universalism was there for all to see in the American Declaration of Independence, which was demanded by "a decent respect for the opinions of mankind" and in the pronouncement of the French representatives of the National Assembly on December 29, 1791, with Nicolas de Condorcet's prompting, that they "owed to Europe and to the whole of mankind [*humanité*]" an explanation for the coming war.[70]

We can see, however, that Best's analysis (following the pattern of the Enlightenment itself) has considerable weaknesses and some major blind spots. First, despite the all-inclusive title (at least in the sense of humanity as the human race) *Humanity in Warfare* is, as he admits, only "a history of the laws and customs by which the *more developed* countries have thought fit to control their conduct of war *amongst themselves*."[71] The problem is that, as Sven Lindqvist and others have shown, conduct in wars against less developed peoples, in so many cases reaching the proportions of genocide, had a huge impact on the way wars between "more developed countries" were managed – certainly during the twentieth century.[72] It is impossible to separate the two spheres – metropolis and empire – much as many scholars would like to and the Enlightenment publicists in fact did. According to the publicist consensus, enlightened ("educated and civilized") people were usually capable of solving conflicts peacefully, whereas the "very uneducated and uncivilized," meaning the peoples of the non-Western world, apparently were not.[73] In fact, Best's narrow approach does not go much beyond what Gustave Moynier, president of the International Committee of the Red Cross (ICRC) said in the winter of

1890–91 on the Geneva Convention. "First of all," he said at a public lecture, "we might note that the Convention has furnished an argument in favour of the brotherhood of men. In subscribing to it, the several factions of *civilized mankind* have ... placed themselves under a common rule, formulated entirely in the light of moral considerations. .... Recognizing that after all they all belong to the same family ... [they] have concluded that they ought to begin by showing some regard for another's suffering."[74]

Best does point to the enemies of the Enlightenment position: increasing nationalist sentiment; imperialism; the impact of the industrial revolution; and the increasing influence from about the 1860s of a harder positivist line, using the language of state necessity, taken by the major powers in international affairs, all of which led in the end to the catastrophes of world war.[75] Indeed, the influence of positivism – that the interests of states are the only guide in the international sphere – increasingly overshadowed ideas of natural law. But rarely does he consider the increasingly direct and negative impact of imperialism and rising racism on his subject: humanity in warfare.[76] Further, he is oblivious to the catastrophic and corrosive impact of the slave trade, which was reaching its peak at the very moment that the sublime thoughts of the great Enlightenment philosophers and publicists were being articulated.[77] Ultimately *Humanity in Warfare* presents a conventional view of the late Enlightenment contribution. The tension between universalist ideals and the more limited and self-serving interests of both the Enlightenment thinkers and the states they lived in is acknowledged but not resolved.[78] For resolution, we must turn to the work of contemporary French philosopher Louis Sala-Molins and Swedish historian Sven Lindqvist.

Sala-Molins makes no bones about highlighting the chasm between theoretical universalism and its provincial practice, simultaneously contained within the eighteenth-century Enlightenment doctrine of man. It was applicable at the most to Europe, and it was highly racialized in order to exclude non-whites. This paradox is at the heart of a devastating commentary and analysis in his *Dark Side of the Light*, with its focus on the European (particularly French) justification of the slave trade and maintenance of the *Code noir*, which regulated African slavery in the French empire, with the concurrent proclamation of the *Déclaration des droits de l'homme et du citoyen*.[79] The slave trade, in essence, "banished humanity from an entire continent" from the genesis of the modern period. It was "a form of genocide that did not take place on the sly but in full view of everyone"; a devastation whose efficiency derived "from very Christian members of royalty, solemn decrees and privileges, and from a legal code drawn up in clear language publicized everywhere and readable by all."[80] Sala-Molins asks us, "Can the black man demand, if not for that period then at least for today, that the so-called universal significance of a thinking that chose to ignore him – and that in so doing dislodges him from the category of the human – be appraised in light of the centuries-old, transcontinental disaster of the slave trade and slavery?" For,

> The Enlightenment composes the music, fills it with the most beautiful harmonies of a grand symphony to the glory of Reason, Man, the Sovereignty of the individual, and universal Philanthropy. This score is being beautifully performed until suddenly a black man erupts in the middle of the concert. What at that point becomes of Man, Sovereignty, Reason, Philanthropy? They disappear into thin air. And the beautiful music pierces your eardrums with the gratings of sarcasm.[81]

The Enlightenment, then, even as represented in the works of the supposed friend of the Africans, Condorcet, can be interpreted honestly only "with the *Code noir* in hand."[82] This is a far cry from Best's very compartmentalized analysis, in which slavery is notable by its absence. The fact was that all the great ideas about humanity at peace or at war did not apply to black (or brown) people. This was partly, as we have seen, because black people, whether in Africa or the Caribbean or elsewhere, whether freed or enslaved, were not seen as making up *peoples* or nations. For Condorcet and others (Montesquieu, Raynal, Rousseau, Voltaire, Diderot, Helvétius), they could acquire political and legal rights only in so far as they ceased to be "black." This could not be envisaged in the circumstances of empire and the slave trade, from which the colonial powers benefited.[83] Thus the *Code noir*, which defined black people as "movable assets," remained in force, undisturbed.[84] They were excluded from the evolving laws of war during the Enlightenment and continued to be excluded during the period of high imperialism, well into the twentieth century. The specificity and the generality of the slave trade aid us in drawing conclusions relevant to our own topic.

Lindqvist is even blunter. The bulk of his famous book deals with the nineteenth-century post-Enlightenment era – the age of positivism, of scientific racism, of high imperialism – and, of course, the twentieth century. Africans, Amerindians, South Sea Islanders, and aborigines everywhere were not only excluded from humanity but also seemed to be disappearing from the face of the earth. Extinction, extermination, and genocide were part of the culture of imperialism and imbued the public consciousness of the time. British Prime Minister Robert Cecil, Lord Salisbury, summed it up in May 1898 when he said, "One can roughly divide the nations of the world into the living and the dying."[85] The leading scientists of the era: Wallace, Greg, Galton, Kidd – perhaps even Darwin – thought it inevitable. Lindqvist writes, "Common to them all was … the desire to excuse and approve genocide.

Extermination was inevitable, apparently vitalizing the exterminators, and it had profound secret causes. Nor was it certain that it was particularly unpleasant for the victims." Galton believed it to be a matter of "listlessness and apathy."[86] By the late nineteenth century, only a minority of Europeans believed that black and brown peoples possessed any rights at all, even the right to life. The conservative German political scientist Heinrich von Treitschke wrote in 1898,

> International law becomes phrases if its standards are also applied to barbaric people. To punish a Negro tribe, villages must be burned, and without setting examples of that kind, nothing can be achieved. If the German Reich in such cases applied international law, it would not be humanity or justness but shameful weakness.[87]

To think that the laws of war could have any relevance in the process of imperial conquest would have been inconceivable to those planning it and carrying it out.

Civilian Casualties and the Cost of Empire

"The fact that the Indians also died in the process was unfortunate, but apparently inevitable." This is Lindqvist's ironic comment on the deadlock in the debate at Valladolid over the justification and costs of Spanish imperialism in the Americas, which wiped out tens of millions.[88] It resonates with current NATO and American excuses for civilian deaths in Iraq and Afghanistan. U.S. ambassador to the United Nations Zalmay Khalilzad was reported to have described the killing of some 300 Afghan civilians by NATO and American forces in the first half of 2007 as "unfortunate." American and international forces "did their best to avoid hitting civilians"; "sometimes it happens that weapons go awry, and war is not a perfect science."[89] In a further incident just days after Mr. Khalilzad made known his regrets, Afghans in Kunar province said thirty-five civilians had been killed in two air strikes by aircraft from the NATO International Security Assistance Force (ISAF). The second strike occurred when villagers in Watapour were burying ten people killed in the first. The original ten included nine members from one family. What was the response of ISAF to the claims? "At this time there is no reason for us to believe that there are any civilian casualties of any type," said spokesman Major John Thomas.[90] Nearly a year later, in May 2008, the message from Afghanistan was just the same. The 24th American Marine Expeditionary Unit had been parachuted into parts of Helmand province to clear Taliban forces from important transit routes. Reports soon emerged from NGOs, including the Red Cross, that several thousand civilian families had fled their homes into the desert and accused the Americans of "extensive civilian displacement, innocent casualties and aggressive marine tactics, all of it arousing anti-American sentiment."[91] The marine commander had to go to Kabul in order to "quash" the reports and proclaim the mission's success. Journalist Rosie DiManno reports, "According to Lt.-Col. Kent Hayes, the known scoreboard reads thusly: Marine casualties: 0. Civilian casualties: 0." The civilians were already leaving before the marines arrived. "I can't even speculate why," said Hayes. The British in Helmand admitted to only two displaced families, contradicting Hayes.[92] The pattern is clear: civilian casualties ("collateral damage") are unfortunate but inevitable, or else they did not happen.

The official military response in these cases is strikingly similar to the Pentagon's initial flat rejection of the charges concerning the massacre of refugees during the Korean War by American units at No Gun Ri, published in 1999 by Associated Press journalists, as well as its subsequent damage control. Historian Marilyn B. Young's account of the military's grudging investigation is worth quoting at length. The final army report of January 2001, she writes, is an

> artful acceptance and denial of what happened that summer day fifty years ago. The report acknowledges that "an unknown number of Korean civilians were killed or injured" at No Gun Ri but insists that "what befell civilians . . . was a tragic and deeply regrettable accompaniment to a war forced upon unprepared U.S. and ROK [Republic of Korea] forces." Rumors of North Korean infiltrators, fearful and untrained American soldiers, and the confusion of combat were sufficient to explain the deaths at No Gun Ri. Charles Cragin, the deputy assistant secretary of defense, told a reporter that the U.S. team found nothing to the record that "rose to the level of criminality." "Unfortunately, in the fog of war," he explained, "and in war, innocent civilians die." The army report cast doubt on the memories of those veterans who claimed to have received orders to fire, but accepted the reliability of those who did not remember having received orders. The documents AP reporters had found in the archives were either not mentioned or selectively quoted.[93]

The Associated Press report cites Korean survivors, American veterans, and declassified U.S. army documents and describes the massacre at No Gun Ri as follows. On July 26, 1950, 660 soldiers of the 7th Cavalry Regiment were dug in close to a railway bridge, expecting a North Korean attack. Nearby were several villages, whose inhabitants, survivors state, were ordered to leave their homes. The villagers approached the railway bridge under guard but were then forced off the road by the Americans and onto the railway line so that

American vehicles could pass. After resting for some time, the group of villagers (Young calls them refugees) were attacked by American planes, strafing along the railway track. The survivors ran in panic, abandoning their dead and severely wounded, and hid in a culvert under the tracks. There they were found by American soldiers, who then checked the wounded for signs of life and shot them if they moved. Several hundred – perhaps 400 – Korean civilians were killed, although no one knows the exact number.[94]

A wider pattern of deliberate American attacks on fleeing Korean refugees has been well established, sanctioned by clear orders from commanding officers: "No refugees to cross the front line. Fire everyone trying to cross lines. Use discretion in case of women and children." Major General William Keen of the 25th Infantry instructed his soldiers, "All civilians in this area are to be considered as enemy and action taken accordingly." As in similar cases elsewhere, some American soldiers followed orders, while others refused to.[95]

But we deviate in time, if not in circumstance, and will concentrate now on what happened to non-combatants during the period of the great modern colonial empires, in the nineteenth and twentieth centuries, from North America to China. The vastness of the subject forces us to be illustrative. Through the later part of this period the illumination of the Enlightenment was fading, and in rapid turn positivists, racists, Social Darwinists, imperialists, and fascists, not to forget socialists, came to dominate Western public discourse. But was the difference from the previous age of Enlightenment all that great when the outlook for non-Western peoples is considered; when, during the eighteenth century, India was under attack, Indonesia and the Philippines largely subjugated, the Caribbean and much of North and South America a vast slave labour camp, and the slave trade at its peak, either defended outright or shamefacedly excused by Montesquieu, Condorcet, Diderot, Kant, Hegel, and the rest? By the early nineteenth century in many of the new white settler colonies, genocide was in the air, fuelled by greed, fear, racism, and government policy. In 1820s Tasmania, the local newspapers demanded the government "move" the indigenous Tasmanians, who otherwise must be "hunted down like wild beasts and destroyed."[96] In the Denver, Colorado, press in 1863, of twenty-seven articles concerning Indians, ten directly urged their "extermination." Just two referred to them positively.[97] The point here is not to rehearse the multiple genocides and massacres resulting from white settlement but to remind ourselves of nineteenth-century attitudes in the colonies toward the "other." Such policies and attitudes did not disappear with the indigenous peoples of Tasmania or the American West or, for that matter, the southern parts of South America or southern Africa.

In 1832, the destruction of the Amerindians of Argentina was still not complete. In August of that year, the young Charles Darwin was an appalled witness to the policy of extermination of the Pampas Indians initiated by the Argentine government in order to clear the land for settlement. At Bahía Blanca he met some of the forces of General Juan Manuel de Rosas, in charge of the program, and interviewed a commander. The army strategy was to brutally obtain information from captured Indians on the whereabouts of surviving groups, who were then hunted down. Darwin wrote:

> The Indians are now so terrified that they offer no resistance in a body, but each flies, neglecting even his wife and children; but when overtaken, like wild animals they fight, against any number to the last moment. One dying Indian seized with his teeth the thumb of his adversary, and allowed his own eye to be forced out sooner than relinquish his hold.
>
> This is a dark picture, but how much more shocking is the undeniable fact that all the women who appear above twenty years old are massacred in cold blood! When I exclaimed that this appeared rather inhuman he answered "Why, what can be done? They breed so!"
>
> Everyone here is fully convinced that this is the most just war, because it is against barbarians. Who would believe in this age such atrocities could be committed in a Christian civilized country.
>
> General Rosas' plan is to kill all stragglers and having driven the remainder to a common point, to attack them in a body in the summer, with the assistance of the Chilenos. The operation is to be repeated for three successive years.[98]

Indians, wild animals, barbarians. To General Rosas, his commanders, and the Argentine political elite, what was the difference? The program of genocide in the Pampas continued into the 1870s. For Native Americans, little had changed since the arrival of the *conquistadores* in the north of the continent nearly 400 years earlier, despite the powerful protest of de las Casas' writings.[99]

The similarities were striking in the far West of the expanding United States, as settlers demanded extensive lands. In 1864, the 3rd Colorado Volunteer Cavalry Regiment was formed specifically to kill Cheyenne, Arapaho, or any other "Indians" its soldiers might find over a period of 100 days, the length of their enlistment. On August 10, the Colorado governor, John Evans, arguing that most Indians on the Plains were "hostile," published a proclamation calling on whites to "organize to pursue, kill and destroy" Cheyennes and Arapahos anywhere they were found. The commander of the 3rd Colorado Volunteers, Colonel John Milton Chivington, previously a Methodist minister, said, "My intention is to kill all Indians I may come across," including women, children, the elderly, and babies.[100] His justification for killing the newborn, now notorious, was that "nits make lice." Over the next months and as the enlisted men's 100-day engagement began to expire, the colonel's plans for extermination had disappointingly meagre results. Most of the "savages" in the area were under "peace chiefs" Black Kettle, White Antelope, and Left Hand. They were supposed to be protected by the 1st Colorado Regiment, commanded by Major Edward Wynkoop, at Camp Weld, just outside Denver, on condition of handing in their weapons and accepting what Ward Churchill terms "de facto internment."[101]

In mid-November the frustrated Chivington and his men agreed with a proposal from the newly promoted General Patrick Edward Connor (promoted after his "achievement" at the Bear River massacre of 500 Shoshoni men, women, and children in Idaho in January 1863) to extend their terms of service with the aim of attacking the peace chiefs and their people at Camp Weld. The day before the attack, Wynkoop was absent, innocent of the impending disaster. Chivington first had his men confine Wynkoop's small force to their barracks in order to ensure complete "surprise." (To their credit, two of Wynkoop's subordinate officers, Captain Silas Soule and Lieutenant Joseph Cramer, tried to prevent the attack. Soule was later murdered prior to giving evidence against Chivington.) Then, on the night of November 27, Chivington led his 900 men to Camp Weld. They were instructed to "kill and scalp all, little and big." At dawn the regiment attacked, ignoring the American and white flags fluttering above the sleeping village. The inhabitants fled in panic, most of them trying to escape up a creek bed. There they tried to hide by digging in the sand. Most of them were women and children. Churchill quotes an eyewitness, Robert Bent, the son of a local white trader and Cheyenne woman, who gave evidence before a Senate investigation:[102]

I saw five squaws under a bank for shelter. When the troops came up to them they ran out and showed their persons, to let the soldiers know they were squaws and begged for mercy, but the soldiers shot them all. . . . There were some thirty or forty squaws collected in a hole for protection; they sent out a little girl about six years old with a white flag on a stick; she had not proceeded but a few steps when she was shot and killed. All the squaws in the hole were afterwards killed. . . . The squaws offered no resistance. Every one I saw dead was scalped. I saw one squaw cut open with an unborn child, as I thought, lying by her side. . . . I saw quite a number of infants in arms killed with their mothers.[103]

Other Indians were killed as they tried to escape, some several miles away. A few who had been taken prisoner were executed. Then all the dead – 500 or 600, according to some reports, although 200 according to the Cheyenne – mostly women and children, were systematically mutilated. Another witness (actually a participating officer from the New Mexico Volunteers) testified at the Senate hearings:

> I did not see a body of a man, woman, or child but was scalped, and in many instances their bodies were mutilated in a most horrible manner – men, women and children's private parts cut out, &c; I heard one man say that he had cut out a women's private parts and had them for exhibition on a stick; I heard another man say he had cut off the fingers of an Indian to get the rings on the hand. . . . I also heard numerous instances in which men had cut out the private parts of females and stretched them over the saddle bows and wore them over hats while riding in the ranks.[104]

Years later, President Theodore Roosevelt referred to the Sand Creek massacre "on the whole, as righteous and beneficial a deed as ever took place on the frontier . . . despite a certain amount of temporary suffering."[105] It was not an isolated incident. Hundreds of similar massacres, large and small, took place during the settlement of the American West. There was no distinction between combatant and non-combatant when it came to Native Americans. There was no attempt to apply the doctrine of double effect.[106] There was no law of war, as was applied by the Union side (even if only in theory) in the American Civil War, as Scott Nelson shows in Chapter 3. As Mark Grimsley observes, it is not a new conclusion, at least for some historians, that the United States has two ways of fighting wars: "one for enemies who are similar to white Americans in culture and ethnicity, one for enemies who are not."[107] Yet the dominant view among historians of America, even now, is denial.

The Philippine-American War of 1899–1902 is a case in point. Historian Richard E. Welch concludes that "there is sufficient evidence to persuade any student" that the war would have been fought very differently if the Filipinos had been white: there would have been fewer Filipino casualties than the roughly 250,000 that resulted, and they would have had more impact on the conscience of Americans. Instead, the American public was largely too insulated by racism and distance to express significant concern over reported atrocities committed by their troops.[108] In fact, both American troops and most civilians at home considered Filipinos to be "niggers." This is clear, according to Welch, in the racist depictions of Filipinos in cartoons in a variety of mainstream publications. Perhaps this was not surprising in the era of Jim Crow.[109] H.L. Wells, Manila correspondent for the *New York Evening Post*, was largely understanding of the difficult conditions faced by American troops in the conflict. Yet he did not flinch from describing the racist contempt that they felt for their Filipino enemies:

There is no question that our men do "shoot niggers" somewhat in the sporting spirit, but that is because war and their environments have rubbed off the thin veneer of civilization. . . . Undoubtedly, they do not regard the shooting of Filipinos just as they would the shooting of white troops. This is partly because they are "only niggers," and partly because they despise them for their treacherous servility. . . . The soldiers feel that they are fighting with savages, not with soldiers.[110]

One American officer may have represented his fellow soldiers and his countrymen when he wrote, "I'd sooner see a hundred niggers killed than one of my men endangered."[111]

In southern Africa, settlers were also looking to expand into new lands. In June 1896 in what is now Zimbabwe, the Shona people, united through a common belief in their spirit mediums, rose up in revolt against the British South African Company, which had imposed itself in the region since 1890. Their chiefs began the offensive by rounding up white settlers' cattle and occupying the roads leading to the settlers' capital, Salisbury, and for about three months held the initiative. Chief Makoni, one of the paramount chiefs of central Shonaland, in the meantime made defensive preparations by reinforcing his kraal (a livestock enclosure within a homestead) on Gwindingwi Hill with a loopholed stone wall more than two metres high and storing reserves of foodstuffs in a series of large caves nearby.[112] By early August, the British had brought in reinforcements with seven-pounders and machine guns, and on the 3rd they mounted an assault on Gwindingwi kraal. The results for the attackers were mixed. After an artillery barrage, the kraal was cleared with difficulty, wall by wall, stockade by stockade. Yet the struggle was hardly over. Makoni, with his warriors and the women and children, had retreated into the caves to fight another day. Lieutenant-Colonel Alderson decided to burn the kraal and evacuate his men. Native Commissioner Edwards was scathing: "The surface of the kraal was taken; the natives, however, retired to their caves and made good their position; finding it impossible to dislodge them the Colonel retreated and continued his march towards Salisbury, leaving the natives in full possession, not so much as a sack of grain, which was very plentiful, being taken or destroyed."[113] This was only partly accurate. The position that Makoni and his people found themselves in was far more serious. According to Chief Chipunza, who was present at Alderson's initial assault, 200 of Makoni's men were killed and many more wounded. Makoni therefore offered to surrender on condition of amnesty. The British high commissioner rejected the offer. Terence Ranger argues that this failure to take up an opportunity that might have encouraged other chiefs to make peace contributed to the revolt's dragging on for more than a year, until the end of 1897.[114]

Plans were made for a second attack on Gwindingwi Hill. The best method, according to Alderson, was to drive all the rebels into the caves and leave a strong picket with wagons. All the grain stores in the area would be collected. Then, if the Shona in the caves refused to surrender, the caves would be dynamited. The technique had already been perfected in an earlier attack by Alderson's forces on Chief Manyepera's people, who also took refuge in their caves. Edwards was present and reported events. After the delivery of a wagonload of dynamite to the besieging British forces, "one case was fixed up with a long fuse and lowered down against the downstream entrance. I again warned the natives but as before was laughed at. The fuse was lit and we ran for safety. The explosion blew in the poles and rocks at the entrance and a rebel who must have been on guard there came staggering out. He was a terrible sight. He was skinned from top to toe, but still grasping his rifle." Chief Manyepera again refused to surrender, although he sent out to safety sixty women and children. Edwards continues: "Next day several cases of dynamite were laid along the fissure on top of the caves and fuses timed so that they all went off at once. Again I spoke to the rebels and warned them that this was the last chance they would get, but without any result. The fuse was fired and we retired to a safe distance. The explosion rent the cave from end to end. It was the end as far as the rebels in the cave were concerned. Two natives only escaped."[115]

The technique learned in this way, the British, now under Major Watts, employed it against Makoni and his people, who again abandoned their now destroyed kraals for the caves. They had amassed considerable stocks of food and water, so it was not thought practicable to attempt to starve them out. The assault started with a seven-pounder firing into the main entrance of the caves while the smaller entrances were sprayed by machine guns. Then the dynamiting began, to continue for four days. By that time, the dead in the caves were producing an "over-powering" stench, according to the Mashonaland correspondent of *The Times*. On the second and third days of the siege, groups of women and children emerged from cave mouths lower down the hill, although most of the men still held out. Finally, on the fourth day, Makoni either surrendered or was captured at one of the cave mouths and his surviving people then gave themselves up.[116] The siege was over, although the rebellion was not.

These events, terrible though they were, did not reach the levels of savagery of the genocides on the Pampas, in the American West, or in German South West Africa.[117] The British gave Manyepera and eventually, Makoni, numerous chances to surrender. Yet when they laid siege to the Shona chiefs in the caves they were not attacking warriors alone but whole communities. Non-combatants were probably in the majority. There seems to have been little compunction about killing or wounding significant numbers of women and children in order to crush the revolt. The dynamiting of the caves was indiscriminate, and it is not clear that military necessity required it. Indeed, Cecil Rhodes himself had supported amnesty for Makoni after the first attack on Gwindingwi, hoping that other important chiefs would also surrender. But high officials decided otherwise.

Jeff Guy's work, in Chapter 4, reminds us of the basic reality facing peasant and preindustrial societies defending themselves against aggressive and industrializing imperial powers. Typically, as in the case of the British invasion of Zululand in 1879, the conflict was presented to contemporaries in uncritical, even jingoistic terms, through the mass media and even in specialist writings. "More recently," Guy writes,

> the imperial nostalgia which underlies conventional histories of the invasion has seeped into the world of heritage and tourism with the result that colonial dispossession through warfare is presented as a heroic clash between the noble representatives of different military traditions – savage and civilized – which obscures with a sentimental veneer not just the brutality and injustice of the 1879 war but the fact that the invasion is a key to an understanding of contemporary misery and poverty in rural KwaZulu-Natal.[118]

Such approaches draw a veil of silence behind which the true nature of imperial wars is hidden. As Guy shows, the whole of society, not just identifiable military forces or warrior age-grade regiments, became the target. After the British setback at Isandlwana, Lord Chelmsford, the commander of the British troops in Zululand, was unmistakably clear when he wrote to Sir Henry Bulwer, Lieutenant Governor of neighbouring Natal: "I am satisfied that the more the Zulu nation at large feels the strain brought upon them by the war, the more anxious will they be to see it brought to an end."[119] The enemy now included all Zulu, as well as their homesteads, their livestock, and their crops and foodstuffs. If this was not total war to the British, it was "one-sided total war" to the Zulus.[120]

Precolonial African and Asian societies including those with relatively complex states, even militarized ones such as the Zulu kingdom, typically did not have standing armies in the modern sense. Rather, as Guy argues, the Zulu were an "armed people." The military life of the Zulu *amabutho* (age-grade regiments) was highly integrated into all aspects of life in all the homesteads of the kingdom. Traditional military strategy was subject to the limitations imposed by the demands of the agricultural calendar, and campaigns were usually restricted to the dry winter season. African armies in many regions were dependent on porters to carry supplies, the trypanosomecarrying tsetse fly making it impossible to use pack or draft animals. Campaigns tended to be short, in many places taking the form of raids and counter-raids. In southern and East Africa this usually involved cattle. If conflicts extended beyond this pattern to the destruction of villages, homesteads, and crops, then whole populations were at great risk. Protracted warfare on home territory of the sort imposed by the imperial powers, such as the Zulus faced in 1879, was highly unusual.[121] But this was what many peoples faced during the period of rapid imperial expansion during the late-nineteenth and early-twentieth centuries. Thus, as Guy argues, conventional literature that concentrates on describing pitched battles such as at Isandlwana, Rorke's Drift, and Ulundi misses the main issue, which is the consequence of warfare for whole populations, in terms of not only casualties but particularly the widespread destruction of the productive capacity of the indigenous economy. The main victims, of course, were women and children – whose daily labours underlay social maintenance and reproduction as well as agricultural production – the elderly, and the incapacitated. This was the pattern across expanding imperial frontiers, frequently according to systematic policies targeted at the means of subsistence. In such circumstances, there was little or no attempt to distinguish between combatants and non-combatants. As Helen Bradford has noted for the wars against the Xhosa, "Englishmen waged war primarily against women and children. 'With the Kaffirs, with beasts of prey, you must destroy their earths, their breeding places.'"[122]

In colonial New Zealand, many of the same points applied. The Maori, although innovative fighters and skilled engineers of modern, fortified *pa*, including earthworks, trenches, bunkers, and traps, had no professional warrior class. The economic surplus produced in a country without livestock before white settlement was minimal, and male labour was crucial to most productive activities. As James Belich writes, "The Maoris therefore faced the same problem as any tribal people in conflict with a regular army: a totally inadequate capacity to sustain a war of any length."[123] Even so, the last phases of the New Zealand wars dragged on for twelve years, from 1860 to 1872. Women assisted their men folk in various capacities and were often present during British attacks on *pa* sites.

The sceptical reader may argue that these examples of violent encounters on expanding imperial frontiers are not typical of wars between the West or its offshoots and non-Western peoples and nations. These conflicts instead represent more particular circumstances associated with settler land grabbing, local demands for cheap labour, and racial animosities compounded by the aggression of opportunistic men on the spot. Well-meaning people in London and the home counties, in Buenos Aires, and in New York or Boston would deplore what was done in their name if only they knew. Yet it may be countered, and has been, that the educated classes of the imperial capitals and the white-ruled nations of the New World indeed knew what was happening in the Congo Free State between 1884 and 1907, in Cyrenaica from 1911 to 1917 and again in 1923–32,[124] in Indochina under the French, or in the Iraq of 2003–09 but chose to ignore it.[125] A few did not and sometimes paid a high price for their protest, perhaps another form of collateral damage (see Chapter 7, by Robert Gregg). The test, therefore, is to look at imperial wars elsewhere, where there was little in the way of a settler lobby, few scheming speculators, and where indigenous populations seemed relatively stable or slowly increasing, unlike the Native Americans or the Tasmanians or the Khoisan of southern Africa. Let us consider two more cases from Africa, from the German and French empires, before turning to Indonesia, India, and China, dominated by the imperialist powers, among them Japan, at different stages from the seventeenth to the mid-twentieth century. It will become obvious that during the nineteenth and early twentieth centuries there was little practical difference between the British, French, Dutch, American, or German empires in terms of approaches to colonial war and civilian populations in war zones, although in the earlier decades the responsible authorities perhaps engaged in a little more hand wringing.

German East Africa (including Tanganyika, Rwanda, and Burundi) was the largest and most important possession in Germany's new empire. Although it attracted a few thousand white settlers, it was never in any real sense a settler colony, as were Southern Rhodesia, Algeria, and Angola. Nevertheless, unrelenting German pressure on African communities in the south, including Matumbi and Zaramo peasant farmers, riverine peoples such as Rufiji, and exploiters of forest resources such as the Ngindo, led to a massive uprising, the Maji Maji Rebellion, involving most of the peoples of the southern portion of the colony, from the hinterland of Dar es Salaam to the Rovuma River in the far south. Indeed, Michael Pesek argues in Chapter 6 that in the early years of the colonial state in East Africa, the Germans had no policy in the interior other than to perform a theatre of violence, to brutalize and plunder African societies until they submitted. Nationalist historians writing in the 1960s and '70s argued that the rebellion was an expression of a kind of protonationalism uniting a variety of state and stateless peoples through a common millenarian cult.[126] More recent work shows that local grievances such as the imposition of a brutal government on stateless peoples who had no use for one, forced cultivation of cotton, ill-treatment of local leaders by government functionaries, intervention in local politics, and the denial of access for Africans to traditional forest resources were more important.[127] Whatever the case, from its outbreak in July 1905, the rebellion spread like wild fire. On August 13, the Ngindo destroyed the German *boma* (fort) at

Liwale and killed everyone in it. By late August, believers had carried the *maji* – medicinal water that protected warriors against German bullets – to the powerful Ngoni chiefdoms of the Lake Malawi region, and a rebel assault on the German military station at Mahenge in the west had been beaten off, with huge casualties for the attackers. The rebellion expanded, bringing in the Mwera, Makua, and Makonde in the far south and the Pogoro, Mbunga, and Bena in the west. Several mission stations were sacked and chiefdoms loyal to the Germans attacked.

With the arrival of German reinforcements in October 1905, Governor Graf von Götzen could begin the business of repression, with the deliberate creation of famine as the central plank.[128] Three columns advanced from Dar es Salaam into the interior, concentrating on the destruction of crops and the seizure of foodstuffs rather than conducting a purely military offensive. Captain Wangenheim, commander of the expedition to Mahenge, believed that "only hunger and want can bring about a final submission. Military actions alone will remain more or less a drop in the ocean." After numerous setbacks and brutal fighting, the rebel response through 1906 was to avoid the Germans, confiscate food from loyalists, and plant crops in localities under their control. The rebellion entered a long period of guerrilla warfare, during which the Germans maintained harsh pressure on non-combatants in order to force them to give up rebel leaders. Nevertheless, there were several major engagements, during which the German machine guns caused terrible casualties against warriors ignorant of their effect. Hard core rebels were gradually defeated, everything destroyed in their villages, and their people prevented from cultivating the land so that they starved. The last holdout leaders were finally killed in mid-1908.

The impact of defeat on the people of southern Tanzania was catastrophic. I can do no better than quote John Iliffe, whose work remains without peer:

> Famine covered the land, a famine that killed. The greatest suffering was in Ungoni and the highlands. While [Ngoni chief] Chabruma remained free, Captain Richter in Songea prevented cultivation and appropriated all food for his troops. "The fellows can just starve," he declared. Not until April 1908 was food generally available again in Ungoni. Southern Usagara was described in 1906 as wholly depopulated. Uvidunda was thought to have lost half its population. "What shall I rule?" [Chief] Ngwira asked when he returned from prison. Götzen thought that more than half the Matumbi died in the revolt. A missionary reckoned that more than three-quarters of the Pangwa perished. A careful study of Ulanga made in the 1930s concluded that in the rebel areas, in addition to immediate deaths, "the famine reduced the average fertility of the surviving women by over 25 per cent." Total deaths in Maji Maji and its aftermath are

unknown. Dr Gwassa estimates them at 250,000–300,000, or perhaps one-third of the area's total population, and he may be right. In return the rebels killed 15 Europeans, 73 askari (African soldiers) and 316 auxiliaries.[129]

A glance at the modern map of Tanzania will show that much of the south is still depopulated, with a huge expanse occupied by the Selous Game Reserve.

In French West Africa, similar events were taking place, although not on such a vast scale. The revolt of the Baule peoples of the Côte-d'Ivoire against French authority was the result of heavy-handed intervention into the local economy and system of slavery, the imposition of taxes, and then military requisitions. The French campaign of 1898–1902 had begun as a limited operation against one Baule chief but soon intensified to the level of "a full-scale 'search and destroy' policy against an entire population." According to a French officer, "the complete reduction of this tribe" was necessary. This would be achieved "by seizing or destroying . . . everything that has the greatest value in the eyes of the adversary . . . by methodically destroying all his goods, by requisitioning his herds, by liberating his slaves, by pursuing combatants' families in their refuges and taking important members prisoner, including the women."[130]

In the final phase of Baule resistance, from 1908 to 1911, the French governor, Gabriel Louis Angoulvant, gained a reputation for brutality not only in humanitarian circles in France but also among French businessmen in the Côte-d'Ivoire. One local official feared the emergence of the kind of terrible repression that had recently been the norm in the Congo. In 1908, a colonial medical officer reported on atrocities committed by French officers, including the decapitation and public display of enemy corpses as a warning to other groups.[131] By 1910, the French were once again employing the same kind of search and destroy tactics and destruction of the Baule subsistence economy as they had in the earlier phases of Baule resistance. Timothy Weiskel writes, "Food stores were confiscated, encampments were systematically burned, and new planted crops were uprooted in an effort to bring the Baule to their knees."[132] As in the other campaigns noted, in southern and eastern Africa, the destruction of the food economy – in this case, the annual harvest of yams – targeted whole populations, and starvation drove the resisters into submission. The holdouts, desperate for food, then raided farms in loyalist chiefdoms, thus contributing to civil conflict much as we saw in the case of the Maji Maji Rebellion. After the fighting was over, the loss of property, disarmament, indemnities, and higher head taxes deliberately pushed the Baule into deepening poverty with the aim of forcing them into participation in the colonial capitalist economy. Further, the Baule village system was systematically dismantled. Instead of being permitted to rebuild destroyed villages, the people were forcibly relocated into new village concentrations.[133] The result of close to thirteen years of repression (1899–1911) was a catastrophic collapse of the population in the Baule homeland, from estimates of 1 to 2 million in the late 1890s to about 225,000 in 1916. The causes were not so much casualties in battle, but famine, disease, and outmigration.[134]

In the Ambon Islands, where cloves were the main attraction for Europeans, it took the Dutch several decades in the early seventeenth century to suppress a series of revolts by islanders disaffected by forced labour, bad treatment from Dutch sailors and soldiers, and other grievances. In early 1637, Governor General Antonie van Diemen himself arrived at the islands with seventeen large ships and 2,000 soldiers and sailors. He quickly decided to attack the rebel stronghold at Lusiëla. Perhaps unusually, the soldiers were on pain of death prohibited from looting, burning, murdering, and raping unless officers gave specific permission. Ambonese casualties seem to have been relatively light.[135] Nearly 200 years later, in Java in 1825, the Dutch employed far more ruthless measures when the principality of Yogyakarta and its allies revolted under the leadership of Dipanagara. In 1815, the Dutch had returned after the British had briefly held the territory. For financial reasons they imposed a series of controls on the ruling elite yet failed to improve the position of the peasantry. General Hendrik Merkus de Kock responded to the popular revolt by building a series of fortresses connected by roads. Based at these points, mobile forces then sallied out to ravage the surrounding countryside. As in South Africa and so many other places, "It was a war of attrition for the ordinary people as well as rebels, with immense devastation." Total Javanese deaths from the war and associated famines and epidemics are estimated at 200,000.[136]

India provided a vast field of activity for British officers and soldiers. One of the first words to enter the English language from India was "loot," the distribution of which after battle was conducted, from the early 1800s, in an orderly manner on the basis of rank by "prize agents." The thousands of Indian baggage animal drivers and porters that the British Army required when in the field were impressed and kept in line through mass floggings.[137] Racist attitudes underlay such treatment. In 1848, British and Sepoy regiments were engaged with irreconcilable Sikhs at Multan, in the western Punjab province. In the months before the city could be brought under siege, surrounding villages were "cleared."[138] Then intense shelling of the city and the fortress started, with replying salvoes from the defending Sikh batteries. A contemporary historian wrote, "Seldom or never in any part of the world has a city been exposed to such a terrific shelling as the doomed city of Multan."[139] In January 1849, after a protracted siege that included mining the walls, the city was taken by storm. Women and men were shot, women were raped, and the assailants went on a rampage for loot. A British soldier's diary records that "our men now appeared to be brutish beyond everything, having but little mercy on one another – still less for an enemy. . . . Our native soldiers were much worse, and more brutish; but they were more to be excused, as they were natives." Some of the officers "were equally as brutal as the men."[140]

In 1857, the Indian Mutiny, a "war of races," broke out.[141] Most of the rebellious Sepoy units defended fixed positions, but as these were gradually overcome rebel unity broke down and guerrilla warfare commenced. The British massed troops to besiege fortified urban centres and often found themselves engaged in dreadful street fighting, but then were increasingly forced into counter-insurgency operations. Racial animosity reached extreme levels. V.G. Kiernan writes that on the British side, "Thirst for revenge ensured that all successes were thoroughly followed up, and retreating 'niggers,' as they were habitually called, given no respite. Energetic pursuit was a hallmark of European colonial practice, [Colonel] Callwell was to emphasize. 'Asiatics do not understand such vigour and are cowed by it.'"[142]

There were of course plenty of precedents for the brutal suppression of insurrections, including that of the Santals of Bengal and Orissa, a non-Hindu forest people who as they moved onto the plains found themselves caught between the forces of modernization, bonded labour, and a harsh colonial system.[143] Armed with bows and arrows in 1855, they removed the Raj from three districts, holding out for five months. Their ultimate defeat was devastating and many starved. The solution, some British officials believed, was mass deportation of the Santals overseas. "Liberal" imperialists preferred instead to turn the Santal peasants into coolie wage labourers for the Assam tea plantations or indentured labour in Mauritius and the Caribbean. The larger aim was to utilize the defeat of peasant revolts for broader imperial economic interests. For that to succeed, Santal society had to be forcibly incorporated into the colonial capitalist economy. In reality, the "improvement" offered by wage labour was a chimera. Ranajit Guha writes,

Many of these so-called improvements were . . . the result of sheer wishful thinking or so ephemeral as not to have mattered at all. The connection between usury and bonded labour continued all through the British rule well into independent India. The freedom of the labour market was seriously restricted by the want of competition between British and indigenous capital. The employment of tribal families on tea plantations became a source of cynical exploitation of the labour of women and children. . . . The system of indenturing helped rather less to liberate servile labour than to develop a sort of second serfdom, and so on.[144]

From the imperial standpoint, rebellions were envisaged as opportunities to remake offending peoples into satisfactory contributors to the imperial project. In the Santal revolt and in many others around the world, the distinction between combatants and non-combatants never had any meaning. The imperial context made sure of that, even if the Santals were not as united as nationalist historiography sometimes suggests. Indeed, in later times, as Smita Tewari Jassal shows us in Chapter 10, tribal peoples' memories of collective suffering, idealized, could become a badge of honour, to be used in claims against the postcolonial state.

On the northwest frontier of the British Indian empire, there was almost perpetual fighting for more than a quarter of a century as the British attempted to subdue Afridis and other Pashtuns (Pathans).[145] The relatively decentralized nature of these societies made it difficult to enforce authority. A variety of strategies were developed to pacify the frontier districts: blockades, modest fines if there was co-operation, and large-scale expeditions in which Mahsuds or Wazirs were forced back into the mountains and their crops and settlements destroyed. To give two examples, in 1850 the Afridis were collectively blockaded into their hill refuges and "starved into submission." This seemed to fail, because two years later the British resorted to "the policy of slaying and burning . . . odious to us, as to any of our critics," according to Governor General Dalhousie. In 1897–98, the Tirah campaign involved 40,000 British and Indian soldiers fighting against rebellious tribal levies in the region of the Khyber Pass and was described by the young Winston Churchill as a "war without quarter."[146] Both sides committed atrocities. It is not clear what the full impact on non-combatants was, but given British tactics elsewhere in the colonial world, women and children must have suffered terribly.

At the top there were occasional pangs of conscience over the human cost of these campaigns and also recourse to political realism concerning military measures in the colonies. A contemporary expert wrote that over a decade after the revolt of the Santals, officers involved in the pacification preferred silence rather than discussion of British measures. As for the Indian soldiers employed in this work, "There was not a Sepoy . . . who did not feel ashamed of himself."[147] A more remarkable example of imperial conscience is found in the career of James Bruce, eighth Earl of Elgin and twelfth Earl of Kincardine, the British Plenipotentiary with the Anglo-French expeditionary force to China in 1857–58 and 1860, during the Second Opium War.[148] The *Arrow* incident, in which Chinese officials boarded a suspected smugglers' ship that the British claimed to have been flying a British ensign, was a trumped-up *casus belli* of British aggression and, in Elgin's own words, "a scandal . . . and is so considered, I have reason to know, by all except the few who are personally compromised."[149] Yet the telling fact is that his conscience did not deter him one iota from his imperial duty. As John Newsinger notes, Elgin's own writings provide a remarkable commentary on aspects of the psychology of imperialism. On December 22, 1857, Elgin's diary entry records his anguish as a fleet of thirty-two British warships prepared to pound the city of Canton.

> I never felt so ashamed in my life, and Elliot [Newsinger, the ship's captain] remarked that the trip seemed to have made me sad. There we were, accumulating the means of destruction under the very eyes, and within the reach of a population of about 1,000,000 people, against whom these means of destruction were to be employed! "Yes," I said to Elliot. "I am sad because when I look at that town, I feel that I am earning for myself a place in the litany immediately after 'plague, pestilence and famine.'" I believe, however that, as far as I am concerned, it was impossible for me to do otherwise than as I have done.[150]

Six days later, the massive bombardment of shells and rockets began, "without almost any reply from the town," Elgin wrote. Another British observer, a correspondent of *The Times*, took a different attitude toward the destruction, and eagerly recorded how the city by night became "a plain of fire."[151] Although the British and French aimed to concentrate their fire on the city walls, hundreds of civilians were most likely killed. Elgin's secretary, Laurence Oliphant, said 200, but one wonders how he could know. Certainly, the heavy bombardment went well beyond the walls, and Oliphant wrote that it had a terrible effect "upon certain parts of the city." Oliphant was most satisfied with the result; the bombardment had made "a deep impression upon a population whose habitual insolence to foreigners had rendered it extremely desirable that they should be made aware of the power we possessed."[152] This typically belligerent imperial mindset made little distinction between combatants and non-combatants. Elgin's conscience said otherwise; he was distressed by the behaviour of the British and French soldiers and sailors, and in mid-January 1858 recorded in his diary that he could not "accept the office of oppressor of the feeble." When the allied expedition sailed away from Canton he self-righteously wrote of his efforts at "checking . . . the disposition to maltreat this unfortunate people."[153] Six months later, after the capture of the Dagu Forts and the occupation of Tianjin, Elgin could write that though "I have been forced to act almost brutally, I am China's friend in all this."[154] After this display of force and the imposition of the Treaty of Tien-tsin (including an indemnity and the opening up of five more treaty ports) on the imperial government, Elgin returned to Britain in May 1859.

In his absence, the British suffered a major setback at the hands of the Chinese. The new ambassador to Beijing, Elgin's brother, Frederick Bruce, believed that imperial prestige required sending a large force to Beijing to cement the treaty. The Chinese proposed a smaller force and a different route. To Bruce, this was unacceptable: the Chinese had to be shown who was boss. At the now reconstructed Dagu Forts, guarding the route up the Baihe River to Beijing, the British suffered almost 1,000 casualties. When Elgin returned to China in April 1860 he was instructed to restore the British position in China and if necessary to occupy Beijing. This necessitated a third assault on the Dagu Forts, this time by 20,000 British and French troops. The campaign relied heavily on barrages by the new Armstrong artillery (used also in the New Zealand Wars). According to Newsinger, the "use of artillery to ensure against defeat turned the campaign into a series of technological massacres, interspersed by periods of looting," as well as the execution of prisoners and atrocities against the civilian population.[155] The culmination was the infamous destruction of the Emperor's Summer Palace complex of more than forty buildings, described by a participant, Charles Gordon, as "wretchedly demoralizing work."[156]

Throughout, as Newsinger has shown, Elgin expressed private remorse for many of the consequences of British actions in China and in India: "How did Elgin sustain the lifelong contradiction – in many ways so emblematic of liberal England – that left him lamenting in private actions which he relentlessly pursued in public?" The answer, Newsinger suggests, was partly the self-interested building of a highly successful career in imperial diplomacy and politics, and partly the belief that he could moderate the consequences of admittedly brutal policies. Yet as Newsinger so rightly points out, there was little in the way of mitigation in imperial wars. He quotes another observer of the events in China in 1860, Henry Brougham Loch. In the town of Pehtang, which had a population of about 20,000, the military occupation

> necessitated the ejectment of many of the inhabitants from their houses; this was done as kindly as possible. . . . Whole streets had to be pulled down; the people had nowhere to go, no money and no food; old women who for years had never been outside their door suddenly found themselves without a roof to cover them and wandered tottering along in helpless misery.

Loch continues, "what became of a large majority of that population we could never ascertain."[157] In my view, it is precisely the "liberal" imperialist thinking of men such as Elgin that we frequently see reflected in twentieth- and twenty-first-century approaches to war and civil populations in conflict zones, eventually necessitating the alibi of collateral damage.

In the late nineteenth and early twentieth centuries, the age of positivism and high imperialism, the liberal conscience still existed, but its public expression was usually limited to condemnation of excesses in other people's colonies: German support for the Boers in South Africa as the imperial armies ground them down, British horror at King Léopold's atrocities in the Congo (although British concessionary companies were also responsible), and French cynicism concerning British colonial policies. The apparent exception, the South African War of 1899–1902, was viewed by both sides as a "white man's war." Yet it was not an exception according to the British commander-in-chief at the War Office: the laws of war as applied to "civilized" nations were irrelevant in South Africa.[158] Chris Madsen, in Chapter 5, argues that British (and Canadian) behaviour in South Africa was in fact legal according to British military manuals at that time. The military code was enforced by the disciplinarian Horatio Herbert Kitchener, the first Earl Kitchener, yet it often veered into brutal excesses that would in hindsight be termed war crimes. Boer non-combatants suffered in many of the same ways that people caught up in colonial wars elsewhere did: this was, from the Boer perspective, very much a war against women and children. Yet almost all accounts of the war are silent on what Helen Bradford cites as the "occupation of most British troops" and the "principal activity of the British Army," which was to "enthusiastically descend ... on feminized spaces to loot cattle, blind sheep, hang cats, hack slices off pigs, fire houses and load black and Boer civilians into carts destined for concentration camps."[159] Such activities were deemed "odious" or "methods of barbarism" and therefore not "real war" as British gentlemen – and most historians – understood it. In Bradford's view, a definition of war should be inclusive of "what the imperial army did most of the time: terrorize unarmed people."[160] The destructive effect of the war on Africans in some parts of South Africa is even less well documented.[161]

The major difference with other colonial wars was that the Boers were given political rights and targeted for rehabilitation after their defeat. Further, this was a war in which popular and visual forms of propaganda played a major role in shaping public perceptions in Britain, as Tom Gretton shows in Chapter 8, although opposing messages were sometimes implicit. In pro-imperialist newspapers such as the *Daily Mail* and *The Times*, and in pamphlets such as those funded by the Imperial South Africa Association, the Boers were described as primitive and tribal, barely European or Western in any recognizable sense. Imperial troops often saw them in the same way, as racialized "others."[162] The propaganda war was not one sided, however, especially as the war dragged on into its guerrilla fighting phase, and the fate of Boer (but not African) non-combatants became a major concern in Liberal circles in Britain after Emily Hobhouse's exposé of conditions in the concentration camps.[163]

Despite its (wrongful) reputation as a war essentially fought between opposing armies, with relatively little direct impact on civilians, the First World War helped to "set the trajectory" toward the catastrophic scale of civilian deaths in the Second World War and the wars of the post-1945 era. Hew Strachan cites a figure of 6 million for the First World War. Up to 750,000 died as a consequence of the British naval blockade on Germany, which led to mass starvation among the old, children, and the ill. More attention is now paid to the genocide of the Armenians, but there was also massive civilian suffering in Serbia, among the Turks of Anatolia and Eastern European Jews, and in parts of Russia after the 1915 defeat.[164] One should also add the huge burdens borne by civilians during the long East African campaign, in a war that was fought on African territory but not on their behalf. At least 100,000 conscripted porters out of the approximately 1 million impressed to carry military supplies and ammunition died of disease, overwork, and starvation. John Iliffe suggests that losses totalled perhaps two or three times that number: "In the second half of 1917 *recorded* deaths were over 2 per cent per *month* and 'wastage' – including every kind of incapacitation and desertion – was reckoned at 15 per cent per month." Porter deaths outnumbered casualties from all military units put together.[165] Uncountable numbers of innocent people starved as a consequence of requisitions of food crops and livestock for the British imperial armies, the Belgian Force Publique, and the German Schutztruppe. War left famine and disease in its wake.[166]

During the interwar period the momentum toward the massive catastrophes of the Second World War, Korea, Vietnam, and Cambodia, and then the anti-colonial liberation wars in Portuguese and southern Africa – intensified as they were by Cold War interventions – increased. The Italians, not to be outdone by the British and the French, sought for the second time to expand their empire in the Horn of Africa. On the October 3, 1935, an Italian army crossed the Mareb River, which divided their colony of Eritrea from Ethiopia (then known as Abyssinia), and began the invasion of the last independent African country.[167] In 1928, Italy had ratified the 1925 Geneva Protocol outlawing the use of asphyxiating gas. Yet Mussolini was willing to abandon any pretence of following the laws of war and equipped the invading army with an air force and a large stockpile of war chemicals and poison gas. In addition, thousands of C 500-T yperite and C 100-P arsine gas bombs and 76,000 arsine artillery shells were shipped to Eritrea and Somalia for use by the invading forces. From October 1935 through 1936, the Italian Air Force dropped approximately 1,600 C 500-T bombs on the Ethiopians and another 500 during the resistance phase from 1936 to 1939.[168] The Italians also bombed Red Cross ambulances, hospitals, and civilians.

The Italians defended these violations by stating that they were in response to atrocities committed by the Ethiopians against Italian troops, as well as the Ethiopian abuse of the symbol of the Red Cross. Such arguments have always been made in imperial wars. General Rodolfo Graziani, for example, used the language of imperialism when asking Mussolini for permission to use gas "against the barbaric horde ready to commit any kind of horrors."[169] We have already seen how propaganda played a major role in influencing British public opinion during the South African War. In response to international concern about the bombing of Red Cross facilities, the Italians mounted a major counter-propaganda campaign to publicize and exaggerate Ethiopian excesses, especially emasculation and the use of dum-dum bullets by Ethiopian troops. At the same time the Fascist propaganda machine at home proliferated similar ideas or else belittled Ethiopian culture and fighting spirit. Much of this propaganda emphasizes the conquest of Ethiopian women.[170] But as Alberto Sbacchi argues, "the acts that appeared 'barbaric' were desperate actions of defenseless people who tried to defend themselves the best way they knew how."[171] The relatively few mutilations of Italians that occurred were played for all they were worth, and the use of dum-dum bullets was wildly exaggerated. In response to both excesses, the Italians used poison gas. Sbacchi writes,

> Italian use of poison gas was facilitated by Ethiopia's absence of retaliatory capability and by the fact that the war was fought in a faraway country whose inhabitants were considered inferior. The Fascist propaganda that gas was used to retaliate against Ethiopian atrocities is only partially correct. In reality Italy considered chemical weapons as a means of legitimate warfare.[172]

Poison gas was used not only against Ethiopian troops but also on Ethiopian villages far from the fighting. From November 1935, General Pietro Badoglio mounted an air campaign against cities, roads, hospitals, and Red Cross compounds. Yperite gas was sprayed on villages, lakes, rivers, herds, and fields. The northwestern regions from the Takkaze River and northern Gondar to Axum and Adwa in Tigre province were particularly badly hit, as were parts of the southern front.[173] The effects on victims were not only suffocation but also terrible ulcers and blisters over the whole body, as well as blindness. In many other cases civilians had not been directly exposed to the gas but suffered from intestinal poisoning after drinking contaminated water. This happened at Lake Aschanghi, for example. Besides killing non-combatants directly and indirectly, yperite killed many mules and horses that were essential to transportation in Ethiopia, and large numbers of cattle.[174] International organizations carry a high degree of responsibility for the continuing Italian use of poison gas as a weapon of terror in Ethiopia. The International Red Cross failed to speak out even though it had considerable evidence, believing it more important to protect its neutrality. The League of Nations was indifferent to Italian aggression in the first place. Clearly, however, Italian civil and military officials were ultimately accountable.[175]

Empire was not a habit of Western peoples alone. The Japanese conquest of China from 1937 and other examples suggest that the social construction of out-groups or "othering" is based not only on imperial fantasies in the metropole and the building of "racial" or cultural hierarchies to highlight the alleged inferiority of potential subject populations but on the very acts of conquest and subsequent domination themselves. The pattern of abuses of civilians in imperial wars is quite consistent, as we have seen so far. Recent research even suggests that there was relatively little difference between democracies and dictatorships in this regard during the twentieth century.[176] National cultural differences between metropoles are not sufficiently explanatory. We do not always need to search for specific cultural characteristics or special circumstances to explain bloodthirsty behaviour by imperial armies in far-off lands, as has often been attempted in the case of Japanese atrocities in China, although these may be relevant. As historians Yang Daqing and Callum MacDonald argue in independent analyses, even extreme events such as the Rape of Nanjing (Nanking) need to be placed in comparative context and not treated in isolation.[177]

More broadly, a reassertion of imperial domination leads directly to the revival and elaboration of older stereotypes and prejudices that contribute to a climate fostering widespread abuse of civilian populations. This is clearly the case in the Middle East in the twenty-first century. The histories of orientalist constructions of the East are now quite well known, even if such constructions were not uniform and were sometimes contested by alternative world views within the West influenced by interaction with the colonized world.[178] We have seen older anti-Arab and anti-Muslim images resurrected in their crudest forms in recent years. But the act of conquest and the mental conditioning required to make it happen bring with them contempt and a new justification for violence directed against occupied peoples. At the same time, the deliberate use of a strategy to create maximum terror by invading and occupying forces means that widespread abuses are often state sanctioned.

With the end of formal empire after the wave of decolonization from the 1940s through the 1960s and the demise of scientific racism – despite its lingering effects in sections of Western societies and institutions – yet with Western and now Eastern bloc intervention continuing in many parts of the world, an alibi was now required, the alibi of collateral damage. From the 1960s, with the enormous new influence of television, public opinion in democratic societies would not tolerate the open continuation of wartime abuse of civilians, most clearly seen during the Vietnam War. But in 1937, still the age of high imperialism, no alibi was necessary. Nor did the Japanese at first hide the enormity of their atrocities in Nanjing, which were openly celebrated in the home media.[179] Japanese attitudes toward China had hardened since the first defeat of China in 1895, particularly in the military. The acceptance of Social Darwinist and imperialist views in Japan from the late nineteenth century contributed to the emergence of an attitude of contempt for other Asian peoples.[180] Conquest itself further contributed to hatred for the defeated and subject population and thus to massive abuses, and conversely to great fear in the minds of the Chinese. In Nanjing, a city of over 1 million people before the Japanese invasion, somewhere between 260,000 and 350,000 Chinese civilians were killed by Japanese soldiers from December 13, 1937, to early 1938. Tens of thousands of Chinese POWs were executed, including many used for bayonet practice. Somewhere between 20,000 and 80,000 women were raped, mutilated, and tortured, often to death, by Japanese troops with the connivance of their officers. Aerial bombardment from July that year had already terrorized the population.[181] But Nanjing is merely the best known of hundreds of massacres that terrorized the Chinese population and remain lost to history, buried in silence.

The terror resulting from heavy bombing and the atrocities in Nanjing swiftly spread into neighbouring regions. Diana Lary writes of the city of Xuzhou (Suchow) in Shandong province, to the northwest of Nanjing, that its population "sank into chronic anxiety" as news of events to the south reached them. A Québécois missionary – one of twenty-five who bravely remained in the city as most of its population fled in advance of the Japanese entrance – recorded in his journal, "Everywhere *rumour* reigned. It spoke only of the atrocities committed by the Japanese, women raped, pregnant women killed to help to wipe out the Chinese race, young men shot for having been soldiers, or to prevent them from becoming soldiers, students, prisoners, wounded, massacred."[182] Both events and rumour contributed to such fear that "many civilians were convinced that they too would be killed simply because they were Chinese, and that Japan was engaged in a race war against China."[183] The contempt, hatred, and fear occasioned by conquest, domination, and submission added misery upon misery onto the Chinese.

Yet there were further similarities with imperial conflicts in other contexts and ages. In Chapter 9, Tim Brook shows how some Japanese officials were bemused by the damage and suffering they had helped to create, and in the wake of great atrocities reacted in complex ways. Takada Mitsusaburō, a leader of a civilian pacification team in Danyang in the western Yangtze Delta, worked earnestly in what he thought were the interests of the Chinese people of the area. Was Takada very different from well-meaning officials in the French, British, or American empires, determined to put a human face on the indefensible?

The plight of refugees deserves attention. Given the nature of total, totalitarian warfare in imperial contexts and the deliberate destruction of civil populations, the creation of millions of refugees was a predetermined outcome. In Shandong, as the Chinese armies withdrew in May 1938, the towns and cities emptied out as people fled the advancing Japanese. Lary notes that families with girls and young women were often quick to flee to the West, but at the same time refugees from areas to the east of Xuzhou were just arriving. One of the Canadian priests described the scene on May 14 just south of Xuzhou:

> On the road to the southwest, a long ribbon of ox carts stretches without interruption. This is the whole population of the North in flight. The women and children are on the carts, in the middle of bundles, baskets, sacks, chicks, goats, etc. Many are in tears, the children are crying. The men beat the oxen. Impossible to stop, only to go on. In the middle of all this are incredible numbers of soldiers. To go faster, they pass through the wheat. One would say that there is no air. All is gloom. One only breathes dust.[184]

But there was no safety as the Japanese attacked from the air any groups they found on the road. Civilians were targeted exactly the same as were military units. Those who did not have the resources to escape were then subject to what Lary terms "an orgy of brutality" for two weeks after the arrival of Japanese troops in the middle of May, characterized by the burning of towns and villages, massacres, and rapes.[185]

According to Lary and Stephen MacKinnon, *conservative* estimates put the Chinese loss of life from 1937 to 1945 at 20 million, with 100 million civilians displaced.[186] They put this massive figure into the context of a longer history of nearly continual civilian wartime suffering in China from the Taiping Rebellion (1851–64) onward. Yet the Japanese invasion in 1937 (actually, beginning in 1931) follows the pattern of imperial wars elsewhere more than of internal conflicts spawned by the weakening and collapse of the Ch'ing dynasty and then the civil war between the Communists and the Guomindang.

Historians of the Anti-Japanese War in China have contributed to an important debate about the causes of extreme violence against civilian populations. The Rape of Nanjing was well publicized by the media in China, Japan (initially), the United States, and elsewhere in the West.[187] Yet from the perspective of this essay, the most illuminating argument is that the events in Nanjing, the Yangtze basin, and elsewhere in eastern China were a deliberate part of a Japanese campaign to create terror among the Chinese rather than the result of lapses in discipline. The first to reach this conclusion seems to have been *Manchester Guardian* correspondent Harold Timperley in 1938. In

1939, American officer Haldore Hanson went further to argue that the Japanese employed a form of "totalitarian warfare."[188] Many Chinese authors also saw the massive scale of Japanese brutalities against civilians as deliberate and not "a temporary relapse in Japanese military discipline ... brought about by the heat of the battle."[189] The point about totalitarian warfare is important, not because it was new in 1937 but because it was in fact old. One must shift perspective from the world view of the major industrialized powers to that of colonized peoples. Imperial war from the perspective of the Pampas Indians and the Cheyenne, the Zulu and the Herero, the Matumbi and the Baule, the Afridis, Chinese and Vietnamese peasants was total war, totalitarian war. MacDonald is very clear on the links between Japanese atrocities throughout their empire, racism fostered by imperialism, and imperialism more generally:

> In the wider context of the Yangtse campaign and of earlier examples of Japanese atrocities in Taiwan, Korea and Manchuria, it [the Nanjing massacre] is revealed as part of a considered policy, already long established, of punishing "inferior" races. In this respect racism and imperialism were intimately associated with atrocity which was a fundamental element of the punishment expedition wherever it appeared. What was dismissed by the West during the war as typical Japanese conduct reflected a more universal tendency inherent in the idea of an imperial "civilizing mission."[190]

John W. Dower is more specific in comparing Japan's war in Asia and the U.S. war in Indochina in terms of the mass atrocities committed, pacification strategies – the Americans studied Japan's use of scorched earth tactics in rural China – the experience of dishonour faced by returning soldiers, and, of course, defeat. The difference lies in the double standard that still burdens the Japanese when questions are raised about responsibility and atonement, despite American collusion for political reasons in the concealment and downplaying of Japanese war crimes.[191]

From Colonial to Postcolonial Wars: Collateral Damage Comes into Its Own

> In terms of what is legitimate in warfare and administration, there has been rapid deterioration. It began long ago, in holes and corners, and grew deviously, unrecorded.[192]

I have heard an officer say, "Well, so we zap." (The word zap means kill here.) "So we zap the whole village, oh it hurts me a little but what the heck, there are communists in it and we've got to do it, and that's it." Well, this sort of rationale is a respectable rationale for fighting men. But how long can you keep on doing it. How many villages can you zap?[193]

Since 1945, the United States has emerged to be the major economic, techno-logical, and imperial power; indeed, a superpower. The post-Second World War period coincides with the greatest technological development deriving from military industrialism in terms of weaponry of all kinds, logistics, com-munications networks, and inflated military budgets. Further, the period wit-nessed a return to a kind of quasi-religious fundamentalism recently exhibited in the War on Terror. These developments (and of course they began well before 1945) have outstripped the capability of traditional restraints in war-fare, including the doctrine of double effect and the laws of war, to rationally control the devastating impact of modern (or postmodern) wars on non-combatants. This is despite the emergence of a humanitarian response like no other in any period of history and the implementation of the 1949 Geneva Conventions with the aim of protecting the victims of war, the 1977 Addi-tional Protocols, the 1997 Ottawa Convention on the Prohibition of the Use, Stockpiling, Production, and Transfer of Anti-Personnel Mines, and now recent efforts to outlaw cluster bombs.[194]

We have seen that the laws of war and the doctrine of double effect never in fact applied to wars between the industrializing/industrial West and the peoples of Africa, Asia, and the Americas. When the non-Western countries, the former colonies, and "uncivilized" parts of the world obtained their inde-pendence from the great European, American, and Japanese empires, they suddenly entered the world of European-style nation states. They entered the realm of international law. They applied for and gained seats at the United Nations. For the very first time they were even able to influence the making of international humanitarian law, which they had suffered most from the lack of in earlier decades and centuries, through the negotiations over the 1977 Additional Protocols to the Geneva Conventions.[195] What was formerly deemed legitimate became illegitimate in international law and according to public opinion. Further, their peoples became human. In Bamako, Mali, at a unique celebration of the bicentennial of the French Revolution, a famous lawyer, Mr. Diallo, took the floor and described the process:

"I remember that when I was a monkey . . ." The hall burst into laughter and applauded noisily. Mr. Diallo continued his remarks, narrating his memories as a monkey. He was not present during the great period of the triangular trade and therefore could not remember it. He was not present at the time of the Berlin Treaty any more than he was in the days of Jules Ferry, in the era of Jules-Ferryism. No, at the time of the Native Code (*Code de l'indigénat*), he was a monkey, according to him, and so remained between the end of the Native Code and the day his country became independent.

"I became a human being the day, hour, and minute my country attained sovereignty, the day I became, in my country, a citizen of my country; the day the language of the colonizer ceased to speak on my behalf, to define me."[196]

This is why collateral damage as euphemism became necessary. Indeed, it was born as soon as serious claims were made to national sovereignty.

Yet most wars did not change in practice, as Korea, Kenya, Vietnam, Algeria, Malaya, Iraq, and many others show. Much of the deterioration referred to by Kiernan took place during the 1950s and 1960s in the midst of "decolonization,"[197] and during or after the negotiation, signing, and ratification of the 1949 Geneva Conventions by the remaining colonial and imperial powers.[198] We have briefly considered American atrocities in Korea. Besides Vietnam, two other conflicts in particular contributed to the emergence of collateral damage: Mau Mau in Kenya and Algeria.

The new and painstaking research of American historian Caroline Elkins shows that the suppression of the Mau Mau revolt was much less a counter-insurgency operation against anti-colonial rebels than a war against the whole Kikuyu civilian population. It was only just beginning in 1954, as the armed conflict in the forests was coming to an end. The British Army, with local troops, had taken care of military operations, but the war against the people was in the hands of the colonial government, backed by London. An estimated 90 per cent of the Kikuyu population of about 1.5 million had taken an oath of allegiance to the resistance movement. The government now aimed to break the will of the people and force them to renounce their oaths and "rehabilitate" them to colonial society. The means were brutal and totalitarian, consisting of massive forced removals, deportations, the imprisonment of thousands, and confinement of up to 320,000 more in detention camps. Up to another million civilians, mostly women and children, were detained in approximately 800 concentrated Emergency villages, surrounded by barbed wire, trenches, watchtowers, and armed guards. There they carried out forced labour and starved. Thousands of women were beaten, raped, tortured, and killed by armed white settlers such as the notorious Kiboroboro ("Killer"), by Kenyan soldiers, and by members of the Kikuyu loyalist Home Guard, encouraged by the British. In Kikuyu areas, people were subject to a reign of terror with random shootings, torture, and executions taking place on a regular basis. Movements of Africans were strictly controlled, and screening processes known as the "Pipeline" were established to separate the "sheep from the goats." Screening relied extensively on beatings, torture, and endless humiliations.[199] The official figure of Mau Mau deaths was 11,000. Elkins believes the real figure was many times that, perhaps hundreds of thousands.[200]

It was perhaps no coincidence that Britain delayed ratifying the Geneva Conventions until September 1957 because in Kenya, although the shooting phase of the Mau Mau uprising was largely over by the end of 1954, the State of Emergency was maintained until January 1960. Nevertheless, the British did consider the impact of the application of international human rights law to the conflict, particularly the European Convention on Human Rights, which applied to British territories including Kenya from October 1953. But the Convention had an opt-out derogation clause that allowed suspension of its provisions during an extreme emergency that endangered the nation. This was why the Emergency was kept in place, because the derogation made detention without trial possible. Despite this superficial attention to the niceties of international law, the British systematically broke European Convention and U.N. Declaration of Human Rights prohibitions on torture during the Mau Mau war and Emergency. They also contravened the Geneva Conventions through their policy of mass communal detentions aimed at breaking Kikuyu resistance. In fact, the British had no intention of any adherence to the human rights standards of the post-Second World War era. They did not believe that Africans, let alone Mau Mau supporters, had any right to the protections of international human rights conventions. They argued instead that Mau Mau threatened the life of the colony and indeed "British civilization."[201] An official propaganda war dwelled extensively on Mau Mau (African) "savagery" and made liberal use of vicious racist language, creating what has been described by scholars as the myth of Mau Mau.[202] White settlers were if anything more extreme. Elkins shows that during the conflict there was a shift from the typical colonial attitude of white supremacism to one that was "overtly eliminationist." She writes, "In the settler imagination, Mau Mau adherents were scarcely part of humanity's continuum; they were indistinguishable in local thought and expression from the animals that roamed the colony."[203] These attitudes also infected many government officials. Anthony Sampson, a journalist who visited Nairobi in 1954 (later the distinguished biographer of Nelson Mandela), noted "the dehumanization of the enemy" by both settlers and colonial officials: "I heard it everywhere I went. 'How many Kukes had to be gotten rid of, how many Kukes did you wink today?' "[204]

In the Algerian liberation and civil war from 1954 to 1962, the differences from Kenya were more apparent than real. For most French people in the 1950s, including a Socialist prime minister, Algeria was not a colony but part of French territory. François Mitterrand, minister of the interior when the revolt began in November 1954, declared that "Algeria is France." Nine million Algerians legally had French citizenship before it was taken from them in 1963.[205] For four decades the war, which killed nearly 500,000 people, mostly Muslim Algerians but including 25,000 French soldiers, was officially considered not a war but a police action.[206]

In 1956, the government decreed the establishment of three zones in Algeria: an operation zone, a pacification zone, and the so-called forbidden zone. In the forbidden zone, the aim was to forcibly remove the population to "settlement camps" controlled by the army. Over 2 million peasants were displaced in this way.[207] Here was a standard strategy in colonial wars: physically remove the people so that they could not support the *mujahideen* of the Armée de Libération Nationale (ALN) and other factions by providing food, shelter, and intelligence, and thus attempt to isolate the enemy in order to engage it with total war. The similarities to the concentration camps in the South African war, village concentrations in the Côte-d'Ivoire, Emergency villages in Kenya, and the "strategic hamlets" and "free fire" zones that so disfigured the American war in Vietnam are obvious. At the same time the practice of torture "as an ordinary feature of 'pacification'" became widespread. A handful of brave officers opposed it but were ignored. General Jacques Pâris de Bollardière was imprisoned for sixty days as his reward. In the Battle of Algiers of 1957 over 3,000 Algerians disappeared, according to Paul Teitgen, secretary general of the Algiers police. He resigned in September, disgusted by the brutalities of General Jacques Émile Massu's paratroopers.[208] Toward the end, in 1962, the settler paramilitary group the Organisation Armée Secrète (OAS), embittered by the Evian accords, instituted a campaign of terror in Algiers, Oran, and elsewhere, partly against the French security establishment but even more against Muslim civilians, schools, clinics, even the Algiers public library.[209] Then came the well-known French betrayal of the *harki*, the pro-French Muslims, whose main concern as former peasants was to protect or recover their land rather than fight for France, and the vengeful massacres after Algerian independence.[210]

France's war in Algeria, like that of the British in Kenya and the Americans in Vietnam, took place at a key moment in modern history. This was not only the era of "decolonization," whether admitted or not, but of massive economic, social, and cultural change in the Western centres of power, and that had major implications for attitudes toward war. Benjamin Stora captures this shift in the French context:

> Only ten years after the end of the Occupation, political space was determined less by ideological markers than by sociological ones: the upheaval of the agri-

cultural landscape and the end of the peasant world, the urban explosion on the periphery of the cities, the massive intrusion of television into homes, the beginning of the nuclear revolution. That nascent modernity concealed the issues born of the "Algerian years."

. . . Everything joined together to lead to an entirely new approach to the problems of a war waged outside the Hexagon. Society knew, but was content to keep, the secret of an undeclared war. The relation to death was wholly private and excluded from public life: no funeral orations, no specific tombstones, no particular inscriptions on city and village monuments celebrated the merit of those killed "over there." That tendency to exclude and conceal death led people to renounce the effort to come to terms with that war. The age of consumer society and the society of the spectacle had sounded.

At the same time, the war served as a revelation. What was being born under the thick mask of indifference was hostility toward the man living in or coming from the south. That mysterious "other" had resisted, had wanted to obtain a nationality of his own; here was a man whose life, hopes, and history no one took the trouble to find out about. How very distant and strange the Aurès and their inhabitants seemed to the French. With the Algerian War, colonial racism began its crossing of the Mediterranean.[211]

These wider social, cultural, and technological processes with their links to older ideas about "progress" have served to distance the majority of us who live in the comfortable West from the only surety in life: death. As Manuel Castells writes of the late twentieth century, "the attempt to exile death from our lives" is a central feature of our era of rapid innovation in medical technology and biological science. We act out our lives as if we are immortal: "By so doing, the ultimate subversion of the lifecycle is accomplished, and life becomes this flat landscape punctuated by chosen moments of high and low experiences, in the endless boutique of customized feelings. So when death does happen it is simply an additional blip on the screen of distracted spectators."[212] The implications for the emergence of collateral damage as alibi in faraway Aurès or Mukaradeeb, Chechnya or Panama City are clear.

U.S. escalation in the Vietnam War was on the cusp of these post-Second World War transformations. The war itself was prosecuted in a manner representative of contending social and cultural forces in American society. African Americans, Hispanic, and Native American soldiers were overrepresented in the American military, usually commanded by white officers, who were often racist, and suffered high casualties.[213] Here was a throwback to the role of the Irish in the British Army: a colonized group driven by economics and oppression into imperial service. Death was omnipresent, the television networks only partially tamed. The American war was primarily and transparently one against civilians. The statistics alone are horrific: 8 million tons of bombs (four times the weight used in the Second World War) were dropped on Vietnam alone, much more if Cambodia and Laos are included.[214] In just one month of one year (January 1969), 4 million people, one quarter of the population of South Vietnam, were exposed to air strikes less than three kilometres from their hamlets. Ten million gallons of the defoliant Agent Orange were sprayed on the country's forests and peasant holdings. As early as August 1971, 335,000 civilians had been killed and 740,000 wounded.[215] There were 5 million refugees in Vietnam and 1 million in Laos. Republic of Vietnam (South Vietnam) government figures are higher: 7 million. By the war's end in 1975, deaths in both North and South Vietnam totalled approximately 2 million. There were 400,000 prostitutes in Saigon alone, and the city was described by U.S. Senator William Fulbright as a huge brothel. In 1975, about two-thirds of the total population of Cambodia were refugees – 4 to 5 million people.[216]

Philip Jones Griffiths, whose searing photojournalism brings home the meaning of late-twentieth-century imperial war, writes of the Vietnamese civilian wounded:

Perhaps nothing more clearly reveals the extent of American indifference toward the suffering of the Vietnamese people than the enormous disparity between the money and effort expended to kill the Vietcong and that used to treat and care for civilians wounded – in theory accidentally – by U.S. forces while being protected from the VC. Wounded GIs had the best medical care possible lavished upon them, but the Vietnamese were allowed to lie dying in desperately overcrowded hospitals.[217]

The difference between such realities and the image projected by the U.S. military is staggering. Even now, there seems to be a state of denial in military publications. Major Jefferson D. Reynolds, for example, argues that collateral damage in Vietnam was essentially the consequence of a strategy by the Viet Cong of "concealment warfare" by which legitimate military targets were deliberately hidden amongst the civilian population:

Vietnamese leadership described the Vietnam conflict as a "people's revolution," requiring the incorporation of the entire Vietnamese population into its defense. The strategy to incorporate the populace into the conflict increased the difficulty in distinguishing between civilian and military objects, and promoted collateral damage. The Vietcong commonly took advantage of objects normally legally immune from attack to conduct military operations and to obtain sanctuary for military personnel, equipment and supplies. Such objects included religious and historical buildings, private dwellings or other civilian structures.[218]

On the surface this is at least partly true. However, to argue that the utilization of classic guerrilla war strategy somehow shifts responsibility onto the National Liberation Front (NLF) for massive civilian casualties directly caused by American actions misses the context of a national liberation war against foreign occupation and is entirely self-serving. It was the United States that intervened and occupied South Vietnam in a war of aggression and committed innumerable atrocities in the process. It is hardly surprising then that the NLF and the government of North Vietnam were able to use American atrocities in a successful international propaganda war.

Reynolds' suggestion that attacks on civilian food supplies should be legitimate and allowed under the laws of war must be exposed to the evidence of history and vigorously opposed. His argument is one that resonates with the strategy and tactics used in colonial wars over the centuries and has been highlighted here. In short, Reynolds argues that rural or even urban inhabitants where "concealment warfare" is supposedly practised should be coercively denied access to "infrastructure and sustenance" (food and water) and thus forced into "secure exit points," where they can be disarmed and receive the infrastructure, food, and water that they require: "Coercive denial of infrastructure and sustenance requires that a defensible cordon can be established around the contested area, and occupants leaving the area can be effectively managed."[219] He argues that such a strategy would reduce collateral damage, "diffuse" the conflict, enable civilians to receive the services, shelter, and sustenance they require, and secure the area. He recognizes that such practices are against article 54 of Additional Protocol I of the Geneva Conventions, which outlaws the denial of food and water to civilians and which the United States has not signed or ratified, but states that "responsible use of coercive methods necessitates rejection" of this provision of the law of war.

Of course the reason for supporting denial of food, water, and other necessities and forced relocation of civilians to "secure" points is based on an unstated understanding of counter-insurgency operations. Guerrilla forces involved in anti-imperialist and anti-colonial liberation struggles against vastly superior forces rely on access to the populace not only for food but also for intelligence, hiding places, and so on. In the formulation of the great strategist of guerrilla warfare against the Portuguese, Amílcar Lopes Cabral, "Our people are our mountains." Counter-insurgency theory recognizes this basic point and thus aims to violently separate non-combatants from the guerrilla movement, thus denying it necessary resources, and at the same time exert domination over civilians. It is clear that the welfare of civilians is hardly the real motivation when their fate after relocation is considered. Further, even when great coercion is used, as in Vietnam, many civilians preferred to stay in their homes in order to protect their property and livestock and to harvest their crops. General knowledge of the typically brutal conditions in concentrated villages or concentration camps also acts as a deterrent. Those who resist forcible relocation thus become the enemy, even if they choose to remain for the most prosaic domestic and economic reasons. Thus the inherent logic of counter-insurgency strategies of this type is the waging of war against the civilian population, whether they comply with forced relocation or resist, just as was the destruction of crops and scorched earth policies practised in earlier wars.

The history of such strategies, as we saw, shows very different results from those expected by Reynolds when we consider concentrated villages in the Côte-d'Ivoire, concentration camps in South Africa, Emergency villages in Kenya, and "settlement camps" in Algeria. In every case, they were both the product of a war on civilians and a licence for further systematic abuses of non-combatants, mostly women and children. In Vietnam, the strategy was taken to its extremes, with "relentless, terrible structural consequences" flowing from a mix of counter-insurgency and pacification programs.[220] (It must be said that it is astonishing that military experts such as Reynolds remain ignorant of this history.) A very large proportion – at least half – of the South Vietnamese peasantry was forced at gunpoint off the land and into refugee camps or to the urban areas. This process transformed Vietnamese society permanently.[221]

A significant step was the Republic of Vietnam's "strategic hamlets" program, initiated in 1962. The aim was to control the rural population, remove them from NLF influence, and destroy the rural infrastructure. Most of the 11,300 hamlets in South Vietnam were to be fortified and the peasant population moved into them. The program was brutal but largely ineffective. Peasants were forced to leave their homes and lands and moved to often far-off, defensible hamlets. There, they frequently were forced to construct stockades and other structures. They were given neither adequate building materials nor enough cash for sustenance. Republic of Vietnam officials then used their power to "loot, collect back taxes, reinstall landlords, and conduct reprisals against the people." If peasants resisted forced removal to the strategic hamlets, the South Vietnamese Army (ARVN) shelled and bombed their communities. Many young men then joined the NLF, the opposite of what the program aimed to achieve. By late 1963, NLF forces had dismantled 2,500 of the approximately 6,000 existing strategic hamlets. By 1964, the ARVN admitted that it controlled just 1,200.[222]

From March 1965, the United States was fully involved in the conflict. By early 1967, General William Westmoreland was most concerned about the central highlands, and in particular Quang Ngai province, fearing that the NLF in this narrow band of rugged territory would be able to prevent the United States from moving supplies to troops in the demilitarized zone separating North from South Vietnam. For two years, the government of South Vietnam and the U.S. military had been establishing relocation camps throughout the province in an effort to force 300,000 peasants from their smallholdings so that they could not support NLF guerrillas, a revival and more extreme version of the strategic hamlets program. There was considerable resistance, and many people escaped the camps to return to their homes or join the Viet Cong.[223] Careful research by journalists Michael Sallah and Mitch Weiss documents the disturbing pattern of war crimes that followed in one locality, the Song Ve River valley. The Tiger Force reconnaissance unit of Task Force Oregon tried to clear remaining civilians out of the valley and destroy their rice crop before harvest. Superior officers encouraged the atrocities and the U.S. military subsequently engaged in a cover-up. General Westmoreland himself briefed Tiger Force soldiers on the operation: "If the people are in relocation camps, they're green, so they're safe" he explained. "We leave them alone. The Vietcong and NVA [North Vietnam Army] are red, so we know they're fair game. But if there are people who are out there – and not in the camps – they're pink as far as we're concerned. They're Communist sympathizers. They were not supposed to be there." Decades later, Tiger Force platoon commander James Hawkins said to one of the reporters, "I killed people I had to kill. If they were in a free-fire zone, they were fair game."[224]

One example of the hundreds of brutalities that followed the forced relocations and declaration of a "free fire" zone in the Song Ve valley is sufficient to illustrate the pattern of murder, rape, and mutilation of Vietnamese men, women, and children that Tiger Force engaged in over a period of several months in 1967:

Suddenly, before Green could join Ybarra, the point man had raised his hand and motioned for the platoon to halt. Crouching down, he had pointed toward a rice paddy about two hundred meters away. After staring a few more seconds at the field, Ybarra had sprung up and motioned for the others to follow.

He had turned around and, while still walking, whispered something to Green. Green then slowed down long enough to tell the man behind him what Ybarra had spotted.

The third man turned around and told the fourth, and the fourth turned and informed Hawkins. The commander hadn't hesitated. Instead, Hawkins had wheeled around and passed the word: "Fire on my orders."

After a couple of minutes, the soldiers were now well within sight of the villagers, but for some reason the Vietnamese weren't moving. Several were hunched over, their backs to the soldiers. Two of the men continued to drive the water buffalo along the beds.

"They looked to be older, about half of them men, half women," Carpenter recalled. Shaking his head, he looked around to see the other soldiers' reaction to the order. Wood and others were dumbfounded. It was one thing to open up on enemy soldiers, or prisoners, or even people running away. But these people weren't moving – they were just farming.

Before anyone had a chance to say anything, Hawkins raised his CAR-15 and pulled the trigger. Immediately, Doyle, Barnett, and Green fired.

From the thicket of bamboo, Kieu Trak watched as his father and others initially looked up, appearing almost startled, before they began running. Some fell in the muck. Others made it to the dike before dropping. The helicopter soaring overhead began circling the rice paddy, then firing down on the chaos below.[225]

In this massacre of peaceful peasant farmers, five elderly men and five women were murdered.

Reynolds seems less certain on other topics. In a short discussion of the American use of Agent Orange in order to destroy hundreds of thousands of acres of food crops he writes,

> Although the program was directed at enemy Vietcong forces, it effectively destroyed and denied food to neutral civilian communities because the Vietcong regularly seized food from these communities to support their operations. Although destroying supply lines and denying food is an effective strategy to degrade enemy forces' morale, the crop destruction program did not have the desired effect of denying food to the Vietcong because of their coercive access to rice at the consumer level.

Responsibility for the obvious consequences of the destruction of civilian farms and food supplies – including starvation – is thus shifted by a sleight of hand onto the Viet Cong. (One wonders, incidentally, where guerrilla forces such as the Viet Cong in a country under occupation were supposed to get food supplies if not from peasant farmers.) Reynolds continues, "The affected civilian communities resented the program because it destroyed their livelihood, exposed them to a toxic substance, and had limited success in achieving the objective of denying food to enemy forces."[226]

In the mass of publications about the Vietnam War relatively few deal substantively with Vietnam and the Vietnamese, let alone the question of civilian casualties. American interests, American perceptions, and American politics overshadow all else. The wider lessons of the war seem to have been largely forgotten. In the 1960s and 1970s, American "exceptionalism" remained largely untouched. This is clearly shown in a recent study of Vietnam reporting by three major American weekly news magazines: *Newsweek*, *Time*, and *U.S. News & World Report*. Not surprisingly, the coverage on civilian casualties varied in quality but rarely was the civilian war taken seriously, and in a paucity of articles. From 1965 to 1967, just seventeen newsmagazine articles, 3 per cent of those on combat, covered civilian casualties caused by American actions.[227] James Landers notes that

> not until November 1971 did a newsmagazine correspondent investigate the discrepancy between the number of enemy dead claimed and the number of enemy weapons seized, a sure indicator of civilian deaths. A *Newsweek* correspondent checked statistics for Operation Speedy Express, a months-long mission in the Mekong Delta some three years earlier. The Army claimed the Ninth Infantry Division had killed 11,000 guerrillas and captured 700 weapons, an incredible gap. No journalists sought an explanation at the time.

Even after the correspondent filed the story, it was not published for another five months, as it was old news. The article, when it finally ran, stated that "a staggering number of noncombatant civilians" were killed, as many as 5,000.[228]

It was worse than that. As the Paris peace talks geared up, Operation Speedy Express ran from December 1968 to May 1969 with the aim of pacifying large tracts of countryside in the Mekong Delta and ensuring that the government of South Vietnam controlled the civilian population. The operations of the 9th Infantry Division were backed by helicopter gunships and B-52 bombers.[229] In May 1970, and a few months after the My Lai massacre entered the public consciousness, a veteran of Operation Speedy Express wrote a series of letters to General Westmoreland. They were anonymous and signed only "Concerned Sergeant." In the first of these letters, Concerned Sergeant wrote that the atrocities committed by the 9th Division amounted to "a My Lai each month for over a year."[230] He referred to massacres of non-combatants by helicopter gunships, air strikes on villages, and farmers shot in their fields by snipers. Frequently air strikes were called in even if there was no defensive fire from villages. Anyone who ran was a target. The casualties were typically women, children, and old people. Civilians were forcibly used to trip Viet Cong booby traps. The discrepancies between the very high body count and the very small numbers of captured Viet Cong weapons were covered up in reports by references to weapons being destroyed in fire fights or lost in canals. Detailed research by historian Nicholas Turse using confidential letters, secret Pentagon briefings, National Liberation Front sources, original interviews with Vietnamese survivors and 9th Division personnel carried out by the *Newsweek* journalists, and more recent interviews has verified these claims. These sustained atrocities were, in Turse's words, "no accident or aberration. They were instead the result of the command policies that turned wide swaths of the Mekong Delta into 'free-fire zones' in a relentless effort to achieve a high body count."[231] There is extensive evidence that Major General Julian Ewell and his chief of staff, Colonel Ira Hunt, and other officers were obsessed with achieving a high body count at all costs. There was no effort to distinguish between civilians and combatants. The racist "mere gook rule" and "its attendant dictum: 'If it's dead and Vietnamese, it's VC" added to the catastrophe experienced by Vietnamese civilians.[232] More than one lower ranking officer was highly critical of the pattern of atrocities and the body count mentality. Louis Janowski, an adviser in the delta during Operation Speedy Express and very familiar with associated helicopter operations, in his end-of-tour report referred to them as a form of "non-selective terrorism." Further, he wrote that "the percentage of Viet Cong killed by support assets is roughly equal to the percentage of Viet Cong in the population. . . . That is, if 8% of the population [of] an area is VC about 8% of the people we kill are VC."[233] Another adviser, Jeffrey Record, saw in one case how helicopter gunships targeted water buffalo and the children watching them, destroying both innocents and vital assets for peasant farmers. In a few seconds the paddy field was "transformed into a bloody ooze littered with bits of mangled flesh." He added, "The dead boys and the water buffalo were added to the official body count of the Viet Cong."[234] At the end of Operation Speedy Express, General Ewell was promoted and he and Hunt were asked by the Army chief of staff to set down their approach to combat in order to help develop "future operational concepts." No member of the 9th Division was ever charged in relation to war crimes committed in the Mekong Delta.[235]

Responding to the initial publication of Sallah and Weiss' research in the *Toledo Blade* newspaper, Turse observes, "Military records demonstrate that the 'Tiger Force' atrocities are only the tip of a vast submerged history of atrocities in Vietnam." Similarly, Marilyn Young writes that Sallah and Weiss' *Tiger Force* "reinforces the sense of a bottomless pit of unknown war crimes."[236] She quotes Patrick Hagopian on the pardoning of Lieutenant William Calley of My Lai infamy and the wider failure to prosecute and punish American war crimes. Consequences included the accumulation of a "residue of 'unallocated blame' that seemed for a time to stigmatize all Vietnam veterans," and "the disappearance of 'public understanding of the Vietnam War into a moral void.'"[237] Thus when the Tiger Force story was first published in the *Toledo Blade* the public and the wider media largely ignored it.[238] Again, in Castell's formulation, we see death as "additional blip on the screen of distracted spectators," an indifference to suffering in far-off countries.[239] Young concludes,

> Everyone now knows that, in Vietnam, the United States fought a war of great violence in a small country whose national choices could not have affected the safety and security of the United States in any way. Everyone now knows that terrible crimes were committed in the course of that war: the specific crimes of rape, torture, massacre, the more general crimes of unparalleled bombing of civilians. But this knowledge has had few long-run consequences.[240]

After Vietnam, the U.S. military quickly abandoned the body count as a measure of success. Yet, in Somalia, Afghanistan, Iraq, and other post-Vietnam wars of the West, civilian casualty rates remain extraordinarily high. Beyond the historical, ideological, racial, and other factors already discussed here, are there structural or political changes in the post-Vietnam era in the way that militaries of the West and other industrialized countries fight in Asia, Africa, and the Americas? A number of recent works in the sub-field of the sociology of war illuminate these issues. The most sophisticated of these is Martin Shaw's *The New Western Way of War: Risk Transfer War and Its Crisis in Iraq*, with its highly conceptualized and theorized understanding of the recent evolution of Western warfare.[241]

The central argument is the following: since Vietnam, the West has evolved a way of war that has as a central characteristic – beyond the aim of destroying the enemy – an aversion to Western military casualties. This new way of war does not originate in technological innovations but is the outcome of longer-term social, political, and military developments. The decline of mass armies and the shift of military personnel into various skill categories meant that "skilled professionals, in whom militaries made considerable training investments, could not be treated as cannon-fodder." Whereas Western military casualties have become an anathema, civilian casualties that occur in wars of the West are always deemed "accidental." But if the price of reducing Western military casualties is to add to the risk that innocent civilians are exposed to, then they have no choice but to bear that risk. Shaw calls this "risk-transfer war" because it aims to shift the risk of war away from the military and consequently away from the political and electoral risks that politicians might otherwise face if Western publics view military casualties as too high. Defenders of the new way of war always tout precision weapons and sophisticated command and control systems as the way to avoid civilian casualties. In contrast, critics point to the way that civilian casualties are downplayed in the Western media and hidden from the public. Shaw argues that the reality is more complicated, with some truth on both sides.[242] Even with euphemistic terminology and the visual "cleansing" of war-related images, Western wars still kill civilians in large numbers.[243] The new Western way of war thus remains as degenerate as the total war of earlier decades because of the high costs of risk-transfer for those who have no choice but to accept them.[244] Shaw argues that although military commanders attempt to distinguish between military and civilian targets, "the significance of continuing civilian deaths was that they occurred *despite* and even *because of* these *new* methods and ideologies of Western wars.[245] Further,

> In minimizing the risk to its own combatants, the West consistently adopts methods of war that effectively transfer risk from its own personnel to civilian non-combatants, so that far more civilians are killed, injured and otherwise harmed than Western military personnel. In any situation where the question of priority arises, the West is likely to put its own soldiers' lives before those of civilians.[246]

Three major conclusions follow:

> Given the central priority of minimizing Western casualties, which in turn derives from the core media-political context within which governments fight war, these transfers are a large part of what the Western way of warfighting is now *about*.
>
> The transfers are understood, accepted and to that extent consciously *intended* by Western governments, military planners and the military operatives who carry them out.
>
> These transfers bare a fundamental contradiction between the norm of civilian protection and the reality of Western warfighting, and so make the *legitimacy* of this way of war fundamentally problematic.[247]

Shaw's overall argument is therefore similar to my own although does not deconstruct the meanings of collateral damage. Instead, he uses the concept of risk-transfer: "Looking at global society as a risk society, it is difficult not to be impressed chiefly by gross inequalities of life-risks, and it is sobering to recognize these as artifacts of power."[248]

If there is a weakness in this analysis it is that continuities from the nineteenth and early twentieth century are not fully examined. Further, Shaw underestimates the evidence for massive civilian casualties in Iraq, although this is corrected in the postscript, with the publication of the first *Lancet* report on Iraqi casualties in October 2004.[249]

And when what had been done in the heart of darkness was repeated in the heart of Europe, no one recognized it. No one wished to admit what everyone knew.[250]

Reflection, analysis, and even language itself seemed inadequate, indeed improper, when one was confronted by the magnitude of the horror. The muses had been silenced. Only the second-rate had the courage to speak. Only the mindless claimed to understand.[251]

The Army brief concluded that despite the evidence, "nothing beneficial or constructive could result for prosecution at this time." Four commanders were asked to read the final report of the Tiger Force case, but no action was to be taken in those cases. The investigation would now be closed, the documents shipped to a storage room at CID [Criminal Investigation Division] headquarters. The longest war crimes case of the Vietnam War was over. There would be no charges. There would be no press conferences. There would be nothing at all. It would be as if nothing had ever happened.

And so it was.[252]

Much recent historical literature on war and conflict is framed around concepts of memory. Geoff Eley writes that the 1990s saw a "boom" in memory. In part this was a "nostalgia for the present" (after Fredric Jameson) resulting from apprehensions about rapid social and cultural change "in which representations of the past, the narration and visualizing of history, personal and collective, private and public, spell the desire for holding on to the familiar." Thus, " 'memory' becomes the crucial site of identity formation in the late twentieth century, of deciding who we are, and of positioning ourselves in time, given the hugeness of the structural changes occurring in the world."[253] The growth of the mass media, with its rapid postmodern transmission of signs, quickly moves historical material in electronic form across previously separate formats. There is also the parade of anniversaries and commemorations (the abolition of the slave trade being one of the most recent) and the growth of interdisciplinarity in academia. The relationship between history and memory has become a staple for historians.[254] Yet for our topic, memory is usually absent. Instead, the present and the past are filled with silences. Our identities and awareness of the world are shaped as much by silencing and forgetting as they are by remembrance.

African and (some) Africanist historians know only too well the power of silence. Marjorie Perham, grande dame of British imperialism in Africa, saw

African peoples as "a collection of primitive 'tribes' with no clothes, no brick wall dwellings, no major historical monument, and therefore No History!"[255] She was hardly alone, as Professor Hugh Trevor-Roper later infamously reminded us, with his pronouncement on African history as the "unrewarding gyrations of barbarous tribes." This is a classic example of how the production of knowledge lies in strict conformity to relationships of power and subordination. It was only with decolonization, both political and of the mind, that African historians and sympathetic outsiders were able to take on the task of reconstructing the history of the African continent and its peoples. Yet, Ibrahim Abdullah argues in his preface to Congolese historian Jacques Depelchin's *Silences in African History*, "The representation of Africa, Columbus style, survived the demise of formal colonial domination. Inherent in this missionary project is a simple but powerful claim of superiority versus inferiority founded on colonial/post-colonial power and arrogance."[256] Abdullah continues:

> As Depelchin shows again and again in *Silences*, it is not enough [for Western Africanists] to talk about sources and methodology; it is just not enough to continue to bemoan archival sources or belabour the point that such sources overwhelmingly recount the deeds of victors. Africanist historians would do better if they take seriously the injunction that they come from the dominant and dominating cultural milieu (read power), whose very existence is much at odds with the production of an emancipatory history capable of speaking to the complex issues of individual and collective survival that has shaped the existence of the colonized/post-colonial world since it was constituted almost six hundred years ago.

Instead, what is required for an emancipatory history is to "transcend and subvert what Depelchin calls paradigmatic silences: silences that are difficult to detect because they are framed in such a way that they evade crucial theoretical questions."[257]

The above discussion concerns African history. Yet it has wider relevance. This book is about the violence done to the silenced and the forgotten, a huge proportion of whom are Africans, Asians, Native Americans, and other colonized peoples. Further, the history of this violence has been subject to the kind of "paradigmatic silencing" that Abdullah and Depelchin refer to. In the very formulation of this project at the 2004 conference on collateral damage in Toronto, a paradigmatic silence intruded. At the initiative of an inquisitive correspondent, American National Public Radio (NPR) was to cover the conference, given its seeming relevance to contemporary events in the Middle East and Afghanistan. Several conference participants and I were interviewed for NPR. Yet once the NPR editors received the details of presenters and topics they reacted immediately. No interview material was broadcast. The ideas and methodology of at least one of our contributors, Marc Herold, were deemed by NPR to be too troubling; they had been savagely attacked by supporters of the invasion of Afghanistan and Iraq, and Herold had been accused of wildly over-estimating Afghani civilian casualties caused by American bombing. In fact, it was Herold's critics who were way off base, often misreading his work, using uncritical and illogical pseudo-analysis, and deploying imperialist and racist assumptions.[258] At the Carr Center for Human Rights Policy workshop on collateral damage in 2002, an unnamed reporter referred to the way that the U.S. military had "all but ceded public debate about deaths in Enduring Freedom to an academic who simply compiled estimates from foreign news reports," an "inherently suspect analysis." The reference is clearly to Herold.[259] The irony is that Herold's methodology is now the most conservative used to count or estimate civilian casualties. Iraq Body Count, which uses a methodology (similar to Herold's) of cross-checking multiple independent media reports on violent incidents, has far lower figures for casualties in Iraq (43,491–48,283 from the start of the invasion to September 26, 2006; 84,723–92,414 as of June 20, 2008) than do, for example, the household surveys of the Iraq Family Health Survey Group, sponsored by the World Health Organization and the Iraq Health Ministry.[260] The Iraqi government accepts the conclusions of the Survey Group's research: 151,000 violent deaths, from March 2003 to June 2006.[261] A more complete study also using a household survey methodology, carried out by a team from Johns Hopkins Bloomberg School of Public Health and the School of Medicine at Al Mustansiriya University in Baghdad and published in *The Lancet*, estimated a post-invasion violent death total of 601,027. Its methodology is superior because its results were validated with death certificates.[262] Herold's work, including his chapter in this book, should now be seen as seminal, path-breaking, and courageous.[263]

Analysis of civilian casualties in Iraq requires far more space than is available here. Despite close control of the media in Iraq and systematic attempts by the military to hide the true extent of civilian casualties,[264] numerous important source materials apart from the various numerical estimates are available. These include 479 files from the U.S. Foreign Claims Commission of the Department of Defense obtained by the American Civil Liberties Union.[265] These files date from early 2003 to late 2006 and cover claims for damages made by the families of civilians killed or wounded by American and Coalition forces. Another seventeen files relate to Afghanistan. The ACLU believes that many more such files are being withheld, probably the majority.[266] Of the total of 496 files, 198 were denied consideration for compensation because, according to the Commission, the deaths and injuries arose "from action by an enemy or resulted directly or indirectly from an act of the armed forces of the United States in combat." The U.S. military refers to this as "combat exclusion."[267] The following file summaries are typical examples:

Al Duluyia, Iraq. 7/7/2005. Claim on behalf of several Iraqis [Redacted]. Claimant and his family were traveling from their orchard to the market with fruit. Coalition Forces (CF) fired artillery at their car, killing the son, injuring the wife and daughter, and completely destroying the car. "The car was thoroughly perforated with artillery fragments." SIGACTS revealed no similar activity. Army Memo: "CF regularly conduct artillery strikes on orchards such as Claimant's orchard." Finding: denied due to combat exception. Condolence payment granted: $5,200 U.S. (2,500 for death, $1,200 and $1,000 for injuries, $500 for car.)

Balad, Iraq. 2/25/2006. Claim on behalf of Iraqi [Redacted] by parent. [Redacted], a six year old girl, was shot and killed by Coalition Forces who shot into a crowd celebrating a wedding. The crowd fired celebratory shots and CF responded by returning fire. SIGACTS revealed no similar incident. Finding: denied due to lack of evidence.[268]

Ninety-two of the files concern deaths at American checkpoints or in the vicinity of U.S. military convoys. Obviously the files represent only a small proportion of the total civilian deaths and injuries caused by American and Coalition forces. As noted, incidents "directly or indirectly" related to combat do not qualify for compensation and so relatively few claims would be heard or recorded in such cases. Second, cases regarding deaths and injuries caused by bombing and air strikes are not included in the files. Third, Iraqi civilians would not always know that they could lodge claims or have safe access to Commission offices.

A source of a different kind for Iraq is the series of interviews recorded by journalists Chris Hedges and Laila Al-Arian with fifty American combat veterans: soldiers, sailors, and marines.[269] The aim was to analyze the impact of the invasion and occupation on "average Iraqi civilians." The compilation of the interviews provides a picture very much at odds with the great majority of mainstream television and newspaper reports of the war: "Dozens of those interviewed witnessed Iraqi civilians, including children, dying from American firepower. Some participated in such killings; others treated or investigated civilian casualties after the fact. Many also heard such stories, in detail, from members of their unit." However, the interviewees also stressed that many American troops did not take part in "indiscriminate killings," and many of them said that only a minority were responsible. Nevertheless, such atrocities were common, were often not reported to military authorities, and were almost never punished. Iraqi civilians were typically thought to be hostile. Hedges and Al-Arian conclude from their analysis that "fighting in densely populated urban areas has led to the indiscriminate use of force and the deaths at the hands of occupation forces for thousands of innocents." They also make a direct comparison with the French colonial war in Algeria, the Vietnam War, and the Israeli occupation of Palestinian territories.[270] Yet American military officers complain today that they are expected to comply with a *higher* standard than international humanitarian law demands.[271]

The vast majority of the violent deaths blandly enumerated in statistics, coldly described in military files like those above or witnessed by occupying soldiers, occurred far from the media gaze. The perpetrators knew what they had done, or what had been done in their name, but willed themselves to forget. Occasionally a voice of conscience emerged: Roger Casement, for example, who was hounded to the grave by his enemies, or Bishop John and Harriette Colenso, who gave decades of their lives and family fortune in the Zulu cause.[272] The victims also, shamed and humiliated, frequently prefer silence. Forgetting was sometimes a collective willing of national amnesia.

No better example is to be found than in the culture and history of Italy, where despite an earlier history of colonial discourse, its existence with reference to Italian conquests in Africa is only latent. Patrizia Palumbo writes that its complex and varied expressions in relation to the conquest, occupation, and cultural domination of parts of North and East Africa "are some of the least-known aspects of Italian history."[273] One must quote the searching critique by historian Angelo del Boca of the fifty-volume post-Second World War publication of the Ministry of Foreign Affairs, *L'Italia in Africa*, whose advisory committee consisted of fifteen former colonial governors and a handful of pro-colonial historians:

> The operation of the committee, conducted so arbitrarily, unavoidably led to the silencing or even the confutation of the many mistakes and crimes committed during the wars of conquest, from the very high price paid by the subjected populations, to the attempt to deprive them of their own cultural and national identities, or even, as in Cirenaica, to their physical elimination. There are no traces, in fact, in any of the fifty volumes of *L'Italia in Africa* of the massive employment of chemical weapons in Ethiopia between 1935 and 1940, not a single reference to the lethal concentration camps in Libya, Somalia, and Eritrea. Absolute silence is maintained concerning the decimation of the Coptic Church after the attempt on Rodolfo Graziani's life on February 19, 1937 – an operation led by General Maletti with such zeal and professionalism that it caused the death of 1,200 deans and priests.

The result of the failure in Italy to seriously debate the reality of colonialism and its cost to subject peoples has been a collective amnesia and the retention of colonialist myths that emerged a century or more ago. All those who participated in the terrible crimes perpetuated in North and East Africa have therefore escaped justice or public censure.[274]

The same can be said for the British officials, both military and civilian, who were responsible for the war on non-combatants and the massive human rights violations during the Mau Mau revolt and Emergency.[275] The British and Kenyan colonial governments systematically destroyed hundreds of thousands of files relating to detention camps, particularly on the eve of independence in 1963, when "countless" files were burned. Records were removed from the Public Record Office in Kew and the Kenyan National Archive. For example, Elkins' research shows that for each of the 80,000 Kikuyu detainees in the detention camps (and official figures were grossly low because they accounted for "daily average" detentions, rather than the total number of individuals who had been detained), three government departments kept a file. Thus there should have been a minimum of 240,000 files in the archives for this category alone. Yet the Public Record Office has no such records, and the Kenyan archives only some hundreds. Further, many surviving documents were still not available to researchers fifty years after the end of the war.[276] The colonial archive was largely erased; the war on Kenyans never happened – atrocities and civilian casualties hidden, silenced, but not forgotten by the Kikuyu.

Just as troubling, but now better known, is the history of official suppression of debate concerning France's actions in Algeria during the liberation and civil war of 1954–62. This history of silencing began early. Roland Barthes noticed it in the French press in the mid-1950s, when euphemisms or code words were used to sanitize the atrocities committed by the French army. The result was the construction of myths out of ideology through the manipulation of language. Barthes agonized, "In the account given of our present circumstances, I suffered at seeing Nature and History confused at every turn, and I wanted to track down, in the decorative display of *what-goes-without saying*, the ideological abuse which, in my view, is hidden there."[277] After the war ended, its memory was contained "as if within an invisible fortress." A series of amnesties in France allowed the public to forget the atrocities, and there were no commemorative ceremonies. The first amnesty was in December 1964, and they continued at regular intervals – for those responsible for atrocities and torture, for OAS (Organisation de l'armée secrète) members, for those French military officers who had supported the OAS and acted against the Republic – until November 1982.[278] It was only in the 1990s and first years of the new millennium that decades of deliberate forgetting came to an end, as if a mental archive had been prized open and its contents revealed. Michael Haneke, an Austrian, brilliantly captures this process in his dramatic film *Caché* (Hidden), in which recessed and layered memories in relation to the Paris massacre of October 17, 1961, gradually resurface four decades later under the influence of new forms of trauma. On that day, up to 200 Algerian protesters were murdered by the French police and many thrown into the River Seine. The government systematically worked to hide the true nature of the massacre, and police records were off limits to historians until 1999.[279]

There are other kinds of forgetting. Repression of memory by those who suffered or witnessed unspeakable violence is one of them. This is a theme in W.G. Sebald's *On the Natural History of Destruction*, a meditation on the silences in German literature concerning the destruction of 131 German cities and towns by the Royal Air Force and the United States Air Force during the Second World War and the deaths of 600,000 German civilians.[280] A "conspiracy of silence" encased German culture in the following decades, even though a very large proportion of the German population was exposed to the bombing campaign for months, even years, on end. "The destruction, on a scale without historical precedent, entered the annals of the nation, as it set about rebuilding itself, only in the form of vague generalizations. It seems to have left scarcely a trace of pain behind in the collective consciousness."[281] Sebald senses something else at work, a numbing of the spirit even in the immediate aftermath of the catastrophic events, when mounds of rubble – 42.8 cubic metres for each inhabitant of Dresden – remained uncleared, and the smell of death was everywhere.[282] "But these things obviously did not register on the sensory experience of the survivors still living on the scene of the catastrophe."[283] Among German writers in the late 1940s, "the darkest aspects of the final act of destruction, as experienced by the great majority of the German population, remained under a kind of taboo like a shameful family secret."[284] Only a small handful of writers went beyond this self-imposed limit on what could be said. Was this because Germany, responsible for the Holocaust and the enslavement and murder of millions, had no right to question the logic of the bombing campaign? Or was it that victims of the "obvious madness" of the air raids could nevertheless see in them some sort of "just punishment?"[285] In the English-speaking world, the debate over the destruction of German cities has been rather more adversarial, and here is joined by Sven Lindqvist, famous for his work on the history of bombing.[286]

In China also, the experience and cost of war have remained veiled, although not because of any sense of collective guilt.[287] Lary and MacKinnon note that although the Rape of Nanjing is to some extent known by the Chinese,[288] the huge number of massacres committed during the war against Japan and the losses resulting from Japanese bombing and Chinese defensive strategies are not. Despite the large scale of the hundreds of war crimes, until the recent past in China there has been "a reticence verging on denial" to discuss publicly the massive civilian suffering that resulted. Similarly, people outside China are probably more aware of Japanese civilian casualties resulting from the use of nuclear weapons at Hiroshima and Nagasaki than they are of the 20 million Chinese dead.[289] The inhibition on opening up discourse is the same in Taiwan as it is on the mainland. The traditional ruling party, the Guomindang, lost the civil war to the Communists, and hence has little interest in opening up a close examination of its own failures. Similarly, the Communist Party has no interest in initiating a debate that might lead to comparisons of suffering during the Sino-Japanese War with the chaos of the Cultural Revolution, instigated by Mao Zedong. Thus media coverage of wartime suffering is muted in both cases, and calls for compensation from Japan by activists on the mainland are suppressed.[290]

Memory is also suffocated by the sheer banality of civilian suffering in modern Chinese history, beginning in the mid-nineteenth century with the estimated 30 million casualties of the Taiping Rebellion, numerous other peasant disturbances, the Opium Wars, and other nineteenth-century wars of imperialism, including the war with Japan of 1894–95 and the suppression of the Boxer Rebellion by the Western powers; then the period of warlordism and civil war prior to and coterminous with the Japanese invasion. Further, for outsiders in particular, the vast size of the Chinese population has had the effect of creating a disjuncture with the huge scale of civilian suffering, thus apparently reducing the extent of the true horror of the war. This has affected historical writing by both Chinese and foreign scholars. Individual massacres – even those involving thousands of people – are mentioned only briefly in histories, with phrases such as "heavy casualties." Foreigners too often have resorted to stereotypes such as Chinese "fatalism" to explain resilience in the face of such events. As Lary and MacKinnon note, these are insulting and far from the truth. Rather, extreme trauma and "the ever-present possibility of arbitrary death" have made it almost impossible to express adequately in words the scale of the horror. But for the victims of such events and their descendants, history is not a void. Memories have survived and even accumulated, though there are few sites of mourning such as war cemeteries where the survivors can visit graves of family members.[291]

China has much in common with other countries where imperialist domination and occupation by foreign invaders contributed to collective amnesia. Emotions of shame and dishonour, even though Japan was eventually defeated, have permeated into the present. The terrible suffering and humiliation caused by years of defeats by the Japanese, the inability of the Guomindang armies to defend the country, and the systematic abuse of civilians have contributed to a fragmented, equivocal approach to commemoration and remembrance. A mix of "memory, amnesia, and suppression or avoidance of memory" burdens the few books, films, and commemorations dealing with the war.[292] "Good" memories are manufactured or exaggerated while the "bad" are neglected and thus become buried by overlapping experiences and political imperatives.

Questions of history and remembrance are fraught in Kenya too, as in so many former colonies and occupied territories trying to cope with the trauma of imperial wars. One is reminded of the approach at independence of Kenya's first president, Jomo Kenyatta, to healing the wounds of Mau Mau. "Forgive and forget," he urged, referring to the memories of the brutalities of the loyalist Home Guard and the self-enrichment of Kikuyu elites while 90 per cent of the Kikuyu population was being interned, forcibly relocated, raped, starved, or tortured. "We all fought for *uhuru* – freedom," he asserted, keeping up what John Lonsdale and E.S. Atieno Odhiambo call the "momentum of therapeutic oblivion."[293] Historian David Anderson writes, "In Kenyatta's Kenya there would be a deafening silence about Mau Mau."[294]

The experience of dishonour and humiliation is perhaps nowhere more present than in cases of widespread and targeted sexual violence against women in the context of wars of conquest or expansion. The shame associated with sexualized violence accompanying or central to the aims of conquest and domination leads to another kind of silence, as Marlene Epp shows in Chapter 11 in this volume. Nowhere is this more marked than in the mass rapes on the American frontier. The genocides of Native people in the Pampas of Argentina and in the U.S. West, mentioned above, featured massive sexual violence against women, children, and men. In his forthcoming dissertation, Benjamin Madley provides evidence of over 200 instances in which whites killed five or more Californian aboriginal people. These events included battles, mass killings, executions, and outright massacres.[295] Almost certainly many also involved rape and mutilation. Mark Grimsley contrasts this widespread pattern with the rarity of rape committed by Union soldiers against Southern women during the same period of American history.[296]

In an extraordinary book, Kass Fleischer mines the subterranean fragments of memory and denial relating to one such case, the massacre on January 29, 1863, of 300 Northwestern Shoshone men, women, and children on the banks of the Bear River, Idaho, by Colonel Patrick Connor's Union troops, and the accompanying rapes.[297] Recent commemoration of the massacre by the U.S. National Parks Service controversially ignores mention of the rapes. Fleischer's analysis of the evidence is remarkable for showing that in this case, some white male historians acknowledge the rapes while female Shoshone historians working with oral traditions deny that they occurred. The unusual contradiction probably derives from the enmity between Mormon settlers in the area and the Union troops. Fleischer speculates that "the motivation for documenting the rape at Bear River finds its source in tensions regarding sexual behavior. If Connor was going to blast Mormons for polygyny, then Mormons were going to take note of the rape committed by Connor's soldiers."[298] In a wider culture that systematically ignored the rape of black, indigenous, and colonized women through long periods of history, there is little space between victims' shame and forgetting.

Such histories suggest a need to understand sexual violence in wars where enemies attempt to remake or reinforce ethnic or racial categories. The mass rape of Bosnian Muslim women by Bosnian Serbs stimulated scholars such as Catharine MacKinnon and Susan Brownmiller to think more deeply about the relationship between war and sexual violence.[299] Yet according to Darius Rejali, both analyses have their limitations. MacKinnon emphasizes unequal gender relations expressed in the eroticized body and the licence that war offers men to rape. She does not address the constructed ethnicity literally embodied in the enemy. Brownmiller, on the other hand, concentrates on rape as a weapon of ethnic war. The female body is a marginalized object in an ethnic conflict between men. In this view, the eroticization involved in torture is not addressed.[300] In Rejali's view, addressing the specific context of each conflict and seeing sexual violence in war as multifunctional can transcend these problems. Further, there are key distinctions between conflicts in which the ethnic populations are relatively equal according to prewar status and distribution in economic niches and there is no obvious pattern of dominance by one group, and conflicts in which a clear hierarchy coexists with ethnicity or race. Bosnia represents the first category and Peru the second.[301] He cites the example of the rapes in Peru in the 1980s, quoting Julie Philips:

> "If traditional 'women's work' – tending families, raising children – holds communities together, assaults on women do much to tear the social fabric apart. When you are out to subdue a population, women are the population." Rape may be used as a terror tactic to force confessions or destabilize whole areas. In the case of female guerrillas, rape provides a particularly vicious means of reinforcing the gendered division of labor. Rape also imitates and reinforces ethnic and racial divisions: in Peru, *mestizo* guerrillas are raped by *mestizo* and white soldiers, whereas Indian guerrillas are raped by dark-skinned as well as *mestizo* soldiers.[302]

The racial and ethnic hierarchies mentioned here are largely derived from and consistent with the earlier colonial experience in Peru. Further, we can see a clear link with the conclusions earlier in this essay concerning the way in which imperial violence (and violence in ethnic or national wars) targets whole communities and the means of production and reproduction.

Rejali concludes, "In a war context, racial and ethnic distinctions have particular salience because they are violently renegotiated, complicating the relationship between ethnicity and gender."[303] Ethnic and racial categories in wartime are not a given but are themselves being forcibly remade:

> Rape constitutes an ethnomarker. . . . If ethnic groups identify themselves mainly in relation to one another, if ethnic war renegotiates these relations, and if rape marks the new boundaries of those relations, then we can expect rape to vary with the kind of ethnic system we are dealing with. In conflicts involving ranked ethnic systems, rape marks how groups are subordinated and superordinated.[304]

We could paraphrase the last sentence to read: In imperial and colonial conflicts rape defines the racialized parameters of subjugation and domination. This is borne out in Joshua Cole's powerful examination of the forgetting and remembering of torture and rape in French Algeria:

> Torture and rape were about establishing a particular relationship between French soldiers and Algerian Muslims, one in which the most essential parts of victim's personality – the integrity of their bodies, their relations with their families, their connection to a religion, a cause – were annihilated. . . . The French military . . . was determined to use the trauma of torture and rape as a kind of primal scene, that would forever define the relationship between the state and its colonial subjects, between the torture-ers and the torture-able.[305]

Kenya was no different. Elkins' *Imperial Reckoning* includes copious evidence of the most horrific mass rapes, sexual torture, mutilation, and forced labour meted out by British and African soldiers, white settlers, Kikuyu loyalists, and Home Guards to Mau Mau detainees, both male and female, and Kikuyu women imprisoned in the barbed wire villages.[306] The Home Guards took their cues from the British. Torture, rape, and mutilation were central to the "particular relationship" – as described by Cole for Algeria – that the British colonial administration and the settlers aimed to establish between themselves and the Kikuyu:

> The women detained in the villages called Britain's security forces *haraka*, "the fast ones," because of the speed with which they could inflict damage on the local population. "Whenever those groups came into the villages," recalled Shelmith Njeri, "they would wreak havoc within no time. They would be every-

where within a short period, turning houses inside out, burning houses, and raping women. It was so fast that a person in one house would have no time to know what was happening in another. As soon as she heard the screams, they had already burst into her house and begun tearing it apart."[307]

Although some Kikuyu women knew the difference between the military and paramilitary units and could identify whether whites belonged to the Kenya Police Reserve, the King's African Rifles, or the Kenya Regiment, many women called them collectively "Johnnies" or "British savages." Elkins continues,

Women suspected of continuing to feed the Mau Mau guerrillas were sometimes brought into the village square and shot or hung as an example to the rest. Sometimes they were beaten first with clubs and rifle butts, and sometimes raped. On other occasions members of the security forces would take captured Mau Mau fighters, rope them to the back of Land Rovers, and drive them around the villages, leaving bits of body parts in their wake. Young children were slaughtered and their remains skewered on spears and paraded around the village squares by the Home Guards. Excrement-based torture was also widespread. "The Johnnies would make us run around with toilet buckets on our heads," recalled one woman. "The contents would be running down our faces, and we would have to wipe it off and eat it, or else we were shot."[308]

Women of all ages feared sexual violence. British and Kenyan soldiers sometimes raped mothers and daughters of the same family together. One of Elkins' informants told her,

The white officers had no shame. They would rape women in full view of everyone. They would take whomever they wanted at one corner and just do it right there. Whenever those soldiers came into the village, I remember I used to sneak into our house and smear ashes all over my body so they would not fancy me. Then, when they saw me, they would say, "Now look at this one, what is wrong with her?"[309]

Such testimony brings to mind the Rape of Nanjing, when women desperately tried to avoid rape, torture, and death at the hands of the Japanese by rubbing soot on their faces in order to seem old or disfigured.[310] Nevertheless, many Kikuyu women could not avoid rape, which was frequently chosen instead of death.

In the wake of successful Mau Mau actions, the Johnnies and the Home Guards were especially sadistic, combining revenge with interrogation of villagers. Elkins' informants remembered that women sometimes suffered their breasts being squeezed with pliers, being swung by their hair, or being tortured as they lay prone on the ground with a soldier's boot on their necks. Women beaten into unconsciousness were revived with buckets of water, only for the torture to start again. Those women and men who refused to confess were sometimes forced into sacks that were doused with petrol or paraffin. A terrible death followed. Rape was frequently accompanied by penetration with bottles – in some cases filled with pepper and water – rifles, or vermin.[311]

As in other instances of mass rape and torture during colonial and civil wars, in Kenya the aims and the effects were multiple. Once the worst of the repression was over and detainees were able to return to their villages, couples and families had to deal with the consequences of extreme trauma. Many raped women had given birth to children and could not easily welcome their husbands home if they had survived. Some of these children were mixed, the offspring of white rapists. Sometimes these babies were forcibly removed from mothers who had decided to keep them. Many children conceived during rape were visibly related to Home Guard neighbours of the victims.[312] Many women could not successfully carry their babies because they had been starved in the concentrated villages. Others were made infertile by the violence and disease they had suffered. There were numerous cases of suicide of men who had come home after experiencing the worst of the Pipeline, but then could not cope with the destruction of their families in their absence or with finding their wife with a mixed-race baby. Both men and women coped with the shame through silence, the "widespread remedy" for which there was no alternative if they were to survive through the ongoing Emergency and eventually re-establish "normal" life.[313]

One hundred years after Bear River, silence reigned over similar American atrocities in Vietnam. Some time in 1967, U.S. Army journalist Dennis Stout had witnessed the gang rape and execution of a Vietnamese woman by American soldiers near Quang Ngai City. He reported the incident to an Army chaplain, who told him to just carry on doing his job. "It was too late to do anything, and it was, the chaplain argued, an isolated incident."[314] It was far from isolated. One veteran, Joe Galbally, gave testimony at the Winter Soldier Investigation in January and February 1971 concerning a gang rape by American soldiers. "This wasn't just one incident," he concluded. "This was the first one I can remember. I know of 10 or 15 such incidents at least." Galbally was in Vietnam just one year.[315] Other soldiers, including Sergeants Jamie Henry and Scott Camil, gave similar evidence about other rapes, torture, and murder of Vietnamese women at the hearings. Henry noted that rape was "SOP," meaning standard operating procedure.[316] The fact that there was another euphemism – "double veterans" – for those who raped and then killed their female victims, speaks to how commonplace the atrocities were.[317] It seems that as yet very little detailed research has been carried out on this aspect of American war crimes in Vietnam.[318]

Carolyn Nordstrom, in her work on girl victims of the civil war in post-colonial Mozambique, a war stoked by Ian Smith's white settler regime in Southern Rhodesia and the South African apartheid government's aid to the RENAMO rebels, makes a related and crucial point. In recent wars around the world, children have been victims of violence almost as much as adults. They are in large numbers killed, maimed, tortured, raped, starved, recruited, and imprisoned. Most information available about juvenile war victims, however, concerns boys. The obvious question, then, is, "Where are the girls?"[319] Women can be found in war zones and their stories can often be collected. Women, as the Mau Mau war shows, are extremely active in conflicts as participants, diplomats, spies, producers, traders, healers, farmers, and activists.[320] But girls, Nordstrom argues from her own research experience, "were largely, dangerously, invisible."[321] They could be found only in the context of the family. Beyond this, "they disappeared from sight; they had no agency to direct their lives, to talk and trade and set up healing programs, they never spoke on the radio, their words were not recorded in newsprint, political scientists did not quote them, non-governmental organizations . . . did not interview them." Girls have remained hidden. Yet of course they were and are actors and casualties of war, along with the adults: "They are targeted for attack, they devise escapes, they endure torture, they carry food to the needy, they forge a politics of belief and action."[322] The problem is silence. Girls, and to a lesser extent boys, have remained largely invisible in the reporting and subsequent analysis of colonial and postcolonial wars. Journalists and researchers very rarely visited rural areas in countries like Mozambique during wartime. Until recently, with the advent of cellular telephones, communications in most parts of Africa and Asia were very difficult. As Nordstrom writes, "The sad truth is that no one knows what occurred in the hundreds of towns and villages in Mozambique (and in thousands of villages worldwide like them)." After the conflict was over, when the question is asked, "Where are the girls?" it is not possible to find an answer, when 1 million people were killed, and there were 200,000 to 300,000 orphans. In many cases, families took in orphan children, but hundreds of thousands disappeared. Many Mozambican girls were sold to white families in neighbouring South Africa for domestic work or sexual slavery. This was camouflaged by popular and media attention on alleged cases of children's body parts being used for "medicine" and threats against the few interested local journalists.[323]

Memory fades like a ruin in the jungle. The lost are forgotten, their graves a desert. Shame petrifies speech. In the stone-faced centres of power, silence reigns.

This is a work of historical comparison. Much of the failure to understand violence against non-combatants in imperial and colonial conflicts comes from a failure to consider the meaning of violence in such contexts.[324] Violence does not exist just as a tool for the conquest of land, material resources, labour: "Colonial violence also creates a specific space in which the violent relationship can be re-enacted and exploited as a kind of existential condition: it is what gives meaning to the social and political relationships that emerge from this violence." Imperial and colonial relationships – meaning the subordination of the "other" by a dominant external power for the latter's alleged benefit – depend ultimately on the continual ability to re-enact and exploit this "existential condition."[325] This is a similar conclusion to my own, which is that violence in colonial and imperial contexts is inevitably and primarily directed against non-combatants, both for structural reasons and because of the inherent nature of the imperial relationship. It is not an unintended side effect of a specific policy goal or the action of overenthusiastic men on the spot: "*It is the goal itself.*"[326] Remember the words of Elgin's secretary, Oliphant: the necessity of making a "deep impression" on the Chinese population. It is this reality that the alibi of collateral damage occludes, hides, and denies.

As I end this piece, the importance of working internationally to reduce civilian suffering is as apparent as ever. Yet we in the West, influenced as we are by deeply entrenched military and political cultures of imperialism, need a change of hearts and minds of our own instead of forcing conformity on others. Given the huge global social and economic inequalities, this seems unlikely in the immediate future. I log on to my computer and check the BBC website where I see the following: "Afghan Strike 'Hit Wedding Party.' At least 20 people have been killed in a missile strike by coalition forces in Afghan's [sic] eastern Nangarhar province. Local people say that the group was a wedding party and that most of the dead were women and children. But the U.S. has denied this, saying those killed were militants involved in previous mortar attacks on a NATO base."[327]

Notes

1 No author, "Mahathir Blasts U.S. at Summits," *Globe and Mail*, March 3, 2003.
2 Mahathir Mohamad, Speech to the Non-Aligned Movement, Kuala Lumpur, February 24, 2003.
3 See the critique of Walzer's position on the war in Afghanistan in Michael Mandel, *How America Gets Away with Murder: Illegal Wars, Collateral Damage and*

Crimes Against Humanity (London and Ann Arbor: Pluto Press, 2004), 46–49. Martin Shaw, in his *The New Western Way of War: Risk-Transfer War and Its Crisis in Iraq* (Cambridge and Malden, Mass.: Polity Press, 2005), 2–3, also combines rigorous analysis with a moral and political argument.

4 Despite the misgivings of the British Attorney-General and a majority in the House of Commons, this was the position taken by the British government in its attacks on China in 1857–58 and 1860. See John Newsinger, "Elgin in China," *New Left Review* 15 (May-June 2002), 128–29.

5 Quoted in Mandel, *How America Gets Away with Murder*, 46.

6 Heather A. Wilson, *International Law and the Use of Force by National Liberation Movements* (Oxford: Clarendon Press, 1988), 6–8.

7 See George Kassimeris, "The Barbarization of Warfare: A User's Manual," in *The Barbarization of Warfare*, ed. George Kassimeris (New York: New York University Press, 2006), 5.

8 The ratio of civilian casualties was about twenty-five to one, or approximately 1,000 killed by the Israelis and 40 killed by Hizbullah. See Amnesty International, "Lebanon: Deliberate Destruction or 'Collateral Damage'? Israeli Attacks on Civilian Infrastructure," August 22, 2006, index no. MDE 18/007/2006, www.amnesty.org/.

9 The sources for violent deaths in Iraq are discussed below.

10 This argument is elaborated at length in Jefferson D. Reynolds, "Collateral Damage on the 21st Century Battlefield: Enemy Exploitation of the Law of Armed Conflict, and the Struggle for a Moral High Ground," *Air Force Law Review* 56 (Winter 2005), www.afjag.af.mil/library/. In 2005 Reynolds was a research fellow at the RAND Corporation and a reserve major in the U.S. Air Force.

11 The concept of "concealment warfare" is commonly deployed by Israeli politicians and military leaders and is central to the propaganda justifying disproportionate civilian casualties in the recent conflicts with Hizbullah and Hamas. The chief audience is Western public opinion, especially in the United States. It is unlikely that the Arab public would be so persuaded.

12 Interestingly, a 2002 workshop on collateral damage attended by military officers, journalists, NGO leaders, and academics also conflates collateral damage with civilian casualties, but without any critical analysis. Nowhere in the workshop report is collateral damage defined or its meanings and use in discourse problematized. See Carr Center for Human Rights Policy, "Understanding Collateral Damage Workshop," John F. Kennedy School of Government, Harvard University, Washington, D.C., June 4–5, 2002.

13 This paragraph in part follows from http://en.wikipedia.org/wiki/Collateral_damage.

14 Ibid.

15 Michael Walzer, *Just and Unjust Wars: A Moral Argument with Historical Illustrations*, 3rd ed. (New York: Basic Books, 2000), 270.

16 Ibid., 274–83, quoted at 276. Even conventional weapons, given their destructive power and the size and nature of the military-industrial complex that develops them, have since the Second World War and especially since 1989, moved beyond the ability of the laws of war to control their use against non-combatants. This is highly relevant to the emergence of the concept of collateral damage.

17 Mandel, *How America Gets Away with Murder*, 46–47.

18 Bryan L. Feary, Paul C. White, John St. Ledger, and John D. Immele, "An Analysis

of Reduced Collateral Damage Nuclear Weapons," *Comparative Strategy* 22, 4 (2003), 305–24.

19 Laurence Martin, "Limited Nuclear War," in *Restraints on War: Studies in the Limitation of Armed Conflict*, ed. Michael Howard (Oxford: Oxford University Press, 1979), 103–21.

20 *USAF Intelligence Targeting Guide*, Air Force pamphlet 14–210 intelligence, February 1, 1998, 180, http://fas.org/irp/doddir/usaf/.

21 Quoted from http://en.wikipedia.org/wiki/Collateral_damage. In reality, of course, the issue of targeting is not at all clear cut. It is very easy to deny subsequently that civilians were indeed targeted.

22 In particular the horrific bombing of the al Firdos air raid shelter. For an account that downplays the extent of collateral damage during the first Gulf War see Murray Williamson, "Not Enough Collateral Damage: Moral Ambiguities in the Gulf War," in *Civilians in the Path of War*, ed. Mark Grimsley and Clifford J. Rogers (Lincoln: University of Nebraska Press, 2002), 251–69. See Reynolds, "Collateral Damage on the 21st Century Battlefield," for a U.S. military perspective on the First Gulf War. Interestingly, Reynolds is rather more measured than Williamson, and cites Human Rights Watch figures of up to 3,000 Iraqi civilians dead from 65 incidents in the war.

23 For a powerful discussion of "the language of slaughter" see Joanna Bourke, "Barbarisation vs Civilisation in Time of War," in *The Barbarization of Warfare*, ed. Kassimeris, 19–38. A useful overview of media management by the U.S. military in recent decades is Thomas Rid, *War and Media Operations: The US Military and the Press from Vietnam to Iraq* (Abingdon, U.K.: Routledge, 2007).

24 Noam Chomsky discusses the development of propaganda in the United States and the use during the Afghanistan and Iraq Wars of euphemisms such as "embedded journalist" and "unlawful combatant." See "Collateral Language: Noam Chomsky Interviewed by David Barsamian," *Z Magazine* (July–August, 2003), www.zmag.org/zmag.

25 Victor Davis Hanson, *Carnage and Culture: Landmark Battles in the Rise of Western Power* (New York: Anchor Books, 2002), 7. The work is flawed conceptually and methodologically by the equation of everything Western with "freedom," by a tendency to absorb uncritically colonial mythology (for example, on the Zulu king, Shaka). Further, the military-industrial complex is deemed irrelevant and the modern West, astonishingly, is assumed to be unmilitaristic. In the later chapters, especially those on Rorke's Drift and Tet, there is a failure to address the power of national culture and ideology: for the Zulus the defence of the *Usuthu*, or royal house, and for the Vietnamese, anti-imperialist nationalism. Non-Westerners, whether ancient Persians, Ottomans, Zulus, or Vietnamese, are assumed to have fought out of fear of their rulers. In contrast, the resilience and character of Western culture, assumed to be essentially unbroken from the ancient Greeks to the present, is at the core of his argument.

26 The last lines read: "The final premise of *Carnage and Culture* – that the chief danger of Western militaries is not their weakness, but their unmatched power to kill – remains the most germane and yet most unrecognized lesson of our current conflict." Hanson, *Carnage and Culture*, 463.

27 Walzer, *Just and Unjust Wars*, 20.

28 Ibid., 144–59. See also Camillo "Mac" Bica, "Collateral Damage: A Military

Euphemism for Murder," April 16, 2007, www.zmag.org for a short discussion of the doctrine of double effect and its weaknesses.

29 Walzer, *Just and Unjust Wars*, 144, quoting M. Greenspan, *The Modern Law of Land Warfare* (Berkeley: University of California Press, 1959), 313–14.

30 Walzer, *Just and Unjust Wars*, 144. The impact of strategic choices on civilians is noted in Carr Center for Human Rights Policy, "Understanding Collateral Damage Workshop," 5.

31 Major Reynolds argues that attacks on civilian food supplies are legitimate according to the laws of war, and may be beneficial to the civilians because they will be forced to evacuate the area! See Reynolds, "Collateral Damage on the 21st Century Battlefield."

32 Walzer, *Just and Unjust Wars*, 146. For the example of submarine warfare and the Laconia Affair from the Second World War, see ibid., 147–51.

33 Non-combatants have been particularly in danger in two types of international conflict: those involving industrialized powers and pre-industrial societies in both earlier and recent periods, and all wars since the 1930s.

34 Thomas Aquinas, *Summa Theologica* (II-II, Qu. 64, art. 7) in Alison McIntyre, "Doctrine of Double Effect," *Stanford Encyclopedia of Philosophy*, July 28, 2004, http://plato.stanford.edu/entries/double-effect/; Walzer, *Just and Unjust Wars*, 152; Bica, "Collateral Damage."

35 Walzer, *Just and Unjust Wars*, 153, quoting Kenneth Dougherty, *General Ethics: An Introduction to the Basic Principles of the Moral Life According to St. Thomas Aquinas* (Peekskill, N.Y.: 1959), 64.

36 Indeed, its principles are written into the war crimes provisions of the 1998 Rome Statute governing the International Criminal Court. See Reynolds, "Collateral Damage on the 21st Century Battlefield."

37 A thoughtful military analyst notes that the doctrine of double effect does not help to morally resolve all cases of potential harm to civilians in war. Chris Mayer, "The Doctrine of Double Effect: Its Relevance to Collateral Damage Cases," www.usafa.af.mil/isme/JSCOPE3/Mayer03.html. However, the examples that Mayer discusses are too conventional to be very relevant to the kinds of highly asymmetrical wars that are currently fought by Western powers.

38 From Walzer, *Just and Unjust Wars*, 153. Mayer provides a similar set of conditions in "The Doctrine of Double Effect," 3. For the formulation as found in the *New Catholic Encyclopedia*, see McIntyre, "Doctrine of Double Effect," 2.

39 Quoted in Walzer, *Just and Unjust Wars*, 129.

40 Most international conflicts since the Second World War involve a highly industrialized and developed nation or coalition of nations on one side and an underdeveloped nation or nations or non-state force on the other.

41 This case comes from Mayer, "The Doctrine of Double Effect," 9. It is not typical for the current era because armies of industrialized powers rely on heavy weapons and ground attack aircraft, both absent from the description.

42 As described and analyzed in Walzer, *Just and Unjust Wars*, 154–56. The quotations are from Reginald Thompson, *Cry Korea* (London: Macdonald, 1951), 54, 142–43.

43 Walzer, *Just and Unjust Wars*, 155.

44 Ibid., 15–16; McIntyre, "Doctrine of Double Effect," 5. I have deliberately stayed close to Walzer's words in this discussion, given the precision required in language as well as in action, and because this is Walzer's major contribution to the debate.

45 Beryl Fox, producer and director, *The Mills of the Gods: Vietnam*, CBC Television, 1965.

46 Sociologist Martin Shaw refers to the "cult of the weapon-system" and an "armament culture" that became particularly prominent after the Vietnam War. See Shaw, *The New Western Way of War*, 37.

47 For further images documenting the devastating impact of the war on ordinary Vietnamese civilians see the work of Magnum photographer Philip Jones Griffiths, *Vietnam Inc.* (London: Phaidon Press, 2001).

48 The analysis comes from Bica, "Collateral Damage," 2–3.

49 See the discussions in McIntyre, "Doctrine of Double Effect."

50 Walzer, *Just and Unjust Wars*, 153; McIntyre, "Doctrine of Double Effect," 6, 9. British Catholic philosopher Elizabeth Anscombe, for example, has offered a searching critique of the usage of the doctrine of double effect to justify civilian casualties in war.

51 Bica, "Collateral Damage," 2. It should be noted that Bica is a United States Marine Corps veteran of the Vietnam War.

52 David Lefkowitz, "Collateral Damage," in *War: Essays in Political Philosophy*, ed. Larry May (Cambridge: Cambridge University Press, 2008), 159.

53 Mayer, "The Doctrine of Double Effect."

54 Philippe Contamine, *War in the Middle Ages*, trans. Michael Jones (Oxford: Basil Blackwell, 1984), 270–80; David Hay, "Chivalry and Crusade: Collateral Damage in Western Thought and Practice during the High Middle Ages," paper presented at the conference " 'Collateral Damage': Civilian Casualties from Antiquity through the Gulf Wars," University of Toronto, May 16–17, 2004.

55 Contamine, *War in the Middle Ages*, 273–74; Hay, "Chivalry and Crusade," 6.

56 Hay, "Chivalry and Crusade," 7, 9.

57 Louis Sala-Molins, *Dark Side of the Light: Slavery and the French Enlightenment* (Minneapolis: University of Minneapolis Press, 2006), 52–53, 84, 159n. 27; John Conteh-Morgan, "Translator's Introduction," *Dark Side of the Light*, xxv; Sven Lindqvist, *"Exterminate All the Brutes": One Man's Odyssey into the Heart of Darkness and the Origins of European Genocide*, trans. Joan Hay (New York: The New Press, 1996), 112. The lawyers failed to come to agreement. For the background to the debate and Las Casas' life and work see Anthony Pagden, "Introduction" to Bartolomé de Las Casas, *A Short Account of the Destruction of the Indies*, trans. Nigel Griffin (London: Penguin, 1992).

58 Hay, "Chivalry and Crusade," 9. See also Contamine, *War in the Middle Ages*, 277–78 on the crusading spirit.

59 David Hay, "Gender Bias and Religious Intolerance in Accounts of 'Massacres' of the First Crusade," in *Tolerance and Intolerance: Social Conflict in the Age of the Crusades*, ed. Michael Gervers and James M. Powell (Syracuse, N.Y.: Syracuse University Press, 2001), 3–10.

60 Geoffrey Best, *Humanity in Warfare* (London: Wiederfeld and Nicholson, 1980), 20. For a similar statement see Anthony Dworkin, "The Laws of War in the Age of Asymmetric Conflict," in *The Barbarization of Warfare*, ed. Kassimeris, 222–24.

61 There were partial exceptions to the attribution "savage" or "barbarous." For example, the *quatre communes* of Senegal, the African residents of which had French citizenship from 1871; and the so-called *assimilados* of Portuguese Africa. It is also important to realize that imperial conquests and security typically relied on the employment of "native" troops. For examples see V.G. Kiernan, *Colonial*

Empires and Armies 1815–1960 (Montreal and Kingston: McGill-Queen's University Press, 1998); Johnson U.J. Asiegbu, *Nigeria and Its British Invaders 1851–1920* (New York and Enugu: Nok Publishers, 1984); Myron J. Echenberg, *Colonial Conscripts: The Tirailleurs Sénégalais in French West Africa, 1857–1960* (Portsmouth, N.H.: Heinemann, 1991); Timothy Parsons, *The African Rank-and-File: Social Implications of Colonial Military Service in the King's African Rifles, 1902–1964* (Portsmouth, N.H.: Heinemann, 1999).

62 Agreeing with Louis Sala-Molins and postcolonial writers such Dipesh Chakrabarty, I do not critique the Enlightenment values themselves. Indeed I embrace them. Rather, I would like the Enlightenment and its legacy to be as truly enlightened and universal as it claimed.

63 Hedley Bull in *World Politics* 31 (1979), quoted in Best, *Humanity in Warfare*, 1.

64 Best, *Humanity in Warfare*, 16–18, quoted at 17.

65 Rousseau from ch. 4, book i of *Du contrat social*, as quoted in Best, *Humanity in Warfare*, 56.

66 Best, *Humanity in Warfare*, 56–9, quoted at 58.

67 John K. Thornton, *Warfare in Atlantic Africa 1500–1800* (London: UCL Press, 1999), 100.

68 Best, *Humanity in Warfare*, 45. For more on necessity see ibid., 43–53.

69 Emmerich de Vattel, *Le droit des gens ou principes de la loi naturelle, appliqués à la conduite et aux affaires des nations et des souverains* (Neuchatel, 1758), quoted in Best, *Humanity in Warfare*, 43. For Vattel's major contributions to humanity in warfare see *Humanity in Warfare*, 32–74.

70 Quoted in Best, *Humanity in Warfare*, 43.

71 Best, *Humanity in Warfare*, 8, emphasis added.

72 Lindqvist, *"Exterminate All the Brutes."*

73 Best, *Humanity in Warfare*, 49–50.

74 *Conférence sur la Convention de Genève* (Geneva, 1897), 29–31, quoted in Best, *Humanity in Warfare*, 10, emphasis added. It is obvious who Moynier and his contemporaries regarded as civilized.

75 Best, *Humanity in Warfare*, 17–18, 46–47.

76 An exception is the brief (and critical) discussion of British embarrassment at The Hague in 1899 over their use of dum-dum bullets, designed to knock down big game and then defended for imperial use: "Nothing less would stop 'savages' like the tribesmen of the Indian North-West Frontier and the followers of the Mahdi in the Sudan." Best, *Humanity in Warfare*, 162.

77 Sala-Molins, *Dark Side of the Light*.

78 This universalism, so provincial in practice, is commonly critiqued by postcolonial thinkers for not living up to its own ideals. For an example dealing with post-Enlightenment and imperialist thought on slavery and labour in Africa, see my own *Carriers of Culture: Labor on the Road in Nineteenth-Century East Africa* (Portsmouth, N.H.: Heinemann, 2006), 8–23.

79 See Conteh-Morgan, "Translator's Introduction," *Dark Side of the Light*, xx.

80 Sala-Molins, *Dark Side of the Light*, 6, 5. For those who wish to interrogate the imagining of genocide during the early Enlightenment, an interesting although, to my mind, highly flawed discussion of Claude Rawson's *God, Gulliver, and Genocide: Barbarism and the European Imagination, 1492–1945*, is found in Robert Alter, "Immodest Proposals," *The New Republic Online*, February 11, 2002, www.thenewrepublic.com/.

81 Sala-Molins, *Dark Side of the Light*, 7, 8. What more relevant introduction to recent events at Westminster Abbey in London, when the solemn ceremony marking the bicentenary of the abolition of the British slave trade, attended by the Queen, the Archbishop of Canterbury, and the prime minister was interrupted by the protests of Toyin Agbetu? See "This Is a Disgrace," *Toronto Star*, March 28, 2007.

82 Sala-Molins, *Dark Side of the Light*, 9. For Condorcet and slavery see 11–53.

83 Ibid., 29, 32, 75, 12.

84 For a formidable analysis of the *Code noir* in relation to the Declaration of the Rights of Man see Sala-Molins, *Dark Side of the Light*, 55–72.

85 Lindqvist, *"Exterminate All the Brutes,"* 140, quoting from J.A.S. Grenville, *Lord Salisbury and Foreign Policy: The Close of the Nineteenth Century* (London: Athlone Press, 1964), 165.

86 Lindqvist, *"Exterminate All the Brutes,"* 139.

87 Quoted in ibid., 157.

88 Ibid., 112.

89 "U.S. Regrets Afghan Civilian Deaths," July 3, 2007, www.news.bbc.co.uk. The second quotation is a paraphrase from the BBC, the third is the BBC quoting Mr. Khalilzad.

90 "NATO Raids 'Killed 35 Afghans,'" July 6, 2007, www.news.bbc.co.uk.

91 Rosie DiManno, "Marines Battle Taliban in Helmand Province," *Toronto Star*, May 15, 2008.

92 Ibid. For background see Declan Walsh, "In Ghost Town Where Afghan War Begins, U.K. Fights Losing Battle," *The Guardian*, May 5, 2008.

93 Marilyn B. Young, "An Incident at No Gun Ri," in *Crimes of War: Guilt and Denial in the Twentieth Century*, ed. Omer Bartov, Atina Grossmann, and Mary Nolan (New York: The New Press, 2002), 256–57.

94 Young, "An Incident at No Gun Ri," 249, 245.

95 Quoted in Young, "An Incident at No Gun Ri," 249–50. For other deliberate American attacks on non-combatants in Korea see ibid., 250–53. See also Bruce Cummings, "The South Korean Massacres at Taejon: New Evidence on U.S. Responsibility and Coverup," *Japan Focus*, www.japanfocus.org, July 23, 2008; Charles J. Hanley and Jae-Soon Chang, "U.S. Wavered over S. Korean Executions," *Global Research*, July 6, 2008, www.globalresearch.ca.

96 Quoted in Lindqvist, *"Exterminate All the Brutes,"* 118.

97 David Svaldi, *Sand Creek and the Rhetoric of Extermination: A Case Study in Indian-White Relations* (Lanham, Md.: University Press of America, 1989), 149–50; also Ward Churchill, *A Little Matter of Genocide: Holocaust and Denial in the Americas 1492 to the Present* (Winnipeg: Arbeiter Ring Publishing, 1998), 228.

98 Charles Darwin, *The Voyage of the Beagle*, ch. 5, quoted in Lindqvist, *"Exterminate All the Brutes,"* 116.

99 Pagden, "Introduction."

100 For detailed accounts of the Sand Creek massacre see Stan Hoig, *The Sand Creek Massacre* (Norman: University of Oklahoma Press, 1961); Svaldi, *Sand Creek*; Churchill, *A Little Matter of Genocide*, 228–34. Churchill also briefly discusses the subsequent Washita and Sappa Creek massacres, 234–38.

101 Churchill, *A Little Matter of Genocide*, 229–31.

102 For the politics of government investigations, see ibid., 235; Svaldi, *Sand Creek*. No one was punished, although it was admitted that Chivington, Evans, and others were responsible for a terrible crime.

103 Quoted in Churchill, *A Little Matter of Genocide*, 233.

104 Quoted in ibid. For similar testimony, see Hoig, *The Sand Creek Massacre*, 177–92. We will discuss sexual violence in war below.

105 Quoted in Thomas G. Dyer, *Theodore Roosevelt and the Idea of Race* (Baton Rouge: Louisiana State University Press, 1980), 79; also quoted in part in David E. Stannard, "Preface" to Churchill, *A Little Matter of Genocide*, xvii.

106 Mark Grimsley, "'Rebels' and 'Redskins': U.S. Military Conduct toward White Southerners and Native Americans in Comparative Perspective," in *Civilians in the Path of War*, ed. Grimsley and Rogers, 142.

107 Ibid., 138. For the distinctions the Union government made between, on the one hand, Confederate soldiers and southern civilians, who were usually treated as if they were the soldiers and citizens of a separate nation, and, on the other hand, Native Americans, who despite being members of separate societies were treated as insurgents with no rights at all, whether resisting or not, see 139–41.

108 Richard E. Welch, "American Atrocities in the Philippines: The Indictment and the Response," *Pacific Historical Review* 43 (1974), 252.

109 Ibid., 252.

110 Ibid., 242, 252–53, quotation at 241.

111 Quoted in ibid., 253.

112 For a more detailed account, see Terence O. Ranger, *Revolt in Southern Rhodesia 1896–7: A Study in African Resistance* (London: Heinemann, 1967), 268–81.

113 Quoted in ibid., 272.

114 Ibid., 273–75.

115 Quoted in ibid., 276–77.

116 Ibid., 277–78.

117 For the comparatively well-known 1904 genocide of the Herero in Namibia, then German South West Africa, see, among others, Horst Drechsler, *Let Us Die Fighting: The Struggle of the Nama and Herero against German Imperialism (1884–1915)* (Berlin: Akademie-Verlag, 1966); Peter H. Katjavivi, *A History of Resistance in Namibia* (London: James Currey, 1988); Jan-Bart Gewald, *Herero Heroes: A Socio-Political History of the Herero of Namibia 1890–1923* (Oxford: James Currey, 1999); Tilman Dedering, "'A Certain Rigorous Treatment of all Parts of the Nation': The Annihilation of the Herero in German South West Africa, 1904," in *The Massacre in History*, ed. Levene and Roberts, 205–22; Jon Bridgman and Leslie J. Worley, "Genocide of the Hereros," in *Century of Genocide: Eyewitness Accounts and Critical Views*, ed. Samuel Totten, William S. Parsons, and Israel W. Charny (New York and London: Garland Publishing, 1997), 3–40; Isabel V. Hull, "Military Culture and the Production of 'Final Solutions' in the Colonies: The Example of Wilhelminian Germany," in *The Specter of Genocide: Mass Murder in Historical Perspective*, ed. Robert Gellately and Ben Kiernan (Cambridge: Cambridge University Press, 2003), 141–62. Hull argues that the normative military ethos of the Wilhelmian army was a major factor in the genocide.

118 Jeff Guy, "Non-Combatants and War: The Unexplored Factor in the Conquest of the Zulu Kingdom," paper presented at the conference "'Collateral Damage': Civilian Casualties from Antiquity through the Gulf Wars," University of Toronto, May 16–17, 2004. Guy's classic work is *The Destruction of the Zulu Kingdom: The Civil War in Zululand 1879–1884* (London: Longman, 1979).

119 Quoted in Jeff Guy, "Non-Combatants and War," 3, 9.

120 Ibid., 11.

121 Ibid., 5–6.

122 Guy refers to Bradford's full, disturbing quotation, highlighting the gendered perspective of Xhosa women, at ibid., 7.

123 James Belich, *The New Zealand Wars and the Victorian Interpretation of Racial Conflict* (Auckland: Penguin, 1988), 22.

124 For the Italian conquest of Cyrenaica and the massive civilian casualties that followed, see Alexander B. Downes, "Democracy and Destruction: Regime Type and Civilian Victimization in Small Wars," paper presented at the conference "'Collateral Damage': Civilian Casualties from Antiquity through the Gulf Wars," University of Toronto, May 16–17, 2004, 22–29.

125 Lindqvist, "*Exterminate All the Brutes.*"

126 G.C.K. Gwassa, "Kinjikitili and the Ideology of Maji Maji," in *The Historical Study of African Religion*, ed. T.O. Ranger and I.N. Kimambo, (Berkeley: University of California Press, 1972), 202–17; G.C.K. Gwassa, *The Outbreak and Development of the Maji Maji War 1905–1907*, ed. Wolfgang Apelt (Cologne: Rüdiger Köppe Verlag, 2005); O.B. Mapunda and G.P Mpangara, *The Maji Maji War in Ungoni* (Dar es Salaam: East African Publishing House, 1969); John Iliffe, *A Modern History of Tanganyika* (Cambridge: Cambridge University Press, 1979), 168–202.

127 Thaddeus Sunseri, "Famine and Wild Pigs: Gender Struggles and the Outbreak of the Majimaji War in Uzaramo (Tanzania)," *Journal of African History* 38 (1997), 235–59; Thaddeus Sunseri, "Statist Narratives and Maji Maji Ellipses," *International Journal of African Historical Studies* 33, 3 (2000), 567–84; Thaddeus Sunseri, *Vilimani: Labor Migration and Rural Change in Early Colonial Tanzania* (Portsmouth, N.H.: Heinemann, 2002); Jamie Monson, "Relocating Maji Maji: The Politics of Alliance and Authority in the Southern Highlands of Tanzania, 1870–1918," *Journal of African History* 39 (1998), 95–120.

128 This account is based on Iliffe, *Modern History of Tanganyika*, 193–202.

129 Ibid., 199–200.

130 See Timothy C. Weiskel, *French Colonial Rule and the Baule Peoples: Resistance and Collaboration 1889–1911* (Oxford: Clarendon Press, 1980), 140, second quotation my translation.

131 Ibid., 196.

132 Ibid., 202.

133 Ibid., 203–04.

134 Ibid., 208–09.

135 Gerrit J. Knaap, "Crisis and Failure: War and Revolt in the Ambon Islands, 1636–1637," in *Warfare and Empires: Contact and Conflict between European and Non-European Military and Maritime Forces and Cultures*, ed. Douglas M. Peers (Aldershot: Ashgate Publishing, 1997), 161–62.

136 Peter Carey, "The Origins of the Java War (1825–30)," *English Historical Review* 91, 358 (1976), 52–78; Michael Adas, *Prophets of Rebellion: Millenarian Protest Movements against the European Colonial Order* (Cambridge: Cambridge University Press, 1987), 3–11; quotation from Kiernan, *Colonial Empires and Armies*, 118.

137 Kiernan, *Colonial Empires and Armies*, 24, 33–34.

138 Ibid., 41.

139 Capt. E. Buckle, *Memoir of the Services of the Bengal Artillery* ed. J.W. Kaye (London, 1852), 555–57, quoted in Kiernan, *Colonial Empires and Armies*, 42.

140 Corp. J. Ryder, *Four Years Service in India, By a Private Soldier* (Leicester, 1853), 127–30, quoted in Kiernan, *Colonial Empires and Armies*, 42.

141 For a short account see Kiernan, *Colonial Empires and Armies*, 47–50.

142 Ibid., 50. Kiernan quotes Col. C.E. Callwell, *Small Wars: Their Principles and Practice*, 3rd. ed (London: War Office, 1906), 80.

143 Kiernan, *Colonial Empires and Armies*, 115–16; Ranajit Guha, "The Prose of Counter-Insurgency," in *Selected Subaltern Studies*, ed. Ranajit Guha and Gayatri Chakravorty Spivak (Oxford: Oxford University Press, 1988).

144 Guha, "The Prose of Counter-Insurgency," 69.

145 The same region currently contested by the government of Pakistan, tribal authorities, and supporters of the Taliban.

146 J.G.A. Baird, ed., *Private Letters of the Marquis of Dalhousie*, 222–23, quoted in Kiernan, *Colonial Empires and Armies*, 69; Churchill in a letter to his mother, quoted in ibid., 70.

147 Kiernan, *Colonial Empires and Armies*, 116. Kiernan refers to Sir W.W. Hunter, *Annals of Rural Bengal*, 7th ed. (London, 1897), 247–48.

148 This discussion is from Newsinger, "Elgin in China," 119–40.

149 J.L. Morison, *The Eighth Earl of Elgin* (London: Hodder and Stoughton, 1928), 212, quoted in Newsinger, "Elgin in China," 130.

150 Theodore Walrond, ed., *The Life and Diaries of the Eighth Lord Elgin* (London, 1872), quoted in Newsinger, "Elgin in China," 120.

151 George Wingrove Cooke, *China: Being "The Times" Special Correspondent from China in the Years 1857–58* (London, 1858), 318, quoted in Newsinger, "Elgin in China," 120.

152 Laurence Oliphant, *Narrative of the Earl of Elgin's Mission to China and Japan* (Edinburgh, 1861), 130, quoted in Newsinger, "Elgin in China," 121.

153 Walrond, ed., *Life and Diaries*, 212, quoted in Newsinger, "Elgin in China," 130.

154 Ibid., 131.

155 Newsinger, "Elgin in China," 135.

156 Demetrius Boulger, *The Life of Gordon* (London, 1896), 46, quoted in Newsinger, "Elgin in China," 138.

157 Henry Brougham Loch, *Personal Narrative of Occurrences during Lord Elgin's Second Embassy to China in 1860* (London, 1900), 29, quoted in Newsinger, "Elgin in China," 140.

158 Helen Bradford, "Gentlemen and Boers: Afrikaner Nationalism, Gender, and Colonial Warfare in the South African War," in *Writing a Wider War: Rethinking Gender, Race, and Identity in the South African War, 1899–1902*, ed. Greg Cuthbertson, Albert Grundlingh, and Mary-Lynn Suttie (Athens: Ohio University Press, 2002), 41.

159 Ibid., 38. For details of British soldiers' looting, vandalism, and confiscation of property see 40–44.

160 Ibid., 38.

161 See for example, John Lambert, "'Loyalty Its Own Reward': The South African War Experience of Natal's 'Loyal' Africans," in *Writing a Wider War*, ed. Cuthbertson, Grundlingh, and Suttie, 115–35.

162 Examples are found in Andrew Thompson, "Imperial Propaganda during the South African War," in *Writing a Wider War*, ed. Cuthbertson, Grundlingh, and Suttie, 307, 319; and Bradford, "Gentlemen and Boers," 39.

163 Thompson, "Imperial Propaganda during the South African War," 317.

164 Hew Strachan, "Strategic Bombing and the Question of Civilian Casualties up to 1945," in *Firestorm: The Bombing of Dresden, 1945*, ed. Paul Addison and Jeremy A. Crang (London: Pimlico, 2006), 4–5.

165 Iliffe, *Modern History of Tanganyika*, 249–50, emphasis in original. For porters see Geoffrey Hodges, *The Carrier Corps: Military Labor in the East African Campaign, 1914–1918* (New York and London: Greenwood, 1986).

166 Iliffe, *Modern History of Tanganyika*, 251, 269–70.

167 This discussion is based on Alberto Sbacchi, *Legacy of Bitterness: Ethiopia and Fascist Italy, 1935–1941* (Lawrenceville, N.J., and Asmara: Red Sea Press, 1997), 55–85.

168 Ibid., 57–60. It is worth noting that the British and French also shipped poison gas to their colonies in East Africa in 1935. See ibid., 71.

169 Quoted in ibid., 62.

170 See the excellent collection of images in Adolfo Mignemi, ed., *Immagine coordinate per un impero Etiopia 1935–1936* (Turin: Gruppo Editoriale Forma, 1984). Most, such as posters, murals, stamps, postcards, cartoons, and films, served propagandistic purposes. Others, more brutally realistic, come from unofficial and private sources. For the feminization of Italian imperial propaganda in order to make the invasion palatable to Italian women see Robin Pickering-Iazzi, "Mass-Mediated Fantasies of Feminine Conquest, 1930–1940," in *A Place in the Sun: Africa in Italian Colonial Culture from Post-Unification to the Present*, ed. Patrizia Palumbo (Berkeley: University of California Press, 2003), 197–224.

171 Sbacchi, *Legacy of Bitterness*, 63–70, quoted at 63.

172 Ibid., 73.

173 See ibid., 60–63, 71 for details.

174 Ibid., 71–72, 77.

175 Ibid., 73–74.

176 Downes, "Democracy and Destruction."

177 Callum MacDonald, " 'Kill All, Burn All, Loot All': The Nanking Massacre of December 1937 and Japanese Policy in China," in *The Massacre in History*, ed. Levene and Roberts, 223–45; Yang Daqing, "Atrocities in Nanjing: Searching for Explanations," in *Scars of War: The Impact of Warfare on Modern China*, ed. Diana Lary and Stephen MacKinnon (Vancouver: UBC Press, 2001), 76–96.

178 Edward Said, *Culture and Imperialism* (New York: Vintage Books, 1993), and the critique by John M. MacKenzie, *Orientalism: History, Theory and the Arts* (Manchester: Manchester University Press, 1995). A very useful introduction to nineteenth-century writing about Arabs in East Africa is Norman R. Bennett, *Arab versus European: Diplomacy and War in Nineteenth Century East Central Africa* (New York: Africana Publishing Company, 1986), 3–17. Note also how the neo-liberal proponents of the invasion of Iraq pushed the views of conservative historian Bernard Lewis to the fore.

179 See Iris Chang, *The Rape of Nanking: The Forgotten Holocaust of World War II* (New York: Penguin Books, 1998).

180 For a clear overview see MacDonald, "Kill All, Burn All, Loot All," 225–30; also Yang Daqing, "Atrocities in Nanjing," 87.

181 Chang, *The Rape of Nanking*, 4–6, 99–104; Yang Daqing, "Atrocities in Nanjing," 76.

182 Quoted in Diana Lary, "A Ravaged Place: The Devastation of the Xuzhou Region, 1938," in *Scars of War*, ed. Lary and MacKinnon, 101, emphasis in original.

183 Ibid., 101. For the impact of Japanese bombing in and around Xuzhou, the loss of civilian infrastructure, destruction caused by the fires started by ground troops on both sides, and economic collapse see ibid., 102–04.

184 Quoted in ibid., 101.

185 See ibid., 107–10 for details. For a more systematic overview of the refugee experience in China see Stephen MacKinnon, "Refugee Flight at the Outset of the Anti-Japanese War," in *Scars of War*, Lary and MacKinnon, 118–34.

186 Diana Lary and Stephen MacKinnon, "Introduction," in *Scars of War*, ed. Lary and MacKinnon, 3.

187 Chang, *The Rape of Nanking*.

188 MacDonald, "Kill All, Burn All, Loot All," 242.

189 Ibid., 241; Yang Daqing, "Atrocities in Nanjing," 77–79. The quotation, p. 79, is from Hsu Shu-hsi, *The War Conduct of the Japanese* (Shanghai: Kelly and Walsh, 1938), 98.

190 MacDonald, "Kill All, Burn All, Loot All," 242.

191 John W. Dower, " 'An Aptitude for Being Unloved': War and Memory in Japan," in *Crimes of War*, ed. Bartov, Grossmann, and Nolan, 217–41.

192 Kiernan, *Colonial Empires and Armies*, xvi.

193 Fox, *The Mills of the Gods*, unknown American voiceover. The film's images at this point are of women and children engaged in peaceful scenes of village life.

194 Adam Roberts and Richard Guelff, eds., *Documents on the Laws of War*, 3rd ed. (Oxford: Clarendon Press, 2000), 645–66. China, India, Pakistan, Russia, and the United States decided not to sign the Ottawa Convention.

195 Geoffrey Best, *War and Law since 1945* (Oxford: Clarendon Press, 1994).

196 Recounted in Sala-Molins, *Dark Side of the Light*, 55–56.

197 "Decolonization" is placed inside quotation marks because it is another term fraught with contested meanings. The standard Western assumption is that decolonization was a gradual process, managed by both imperial statesmen and nationalist leaders in the colonial territories, with the aim of conferring self-government and then eventual independence. In many cases, however, the idea of decolonization was a retrospective invention with the aim of explaining away absolute failures of both colonial integration and imagination in the imperial centres. See, for example, Todd Shepard, *The Invention of Decolonization: The Algerian War and the Remaking of France* (Ithaca, N.Y., and London: Cornell University Press, 2005).

198 Belgium (September 3, 1952); China (December 28, 1956); France (June 28, 1951); Portugal (March 14, 1961); South Africa (March 31, 1952); United Kingdom (September 23, 1957); United States (August 2, 1955); USSR (May 10, 1954). See Roberts and Guelff, eds., *Documents on the Laws of War*, 355–61.

199 Caroline Elkins, *Imperial Reckoning: The Untold Story of Britain's Gulag in Kenya* (New York: Henry Holt and Company, 2005), passim. Estimates for detention camps and concentrated villages are on pp. xiii–xiv. See also Caroline Elkins, "Detention, Rehabilitation and the Destruction of Kikuyu Society," in *Mau Mau and Nationhood: Arms, Authority and Narration* ed. E.S. Atieno Odhiambo and John Lonsdale (Oxford: James Currey, 2003), 191–226.

200 Elkins, *Imperial Reckoning*, xvi, 363–66.

201 Ibid., 96–97, 135, 314. The British took a similar approach to the almost contemporaneous Malaya Emergency, which was also fought as a "police action," in theory freeing the British from the laws of war. See T.N. Harper, *The End of Empire*

and the Making of Modern Malaya (Cambridge: Cambridge University Press, 1999), 151–58. Elkins makes numerous comparisons between the repression of Mau Mau and British counter-insurgency strategies in Malaya.

202 Elkins, Imperial Reckoning, 46–51; Elkins, "Detention, Rehabilitation and the Destruction of Kikuyu Society," 192–94. The work of Bruce Berman and John Lonsdale is particularly helpful on the various mental constructions of Mau Mau. See Unhappy Valley: Conflict in Kenya and Africa, 2 vols. (Oxford: James Currey, 1992), especially vol. 2, Violence and Ethnicity.

203 Elkins, Imperial Reckoning, 48. Thus there is close comparison with the language of genocide. In the Armenian genocide, the Turks referred to the people they were murdering as "dog-food." See Bourke, "Barbarisation vs Civilisation in Time of War," 29.

204 Quoted in Elkins, Imperial Reckoning, 49.

205 Shepard, The Invention of Decolonization, 2, 6–7; Benjamin Stora, Algeria 1830–2000: A Short History (Ithaca, N.Y., and London: Cornell University Press, 2001), 30. Shepard covers French self-delusion and the problems that this created for France and Algeria in his introduction, 1–15.

206 Henri Alleg, "Some Thoughts by Way of a Preface," in Algeria and France 1800–2000: Identity, Memory, Nostalgia, ed. Patricia M.E. Lorcin (Syracuse: Syracuse University Press, 2006), x. For casualties, including civilians, see Stora, Algeria 1830–2000, 107–11.

207 Stora, Algeria 1830–2000, 46, 54, 75.

208 Ibid., 50–52. For the impact of the recent "remembering" of French torture in Algeria see Sylvie Durmelat, "Revisiting Ghosts: Louisette Ighilahriz and the Remembering of Torture," in Memory, Empire, and Postcolonialism: Legacies of French Colonialism, ed. Alec G. Hargreaves (Lanham, Md.: Lexington Books, 2005), 142–59.

209 Stora, Algeria 1830–2000, 97–101. For the origins of the OAS see 81–83.

210 Ibid., 101–03.

211 Ibid., 93.

212 Manuel Castells, The Information Age: Economy, Society and Culture, vol. 1, The Rise of Network Society (Oxford: Blackwell, 1996), 451.

213 Gabriel Kolko, Anatomy of a War: Vietnam, the United States, and the Modern Historical Experience (New York: The New Press, 1994), 363–64.

214 An attempt has been made to standardize metric, imperial, and U.S. weights and measures where practicable. In many cases, however, the original usage from sources has been retained according to the context.

215 D.R. SarDesai, Vietnam: The Struggle for National Identity (Boulder, Colo.: Westview Press, 1992), 86, 95; Kolko, Anatomy of a War, 200, 463–64. Kolko's civilian casualty figures are similar and are based on Pentagon and Senate reports.

216 SarDesai, Vietnam, 86; Kolko, Anatomy of a War, 201.

217 Griffiths, Vietnam Inc., 204.

218 Reynolds, "Collateral Damage on the 21st Century Battlefield."

219 Ibid.

220 Kolko, Anatomy of a War, 131.

221 Ibid., 201–07, for the impact on former peasants in the urban areas.

222 See ibid., 126–37, 231–51, 386–400, for an overview of the war and rural society; 132–34 for strategic hamlets. The quotation from a United States Marine Corps officer is on p. 133.

223 Michael Sallah and Mitch Weiss, *Tiger Force: A True Story of Men and War* (New York: Back Bay Books, 2006), 29. The authors won the Pulitzer Prize for their original research on U.S. atrocities and the subsequent cover-up by the military, first published by the *Toledo Blade*.

224 Ibid., 29–30, 315. This is a reconstruction of the briefing based on interviews of former Tiger Force members.

225 Ibid., 123–24 and passim. The sources used by Sallah and Weiss include U.S. army CID records, and interviews with Tiger Force and Vietnamese witnesses and villagers.

226 Reynolds, "Collateral Damage on the 21st Century Battlefield."

227 James Landers, *The Weekly War: Newsmagazines and Vietnam* (Columbia and London: University of Missouri Press, 2004), 121–22.

228 Ibid., 137–38. For more details on how *Newsweek* gutted the original article, leaving out evidence from Vietnamese witnesses, see Nicholas Turse, "The Vietnam Exposé That Wasn't," *The Nation*, November 13, 2008, www.thenation.com; Nick Turse, "A My Lai a Month," *The Nation*, December 1, 2008, www.thenation.com.

229 This paragraph is based on Turse, "A My Lai a Month."

230 Quoted in ibid. Turse quotes extensively from a source given as "Concerned Sergeant."

231 Ibid.

232 Nicholas Turse, "The Doctrine of Atrocity: U.S. against 'Them' – a Tradition of Institutionalized Brutality," *The Village Voice*, May 4, 2004, www.villagevoice.com.

233 Quoted in Turse, "A My Lai a Month."

234 Ibid.

235 Ibid. The report of the Carr Center for Human Rights Policy, "Understanding Collateral Damage Workshop," 4, uncritically refers to the "body count" as "the measure of enemy dead," thus seemingly perpetuating the notion that Vietnamese civilians were legitimate targets.

236 Nick Turse, "The Vietnam War Crimes You Never Heard Of," *History News Network*, November 17, 2003, http://hnn.us/articles/1802.html; Marilyn Young, "Why Vietnam Still Matters," in *The War That Never Ends: New Perspectives on the Vietnam War*, ed. David L. Anderson and John Ernst (Lexington: University Press of Kentucky, 2007), 5–6.

237 Within three days of Calley's conviction, country singer Tony Nelson sold 200,000 recordings of his song "The Battle Hymn of Lieutenant Calley." For the lyrics, see Bourke, "Barbarisation vs Civilisation in Time of War," 24.

238 Young, "Why Vietnam Still Matters," 6. My own reaction to the *Toledo Blade* stories, then easily accessible on the internet, was astonishment that just one small regional newspaper had the courage to publish them.

239 See also Carl Boggs, "Outlaw Nation: The Legacy of U.S. War Crimes," in *Masters of War: Militarism and Blowback in the Era of American Empire*, ed. Carl Boggs (New York and London: Routledge, 2003), 220–23, for further discussion of this theme in relation to American military dominance and "technowar."

240 Young, "Why Vietnam Still Matters," 8.

241 For a discussion of other key contributions and concepts, including war as a spectator sport and Ignatieff's and Der Derian's ideas on "virtual" and "virtuous" war, see Shaw, *The New Western Way of War*, 29–46.

242 Ibid., 1–2 and passim, quoted at 37.

243 Ibid., 39.

244 For the evolution of the new Western way of war through the Falklands War, the First Gulf War, the intervention in Kosovo, and the War on Terror in Afghanistan and Iraq, see ibid., 4–28.

245 Ibid., 39, emphasis in original. See especially what Shaw refers to as the "Rules of Risk-Transfer War," 71–97, and especially, 79–89.

246 Ibid., 94.

247 Ibid., 95, emphasis in original.

248 Ibid., 97.

249 Ibid., 98–145. See below for the second *Lancet* report of October 2006.

250 Lindqvist, *"Exterminate All the Brutes,"* 172.

251 Modris Eksteins, *Walking since Daybreak: A Story of Eastern Europe, World War II, and the Heart of Our Century* (Toronto: Key Porter Books, 1999), x.

252 Sallah and Weiss, *Tiger Force*, 306.

253 Geoff Eley, "Foreword" to *War and Memory in the Twentieth Century*, ed. Martin Evans and Ken Lunn (Oxford: Berg, 1997), vii.

254 Ibid.

255 Quoted in Ibrahim Abdullah, "Preface" to Jacques Depelchin, *Silences in African History: Between the Syndromes of Discovery and Abolition* (Dar es Salaam: Nkuki na Nyota, 2004), xi.

256 Ibid., xi.

257 Ibid., xii–xiii.

258 As for example, in Lucinda Fleeson, "The Civilian Casualty Conundrum," *American Journalism Review* (April 2002), www.ajr.org/. Fleeson reports without criticism the belief of U.S. war correspondents that they have higher "reporting standards" than "the foreign media" (3, 7). This is a ridiculous assumption, especially given the supine – even unprofessional – manner in which most mainstream American media such as the *New York Times* reported on the invasions of Afghanistan and then Iraq. She caricatures and misrepresents Herold's methodology, which he later capably defended in his chapter in *Censored 2003: The Year's Top 25 Stories*, ed. Peter Phillips and Project Censored (New York: Seven Seas Publishing, 2002). She ignores Herold's argument concerning the military benefits of precision weapons: fewer sorties and lower cost, rather than reduced civilian casualties (6). She approvingly refers to Donald Rumsfeld on civilian casualties in Afghanistan (6). She suggests that only Western media reports should be accepted, which is a slur on the dozens of courageous and very able Afghan, Pakistani, Iraqi, Palestinian, Somali, and other journalists, many of whom have died covering the world's trouble spots in recent years, and a variation of the old imperialist adage that nothing notable happens unless a white man (or woman) has seen it or verified it. She glorifies Western technology, always dangerous in this author's view. Technology should never be a substitute for analysis. She deploys a Cold War type dismissal: Herold's initial report can "only be described as left-wing polemic" (7).

259 See Carr Center for Human Rights Policy, "Understanding Collateral Damage Workshop," 21. Lucinda Fleeson is listed in the workshop program and may be the journalist in question.

260 Iraq Body Count, www.iraqbodycount.org. The website states *"Iraq Body Count* is an ongoing human security project which maintains and updates the world's largest public database of violent civilian deaths during and since the 2003 invasion. The count encompasses non-combatants killed by military or paramilitary action and the breakdown in civil security following the invasion. Data is drawn

from cross-checked media reports, hospital, morgue, NGO and official figures to produce a credible record of known deaths and incidents."

261 See Sarah Boseley, "151,000 Civilians Killed since Iraq Invasion," July 1, 2008, www.guardian.co.uk/. *The Guardian* has since posted a correction to the article; the figure from the report includes combatants as well as civilians. The full report is Iraq Family Health Survey Group, "Violence-Related Mortality in Iraq from 2002–2006," *New England Journal of Medicine* 358, 5 (2008), 484–93.

262 Gilbert Burnham, Riyadh Lafta, Shannon Doocy, and Les Roberts, "Mortality after the 2003 Invasion of Iraq: A Cross-Sectional Cluster Sample Survey," *The Lancet* 368 (October 12, 2006), 1–8. It should be noted that the household surveys do not distinguish between combatant and non-combatant deaths; a considerable proportion of these estimates should be attributed to deaths of members of the various Iraqi armed groups.

263 For Herold's work and the silencing of stories about collateral damage in U.S. media such as CNN, see Norman Solomon, "Mass Media: Aiding and Abetting Militarism," in *Masters of War*, ed. Boggs, 251–52 and passim.

264 Rid, *War and Media Operations*. Reynolds, who is relatively balanced when discussing civilian casualties caused by U.S. and Coalition actions during the First Gulf War, is completely evasive on the massive civilian suffering caused by the American occupation of Iraq. See Reynolds, "Collateral Damage on the 21st Century Battlefield."

265 For an overview see American Civil Liberties Union, "ACLU Releases Files on Civilian Casualties in Afghanistan and Iraq," April 12, 2007, www.aclu.org/. The 1,700 pages of the files are at www.aclu.org/civiliancasualties.

266 See "Payouts Reveal Iraq Civilian Toll," April 13, 2007, www.news.bbc.co.uk.

267 American Civil Liberties Union, "ACLU Releases Files on Civilian Casualties in Afghanistan and Iraq."

268 File summaries from www.aclu.org/civiliancasualties.

269 Chris Hedges and Laila Al-Arian, "The Other War: Iraq Vets Bear Witness," *The Nation*, July 30, 2007, www.thenation.com/. An extended version was published as *Collateral Damage: America's War against Iraqi Civilians* (New York: Nation Books, 2008).

270 Hedges and Al-Arian, "The Other War."

271 Carr Center for Human Rights Policy, "Understanding Collateral Damage Workshop," 11–12.

272 Jeff Guy, *The View across the River: Harriette Colenso and the Zulu Struggle against Imperialism* (Charlottesville: University Press of Virginia, 2002).

273 Patrizia Palumbo, "Introduction: Italian Colonial Cultures," in *A Place in the Sun*, ed. Palumbo, 11.

274 Angelo Del Boca, "The Myths, Suppressions, Denials, and Defaults of Italian Colonialism," in *A Place in the Sun*, ed. Palumbo, 18–19.

275 Elkins, *Imperial Reckoning*, 363–65.

276 Ibid., xii–xiii.

277 Roland Barthes, *Mythologies* (Paris: Éditions du Seuil, 1957), 9, quoted in Lynne Huffer, "Derrida's Nostalgeria," in *Algeria and France 1800–2000*, ed. Lorcin, 228, emphasis in original.

278 Stora, *Algeria 1830–2000*, 30, 112–15, quoted at 113.

279 See Joshua Cole, "Entering History: The Memory of Police Violence in Paris, October 1961," in *Algeria and France 1800–2000*, ed. Lorcin, 117–34.

280 W.G. Sebald, *On the Natural History of Destruction*, trans. Anthea Bell (Toronto: Vintage Canada, 2003).

281 Ibid., 4.

282 For details of the Dresden bombing, see Addison and Crang, eds., *Firestorm*.

283 Sebald, *On the Natural History of Destruction*, 5. One exception – a contemporary account of the destruction of Dresden and its aftermath recorded in a private diary – is the main source for Jeremy A. Crang, "Victor Klemperer's Dresden," in *Firestorm*, ed. Addison and Crang, 78–95.

284 Sebald, *On the Natural History of Destruction*, 10.

285 Ibid., 14.

286 Sven Lindqvist, *A History of Bombing* (London: Granta Books, 2002). For Dresden see Addison and Crang, eds., *Firestorm*, passim, but especially Donald Bloxham, "Dresden as a War Crime," 180–208.

287 I rely for this discussion on Lary and MacKinnon, "Introduction."

288 A recent *Toronto* Star article discusses a new American-Chinese documentary, *Nanking*, about the atrocities. See Bill Schiller, "The Horrors of Nanking," *Toronto Star*, July 7, 2007. A recent BBC article discusses the seventieth anniversary commemorations in Nanjing. See Michael Bristow, "Nanjing Remembers Massacre Victims," December 13, 2007, www.news.bbc.co.uk.

289 Lary and MacKinnon, "Introduction," 3–4.

290 Ibid., 4.

291 Ibid., 5–9.

292 Ibid., 11.

293 John Lonsdale and E.S. Atieno Odhiambo, "Introduction," in *Mau Mau and Nationhood*, ed. Atieno Odhiambo and Lonsdale, 4. Although Lary and MacKinnon's discussion of silence, memory, and forgetting in China is valuable, I believe that the contrast they make with the experience of the European victors of the Second World War is misplaced. A more valid comparison is with the former colonies discussed here, such as Kenya and Algeria.

294 David Anderson, *Histories of the Hanged: The Dirty War in Kenya and the End of the British Empire* (New York: W.W. Norton, 2005), 336.

295 Benjamin Madley, "American Genocide: The California Indian Catastrophe, 1846–1873," (Ph.D. diss., Yale University, forthcoming).

296 Grimsley, " 'Rebels' and 'Redskins,' " 151–52.

297 Kass Fleischer, *The Bear River Massacre and the Making of History* (Albany: State University of New York Press, 2004).

298 Ibid., 248.

299 The analysis of the work of MacKinnon and Brownmiller here is from Darius M. Rejali, "After Feminist Analyses of Bosnian Violence," in *The Women and War Reader*, ed. Lois Ann Lorentzen and Jennifer Turpin (New York and London: New York University Press, 1998)

300 Ibid., 27–28.

301 Ibid., 28, 30.

302 Ibid., 28. The quotation from Philips is from "Crossfire's Targets: Women in Peru Fight Violence from Both Sides," *Village Voice*, July 13, 1993, 28.

303 Rejali, "After Feminist Analyses of Bosnian Violence," 26.

304 Ibid., 30.

305 Joshua Cole, "Intimate Acts and Unspeakable Relations: Remembering Torture and the War for Algerian Independence," in *Memory, Empire, and Postcolonial-*

ism, ed. Hargreaves, 133. Cole tells the harrowing story of Mohamed Garne, born of a sixteen-year-old Algerian woman who was raped numerous times by French soldiers while in a resettlement camp in 1960. As an adult, Garne struggled to prove his paternity, to overcome the shame of both victim and oppressor, and thus to break the conspiracy of silence. See 134–36. For more on torture and rape in Algeria see Durmelat, "Revisiting Ghosts," 152–55.

306 Elkins, *Imperial Reckoning*, 220–21, 244–52, 254, 256–57, 269–71. For sexual torture of Kikuyu men including castration see 208–09, 256.
307 Ibid., 246.
308 Ibid., 246–47.
309 Ibid., 247, also 254.
310 Chang, *Rape of Nanking*, 96.
311 Elkins, *Imperial Reckoning*, 248–49, 251, 254, 258, 244, 245.
312 Ibid., 269.
313 Ibid., 269–70.
314 Sallah and Weiss, *Tiger Force*, 80, 223. For another case committed by Tiger Force see 201–02, 377–78. One wonders why so few rapes were ultimately acknowledged in the catalogue of dozens of Tiger Force atrocities.
315 Karen Stuhldreher, "State Rape: Representations of Rape in Vietnam," *Viet Nam Generation* 5, 1–4 (March 1994), *The Sixties Project*, www2.iath.virginia.edu/.
316 Video of testimony by Galbally, Henry, and Camil from the documentary *Vietnam: American Holocaust* is available on Youtube: www.youtube.com/watch?v=r6yXxvKtnEY. See also Stuhldreher, "State Rape."
317 William B. Ashbaugh, "Atrocities 'R' U.S.," review of Michal R. Belknap, *The Vietnam War on Trial: The My Lai Massacre and the Court-Martial of Lieutenant Calley* (Lawrence: University Press of Kansas, 2002), in *Reviews in American History* 31, 4 (2003), 640.
318 For rape and torture of Iraqi women during the current war in Iraq, see Haifa Zangana, *City of Widows: An Iraqi Woman's Account of War and Resistance* (New York: Seven Stories Press, 2007), 116–25.
319 Carolyn Nordstrom, "Girls behind the (Front) Lines," in *The Women and War Reader*, ed. Lorentzen and Turpin, , 80–81.
320 See Lorentzen and Turpin, *The Women and War Reader*, passim. For an excellent example of women and war during a major postcolonial conflict see Egodi Uchendu, *Women and Conflict in the Nigerian Civil War* (Trenton, N.J.: Africa World Press, 2007).
321 Nordstrom, "Girls behind the (Front) Lines," 81.
322 Ibid., 81.
323 For more see ibid., 82–84.
324 I am influenced here by the argument in Cole, "Intimate Acts and Unspeakable Relations," 129–31.
325 Ibid., 131.
326 Ibid., emphasis in original. Pesek, this volume, also reaches this conclusion.
327 "Afghan Strike 'Hit Wedding Party,' " July 6, 2008, www.news.bbc.co.uk/. Further research shows that the toll was forty-seven or forty-eight civilians, all but two women and children. See Stephen J. Rockel, "Wedding Massacres and the War in Afghanistan," in *A Natural Inclination: The Massacre throughout History*, ed. Philip Dwyer and Lyndall Ryan (New York and Oxford: Berghahn Books, forthcoming).

Part 1

Non-combatants in Civil Wars:
France and the USA

"Only the Sack and the Noose for Its Citizens"

Atrocities and Civilian Casualties during the French Wars of Religion

N ègrepelisse smouldered into the night on June 10, 1622, and the bodies of hundreds of its inhabitants lay strewn in the streets and within the burning buildings of this small southern French town. A contemporary account vividly describes the suffering of Nègrepelisse's residents:

> After a general desolation, most of the inhabitants were dead, their houses having been pillaged, burned, and reduced to nothing [by the soldiers]. The houses and farms of the countryside had been equally burned and ruined, the beasts of labour pillaged, and the grapevines destroyed in such a way that there remained nothing for the beggars; most of them were being constrained, as they are still, to beg for their bread, and others have become wanderers and vagabonds.[1]

This scene of devastation followed a short siege of the predominantly Protestant town of Nègrepelisse by a Catholic army under the command of King Louis XIII. The Catholic artillery had quickly pounded a breach in the walls, and the king's soldiers had broken into the town, killing and pillaging as they went. According to a pamphlet published soon after the siege, the Protestant residents of Nègrepelisse "who remained in the town were killed, others threw themselves from the top of the walls, still others drowned. One saw mothers holding their children in their arms, who jumped into the water." The pamphlet's author claimed that "in a half an hour they were exterminated, and the streets were so full of dead and of blood that it was difficult to walk there."[2]

The Catholic soldiers responsible for this mass killing of civilians had advanced under the eyes of Louis XIII, and the king made no attempt to dissociate himself from the atrocities at Nègrepelisse, instead formulating an elaborate justification for the massacre in a series of letters, acts, and pamphlets that portrayed the killing as legitimate royal retribution against a town that deserved "only the sack and the noose for its citizens."[3] Nègrepelisse was hardly the only town to suffer such a fate during the French Wars of Religion of 1562–1629; dozens of communities experienced massacres and systematic destruction during this period. Even during bitter religious warfare, limits and conventions restrained combatants' application of violence, providing some protections for civilians. Such conventions could break down, however, resulting in the brutal violence against civilians inflicted on the residents of towns like Nègrepelisse.

Surely the best-known atrocity during the French Wars of Religion is the Saint Bartholomew's Day Massacre of 1572, in which probably between 2,000 and 4,000 Huguenots, or French Protestants, were slaughtered by Catholic bodyguards, militia troops, and armed civilians in Paris. Another 3,000 Protestants were killed in successive massacres in provincial towns throughout France.[4] Massacres of civilians during supposedly "peaceful" circumstances and truces occurred periodically throughout the French Wars of Religion, usually when military or paramilitary troops acted in conjunction with civilian co-religionaries against "heretical" enemies.

In this chapter, I avoid focusing on massacres such as Saint Bartholomew's Day in order to cast light on the much more frequent and pervasive violence done against non-combatants during the religious wars.

Early modern European warfare subjected civilians to a broad spectrum of violence, as armies pillaged belongings, burned crops, coerced peasants, raped women, occupied homes, destroyed churches, and sacked cities. This violence against innocent civilians, particularly women and children, was so horrifying that many contemporary Europeans saw atrocities as signs of the coming Apocalypse.[5] The later stages of the French Wars of Religion, from 1610 to 1629, provide an especially interesting case to examine collateral damage during a period in which issues of civilian status and excessive violence were extremely problematic.[6] Although collateral damage is a relatively recent concept, violence against civilians has long been accepted by military organizations as an inevitable – and sometimes acceptable – part of warfare. The term collateral damage is routinely used today to refer to civilian casualties, especially people wounded or killed by aerial bombardment, but it can also describe psychological damage, property destruction, economic loss, and environmental damage suffered by civilians.[7] "Collateral damage" suggests that the killing of civilians is unintended, accidental, and even regrettable. At the same time, the concept implies that such damage is inevitable but that it can (and should be) minimized by participants in warfare.[8]

The analysis here focuses on the *forms* of violence that directly inflicted injuries on early modern French civilians. Our access to early modern civilians' experiences of warfare is always mediated through the perceptions and representations of violence presented in complex sources, however. The early-seventeenth-century letters, reports, pamphlets, memoirs, and journals analyzed here were often highly polemic accounts written by participants in, or advocates for, religious warfare. Just as modern analysts deconstruct Secretary Donald Rumsfeld's use of the term collateral damage, we must also be attentive to the ways in which contemporary language and rhetoric were employed in definitions of non-combatant status, in representations of civilian casualties, and in justifications for atrocities.[9] I want to examine these issues through three related contexts of collateral damage during the religious wars in France: violence against civilians inflicted in war zones, in raiding warfare, and in siege warfare.

Civilian Suffering in War Zones

The armies of the French Wars of Religion inflicted collateral damage on civilians everywhere they marched. Contemporary artist Jacques Callot's engravings on the miseries of war depicted in horrifying detail the sufferings of civilians living in war zones during this period.[10] Protestant and Catholic residents of the religiously mixed communities and neighbouring towns in southern France bore the brunt of the religious warfare in France. The vast majority of French Protestants were concentrated within the "Huguenot crescent," a region stretching from La Rochelle across southern France to Dauphiné, especially in the provinces of Languedoc and Guyenne. Localized disputes and religious tensions transformed this broad area into the key war zone of the later French Wars of Religion. Officials and administrators in Languedoc frequently reported the "disorders, calamities, and extreme miseries of the province." Rampaging troops performed "extortions, larcenies, pillages, public force, ransoms, outrages, murders, burnings, and other enormous crimes," leaving the "sad marks of an entire desolation." The people were "abandoned to this furious license" by the "tolerance and connivance" of some of the warrior noble leaders and military officers.[11] Soldiers raped women living in villages along march routes and in occupied communities within war zones. According to one Protestant source, Catholic forces operating in Bas Languedoc 1622 "ruined the countryside of the surrounding villages and exercised a thousand cruelties and villainies in violating the wives and daughters everywhere."[12]

Catholic and Protestant armies engaged in widespread destruction of civilian property and homes in southern France. When the sick and exhausted soldiers of the royal army retreated from the failed siege of Montauban in November 1621, they burned not only the materials they could not carry but also "all the fields and country houses." The townspeople of Montauban watching their departure "saw at the same time more than a hundred fires light the countryside all covered in smoke, nothing could be seen but fires and flames."[13] Destruction of crops produced food shortages, famine, and disease in war zones, sometimes leading to widespread epidemics. The economic deprivation wrought by armies often forced non-combatants to leave their communities or face starvation.

Noble military commanders were responsible for much of the economic deprivation and violence inflicted on civilians. During the religious wars, nobles normally commanded infantry and cavalry units, exercising broad authority to act as "military entrepreneurs."[14] These officers typically provided food, clothing, and equipment for their troops, either by paying for supplies themselves or by coercing local populations to furnish needed items. Whenever food and supplies were lacking, nobles allowed their soldiers to plunder civilians' homes in the war zones. Noble military officers often condoned pillaging, even profiting personally by stealing the best horses, livestock, clothes, and valuables from their enemies before allowing their troops to ransack and burn the remaining goods, buildings, and crops.[15]

The French monarchical government also bore responsibility for civilian suffering. Armies extracted massive amounts of food and material belongings from civilians living in villages and towns in war zones through taxation, contributions, and billeting. John A. Lynn has quite effectively shown the widespread nature of pillaging in seventeenth-century France and the economic reasons for what he calls the "tax of violence," referring to the use of pillaging by armies and soldiers to compensate for ineffective resource mobilization by the French monarchy.[16]

During civil wars, pillaging also supported the religious and political goals of armies engaged in religious conflict. When armies occupied "enemy" communities, they imposed political changes, enacted military justice, and carried out public executions. Religious upheaval, iconoclasm, and conflict broke down civic religious practices and prevented communities from responding to civilian suffering in a unified manner.[17] Fortress garrisons compelled civilians in occupied towns to supply them, as well as to do forced or underpaid labour on the construction and repair of fortifications.

The armies of the religious wars subjected non-combatants to harsh military justice, involving the arrest, imprisonment, and torture of civilians. Merchants and peasants who continued to carry on commerce in war zones could be accused of supplying enemies. Travellers who did not have a passport from the appropriate military commander, or who carried arms, might be arrested. Towns that surrendered often had to give hostages to armies to ensure that they met the terms of the capitulation agreements. Given contemporary notions of pain and truth, physical violence probably accompanied most interrogations of detained peasants and townspeople.[18] Captured civilian magistrates and religious leaders were sometimes executed by military officials in occupying armies, or handed over to judicial officials for more legitimate execution.[19] Many civilians subjected to this sort of violence and coercion fled war zones as refugees or trailed in the wake of armies as camp followers.

During the French Wars of Religion, non-combatant status was highly ambiguous, since civilians actively participated in iconoclastic attacks, processions, protests, and other collective actions.[20] Civilians' involvement in religious confrontation made it easy for their religious opponents to target them for violence.[21] Following the peace of 1626, the ensign of the duc de Rohan's gendarmes was arrested and then – despite his ostensible status as a civilian – tried and beheaded by the parlement de Toulouse.[22] In the context of civil and religious warfare, the distinctions between combatants and non-combatants became especially blurred.[23]

To label victims "helpless" deprives them of agency and fails to show the choices, however limited, that were available to civilians in the path of war.[24] Even during the religious wars, civilian victims maintained agency, making decisions about whether to stay at home to protect belongings or to flee as refugees. Non-combatants living in war zones sometimes retaliated, attacking the soldiers who were tormenting them.[25] Such retaliation extended to ambushes, assassinations, and raids against military officers and groups of soldiers. Some peasants, presumably Catholic, reportedly attacked many of the Protestant soldiers who fled from Pamiers in 1628, in order "to avenge the maltreatment that they had received in the raids of the rebels."[26] Since peasants and townspeople were not as well armed and trained as soldiers, their potential to commit mass atrocities was certainly less, but they did take action to protect themselves.

Civilians could also collaborate with "friendly" soldiers in attacking their enemies. In March 1628, Protestant troops under the duc de Rohan pillaged the château de Theyrargues, one of the residences of the Catholic marquis de Portes.[27] The destruction of Theyrargues seems to have been motivated by a desire for retribution on the part of the seigneury's tenants and surrounding Protestants. According to one account,

> The residents of the surrounding lands dependent on the château had been, during all the preceding wars and even the peace, very inhumanely treated by their seigneur in hatred of the [Protestant] religion; constraining them with baton blows and stirrup leather to go to Mass, and distressing all the families that God affirmed against this persecution, constraining them to abandon their belongings and homes to his discretion, and going to beg for their bread.[28]

When the château capitulated, the duc de Rohan supposedly attempted to prevent any pillaging, since he "sent in his bodyguards, and then captain Quintun with some soldiers, and ordered that an exact inventory be made of wheat and other foodstuff and belongings [that] were within." However, "when he was far away, the soldiers carried the hate that they had against the seigneur of this place, and because of their desire for the prey that they had before their eyes, they started pillaging." The soldiers may have also been influenced by local peasants' anger, since the same source notes that "it was the desire of all the region that this house be razed," despite some Huguenot nobles' calls for the château to be preserved.[29]

Civilians occasionally managed to overwhelm bands of troops or garrisons, massacring the soldiers and mutilating their bodies. This appears to be precisely what occurred at Nègrepelisse prior to the destruction of the town in 1622.[30] Nègrepelisse had submitted to a royal army the previous year without sustaining a siege, and a Catholic garrison had been installed. The townspeople had to provide for the garrison, and some of the Catholic soldiers may have used religious coercion against Protestant residents. Later, Protestants apparently surprised the Catholic garrison and "cut everyone's throat one night."[31] Outraged Catholic pamphleteers portrayed Nègrepelisse's residents as complicitous in the "massacre" of the town's garrison, rejecting their "innocence" and effectively challenging their status as civilians.[32]

Raiding Warfare against Civilians

Raiding warfare was a pervasive form of conflict during the French Wars of Religion and affected civilians greatly. Raids did not represent minor, peripheral activities; they were vital for controlling population areas and mobilizing resources for armies.[33] In the sixteenth and seventeenth centuries, "small war" or "partisan war" involved continual small-scale attacks by troops operating from fortifications.[34] Bands of soldiers foraged for food, gathered fodder, performed reconnaissance missions, gathered military intelligence, and carried out reprisals on enemies.[35] Raiding was especially extensive in southern France, where religious tensions in a mixed-religion population invited conflict. For example, an intense "small war" raged across the region of Vivarais in 1622, as Protestants and Catholics living in this hilly area targeted their nearby enemies while larger armies operated in other regions.[36] Warrior nobles throughout southern France organized localized attacks and punitive expeditions in the vicinity of their châteaux and governments.

Positional warfare encouraged widespread marauding by troops seeking to control urban spaces.[37] Towns that lay in the midst of a countryside dominated by members of the opposing faith regularly sent out raiding bands.

During prolonged sieges, soldiers ravaged the surrounding areas, seizing food, pillaging belongings, and destroying crops. Raids facilitated the foraging, blockading duties, economic destruction, and relief attempts that were so vital to siege operations. The location of fortifications played a significant role in this small-scale warfare, since raiding was often conducted by small bands of infantry and cavalry that needed to find refuge quickly if a large enemy force appeared to stop their destructive activities.

Control of fortifications along key roads and rivers could severely disrupt civilian merchants' and peasants' movements because it allowed raiding forces to shelter within their walls. When Protestants seized Vals-les-Bains in central Vivarais in 1621, Catholic communities in the region suffered. According to one Catholic noble, "This loss was very important for Vivarais, being in the middle of the Catholics on the road from Velay and from Auvergne – from which all commerce was interrupted – and the liberty of raids and ravages was introduced into this region, which suffered much from this loss."[38] In mountainous regions that had few roads, which usually followed streams and rivers, raiding parties operating from fortifications could easily choke off all communications up the valleys. The weekly market held in the town of Aubenas on Saturdays was frequently interrupted by raiding Huguenot forces, disrupting the lives of the Catholic residents. The garrison of the small town attempted to protect the surrounding roads and allow the market to be held.[39]

Catholic and Protestant forces each attempted to shield artisanal industries and commercial goods from attack by enemy raiding groups and bandits. If raiding parties were able to operate freely, they could easily destroy key aspects of the local economic framework and infrastructure. Catholic troops damaged the economy and threatened the food supply of the predominantly Protestant town of Nîmes by burning its windmills, which were located on a hill outside the city walls.[40] The capacity of troops to destroy crops, trees, vineyards, and agricultural products could be devastating, as when the prince de Condé's troops destroyed vineyards around the town of Rouquecourbe in the diocese of Castres in 1628.[41] Bands of soldiers often targeted livestock, especially in the Cévennes mountains, where the domestication of sheep and cattle was a major part of the economy. For example, a group of Catholic nobles launched a raid in the Alès region in 1621 with at least 200 infantry and 100 cavalry drawn from their châteaux and governments in the area. The goal was local livestock. Assembling at dawn near Alès on the chosen day, this force followed the Gardon River, "ravaging the entire plain of a great many animals." When the Protestant garrison of Alès sent troops out to disperse the raiding Catholics, they were routed, allowing the Catholics to continue their foray.[42]

Civilians were the primary victims of the pillaging and extortion that normally accompanied raiding operations. The prospect of obtaining valuable loot motivated soldiers to fight, and noble commanders had great difficulty in preventing or stopping destruction of captured homes and communities, even when they wanted to do so. While there are frequent descriptions of officers trying to halt pillaging by troops out of control, it seems to have been next to impossible to stop victorious soldiers from smashing and stealing. When Pamiers capitulated in March 1628, the victorious Catholic soldiers "pillaged all the valuables." "It has never been possible to stop them," lamented the author of an account of the siege there.[43] Similarly, when the Protestant defenders of Le Pouzin capitulated, Catholic soldiers occupied the town and began a ransacking orgy. There was "no means of preventing the soldiers from putting the torch to this place, which was entirely burned in two days."[44] However difficult it may have been to stop these sorts of excesses by troops, many nobles seem to have been unwilling even to try to halt looting, instead letting their soldiers carry out their profitable vengeance.

Sometimes armies carried out campaigns of widespread economic destruction reminiscent of medieval *chevauchées*.[45] The Catholic duc de Montmorency directed a systematic destruction of crops in areas of Bas Languedoc in 1628, targeting the area around the Protestant city of Nîmes, which was "entirely in rebel hands, and furnished not only provisions to Nîmes and to the Cévennes ... but also served to refresh the [Huguenot] army of Monsieur de Rohan, who drew on large quantities of money there for his soldiers' pay."[46] In July 1628, Montmorency organized a base of operations at the village of Marguerites and prepared rations and supplies for six days, "during which he burned the wheat, and desolated all the countryside that furnished food or contributions to the enemy." The duc's troops then bypassed Nîmes and proceeded northwest to La Calmette, "from which he torched everything within three leagues." Sources suggest that Montmorency's troops carried out a thorough raiding campaign and give hints at the techniques of destruction they employed. The soldiers "burned large numbers of villages, to constrain the inhabitants to withdraw into the towns, so as to starve them, and particularly all of the barrels, cookware, and presses to make oil, to make them lose the harvests of wine and oil." Montmorency carried his campaign of destruction into the nearby valleys (*la vaunage*), "which is the nursery for soldiers and the best land for the rebels." A battle erupted near the village of Clarensac when Huguenot troops apparently tried to curtail the raids by Montmorency's troops. This attempt failed, however, and Montmorency's army continued its devastating march – the cavalry burning the crops around the towns of Uzès and Alès and forcing the nearby Protestant villagers to take refuge within their walls.[47] After further skirmishing, Montmorency halted his raiding campaign and led his army back to the shelter of Beaucaire. His raid had caused the burning of fifty entire villages or parishes. He placed in hunger not only Nîmes, but also Uzès, Alès, Anduze, and all of the Cévennes. He constrained the residents of all those areas to withdraw into the towns, which can nourish them for a very short time. He deprived Monsieur de Rohan of the power to draw on the money and provisions of these towns; and thus reduced him to being unable to make his army subsist – except if he found himself strong enough to maintain [the army] in Catholic lands – and really discredited him amongst those of his party.[48]

Large-scale raiding campaigns like Montmorency's demonstrated the effectiveness of systematic raiding warfare, but such sustained expeditions could be attempted only when adequate supplies were available and careful preparations could be made.

More often, armies employed raiding warfare against specific targets lying in their path of march, such as the châteaux of enemy nobles. Numerous châteaux were burned, pillaged, and destroyed in this period, and civilian tenant farmers were always affected when their noble landlords' châteaux and seigneuries were targeted. Military units sometimes engaged in punitive campaigns to destroy the properties of their enemies. For example, Catholic soldiers who were angry that the seigneur de Cheylus had recently joined the duc de Rohan's army seized his château de Mauras near Chomérac. "To begin the punishment of his rebellion," read one account, "the said château de Mauras had been pillaged, and afterwards burned and ruined, along with other houses that could favour the passage of rebels from Privas to Le Pouzin."[49] Protestant forces under the duc de Rohan used similar tactics, razing numerous Catholic châteaux in the Cévennes, including the Montfaucon family's fort de Blandas.[50] Frustrated Huguenot nobles sought vengeance on other Huguenots whose neutrality or individual submissions to royal troops seemed like betrayals of the Huguenot cause. Thus, the château de Montdardier, which was owned by the "traitor" Charles de Ginestous, was destroyed on the orders of the duc de Rohan.[51]

The residents of Nègrepelisse became targets in the religious wars partly because of the raiding activities of the opposing armies in the region. Catholic inhabitants of Languedoc frequently complained about the disruptions of trade caused by Protestant troops operating out of Huguenot strongholds such as the nearby city of Montauban, which was referred to by some Catholics as the "magazine of all [the Huguenots'] pillaging."[52] During the 1621–22 civil war, Catholic soldiers sought to block Montauban's communications and prevent towns like Nègrepelisse from aiding their co-religionaries during the siege of Montauban.[53] Raiding warfare and religious politics placed towns like Nègrepelisse directly in the path of armies and their siege guns.

Atrocities in Siege Warfare

Sieges exposed civilians to the most vicious violence of the religious wars, often described by contemporaries in apocalyptic terms.[54] Conventions governing the practices of siege warfare offered certain protections for besieged civilians but also legitimized atrocities under certain conditions. Military commanders in the French Wars of Religion could draw on an elaborate body of sixteenth- and early-seventeenth-century theoretical literature on *jus in bello*, or laws of conduct of warfare, to consider ethical problems of siege warfare.[55] Although the juridical literature dealing with the "law of the siege" argued for restraint in the application of violence against civilians, many authors accepted the mass killing of a besieged city's inhabitants if they resisted after the besieging army summoned them to surrender.[56] Alberico Gentili's simple maxim – "Cities are sacked when taken; they are not sacked when surrendered" – was well known by sixteenth- and seventeenth-century French military commanders yet rarely applied consistently.[57] Most sieges in the religious wars actually involved conventional restraints on violence and near-constant negotiations, even during the fighting. But religious warfare, Counter-Reformation ideology, and royal ideals of justice combined to make "rebel" towns like Nègrepelisse frequently subject to the harsher side of the "law of the siege."

Armies inflicted violence on women, children, and other non-combatants during sieges and when they seized urban spaces. Although such persons were in theory considered neutral and protected by the conventions of war, many atrocities against non-combatants occurred. Incidents of rape seem to have been all too common in the civil wars in southern France. Many sources acknowledged the possibility of women being raped by soldiers and expressed the fear of rape that defenders experienced during sieges.[58] In some situations, Protestant women may have been subjected to systematic group rape. During the skirmishes surrounding the siege of Montpellier, for example, a Catholic cavalry troop reportedly "seized five or six women and girls, sending them back after having raped them."[59] That a cavalry unit would be specifically mentioned in such an account hints that nobles, who normally commanded cavalry units and made up many of the cavalry soldiers, may have condoned, or even committed, rape.

Atrocities often resulted from the difficulty of stopping the killing during victorious siege assaults. Once attacking soldiers had got into a killing frenzy, they often continued even when their opponents were trying to surrender, and combat was transformed into mass murder. This seems to have been the case during the siege of the town of Bonail, or Bonnac, in Haut Languedoc in 1625 by a Catholic army under the command of Pons de Lauzières, marquis de Thémines. After an intense three-day bombardment, the Catholic troops assaulted Bonail from all directions and broke into the town. Catholic soldiers "put everyone to the sword" despite Thémines' orders, which "prohibited that they kill the citizens." The Catholic troops could not be restrained, and "one never saw such execution in so little time."[60] The taking of prisoners must have almost always created tense situations, especially during the hand-to-hand combats that siege assaults produced, when troops were excited and under enormous stress. At Bonail, Thémines apparently did eventually manage to halt his soldiers' killing, but he then instigated summary justice, ordering thirty "principals of the faction" hanged "to serve as an example." Similarly, when the Protestant garrison at Pamiers capitulated in March 1628, 200 Protestant soldiers and inhabitants were killed as the Catholic soldiers pillaged the town. Thirty-seven residents were later hanged and another thirty sent to serve in the Mediterranean galley fleet at Marseilles. The Protestant governor of the town and his lieutenant were sent to Toulouse for public beheading.[61] Atrocities were not hidden but openly performed on the displayed bodies of victims.

As we have already seen, few inhabitants survived the sack of Nègrepelisse.[62] Louis XIII's successive accounts of the massacre focused on the culpability of the townspeople, saying that "the residents of Nègrepelisse having dared to refuse entry to those that we had sent there to prepare our quarters, we carried it in two days by a general assault after which they received the just chastisement and punishment that their audacity and insolence merited."[63] Louis XIII emphasized "the stubbornness of these rebels," but he seemed content that his victorious siege had "put them in their duty." The king justified his army's actions by stressing the exemplary aspect of his vengeance: "Having exercised some necessary justice to reprimand the insolent temerity of these mutinous rebels. I hope that this will shorten my voyage, and that several [towns] that my clemency has not bent, will get into line in their duty by the fear of a similar punishment."[64]

Contemporary pamphlets went well beyond justifying the massacre at Nègrepelisse, publicizing the atrocities and celebrating them. A royalist propaganda pamphlet in 1622 referred openly to "the sack of Nègrepelisse," making no attempt to downplay the scale of the atrocities.[65] One pamphlet described the massacre:

The king ... in the guise of lightening breaks and cuts down only those who resist him – they might have been pardoned, if they demonstrated obedience, but they closed the gates, and disposed themselves in defense, the place was besieged, battered, and its weak walls knocked down. The assault was given from two or three directions, and 10 and 11 June the town was forced and taken by assault, eight hundred inhabitants killed, all the women and daughters violated and massacred, and the town generally pillaged, then burned. The château similarly forced, were still found some forty soldiers within who were all hung and strangled and thus it is to provoke a great king to wrath.[66]

Once labelled as "rebels," the residents of Nègrepelisse were no longer considered civilians but instead represented legitimate targets of the most brutal forms of warfare.

Conclusion

French civilians became direct targets of violence during the French Wars of Religion. Official correspondence and literary works threatened civilians with exemplary violence and provided justifications of atrocities in the name of justice. Massacres perpetrated by Catholic troops at Nègrepelisse, Monheur, and Privas were celebrated not only as properly applied exemplary royal justice but as meritorious acts by Louis "the Just." For example, one pamphlet addressed the residents of Montauban directly, warning them not to hope for mercy:

> "No! No! rebels, you will eat the bread of grief, and will be in continual wakefulness, agitated by the torments of war, and surrounded by the depths of unhappiness, and for the crowning of your demerits, following the example of Monheur, your blood will make the rivers run red, so that there remain the marks inscribed for posterity. . . . Vengeance will be exercised on the rebels."[67]

The rhetoric of rebellion combined powerfully with propaganda against "heresy" to justify religious coercion and violence against Protestant civilians.

Both Catholics and Protestants targeted civilians during the French Wars of Religion, but Huguenots suffered particularly during the later stages. Excessive violence and retribution became pervasive, and a "hard war" developed in which the conventions normally protecting non-combatants collapsed and warfare was often conducted beyond the limits of the laws of war.[68] The dynamics of religious warfare thus produced a particular sort of collateral damage that was ultimately inflicted on the residents of towns like Nègrepelisse.

Notes

1 "Arrêt du conseil," Bibliothèque Nationale de France (hereafter BNF), Manuscrits français (hereafter Mss fr.) 18201, quoted in Louis Batiffol, *Le roi Louis XIII à vingt ans* (Paris: Calmann-Lévy, n.d.), 252–53.

2 *Recit véritable de tout ce qui s'est passé en l'armee du roy depuis le 28 may jusques au*

24 juin; Ou se voit la prise de Nègrepelisse, bruslement d'icelle, & chastiment des re-belles; Avec la reduction de Sainct Anthonin ou cinq des principaux avec le ministre ont esté pendus (Lyon: Claude Armand, 1622), 10–11.

3 *Relation véritable et journalière de tout ce qui s'est passé en France & Pays Es-trangers; Depuis le depart du roy de sa ville Capitale de Paris, jusqu'à present* (Paris: Joseph Bouïllerot, 1622), BNF, Clairambault 378, f° 150–69. Other justifications included the following sources: Louis XIII to parlement de Toulouse, Camp de Saint-Antonin, June 23, 1622, BNF, Brienne 211, Nouvelles acquisitions français 7182, f° 427; *Le grand et juste chastiment des rebelles de Nègrepelisse, mis & taillez en pieces, & leur ville reduite à feu & à sang, par l'armée royale de sa majesté les 10 & 11 juin 1622* (Paris: Pierre Rocolet, 1622).

4 For recent studies of massacres in the French Wars of Religion, especially Saint Bartholomew's Day Massacre, see David El Kenz, "La civilisation des mörus et les guerres de religion: Un seuil de tolérance aux massacres," in *Le massacre, objet d'histoire,* ed. David El Kenz (Paris: Gallimard, 2005), 183–97; Mark Greengrass, "Hidden Transcripts: Secret Histories and Personal Testimonies of Religious Vio-lence in the French Wars of Religion," in *The Massacre in History,* ed. Mark Levene and Penny Roberts (New York: Berghahn Books, 1999), 69–88; Denis Crouzet, *La nuit de la Saint-Barthélemy: Un rêve perdu de la Renaissance* (Paris: Fayard, 1994); Barbara B. Diefendorf, *Beneath the Cross: Catholics and Huguenots in Sixteenth-Century Paris* (Oxford: Oxford University Press, 1991); Natalie Zemon Davis, "The Rites of Violence," in *Society and Culture in Early Modern France: Eight Es-says* (Stanford: Stanford University Press, 1975), 152–87.

5 On collateral damage and violence against civilians in the early modern period, see Andrew Cunningham and Ole Peter Grell, *The Four Horsemen of the Apoca-lypse: Religion, War, Famine, and Death in Reformation Europe* (Cambridge: Cam-bridge University Press, 2000), 92–199; John A. Lynn, "A Brutal Necessity? The Devastation of the Palatinate, 1688–1689," in *Civilians in the Path of War,* ed. Mark Grimsley and Clifford J. Rogers, (Lincoln: University of Nebraska Press, 2002), ch. 3; Theodor Meron, *Bloody Constraint, War and Chivalry in Shakespeare* (Oxford: Oxford University Press, 1998); André Corvisier and Jean Jacquart, eds., *Les malheurs de la guerre,* vol. 1, *De la guerre à l'ancienne à la guerre réglée* (Paris: Éditions du CTHS, 1996); Stephen Porter, *Destruction in the English Civil Wars* (Stroud, U.K.: Sutton Publishing, 1994); Philippe Contamine, *War in the Middle Ages,* trans. Michael Jones (Oxford: Basil Blackwell, 1984); J.R. Hale, *War and Society in Renaissance Europe, 1450–1620* (Baltimore, Md.: Johns Hop-kins University Press, 1985); Myron P. Gutman, *War and Rural Life in the Early Modern Low Countries* (Princeton, N.J.: Princeton University Press, 1980).

6 Key recent studies of violence in the French Wars of Religion include Philip Bene-dict, Guido Marnet, Henk van Nierop, and Marc Venard, eds., *Reformation, Revolt and Civil War in France and the Netherlands, 1555–1585* (Amsterdam: Royal Netherlands Academy of Arts and Sciences, 1999); Stuart Carroll, *Noble Power during the French Wars of Religion: The Guise Affinity and the Catholic Cause in Normandy* (Cambridge: Cambridge University Press, 1998); James B. Wood, *The King's Army: Warfare, Soldiers, and Society during the Wars of Religion in France, 1562–1576* (Cambridge: Cambridge University Press, 1996); Diefendorf, *Beneath the Cross;* Denis Crouzet, *Les guerriers de Dieu: La violence au temps des troubles de religion (vers 1525–vers 1610),* 2 vols. (Seyssel: Champ Vallon, 1990); Arlette Jouanna, *Le devoir de révolte: La noblesse française et la gestation de l'état moderne,*

1559–1661 (Paris: Fayard, 1989).

7   While collateral damage is frequently associated with bombing victims, it can refer to people harmed by artillery, mines, chemical weapons, and small arms. For a sampling of the various uses of the term and related concepts, see Human Rights Watch, *Off Target: The Conduct of the War and Civilian Casualties in Iraq* (New York: Human Rights Watch, 2003); No author, "Art Exhibition Explores 'Collateral Damage,'" *Green Left Weekly*, September 3, 2003; Thomas W. Smith, "The New Law of War: Legitimizing Hi-Tech and Infrastructural Violence," *International Studies Quarterly* 46 (2002), 355–74; Conrad C. Crane, *Bombs, Cities, and Civilians: American Airpower Strategy in World War II* (Lawrence: University Press of Kansas, 1993). The concept of collateral damage is also being applied to destruction of non-human life: Claudia Card, "Environmental Atrocities and Non-Sentient Life," *Ethics and the Environment* 9 (2004), 23–45.

8   Ben Kiernan provides an excellent brief discussion of the modern legal definitions of intentional/unintentional civilian casualties and excessive casualties used by the International Criminal Court. Ben Kiernan, "'Collateral Damage' from Cambodia to Iraq," *Antipode* 35, 5 (2003), 846–55.

9   For analyses of the language and representation of collateral damage, see Dexter Filkins and Edward Wong, "Disputed Strike by U.S. Military Leaves at Least 40 Iraqis Dead," *New York Times*, May 20, 2004; Sandra Silberstein, *War of Words: Language, Politics and 9/11* (New York: Routledge, 2004); Richard Jackson, *Writing the War on Terrorism: Analysing the Language of Counter-Terrorism* (Manchester: Manchester University Press, 2005); Paul Virilio, *War and Cinema: The Logistics of Perception*, trans. Patrick Camiller (New York: Verso, 1997); Carol Cohn, "Sex and Death in the Rational World of Defense Intellectuals," *Signs: Journal of Women in Culture and Society* 12 (Summer 1987), 687–718; Elaine Scarry, "Injury and the Structure of War," *Representations* 10 (Spring 1985), 1–51.

10 On Callot's depiction of pillaging and civilian suffering, see Peter Paret, *Imagined Battles: Reflections of War in European Art* (Chapel Hill: University of North Carolina Press, 1997), 31–39; Paulette Choné, "Les misères de la guerre ou 'la vie du soldat': La force et le droit," in *Jacques Callot, 1592–1635*, ed. Paulette Choné, Daniel Ternois, Jean-Marc Depluvrez, and Brigitte Heckel (Paris: Editions de la réunion des musées nationaux, 1992), 396–410. See also contemporary artistic depictions of the theme of the "massacre of the innocents," including Peter Paul Rubens, *The Massacre of the Innocents* (c. 1609–11), recently sold at Sotheby's, London; Peter Paul Rubens, *The Massacre of the Innocents* (1621), Alte Pinacotek, Munich; Nicolas Poussin, *The Massacre of the Innocents* (c. 1625), Musée Condée, Chantilly.

11 "Commission du roy," Archives départementales Hérault, A 47, f° 201–03.

12 "Memoire ou journal du siege de Montpellier," BNF, Mss fr. 23339, f° 164–65.

13 "Tableau du siege de Montaulban," BNF, Mss fr. 18756, f° 65–66.

14 On the concept of military entrepreneurs, see Fritz Redlich, *The German Military Enterpriser and His Work Force: A Study in European Economic and Social History*, 2 vols., Vierteljahrschrift für Sozial-und Wirtschaftgeschichte, Beihefte 48 (Wiesbaden: Franz Steiner Verlag, 1964–65); David Parrott, *Richelieu's Army: War, Government, and Society in France, 1624–1642* (Cambridge: Cambridge University Press, 2001), 505–46.

15 For an introduction to pillaging in early modern warfare see John A. Lynn, "How War Fed War: The Tax of Violence and Contributions during the Grand Siècle,"

Journal of Modern History 65 (June 1993): 286–310; J.R. Hale, *War and Society in Renaissance Europe, 1450–1620* (Baltimore, Md.: Johns Hopkins University Press, 1985), 179–208; Fritz Redlich, *De Preada Militari: Looting and Booty 1500–1815*, Vierteljahrschrift für Sozial-und Wirtschaftsgeschischte, Beihefte 39 (Wiesbaden: Franz Steiner Verlag, 1956).

16 Lynn, "How War Fed War," 286–310.

17 Cunningham and Grell, *The Four Horsemen of the Apocalypse*, 92–114; Hale, *War and Society in Renaissance Europe*, 179–252.

18 For a study of attitudes on pain and the judicial practices of torture in early modern Languedoc, see Lisa Silverman, *Tortured Subjects: Pain, Truth, and the Body in Early Modern France* (Chicago: University of Chicago Press, 2001), 51–68.

19 These executions can certainly be considered atrocities, and many contemporaries seemed to view them as such, especially if the executions were of co-religionaries or of political and religious leaders.

20 Davis, "Rites of Violence," 182–87.

21 In their work on "civilians in the path of war," Mark Grimsley and Clifford J. Rogers point out the difficulties in defining civilian victims, showing how the notions of helpless, innocent, and non-combatant victims overlap and suggesting that "the language of war is inherently politicized, and no portion more than the language used to refer to its victims." *Civilians in the Path of War*, ix–x.

22 Claude Devic and J. Vaissete, *Histoire générale de Languedoc*, 13 vols. (Toulouse: Privat, 1872–1905) (hereafter *HGL*), 11: 1000–01.

23 James Turner Johnson, "Maintaining the Protection of Non-Combatants," *Journal of Peace Research* 37 (July 2000), 421–48; Michael Walzer, *Just and Unjust Wars: A Moral Argument with Historical Illustrations*, 3rd ed. (New York: Basic Books, 2000).

24 For a discussion of women's agency, see Brian Sandberg, " 'Generous Amazons Came to the Breach': Besieged Women, Agency, and Subjectivity during the French Wars of Religion," *Gender and History* 16 (November 2004): 654–88. Here, my approach to violence against civilians differs somewhat from that of Grimsley and Rogers, *Civilians in the Path of War*, ix–xviii.

25 Peasant retaliation against soldiers also frequently occurred during the Thirty Years' War. See Herbert Langer, *The Thirty Years' War*, 2nd ed. (New York: Dorset Press, 1990), 103–26.

26 "Recit véritable de la prise de la ville de Pamiers Capitale du Pays de Foix, ensemble de Beaufort Lieutenant General du duc de Rohan, Dauros gouverneur de Mazeres et desroutte de toutes les troupes de Foix," BNF, Dupuy 100, f° 298–301.

27 *Les commentaires du soldat du Vivarais; Ou se voit l'origine de la rébellion de la France et toutes les guerres que, durant icelle, le pays du Vivarais a souffertes, divisés en trois livres, selon le temps que lesdites guerres sont arrivées; Suivis du voyage du duc de Rohan en Vivarais, l'en 1628; de la relation de la révolte de Roure en 1670; Et d'une anecdote extraite du journal manuscrit de J. de Banne, chanoine de Viviers* (1908; reprint, Valence: La Bouquinerie, 1991), 119.

28 "Voiage du M. le duc de Rohan en Vivarais," in *Les commentaires du soldat du Vivarais*, 244–45; Jean-Bernard Elzière, *Histoire des Budos: Seigneurs de Budos en Guyenne et de Portes-Bertrand en Languedoc* (Nîmes: Renaissance du château de Portes, 1978), 141.

29 "Voiage du M. le duc de Rohan en Vivarais," 244–45; Elzière, *Histoire des Budos*, 141.

30 Victor-Louis Tapié argues that "only a few weeks previously the people of Nègre-

pelisse had treacherously wiped out Vaillac's regiment which was quartered there, the women showing themselves no less rabid than the men." Victor-L. Tapié, *France in the Age of Louis XIII and Richelieu*, trans. D. McN. Lockie (New York: Präger Publishers, 1975), originally published as *La France de Louis XIII et Richelieu* (Paris: Flammarion, 1952), 121, 125, 126.

31 Louis de Pontis, *Mémoires (1676)*, édition critique par Andrée Villard (Paris: Honoré Champion, 2000), 195.

32 *Recit véritable de tout ce qui s'est passé en l'armee du roy depuis le 28 may jusques au 24 juin*; and *Le grand et juste chastiment des rebelles de Nègrepelisse*. On the notion of outrage, see Philip Benedict, "Settlements: France," in *Visions, Programs, and Outcomes*, vol. 2 of *Handbook of European History, 1400–1600: Late Middle Ages, Renaissance, and Reformation*, ed. Thomas A. Brady, Jr, Heiko A. Oberman, and James D. Tracy (Grand Rapids, Mich.: William B. Eerdmans, 1995), 446–47.

33 On raiding warfare, see John Lamphear, "Toward a History of 'Raiding War,'" paper presented at the World 2000 Conference on Teaching History and Geography, Austin, Texas, February 2000; Lawrence H. Keeley, *War before Civilization: The Myth of the Peaceful Savage* (Oxford: Oxford University Press, 1996); Harry Holbert Turney-High, *Primitive War: Its Practice and Concepts* (Columbia: University of South Carolina Press, 1949), ch. 2; Paul Bohannan, ed., *Law and Warfare: Studies in the Anthropology of Conflict* (Austin: University of Texas Press, 1967).

34 For analyses of partisan warfare in seventeenth-century France, see John A. Lynn, *Giant of the Grand Siècle: The French Army 1610–1715* (Cambridge: Cambridge University Press, 1997), 538–46; George Satterfield, *Princes, Posts, and Partisans: The Army of Louis XIV and Partisan Warfare in the Netherlands (1673–1678)* (Leiden: Brill, 2003).

35 For a discussion of the connections between raiding and military intelligence, see Lynn, *Giant of the Grand Siècle*, 316–18.

36 *Les commentaires du soldat du Vivarais*, 66–69.

37 An examination of the connections between fortifications and raiding warfare in the second half of the seventeenth century can be found in Lynn, *Giant of the Grand Siècle*, 580–87.

38 *Les commentaires du soldat du Vivarais*, 97–98.

39 Ibid., 148–49.

40 Simon Du Cros, *Histoire de la vie de Henry dernier duc de Montmorency; Contenant tout ce qu'il a fait de plus remarquable depuis sa naissance jusques à sa mort* (Paris: Antoine Sommaville & Augustin Courbé, 1643), 183–85.

41 Devic and Vaissete, *Histoire générale de Languedoc*, 11: 1027.

42 *Les commentaires du soldat du Vivarais*, 56–57.

43 "Recit véritable de la prise de la ville de Pamiers Capitale du Pays de Foix, ensemble de Beaufort Lieutenant General du duc de Rohan, Dauros gouverneur de Mazeres et desroutte de toutes les troupes de Foix"; BNF, Dupuy 100, f° 298–301; BNF, Languedoc-Bénédictins 94, f° 216.

44 *Les commentaires du soldat du Vivarais*, 166; Du Cros, *Histoire de la vie de Henry dernier duc de Montmorency*, 156–59.

45 For a recent interpretation of *chevauchées* in the Hundred Years' War, see Clifford J. Rogers, "By Fire and Sword: *Bellum Hostile* and 'Civilians' in the Hundred Years War," in *Civilians in the Path of War*, ed. Grimsley and Rogers, 33–78; Clifford J. Rogers, *War Cruel and Sharp: English Strategy under Edward III, 1327–1360*

(Woodbridge, U.K.: Boydell Press, 2000).

46 *Récit véritable de ce qui s'est passé au degast es environs de Nismes, Uzes, Anduze et Alez, en la préseance du duc de Rohan et de son armée, avec la deffaite de son avant-garde, et le nombre des blessez et pris prisonniers. Par Monseigneur de Montmorency, Duc et Pair de France, Gouverneur pour le Roy au païs de Languedoc* (Paris: Jean Barbotte, 1628), BNF, Lb36 2640.

47 Du Cros, *Histoire de la vie de Henry dernier duc de Montmorency*, 166–68.

48 *Récit véritable de ce qui s'est passé au degast es environs de Nismes, Uzes, Anduze et Alez.*

49 *La prise de la ville de Chaumerac en Vivarests. Par Monseigneur le duc de Montmorency. Avec l'execution de six vingts des rebelles qui ont esté penduz à la veüë du Pousin. Et le pillage & bruslement du chasteau de Mauras, & autres maisons qui pouvoient favoriser le passage des rebelles de Privas audit Pousin* (Paris: Jean Barbote, 1628), BNF, Lb36 2634.

50 Adrienne Durand-Tullou, *Le loup du Causse: La légende d'un compagnon de Rohan (1594–1638)* (Paris: Payot & Rivages, 1994), 166–67.

51 Ibid., 165–68.

52 *L'Estat du siege contre Montauban par l'armée royale de sa Majesté contre ceux de la rebellion* (Paris: Isaac Mesnier, 1621), BNF, Lb36 1730. For an analysis of the economy of pillaging and second-hand trade in armies, see Brian Sandberg, " 'The Magazine of All Their Pillaging': Armies as Sites of Second-Hand Exchanges during the French Wars of Religion," in *Alternative Exchanges: Second-Hand Circulations from the Sixteenth Century to the Present*, ed. Laurence Fontaine (New York: Berghahn Books, 2008), 76–96.

53 *La prise et transport des bleds; et autres provisions des habitans de la Rochelle. Par Monsieur le duc d'Espernon ensemble l'empeeschement des eaux douces en ladite ville, & l'incommodité qu'elles apportent aux Habitans. Les preparatifs des Vendages. Les deffaictes qui se sont faictes és lieux circonvoisins. Et generalement tout ce qui s'est passé à ce subject jusques à présent* (Paris: Isaac Mesnier, 1621), BNF, Lb36 1740. Another source claimed that "M. d'Espernon tient maintenant bloquée du costée de la terre en sorte que personne ne peut y entrer ny en sortir," BNF, Mss fr. 3810, f° 44. However, some communications did continue between La Rochelle and Montauban, since messengers were occasionally able to make it through the siege lines. See BNF, Mss fr. 18756, f° 54; Guillaume Girard, *Histoire de la vie du duc d'Espernon* (Paris: Montalant, 1730), 363–68.

54 On siege warfare in the French Wars of Religion, see Gabriel Audisio, ed., *Prendre une ville au XVIe siècle* (Aix-en-Provence: Publications de l'Université de Provence, 2004); Jean-Paul Desaive, "Les sièges pendant les guerres civiles en Bourgogne (fin du XVIe siècle): Un double témoignage," in *Situazioni d'Assedio/Cities under Siege/États de Siège*, ed. Lucia Carle and Antoinette Fauve-Chamoux (Montalcino: Clio-Polis, 2002), 299–306; Michael Wolfe, "Writing the City under Attack during the French Wars of Religion," in *Situazioni d'Assedio/Cities under Siege/Etats de Siège*, ed. Carle and Fauve-Chamoux, 197–203; Michael Wolfe, "Walled Towns during the French Wars of Religion," in *City Walls: The Urban Enceinte in Global Perspective*, ed. James D. Tracy (Cambridge: Cambridge University Press, 2000), 328–37; David Buisseret, *Ingénieurs et fortifications avant Vauban: L'organisation d'un service royal aux XVIe-XVIIe siècles* (Paris: CTHS, 2000); Wood, *The King's Army*, 205–25, 246–74.

55 For an overview of *jus in bello*, see Johnson, "Maintaining the Protection of Non-

Combatants," 427–30; Meron, *Bloody Constraint*, ch. 4; Maurice Keen, *The Laws of War in the Middle Ages* (London: Routledge and Kegan Paul, 1965).

56 Geoffrey Parker, "Early Modern Europe," in *The Laws of War: Constraints on Warfare in the Western World*, ed. Michael Howard, George J. Andreopoulos, and Mark R. Shulman (New Haven, Conn.: Yale University Press, 1994), 40–58.

57 Alberico Gentili, quoted in Parker, "Early Modern Europe," 51.

58 BNF, Mss fr. 18972, f° 36–38.

59 "Mémoire ou journal du siege de Montpellier," BNF, Mss fr. 23339, f° 188–89.

60 *La prise par force de la ville de Bonail en Languedoc* (Paris: Adrian Bacot, 1625), Bibliothèque municipale (hereafter BM) Montpellier, 30017, f° 5; *HGL*, 11: 992–93. Bonail is also described in some sources as the château de Bonnac.

61 *La prise par force de la ville de Bonail en Languedoc*; *HGL*, 11: 992–93.

62 Some residents did manage to survive the destruction of Nègrepelisse, often because they were protected by officers and soldiers. Pontis, *Mémoires (1676)*, 194–200.

63 Louis XIII again avoided mentioning the massacre, instead describing his clemency in his treatment of the 300 to 400 men the royal army captured, "being content with a chastisement of six amongst them to serve as an example." Louis XIII to the parlement of Toulouse, Camp at Saint-Antonin, June 23, 1622.

64 Louis XIII to Marie de Médicis, Saint-Antonin, June 23, 1622, BNF, Cinq Cens de Colbert 98, reprinted in *Lettres de la main de Louis XIII*, ed. Eugène Griselle (Paris: Société des Bibliophiles François, 1914), 220–21.

65 *La deffaicte de cinq cens hommes de guerre sortis de Montpellier. Par monsieur le duc de Mont-morency. Ensemble la nouvelle arrivé des registres & Lansquenets levez en Allemagne pour le service de sa Majesté en Languedoc*, BM Montpellier, 30239, f° 5. As historian A. Lloyd Moote observes, "Pamphleteers extolled the glories of punishment." Moote, *Louis XIII, the Just* (Berkeley: University of California Press, 1989), 129–30.

66 *Relation véritable et journalière de tout ce qui s'est passé en France & Pays Estrangers*.

67 "Le psaultier des rebelles de ce temps," BNF, Mss fr. 23060, f° 169–72.

68 Mark Grimsley's analysis of the "persistence of restraint" during the American Civil War provokes intriguing questions for historians of early modern civil warfare based on assessing the sources of restraint, evaluating episodes of atrocity and vengeance, and questioning why restraint broke down. See Mark Grimsley, *The Hard Hand of War: Union Military Policy toward Southern Civilians, 1861–1865* (Cambridge: Cambridge University Press, 1995).

3 Scott Reynolds Nelson

An American War of Incarceration

Guerrilla Warfare, Occupation, and Imprisonment in the American South, 1863–65

H istorians of the American Civil War have taken a decidedly partisan interest in the side of the Union. There is a seductive logic here: no one would deny that slavery was wrong, or that a war to protect it led Confederates to do terrible things. But an emphatically pro-Union history of the American Civil War has led historians to ignore the imperialist features of the Union Army, the predecessor of the United States Army. In particular we might miss the constellation of law, authority, and state power that authorized the use of force against civilians in the American Civil War and its later use in America's imperial wars. We might better see the army's role in later wars – in the Dakota Plains, Central America, the Philippines, Korea, Vietnam, and Iraq – as part of a great arch of military and state expansion that had its start in the American Civil War.[1] One keystone of that arch is the legal case the Union Army made for the criminalization of its enemies, which simultaneously justified raids on civilian property and criminalized many forms of military response. In this sense, we should recognize a legal defence of occupation in the last years of the American Civil War that presaged the unconstitutional roundup of enemy combatants in America's wars in Afghanistan and Iraq.

In the six months after President Lincoln shifted his strategy from disproving the theory of state sovereignty to eliminating chattel slavery, his Union commanders began to prosecute the war differently. Two armies, the Army of the Potomac and the Army of the Cumberland, began a war of pacification and resettlement. By then the war had become, certainly, a war of liberation, one that drew on the power of tens of thousands of black soldiers and sailors. It became, to be sure, a war that demanded only brief Union forays into enemy territory, which then allowed slaves to destroy the foundations of plantation agriculture.[2]

But by 1863, the Union strategy was also bent on the gradual subtraction, incarceration, and containment of civilian "effectives," men behind the lines who could stand and fight. At the same time, the Union initiated a regular war on Southern civilians. This was a new war of long marches, fought with engineering corps, gunboats, and torches. It was prosecuted by raiding parties of tens of thousands of men, which gradually removed enemy prisoners from the total forces available to Southern generals and pushed them into long-term holding pens. Confederate effectives captured at Gettysburg and Petersburg were shuffled onto steamers that disembarked at Point Lookout, Maryland. Processed and inspected, the oldest and youngest were reassembled and shipped by boat and railway car to Elmira, New York.[3] The Army of the Cumberland moved south and east toward Atlanta. The Army of the Potomac swept south toward Richmond. Both Union armies functioned as slowly moving engines of liberation, incarceration, and reconstruction. They left in their wake a shattered landscape that took decades to rebuild and inaugurated a policy that criminalized its enemies and enabled future wars of occupation.[4]

The Sentiment

Historian Eric Foner has described how, by the 1850s, anti-slavery Republicans viewed the Southern landscape as barren, wrecked by the slave power.[5] Republicans compared every overgrown field or untended garden with the neat farms of Pennsylvania or Ohio, identifying the "problem" as evidence of the absence of free labour.[6] This grammar of Southern agricultural failure may have conditioned Union soldiers to consider the Southern landscape as empty and wasted and prepared them for the more regular destruction that would come. Union surgeon Dr. Milton Carey, stationed in East Tennessee, described the sentiment of soldiers who had come to hate the South as a foreign place. "It is," he wrote,

> the poorest country that was ever known not an inhabitant for miles & miles & those that have been found are so ignorant that they do not know their right hand from their left. It is truly astonishing. In fact after you leave the Ohio River there is scarcely a civilized inhabitant for over 500 miles.[7]

He described to a friend how this barren landscape could become fearful to soldiers stationed there. A few days before the bloody Battle of Shiloh, Carey described a small farmer's house that made Ohio log cabins look like mansions. Scouts had just visited "an old one story log house which is for the 'bush whacker' & his family to live in there."[8] As geographer Yi-Fu Tuan has said, occupying soldiers sometimes turned the landscape around them into a "landscape of fear," making unfamiliar landmarks into threatening ones. Carey described this "God forsaken country" as not only terrifying but also sickening and worthless:

> If all the Southern States are like this part of Tennessee I would say let the secessionists take it & go for it is not worth the loss of one single life or ten grains of the commonest powder. But enough of this description for it makes me sick to think of it.[9]

Desolate, untended farms, not worth defending, were filled with "bushwhackers," who under cover of the "scrub oak" forests would kill or maim soldiers.

The Raid

The first innovation in warfare practised by the Union Army was the extended raid on civilian property.[10] Most historians have associated this with Sherman's March to the Sea in 1864, but it actually began as early as 1862 in the western theatre, along the Mississippi River, following Union failures in two major European-style battles: Shiloh and Manassas. The raid began with gunboats, steam-powered ships with heavy artillery that could lob shells as far as a quarter mile.[11] Carey described to a friend the carnage that these ships could deliver to a "small one story ware house[,] frame at that." The house seemed well defended, Carey wrote, "but our gun boats shelled them out in about 30 minutes, killing 25 or 30 of them."[12] This was a military target, but as Carey described the expansion of the war, nearly all targets became military.

Carey heard of the new kind of raid from a doctor in another brigade in September 1862, and it excited him. "Dr Brent got back day before yesterday," Carey wrote "& came and took dinner with me yesterday. He had a great many big yarns to tell about his exploits. He said that the brigade traveled about seventy miles, had four fights, took about thirty secesh [secessionist] prisoners and brought in 300 negroes, 30 heads of horses & 40 mules."[13] Raids usually began with gunboats lobbing explosive shells in the direction of larger houses, and then sending in soldiers to empty a house of its contents. Carey described the scene first as an observer from a steamer at Milliken's Landing:

> The sun shines with great force so much so that it is uncomfortable to be on the deck of the boat. The evenings are cool and pleasant. Wherever we have stopped the soldiers have burned everything that they could reach for miles around. Entire towns and plantations have been burned to the ground. All kinds of stock, horses, cows, sheep, mules and fowls have been brought in in abundance.[14]

To themselves, soldiers justified such raids by painting inhabitants with broad, encompassing labels such as "secesh" and "bushwhackers." Union authority in the raids was generally broad, and generals neglected to record their orders. Thus raids into the Mississippi River farms and plantations do not appear in War Department Records and were not recorded in the *Official Records of the War of the Rebellion*.[15] To many military historians of the Civil War, this omission of orders has erased the activity. On the other hand, the set-piece battles of Manassas, Antietam, and Gettysburg, for which orders were recorded, transferred, and filed, loom much larger in the history of the war. This is despite the fact that a very small percentage of soldiers fought in them. For example only 2 per cent of Union soldiers fought at the Battle of Gettysburg, the so-called turning point of the war.[16]

Soldiers and officers saw raids on civilians as crucial to bringing down the Confederacy, for it destroyed the capacity of farms to supply the Confederate government. Thus Carey described a raid on a local judge in which he participated before the house was burned:

> We stopped at a plantation belong[ing] to Judge Griffin who is quite an old man and owns a large plantation and a great many negroes. He has a very fine house and it was splendidly furnished with furniture and everything of modern style. The boys gave him a call, and took everything out of the house that they could carry off. He had a splendid library, a fine piano, but the boys acted very indiscreetly and destroyed things that could do no good in the world. The boys got at least 250 chickens a great lot of bacon & ham, honey by the barrel, sheep, fresh beef & pork.[17]

In many ways, to themselves and to others, soldiers deflected the charge that they pursued a war on civilians. Slavery was first. Because the war was about slavery, plantations with "a great many negroes" could justifiably be burned. When Carey described these particularly brutal acts, he framed them archly in a story of young boys paying a social call, referring to their burning of the judge's house as having "acted very indiscreetly." This ironic phrasing of violence as a visit helped soldiers justify their actions to themselves. Subconsciously perhaps, the violence refused to be disciplined. Carey next told his wife about a frightening dream he had the night after the raid, in which he apparently did some violence to her. Of the dream he wrote,

> It is so bad that it would not do to write it out on paper for fear that it might fall into the hands of some one besides yourself, and it would not read very elegant, so I will postpone it 'till I see you[,] then I will give it in detail.[18]

The result of plantation raids along the Mississippi was to create a humanitarian crisis of massive proportions, borne largely by slaves. W.E.B. Du Bois described the arrivals of thousands of impoverished slaves along the Mississippi in 1862:

> They came at night, when the flickering camp fires of the blue hosts shone like vast unsteady stars along the black horizon: old men, and thin, with gray and tufted hair; women with frightened eyes, dragging whimpering, hungry children; men and girls, stalwart and gaunt, – a horde of starving vagabonds, homeless, helpless, and pitiable in their dark distress.[19]

While many thousands of slaves bravely escaped from Southern plantations during the war to head for Union lines, many more were driven out by the raids of the Union Army. By provoking a humanitarian crisis along the Mississippi River, Union soldiers could simultaneously rob civilians, disrupt food production along the rivers, and end slavery.

The Guerrillas

While all of these actions proved effective in war, the standard argument made by soldiers to justify their attacks on civilian property was that these particular civilians supported or were themselves guerrillas. Thus Carey referred to the log cabin that Union forces shelled as a place for "the 'bush whacker' & his family to live in." The attack on Judge Griffin Carey justified because Griffin was reputed to have helped the guerrillas who captured a Union gunboat. Carey's own relationship to the judge was complicated. Carey's sword and trepanning equipment had been stolen by a Union soldier while Carey was a prisoner of the Confederates. Just as these goods were being shipped back to him on a Union gunboat, the gunboat was captured by men who may or may not have been friends of the judge. "I had a spite at him," Carey wrote, "for I think that he got my 'sword & things'. . . . I have already written about it! Consequently I will not bring the subject up at this time for it is not very pleasant to you & I know it is not for me."[20] To themselves, soldiers justified raids by raising the spectre of the guerrilla. Taking goods from a plantation that *may* have harboured guerrillas was not theft. And animals taken from farms were not seen as savings that would keep families alive but as food that might be eaten by a guerrilla before he attacked a soldier.

If the raids on the Mississippi in 1862, which expanded to the South Carolina coastline by the end of the year, had remained unofficial policy, then we might safely store the matter under "Plantations, Violence Against." But the raiding style of war and the definition of the guerrilla did actually change policy. To understand this we need to understand the growth of guerrilla violence, the Lieber Code, and its role in shaping American rules of warfare.

We should first understand that gunfire was exchanged in Bleeding Kansas, before the Civil War began. Southern irregulars called bushwhackers raided Northern towns and farms; Northern irregulars called jayhawkers raided Southern towns and farms. (The jayhawk was a mythical hawk that allegedly teased its prey before killing it.) After organized regiments formed North and South, Southern guerrillas who could not or would not join regiments attacked Unionist settlements, especially in Missouri. Irregular militias of Union soldiers defended Northern towns, but their methods differed little from the bushwhackers they were allegedly fighting. In Missouri this spiralled into bloody warfare in which both Union and Confederate partisans exchanged uniforms to hunt out civilian supporters of their enemies.[21] Both sides recognized that this kind of violence could turn war into chaos.

Union Commander-in-Chief Henry Halleck considered the existing rules of war too restrictive for dealing with these guerrillas, especially in Missouri. The worst of them travelled in civilian clothing, killed soldiers and civilians indiscriminately, and then when captured demanded to be treated as prisoners of war. Halleck created a separate institution called the military commission, different from a court martial, to deal with guerrillas. This commission could hang men not in "duly-authorized forces" of the Confederacy, if Union officers found them guilty of violating the laws of war. In any case, the military commission itself was freed from obeying the laws of war.[22] This new commission may well have been the precursor to the authority established for Afghan, Iraqi, and other irregular combatants held in Guantanamo Bay and secret prisons in Eastern Europe.[23]

At the start of the war, the Confederacy hesitated to use guerrillas.[24] But by April 1862, as a force of some 100,000 Union soldiers massed outside of Richmond and Union raids on civilians took place along the Mississippi River, the Confederate Congress changed its position. The Partisan Ranger Act authorized any group of mounted soldiers to apply to the Confederacy, gain a commission, and then raid Union supply lines. When captured, these soldiers could claim to be regular soldiers.[25]

As these armed raiders emerged throughout the South, a difficult standoff emerged in August 1862. The Union tried the first set of Confederate partisans by military tribunal, predicting hanging as the result. By travelling without uniform in Union territory and attacking supply lines, and collecting a bounty for stolen goods, such soldiers, according to Halleck, could be hanged by military commission. Confederates threatened to retaliate by hanging Union prisoners of war.[26]

The Lieber Code

Into this difficulty stepped Francis Lieber, a German-American who had followed the emergence of partisans in Russia, Spain, and Italy in the early nineteenth century and recognized the necessity of drawing a line between partisans who were neither commissioned soldiers nor simple bandits and regular troops. But he also thought it right for jurists during wartime "to say a plain and positive word for the *Nation*."[27] In the context of the Civil War, this meant a strongly pro-Union position. After commenting on the rules of warfare in New York newspapers, he came to the attention of the Union Army, which considered the current rules of warfare, particularly those published by authors who favoured secession, too restrictive.

The most troubling legal treatise for the U.S. government was a new commentary by a prominent New York lawyer on Henry Wheaton's *Elements of International Law*, which appeared to support the Confederate position on a number of important issues including, apparently, the right of citizens to defend themselves outside of regiments and limits to the legality of Union seizure and destruction of property.[28] General Halleck wrote to Lieber for advice, calling the new edition "hyper-state right and secessionist." "For 10 or 15 years this will be *the* book," Halleck exclaimed. Worse still, the author had been contacted for a French translation of the work, which would damn the Union war effort in French eyes.[29] General Halleck summoned Lieber to Washington in December 1862 to draw up a new code of war, what became the Lieber Code.[30] Lieber's positive word for the nation was to alter the laws to suit the new Union strategy of raids on civilian property while limiting the legality of Confederate reprisals. He created a new code of war, the current basis for the U.S. code used by soldiers today, which criminalized Confederate rules of warfare and legalized Union raids on civilians.

Lieber altered the code of war around the idea of occupation. Occupiers are necessarily outside of their homes; those occupied are necessarily near them. Article 82 of the Lieber Code defined partisans as soldiers, but if partisans ever made "intermitting returns to their homes and avocations," then they could be killed as "highway robbers or bandits." An occupying army, therefore, had all the rights of soldiers. Those occupied, even if in uniform, could be killed if it could be proven that they had returned home.[31] As Union gunboats moved into a region, providing covering fire to raiding soldiers, Union soldiers could claim to control and occupy that zone. Any raids they made were thus technically inside their own lines. By comparison, nearly all Confederate raids and counter-attacks took place with cavalrymen, who used speed to evade Union soldiers. The only regular Union force to have operated this way would have been General Sheridan's cavalry in the Valley of Virginia.[32] Lieber called those partisans who operated inside another's lines "armed prowlers." These men, who operated by "robbing, killing, or ... destroying bridges, roads or canals, or ... robbing or destroying the mail, or ... cutting the telegraph wires" also stood outside the laws of war and could be summarily executed. Finally, anyone in occupied territory who rose up against occupiers was named a "war-rebel" and could be summarily executed. If he was involved in a conspiracy to rise up against the occupying force, he could also be executed.[33]

Thus, the Lieber Code often legitimized civilian property destruction while criminalizing military attacks by those under occupation. Where one stood, as occupier or occupied, determined whether force was illegal. Partisans could be regular soldiers provided they never returned home and operated only in areas not yet controlled by the Union Army. Union raids against civilian property made by whole brigades that used the covering fire of artillery, on the other hand, could be considered an expansion of occupying lines and its soldiers protected by the laws of war. Legally this provided safety to most Union raiders and criminalized the warfare of most Confederate raiders. Article 37 of the Lieber Code did require occupying soldiers to protect "strictly private property," but all prosecutions for destruction of property were left in the hands of superior officers. While Union military tribunals occasionally prosecuted a private soldier's theft of civilian property, Confederate raids on military supply lines became criminal acts, punishable by death.

Incarceration

By 1863, as the Union Army occupied nearly half of the South, it did not necessarily attack people with impunity. Instead it began to use the oath of allegiance to separate and incarcerate white Southerners. The president created provisional governors in the occupied portions of Southern states.[34] Soldiers then swept into Southern regions, captured suspicious persons, and sorted them out behind the lines. Two proclamations made the strategy successful. Lincoln's Emancipation Proclamation allowed slaves to free themselves by following Union soldiers when they retreated. And the Amnesty Proclamation was just as important in that it forced white Southerners between eighteen and fifty either to swear an oath to support the U.S. government and return to their homes or to be grouped with those who harboured "sympathies and connections" to the Confederacy. The Lieber Code referred to those who refused to swear the oath as "revolted citizens."[35]

The oath helpfully separated those inside Union-held territory for further processing. Oath swearers who later wore a Confederate uniform could be shot. "Revolted citizens" meanwhile could be taxed to support refugees and could have their goods seized up to the value of any Confederate raids.[36] Confederate soldiers captured in uniform would enter prison for the duration of the war and might appeal for amnesty only by enlisting in the Union Army to fight Indians in the West or in the Union Navy to work at sea.[37] Prisoner exchange stopped.[38]

This change in Union strategy altered the war, turning it into a war of captivity. Captivity became a part of the life of most Confederate soldiers. By the end of the Civil War roughly 35 per cent of Confederate soldiers had spent time as prisoners.[39]

Like so many wars of the twentieth century that would follow, the Union had initiated a war of occupation and incarceration, a strategy against which the Confederacy never successfully responded. The Northern strategy of incarcerating, processing, and deploying prisoners would be duplicated in other wars of incarceration and pacification, in the Plains Wars of the 1870s, in the Anglo-Boer War in South Africa, and in the bloody American campaigns to put down insurrection in the Philippines. It was a policy of separation that has echoes in the "reconcentration" made by Spain in Cuba at the turn of the last century, the "strategic hamlets" created by the United States during the Vietnam War, and the villagization program in Rwanda in the 1990s. Raids on civilians, the criminalization of enemy soldiers, and the capture and imprisonment of those criminalized have thus became an important part of how American soldiers have come to control those around them. The Civil War was not the beginning of total war, as some historians have described it, but the inauguration of a series of wars of incarceration.

Notes

1 I borrow the phrase from Philip Richard D. Corrigan, and Derek Sayer, *The Great Arch: English State Formation as Cultural Revolution* (Oxford and New York: Blackwell, 1985).

2 This is the position of much of the current historiography. See James M. McPherson, *Battle Cry of Freedom: The Civil War Era* (New York: Ballantine, 1988), Eric Foner, *Reconstruction: America's Unfinished Revolution, 1863–1877* (New York: Harper and Row, 1988); Ira Berlin, ed., *The Destruction of Slavery*, vol. 1, *Freedom, a Documentary History of Emancipation, 1861–1867* (Cambridge and New York: Cambridge University Press, 1985).

3 On Elmira, see Michael P. Gray, *The Business of Captivity in the Chemung Valley: Elmira and Its Civil War Prison* (Kent, Ohio: Kent State University Press, 2001).

4 This argument is made in Scott Reynolds Nelson and Carol Sheriff, *A People at War: Civilians and Soldiers in America's Civil War, 1854–1877* (New York: Oxford University Press, 2007). I do not take the position that the Union initiated "total war," a phrase that reads back, I think, the innovations of the First World War onto the American Civil War. For the debates pro and con, see Stig Förster and Jörg Nagler, *On the Road to Total War: The American Civil War and the German*

Wars of Unification, 1861–1871 (Washington, D.C., and New York: German Historical Institute and Cambridge University Press, 1997).

5 Eric Foner, *Free Soil, Free Labor, Free Men: The Ideology of the Republican Party before the Civil War* (New York: Oxford University Press, 1970), ch. 5.

6 One of the most readable of such accounts is Frederick Law Olmsted, *The Cotton Kingdom* (1852–56; reprint, New York: Knopf, 1953).

7 Carey to "My Dear Wife," March 27, 1862, Milton T. Carey Papers, Filson Historical Society, Louisville, Kentucky (hereafter MTC-FHS).

8 Carey to John H. Baynes, April 1, 1862, MTC-FHS.

9 Ibid.

10 William Barney, *Flawed Victory: A New Perspective on the Civil War* (New York: University Press of America, 1980), 33–35.

11 The Dahlgren gun with Rodman casting is described in Mitchell A. Wilson, *American Science and Invention* (New York: Simon and Schuster, 1954), 190–91.

12 Carey to John H. Baynes, April 1, 1862, MTC-FHS.

13 Carey to "My Dear Wife," September 14, 1862, MTC-FHS.

14 Carey to "My Dear Wife," December 25, 1862, MTC-FHS.

15 Thus no orders by General Rosecrans and General Wright exist in the Official Records for gunboats like the *City of Alton* (Carey's gunboat). Yet Asst. Quartermaster L.B. Parsons wrote to U.S. Grant in March of 1863 that Rosecrans and Wright would not give up the 25,200 men and the dozens of gunboats and steamers that were directly under their control. L.B. Parsons, Col. and Asst. Quartermaster General, Supt. Transportation to Maj Gen. U.S. Grant, *Official Records of the War of the Rebellion* (hereafter OR) 38: 116–17.

16 Roughly 86,000 Union soldiers fought at Gettysburg. See Gregory A. Coco, *A Strange and Blighted Land, Gettysburg: The Aftermath of a Battle* (Gettysburg, Pa.: Thomas Publications, 1995), 2. There were 4.3 million Union enlistments. See Lonnie R. Speer, *Portals to Hell: Military Prisons of the Civil War* (Mechanicsburg, Pa.: Stackpole Books, 1997), 341.

17 Carey to "My Dear Wife," January 20, 1863 [mismarked as 1862], MTC-FHS.

18 Ibid.

19 W.E.B. Du Bois, "The Freedmen's Bureau," *Atlantic Monthly* 87 (1901), 354–65.

20 Carey to "My Dear Wife," January 20, 1863 [mismarked as 1862], MTC-FHS.

21 The best account of this is Michael Fellman, *Inside War: The Guerrilla Conflict in Missouri during the American Civil War* (New York: Oxford University Press, 1989).

22 Henry W. Halleck, "General Orders No. 1," January 1, 1862, OR 8: 477–8.

23 "U.S. Faces Scrutiny over Secret Prisons," *Washington Post*, November 4, 2005.

24 Many historians have made the mistake of assuming that the Confederacy considered but abandoned guerrilla warfare at the end of the conflict. A popular version of this argument can be found in Jay Winik, *April 1865: The Month That Saved America*, 1st ed. (New York: Harper Collins, 2001).

25 This is discussed in Nelson and Sheriff, *A People at War.*

26 H.W. Halleck to Francis Lieber, August 5, 1862, OR 123: 302.

27 Francis Lieber to Theodore Woolsey, June 2, 1863 [mismarked as 1862 according to archivist], Sterling Memorial Library, Manuscripts and Archives, Yale University, Woolsey Family Correspondence (hereafter WFC-Y), series 1, box 18, folder 318.

28 Henry Wheaton and William Beach Lawrence, *Elements of International Law*, 2nd annotated ed. (Boston: Little, Brown and Company, 1863).

29 See Lieber's note to Woolsey, June 2, 1863, WFC-Y, series 1, box 18, folder 318.

30 Francis Lieber, New York, to Theodore Woolsey, June 1, 1863, WFC-Y, series 1, box 18, folder 318.

31 Francis Lieber, "Instructions for the Government of Armies of the United States in the Field," in *The Laws of Armed Conflicts: A Collection of Conventions, Resolutions, and Other Documents*, 3rd rev. ed., ed. Dietrich Schindler, and Ji rí Toman, Scientific collection of the Henry Dunant Institute (Dordrecht and Boston: Nijhoff, 1986).

32 A good overview of cavalry raids is Edward G. Longacre, *Mounted Raids of the Civil War* (South Brunswick, N.J.: A.S. Barnes, 1975).

33 Lieber, "Instructions," articles 84–85.

34 Senator Andrew Johnson was placed over Tennessee, former senator Edward Stanly over North Carolina, General George F. Shepley over Louisiana, and former Missouri congressman John S. Phelps over Arkansas. In 1863, Lincoln added former congressman Andrew J. Hamilton to control Texas.

35 Lieber, "Instructions," article 156.

36 For the application of this rule in Tennessee, see Peter Maslowski, *Treason Must Be Made Odious: Military Occupation and Wartime Reconstruction in Nashville, Tennessee, 1862–65*, KTO Studies in American History (Millwood, N.Y.: KTO Press, 1978), 60–66.

37 Wm. H. Smith to Genl. Marston, Point Lookout, October 31, 1863, William L. Clements Library, University of Michigan, Pt. Lookout Papers.

38 The change in Union policy toward prisoner exchange has been attributed to the Union army's recruitment of black soldiers. It is certainly true that the Confederacy refused to exchange black soldiers (treating them as escaped slaves) and often killed them after surrender, as in the Fort Pillow Massacre. But there was also a larger logic to ending the war by incarcerating Confederate soldiers, namely to sweep through the Confederacy and remove all effective soldiers. As Grant wrote, "It is hard on our men held in Southern prisons not to exchange them, but it is humanity to those left in the ranks to fight our battles. Every man we hold, when released on parole or otherwise, becomes an active soldier against us at once either directly or indirectly. If we commence a system of exchange which liberates all prisoners taken, we will have to fight on until the whole South is exterminated. If we hold those caught they amount to no more than dead men. At this particular time to release all rebel prisoners North would insure Sherman's defeat and would compromise our safety here." Grant to Benjamin F. Butler, August 18, 1864, *OR* 120: 607.

39 The Confederate Army had between 1.2 and 1.4 million soldiers. Of those, 463,000 were captured, including those at the war's end. See Lonnie Speer, *Portals to Hell*, 341.

Part 2

Collateral Damage in the Partition of Africa

Non-Combatants and War

The Unexplored Factor in the Conquest of the Zulu Kingdom

I n 1879, British imperial and colonial forces invaded the Zulu kingdom, and the two armies fought a number of pitched battles – among them Isandlwana and Rorke's Drift – which have become for millions around the world emblematic of two fundamental aspects of imperial warfare: the superior weaponry and unflinching discipline of European troops confronting superior numbers, and reckless African savagery. Ever since the 1879 invasion, a voracious and uncritical reading public has consumed a vast accumulation of accounts of courageous redcoats meeting the massed Zulu charge with ranked volley firing. Even attempts at serious analysis have failed, to my mind, to break with the imperial narrative largely because the authors are so mesmerized by the idea of men killing men that they fail to contextualize the conflict effectively.

More recently, the imperial nostalgia that underlies conventional histories of the invasion has seeped into the world of heritage and tourism, with the result that colonial dispossession through warfare is presented as a heroic clash between the noble representatives of different military traditions – savage and civilized – which obscures with a sentimental veneer not just the brutality and injustice of the 1879 war but the fact that the invasion is a key to an understanding of contemporary misery and poverty in rural KwaZulu-Natal.

I have dealt with this elsewhere,[1] and in this essay I examine other aspects of the 1879 invasion by trying to bring into focus people who, although they inhabited the margins of depictions of the 1879 war, formed the majority of those directly affected by it – the Zulu non-combatants. A detailed analysis is impossible: for the most part one is forced to speculate on what is implied in the sources because the historical record is dominated by that all-consuming topic, men at war. Nonetheless it seems to me worthwhile to make an attempt to supplement the vast literature on what are often called the Zulu wars with some examination of those who, while they did not fight, not only suffered but also played a major role in these conflicts and their outcome.

The Nation at Large

It is possible to group discussions on civilian casualties in wartime into a number of rough categories, used both singly and in combination. First is the argument that there can be no justification: that civilian casualties in warfare are (1) *unacceptable*. This argument is used for (1a) tactical and (1b) humanitarian reasons, although the former is often clothed in terms of the latter. Second is the idea that civilian casualties are (2) *regrettable*: the term "collateral damage" often falls into this category as "destruction or injury beyond that intended or expected, esp. in the vicinity of a military target."[2] Third, at the start of his history of the twentieth century, Eric Hobsbawm gives an instructive example of the argument that civil casualties in modern wars are (3) *inevitable*:

> It may be thought better, in view of the allegations of "barbarity" of air attacks, to preserve appearances by formulating milder rules and by still nominally confining bombardment to targets which are strictly military in character . . . to avoid emphasizing the truth that air warfare has made such restrictions obsolete and impossible. It may be some time until another war occurs and meanwhile the public may become educated as to the meaning of air power.[3]

But world history is replete with examples of the argument that war has to be taken to the enemy in its social and economic entirety, and as a consequence civilian casualties are (4) *justifiable, desirable,* and *necessary*. For Hobsbawm this is the inhuman essence of an inhumane century.

I want to offer an earlier version of this fourth category from the man who commanded the British troops in Zululand in 1879, Lord Chelmsford, who after an initial defeat on the battlefield changed from the tactical variant of *unacceptable* to *necessary*: "I am satisfied that the more the Zulu nation at large feels the strain brought upon them by the war, the more anxious will they be to see it brought to an end."

This statement was made in the context of an argument between Chelmsford and Sir Henry Bulwer, lieutenant governor of the neighbouring Colony of Natal. Chelmsford had invaded Zululand at the beginning of the year in order to terminate the rule of the Zulu king Cetshwayo kaMpande as an initial move in a plan to facilitate the creation of British-dominated union of southern African states. His force of some 5,500 British regular troops, over 1,000 white colonial volunteers, and 9,000 African levies had entered the kingdom in three columns. On January 22, while camped at Isandlwana, the headquarter column had been attacked by the Zulu army. Weight of numbers, bravery, and the failure of the imperial force to concentrate its fire enabled the Zulu to penetrate the British lines and use their assegais to destroy the camp and its defenders. It was the greatest defeat that Queen Victoria's army had suffered in its "little wars" of imperial conquest. That night, a portion of the Zulu force attacked a nearby British position at Rorke's Drift and was driven off. To offset the military humiliation at Isandlwana, Rorke's Drift was depicted as the military victory that saved white Natal from Zulu invasion and to this day represents phlegmatic British valour in the face of adversity. But the significance of Rorke's Drift lies in imperial mythology, not in the campaign itself, for the Zulu king had no intention of invading Natal. In the months that followed, while the king attempted to negotiate a peace, the British force fell back into Natal where it could await reinforcements.

During this lull, Chelmsford extended his definition of the enemy from Zulu soldiers to all Zulu, along with their homes, crops, and foodstocks.[4] The looting of cattle had always been accepted as a legitimate military practice. Chelmsford now also sought to encourage Africans living near Natal's border with Zululand to harass their Zulu neighbours by mounting cross-border raids. Natal's Lieutenant Governor Henry Bulwer, fearing retaliatory raids, resisted this and in so doing provoked Chelmsford's response that "the Zulu nation at large" should "feel the strain" of war.

Once reinforcements had arrived and a number of pitched battles had been fought, Chelmsford managed to drag his army to the centre of the Zulu kingdom and on July 4 provoked a Zulu attack. Conventionally, and wrongly in my opinion, this is seen as the Battle of Ulundi that ended the "Zulu war."[5] This essay revisits the significance of the specific violent conflicts between organized bodies of armed men with which writers on the invasion are obsessed by situating them in a wider context – by looking at the consequences of military violence and occupation on the people of the kingdom as a whole.

An Armed People

The essential features of the Zulu kingdom before conquest were not dissimilar from those of other southern African farming societies. People lived in spatially discrete homesteads (*umuzi/imizi*), headed by the husband of a number of wives, each residing in her own house with her children within the protective boundaries of the homestead. Central to the homestead was its holding of livestock, which provided dairy products that were essential to the owners' daily diet, meat on occasion, and by-products, leather especially. As bride wealth, cattle played a key role in social organization and differentiation: they were used to bring women into the homestead as wives, and the exchange of daughters for cattle increased the homestead's holding of livestock, a process of labour-power exchange fundamental to the economic structure of the kingdom.

The division of labour was based on gender. Men were responsible for animal husbandry, and certain craft skills often developed as a result of living in areas that provided the necessary materials: metalworking; the forging of hoes and spears; leather-, wood- and basketwork; and making medical products, for example. There was a certain amount of barter of the products made by those with traditional skills, but in general terms homesteads were economically self-sufficient.

Cereals – maize, millet, sorghum – were planted with the spring rains, reaped from mid- to late summer, and stored within the homestead. These were supplemented by vegetables, tubers, melons, and pumpkins mixed with fermented dairy products and garnished with a range of leafy greens. The process of food production, cultivation, gathering, and preparation for consumption and the making of ceramic wares were considered women's work. In charge of the homestead was the husband/father. Homesteads were linked vertically through the male line from a house in the previous generation's homestead, and in time the existing houses would separate from the parent homestead to form new homesteads under sons. Horizontal links between different lineages were created when wives were brought into the homestead or daughters given to other lineages in exchange for livestock. Aggregations of homesteads were organized politically under district chiefs responsible ultimately to the dominant chiefly line: the Zulu, whose head, in English terminology, was the king.

The power of the king was considerable and depended on a particular social feature that was common in southern Africa's farming societies but particularly well developed among the Zulu – its military system. This was based on age sets that would be gathered together by the king every few years and formed into regiments (*ibutho/amabutho*). Members of a particular regiment trained and worked together at one of the king's homesteads (*ikhanda/amakhanda*).[6] Here the gendered division of labour did not apply, as young men carried out a range of agricultural tasks. It was only after a number of years that the king granted permission for the members of a particular regiment to build their own homesteads – that is to marry. The so-called Zulu military system gave the king tremendous power not only over the military capacity of his people but also over their economic activities, for the laws governing the lives of his soldiers determined when new homesteads were to be established and it was in the homesteads that the essential productive processes of the kingdom took place.

The homesteads, as the site of production, and the army, as the means by which production was ensured: these two elements have to be considered as part of one process. Throughout the history of the kingdom (c. 1816–79), but increasingly as the nineteenth century progressed and the surrounding territories were colonized and settled, the existence of the Zulu army gave protection to the 250,000 people who made up the kingdom, ensuring political autonomy, economic independence, and social continuity. But it is misleading to see this vital organization as a standing army: the point was made at the time that it was better to describe the Zulu as an "armed people" in the sense that the military system was integrated into every aspect of the life of every homestead in the kingdom. For this reason, the mobilization of the army had direct and immediate consequences for the whole populace.

Traditionally military strategy was determined by parameters set by the demands of the agricultural cycle. Military campaigns were best carried out in the winter, when the grain stores had been gathered and labour demands were low. Boys travelled with the soldiers, carrying their weapons, sleeping mats, and basic necessities, but very few supplies could be carried with the army, which had to depend on foraging and what it could seize from the enemy. Campaigns had to be of limited length and organized as raids. By the end of the winter, grain stores were low, land had to be prepared for the new growing season, and the demands of the labour-intensive agricultural cycle had to be attended to as soon as the spring rains broke. Without the capacity to store their means of subsistence for extended periods, the Zulu had to keep the cycles of production, closely determined by the annual change of the seasons: planting in the early summer with the coming of the rains, weeding and protection from vermin as the cereals grew and matured, reaping and storing foodstuffs in the autumn.

Pre-industrial farming societies were vulnerable to the vagaries of the weather and to social disruption, of which war was the most intense. The vast and catastrophic series of conflicts and disruption in the opening decades of the nineteenth century, conventionally referred to as the mfecane, demonstrate what happened when different communities were deprived of access to land and food stocks and a vicious, self-perpetuating process of ever-increasing violence was initiated as people were forced to raid to survive. Conventionally, military action was restricted to short-term campaigns at very particular periods in the productive cycle. Military attacks that moved beyond armed conflict and cattle raids to the burning of homesteads and the destruction of property and food stores could quickly turn to disaster for the whole population, and even extermination if the conflict was not resolved by the coming agricultural season. Mobilization was one thing, protracted warfare another. But protracted warfare fought on its own soil was unprecedented in the history of the Zulu kingdom. And this is what the Zulu had to confront in 1879. The social and economic implications of this provide the context of the formal battles.

Histories of the British invasion of the Zulu kingdom in 1879 concentrate on the pitched battles: Isandlwana (January 22), Rorke's Drift (January

22–23), Khambula (March 29), Gingingdlovu (April 2), and Ulundi (July 4) where, it is conventionally argued, ranked volley firing supported by Gatlings, rockets, and light artillery, topped by a cavalry charge, finally persuaded the Zulu army to accept defeat. I do not dismiss the importance of these pitched battles, but I do believe that their significance can be assessed only within the context created by the effects on the cycle of agricultural production and social continuity by the presence of an invading army in Zululand: of the social, economic, and political impact of the British force on all the people of Zululand as it traversed and destroyed the productive capacity of large tracts of the Zulu kingdom, or threatened to do so.

An Unexplored Theme in Southern African History

Attacks on civilians, looting, raiding, and the burning of stock and stores and the homes of non-combatants is a running theme in history of the conquest of southern Africa. But because of the capacity that guns in the hands of men have to divert attention from hoes in the hands of women, insufficient attention has been paid by most historians to this violence. Part of the problem lies in the sources themselves: when dealing with armed men they are replete with information on casualties, communication, and costs; information on attacks on civilians and casualties incurred is vague and referred to only in passing.

Even a cursory look at what are called the frontier wars of the eastern Cape, or the conflicts between the Boers and Basotho, shows that attacks on African food stocks, living spaces, and productive capacity were a fundamental strategy. Specific terrains determined the tactics involved. The kingdom of Lesotho was built around the defensive capacities of flat-topped mountains to which Free State Boers laid siege and shelled while they ravaged the crops in the valleys. On the frontier of the eastern Cape extensive tracts of bush on the coast and along the river valleys and forested mountain ranges were key features in Xhosa defensive strategies – and consequently of the decision of their enemies to attack homesteads rather than pursue soldiers. As Jeff Peires has written, in 1852,

> a massive campaign designed to systematically eliminate the Xhosa means of subsistence was launched. The burning of crops and dwellings had long been part of frontier warfare. Throughout the period of Smith's command in 1851, the British troops had destroyed and laid waste wherever they had passed. What made the campaign of January-March 1852 so different was that it was a coordinated, deliberate plan aimed exclusively at Xhosa fields and gardens. Unable to gain a straight military victory over an active and elusive enemy, the British Army now turned its attention to the exposed and immobile host of maize and

sorghum located in the Amathole Mountains.[7]

Helen Bradford has extended this using a gendered perspective:

> Approaching frontier wars from the perspective of Xhosa women is illuminating. The imperial army left much armed combat to Khoi and Mfengu allies; Englishmen waged war primarily against women and children. "[W]ith the Kaffirs, with beasts of prey, you must destroy their earths, their breeding places." Soldiers were often little more than robbers, cattle herders, arsonists. Men would reduce homesteads to burnt skeletons: 1,200 huts could be fired in three days. They would cut down crops: "the whole force is constantly employed in destroying prodigious quantities of Indian corn and millet." They would plunder grain pits, seize goats, appropriate horses, steal women's jewellery. They would, above all, loot cattle.[8]

Along the frontier to the northeast in the nineteenth century, the homesteads that made up the different African societies in what was to become KwaZulu-Natal were particularly vulnerable to organized violence. In the Colony of Natal about half the African population lived in some 12 per cent of the territory, with the homestead deliberately preserved as part of the colonial economic structure. When, in 1873, one of Natal's most powerful chiefs, Langalibalele of the Hlubi, was threatened by the colonial authorities, he had no doubt of his vulnerability. He and the able-bodied members of the kingdom and their stock abandoned their homesteads and the land on which they were built and made their away across the mountain passes of the Drakensberg to seek refuge in Lesotho. Those unable to undertake the journey – the very young, the very old, the ill, and the pregnant – were placed in caves in the foothills. Here they were found by the colonial forces, shot or smoked out if they resisted, and the survivors marched to the colony's capital for distribution as labourers. This decision to flee the colony rather than accept the consequences of defending their homesteads is known conventionally as the Langalibalele "rebellion." But regardless of Langalibalele's intentions, fundamental to an understanding of his decision is an understanding of his strategic weakness, of the impossibility of resistance given the parameters determined in the final instance by the demands of decentralized homestead production.

Even in the rebellion that took place thirty years later – the Bhambatha Rebellion of 1906 – it is clear that the exposed vulnerability of the homestead was a major factor in the decision to rebel, or as happened more often, not to rebel. Bhambatha himself had to abandon his homesteads and establish a base in the Nkandla forest. In the case of two rebel chiefs whose role in the rebellion I have recently been researching, crucial to their decision to rebel and their tactics was the relation of their homesteads to access roads, and above all to thick bush through which the colonial militia could not move. But the framework in which their strategic decisions were made was determined by the extent to which their people and their productive resources lay exposed to colonial attack.

Chelmsford in Zululand

Lord Chelmsford had been appointed officer commanding British troops in South Africa at the beginning of 1878, and his theatre of operations was the eastern Cape frontier. In preparation for this he received portentous advice from an old frontier hand General Sir John Michel:

> No plan or operation of yours can in any way circumvent the Caffre. He is your master in everything. He goes where he likes, he does what he likes, he moves 3 miles whilst you move one, he carries no commissariat or only a day's supply. You possess only the ground you stand on, All you have got to do is take cattle, annoy him by burning his kraals, and eventually destroy his crops.[9]

But initially, Chelmsford adopted a different strategy against the Zulu. Officially the British announced – as so many aggressors have done before and since – that this was a war of liberation: it was being prosecuted against the Zulu king, not against the Zulu people. Although from the moment they entered Zululand British troops looted cattle and burned homesteads, this was done with some restraint in the hope that while indicating to the Zulu people the strength and resolve of the invading force it would not so antagonize them that it reinforced their loyalty to the Zulu king (see argument 1b above). But such attacks on homesteads were a tactical diversion from the thrust of Chelmsford's strategy. Persuaded that the Zulu would retain the traditional massed charge, and knowing that, properly deployed, his men had the firepower to inflict devastating casualties, Chelmsford marched three columns from different points in the direction of the king's homestead in the centre of the kingdom, hoping to provoke an attack. He was successful in provoking the charge but was unable to keep it at bay, and on January 22, 1879, at Isandlwana the Zulu army annihilated the headquarter column.

When it reached England, the news of the defeat began a process that eventually destroyed the political policy that had brought the war about. But the war itself had to continue: military, national, and racial reputations had to be reasserted, and this meant the Zulu had to be defeated with a violence comparable to that which they had used in defence of their sovereignty and independence. Frightened and humiliated, most of the British force had to wait on the Natal border for reinforcements before the invasion could be resumed. And during this time Chelmsford abandoned his strategy of "restraint" and began to prosecute a war against the people:

> After what has occurred since the war in Zululand commenced, I cannot understand the argument of the Lieutenant-Governor of Natal that we are not waging war against the Zulu nation. At its first commencement, such an announcement was politic and proper, as it afforded an opportunity to those Chiefs who were averse to Cetywayo's rule to come over to our side. Since then, however, our troops have had to contend with the whole strength of the Zulu nation, and it would be madness to refrain from inflicting as much damage as possible upon our enemy, because it was thought desirable, in the first instance, to declare that our quarrel was with Cetywayo alone. . . .
>
> The argument . . . that "if we make war against the whole Zulu people, and if we so act as to cause every Zulu to believe that we are his enemies," we run a risk of driving every Zulu into a desperate defence of his country, "and thereby incur the further risk of making the war a long and tedious one," is totally opposed to all the experience of former Kafir wars.
>
> I am satisfied that the more the Zulu nation at large feels the strain brought upon them by the war, the more anxious will they be to see it brought to an end.[10]

Although the significance of this change has never been analyzed in sufficient depth, references to it can be found in the primary and the secondary sources. I have taken the following examples from the work of a contemporary authority on the history of the invasion:

> An integral element in Chelmsford's strategy was his intention systematically to destroy all the amakhanda [royal homesteads] he could reach. As rallying-points for the amabutho [regiments] and depots for their supplies, their destruction, culminating in that of oNdini [Ulundi], would ensure the reduction of the king's capacity to resist and fatally damage his ability to exercise authority. Unfortunately for the Zulu, the elimination of these "legitimate" military targets was soon extended to include ordinary imizi, and involved the pillaging of grain stores and the capture of livestock. Chelmsford well understood that one of the most effectual ways of defeating a people such as the Zulu was "through the stomach," which sanctioned the complete destruction of the enemy's means of subsistence along the British line of march.[11]

Although there are some problems with this paragraph,[12] it does introduce a fundamental theme that appears repeatedly in the book. To take just some examples from different stages of the campaign:

> Abandoning the fiction that the war was against the king alone, and not his subjects, the British burned all the imizi along their route to show their displeasure at being attacked.[13]

> They drove off 300 cattle and 100 sheep, killed twelve Zulu and captured a number more, besides burning twenty-four imizi. These far-flung and ruthless patrols by Buller's irregular horse were to clear the country between Conference Hill and Rorke's Drift of all Zulu, whether civilian or under arms. . . .
> The women and children swarmed out of the imizi, making for the nearest mountain with their possessions on their heads. Here as elsewhere, the British found the imizi which they routinely destroyed near the line of march deserted, though the large supplies of corn which they regularly contained suggested they had been precipitately abandoned.[14]

> They scoured the countryside . . . driving the Zulu and their cattle into the sanctuary of the Ngoye forest. In the course of these punitive sorties, in which the Zulu made little attempt to resist, but fled leaving their stores of mealies intact and their potatoes sown, the British killed five Zulu and captured many others, besides lifting 378 cattle, 27 sheep and 29 goats. They also destroyed over fifty imizi.[15]

One-Sided Total War

As I have stated above it is more accurate to consider the Zulu as an armed people than as a military kingdom with a standing army. As a result, war directly affected all aspects of everyone's social existence. And I hesitate to stress a further, related, point, at least without the academic camouflage of phrases like "spatial distance and the pre-modern." But, given that it is of such significance and usually ignored it necessary to make the point that while the "Zulu war" of 1879 affected Great Britain profoundly – from the families who lost men folk, the regiments their colours, and the officers their military reputations to the Conservative government that lost the next election – it was nonetheless a distant and limited conflict, spatially remote from the lives of British non-combatants. This was not so for the Zulu non-combatants: the children, the women, and the old who lived and worked in the tens of thousands of homesteads of the kingdom and felt the consequences of war immediately and directly.[16]

This is not to say that they were affected uniformly: although all homesteads had men serving in the army, border homesteads took the brunt of the attack; homesteads on the line of march were looted, burned, and their cattle taken; homesteads in the north and east felt the pressure less. One reason Chelmsford invaded in mid-summer was that he wanted to make sure there would be grazing for his draft animals. But another was that he knew it would place an extra strain on the Zulu economy, for it coincided with the time to reap the crops and homestead labour needed to be mobilized to assist in the gathering of the crops. This was even more urgent in 1878–79 as the summer rains came late and the previous season's food stocks had been depleted well before the new season's had matured. As a result, when the British entered the kingdom in January the ripening crops still had to be reaped and stored. For this reason the defeat of the headquarter column at Isandlwana was more than a military victory; it halted the invaders and gave women the chance to proceed with the urgent tasks of reaping and storing, although many lost the fruits of their labour when the invasion resumed in May.

What of the people attempting to replenish and guard these resources? Let us assume that the unmarried sons of the homestead were with the *amabutho* and the homestead head was serving as an officer, or *indunai*, in his regiment. Left behind were the children, boys and girls, the married women, and the old. Their specific duties and responsibilities might seem so commonplace that they lie beneath the magisterial vision of the historian, but they were essential tasks: if they were not carried out the survival of the homestead's occupants was threatened. They included milking and herding, food collection and preparation, carrying water, cooking, washing, and minding the young, the old, and the infirm. Such labour is in a sense unremarkable – but it has to be carried out day in and day out if life is to continue. It is not merely "domestic labour" in any bourgeois sense; the division of labour was not sufficiently developed for this. It is heavy work from which there is no respite, demanding a wide range of skills. And it is labour that for the most part is ignored by historians – although not by the military men when their objective was to make the whole Zulu nation "feel the strain" of war – although later it was played down, if not excluded, from the accounts of their military exploits.

The invasion profoundly disrupted these essential social and economic processes even before the Battle of Isandlwana took place. After this as they made their way to Ulundi, the troops turned their attention to the homesteads: looting cattle and prodding their bayonets into the floors to expose grain pits before torching the huts and whatever was left in them. Cattle were raided and either consumed or sold. Cattle raiding is generally treated in the literature as an accepted part of warfare; references to hundreds, even thousands, of head raided and sold are commonplace. They are considered to be the property of the enemy and as such are legitimate targets. And it is rare to find any reference beyond their value as livestock to their role of milch cows. But Harriette Colenso was very aware of the further consequences of cattle raiding: an extract from a letter on the consequences of a punitive raid in 1906 will have to represent a lifetime of bitter and direct experience of violence against and among the Zulu: "What with short crops from the dry summer, & the destruction of what they had, beside the loss of milk, the babies & old folk will suffer sadly."[17] The historical imagination will have to apply a gendered perspective to "livestock" before it is able to make history out of the endless references to "cattle raids" in South African sources.

Even the retreat into strongholds and hiding places could only be a temporary measure and always came with a cost: the abandonment of crops or food reserves, often of cattle, and therefore shortages in basic foodstuffs. Sanitation very soon became a problem, manifested by disease in both the summer (intestinal) and winter (pulmonary), exacerbated by inadequate diet and the shortage of food. And always there were the extra difficulties caused by having to care for the very young and the very old in such conditions. This would normally be the responsibility of women, with men helping with heavy work, but in times of war there could be no assistance from the homesteads' active men, who would be serving in the army. Despite the fact that such matters receive little mention in the sources they have to be considered when constructing any account of these wars of dispossession. To give one of the few specific examples that I have come across (although this applies to a consequence of the invasion, not the invasion itself), during the Zulu civil war a trader visited

> the rocks and caves, where they were living in a most deplorable state, dying in dozens from deprivation and dysentery, children perishing at their mother's breast for want of nourishment, and each person covered with the itch and otherwise emaciated, and if nothing is done to relieve them before the winter sets in there will be scarcely a soul alive, for all their crops were then cut and trodden by Usibepu's forces.[18]

Such situations were replicated countless times during the nineteenth-century wars of dispossession and must be kept in mind in order to decode such statements as "All you have got to do is take cattle, annoy him by burning his kraals, and eventually destroy his crops."

It was the pressure of such conditions, or the fear that such conditions might arise, and the realization of what the end would be if they did, which was a major concern of African military leaders. And such conditions were the result not only of the presence of British troops on African soil but also of the mobilization of huge numbers of the Zulu soldiers. Feeding and supporting the Zulu army when mobilized was always a problem: soldiers attending state functions at military homesteads were often hungry, and such events were on occasion terminated because of the difficulty of supplying the large numbers of men with food. There are many references in the literature on the invasion to the hunger suffered by men in the army and some to the considerable damage this did the resources of the areas through which they marched. After a battle it was assumed that Zulu soldiers would return to their homesteads for ritual purposes and to restore their physical strength after what was often a time of extreme privation while in service. The consequences of this for the Zulu military tacticians were of course profound: above all it made it impossible to conduct a protracted campaign that would sustain uninterrupted pressure on the invaders. But references to the women who ensured that the basic processes of survival continued in the homestead, or caring for others while scrambling to places of safety, or in the hiding places themselves are rare indeed.

By July 1879, Chelmsford had managed to get his troops into the valley of the White Mfolozi, in the vicinity of the royal homesteads built there. On July 4, Chelmsford assembled 5,000 men into a square; the Zulu attacked and were driven off. The encounter came to be known as the Battle of Ulundi and was declared to have ended the Zulu war and the reign of the Zulu king. I have long argued that this is a misinterpretation: that to understand the significance of the battle one has to situate it in a broader context. By July 1879, both sides in the conflict needed peace. With their supply lines extended to their limit, the British could not continue the military occupation of the country, and to inflict a more thorough defeat on the Zulu would have required a radical change in military leadership and tactics that was impossible politically. The Zulu also needed an end to the conflict and the withdrawal of the British troops. Their suffering had been severe as a result not only of direct military action but also of the measures taken against the people and their homes, stock, and property. It was now midwinter; if they were to survive in the longer term there had to be peace before the spring rains and the time for planting began.

The opportunity for both sides to reach some sort of accommodation came with the resignation of Lord Chelmsford after the Battle of Ulundi and the arrival of Sir Garnet Wolseley with instructions to make peace with the Zulu as soon as he could. He revived the old justification for the war that Chelmsford had abandoned: the British "were not & had never been at war with the Zulu people: our dispute was with Cetshwayo."[19]

So here, at the end of an invasion that killed thousands in battle and had a catastrophic effect on Zulu society as a whole, and during which military force was used deliberately against the civilian population, the original justification for the war was revived. Attention was shifted away from the civilian population to its leaders: the war took the form of a number of pitched battles between armed men led by heroes created and recreated by military historians, their readers, movie makers, tour guides, hoteliers, and journalists ever since. The day-to-day struggle of the people of the Zulu kingdom, whose lives and deaths were of such significance and concern to the military of both sides, is demoted, closed off from consideration, and then forgotten.

But I make this point not just to draw attention to the forgotten humanitarian consequences of the war but also to argue that the conventional concentration on the battles in the conflict is both bad social history and bad military history. Thus in his discussion of the reasons why Zulu chiefs surrendered after the Battle of Ulundi, the most prominent historian of the war writes that they were "realistic," "pragmatic," and based their decision on a "rational calculation on how best to enhance personal power and independence."[20] In this way, in a book that seeks to advance the "Zulu dimension of the struggle," he explains Zulu motives in terms that could apply equally to any MBA student today.

In this essay I have tried to emphasize the need to contextualize military confrontation by drawing attention to the consequences of the attacks on the sites of production and means of sustenance of non-combatants in the wars of dispossession in southern Africa generally and in the conquest of the Zulu kingdom in particular. This strategy weakened African resistance by undermining the social and economic structures on which the military depended. But for the military and their historians, war – or at least war as it is presented to the wider public – is armed confrontation between armed men, and victory comes to the side that applies direct, military violence most successfully. The dependence of the military on outsiders, the infliction of violence on those without arms, and the consequences of social disruption on the very young and the very old and the women who look after them are themes that are steadily pushed to the margins in conventional accounts, leaving at the centre men: men in command, men who predicted the war, men who successfully analyzed the situation, men who effectively applied the weaponry at their command to kill other men. Of course, historians have dislodged these victors from their podiums in many cases. But I believe that this still has to happen in South African historiography.

Postscript

This essay was written over the Easter weekend 2004 with one ear on the news coming out of Iraq as resistance to invasion and occupation built up. Of course, the situation there was not directly comparable with the one I have dealt with here.[21] But there are shared resonances in these very different struggles in the history of imperialism, in the military posturing and cultural arrogance, in the determination of the invaders to present themselves as in control when the evidence suggests they are not, in their absence of self-criticism, their inability to see either military or moral capacities in those they have invaded, and the confidence with which they represent the views of the people whose interests they assert they are defending. It is dangerous to make comparisons like this over such wide reaches of time, space, and cultures, yet there are surely useful links to be made, if not in the histories of war then at least in the histories of imperial warfare. I hope that the different areas of specialization of the contributors to this book will facilitate such comparisons. It seems to me an urgent task as military force and military argument, as limited as ever in its range and understanding, gains such a grip on our lives in the opening years of the twenty-first century.

Notes

1 In "Battling with Banality," *The Journal of Natal and Zulu History* 18 (1998), 156–93.

2 *The New Shorter Oxford English Dictionary on Historical Principles* (Oxford: Clarendon Press, 1993).

3 "Rules as to Bombardment by Aircraft, 1921," quoted in E.J. Hobsbawm, *The Age of Extremes: The Short Twentieth Century 1914–1991* (London: Michael Joseph, 1994), 21.

4 See correspondence in *The London Gazette*, March 28, 1879.

5 My argument that the significance of the Battle of Ulundi was distorted by the British officers who needed such a victory to restore their reputations drew on the contemporary correspondence of John Colenso, Bishop of Natal, and was first put forward in "A Note on Firearms in the Zulu Kingdom with Special Reference to the Anglo-Zulu War 1879," *Journal of African History* 12, 4 (1971), 557–70. It has been contested by John Laband in *Kingdom in Crisis: The Zulu Response to the British Invasion of 1879* (Pietermaritzburg: University of Natal Press, 1992), 221.

6 The conventional translation "military kraals" is misleading in that it obscured the fact that they were royal homesteads in which numbers of non-combatants lived and worked.

7 Jeff Peires, *The Dead Will Arise* (Braamfontein: Ravan Press, 1989), 21.

8 Helen Bradford, "Through Gendered Eyes: Nongqawuse and the Great Xhosa Cattle-killing," paper presented at a University of the Western Cape/African Gender Institute seminar, Cape Town, October 9, 2001.

9 Gerald French, *Lord Chelmsford and the Zulu War* (London: John Lane, 1939), 10–11.

10 Bulwer to Hicks Beach, April 16, 1879, and encl. 2, Chelmsford to Secretary of State for War, April 11, 1879, British Parliamentary Papers, Cd2318, no. 13.

11 John Laband, *Rope of Sand: The Rise and Fall of the Zulu Kingdom in the Nineteenth Century* (Jeppestown: Jonathan Ball, 1995), 210.

12 In my opinion, too much significance is given to the *amakhanda*'s military and not enough to its residential and productive role: Chelmsford's justification for attacking civilians and their property changed after Isandlwana, from justifiable but regrettable to desirable. I don't see why "people such as the Zulu" are more vulnerable to starvation tactics than any others.

13 Laband, *Rope of Sand*, 246.

14 Ibid., 292–93.

15 Ibid., 300. These points are repeated and emphasized in *The Illustrated Guide to the Anglo-Zulu War* (Pietermaritzburg: University of Natal Press, 2000), in which it is possible to detect some shifts of emphasis. See 43–44 especially, where argument 3 is suggested in "Inevitably, civilians were the greatest victims of this policy."

16 The point being made here is recognized in a recent reader in which it is said of "colonial warfare" that "the ruthless destruction of lives, property, and crops revealed the emergence of total warfare for the local people however limited an affair it might be for the invaders." Martin Navias and Tim Moreman, "Limited War and Developing Countries," in *War*, ed. Lawrence Freedman (Oxford: Oxford University Press, 1994), 309.

17 Harriette Colenso to Frank Colenso, March 16, 1906, Rhodes House, Colenso collection RH 1286 (1).

18 Quoted in Jeff Guy, *The Destruction of the Zulu Kingdom* (London: Longman, 1979), 219. For some examples from the invasion, refer to the appalling W.E. Montague, *Campaigning in South Africa: Reminiscences of an Officer in 1879* (Edinburgh and London: William Blackwood, 1880), 183, 195, 217.

19 Ibid., 61.

20 Laband, *Kingdom in Crisis*, 245. The relevant passage was amended slightly and used in the same author's *Rope of Sand*, from which I have also drawn.

21 I tried to deal with some of these historical resonances in the events just before the invasion of Iraq in an article in the *Mail & Guardian*, March 7, 2003, entitled "Lessons from Imperial History," which was published subsequently in the *Mail & Guardian Bedside Book 2003* (Bellevue: Jacana, 2003).

5 Chris Madsen

Between Law and Inhumanity

Canadian Troops and British Responses to Guerrilla Warfare in the South African War

ounter-insurgency ranks among the most difficult types of military operations that conventional armies face. For Western military professionals, trained to seek quick decision through material and technological advantage, the patience and flexibility accorded the human element in insurgencies, when combined with clear strategic and operational thinking, can almost prove insurmountable. Such conflicts are usually protracted, messy in conduct, and make it hard to distinguish between combatants and non-combatant civilian populations. Mao Zedong, the leading military theorist and practitioner of this form of warfare, made virtues of these characteristics in formulating a strategy for the weak to win over the strong. Guerrilla warfare, a sub-set of insurgency, represents a stage or concept of operations designed to wear down, drain the strength, and undermine the resolve of an occupying military force. Conventional armies do not have a monopoly over warfare. Whether adopted by choice or by circumstance, guerrilla operations rely on support and sustenance from the civilian population, for whom guerrillas claim to be fighting. Consequently, civilians often become targets for policies and reprisals by armies fighting irregular forces. Though great progress was made with the additional protocols to the 1949 Geneva Conventions, absolute protection for civilians in time of war or armed insurrection still remains tenuous under today's law of armed conflict. Military forces in Iraq and Afghanistan confront tactics and choices remarkably similar to those faced by British generals and troops from the self-governing colonies during the later stages of the South African War of 1899–1902, when another enemy refused to give up. Civilians, then and now, typically suffered most as part of a co-ordinated military campaign.

Most Canadians, accustomed to celebrating their soldiers as peacekeepers, would be very surprised to learn that their soldiers engaged in harsh and cruel measures under official British orders. Military books and sanitized regimental histories leave the impression that Canadians fought the Boers with little impact on civilians, who are hardly mentioned. Reality was far different, since a policy of deliberate destruction in such a harsh and inhospitable countryside was tantamount to slow death by starvation, exposure, or disease. As the Canadian Armed Forces slowly shed the garrison mentality of the Cold War and return to imperial policing under coalition and United Nations auspices, South Africa and, more recently, Somalia (Canada's My Lai) remind Canadians that no armed forces is above mistreating civilians, if afforded the opportunity. Adherence to the rule of law, to which Canada subscribes domestically and internationally, enforcement of military discipline, and vigilance from an informed public provide safeguards against the worst abuses in the military context. The Canadian experience in the guerrilla phase of the South African War has direct relevance to current and future military operations in the modern world and the multiple ways in which Canadian troops might interact with civilians abroad.

In retrospect, the conduct of the British and Canadians during the South African War may seem brutal and barbarous to people appalled at "pacification" by the Americans in Vietnam, "ethnic cleansing" by the various warring sides in the former Yugoslavia, or recent events in Iraq. It was also undoubtedly so to some contemporaries in Great Britain and Canada at the beginning of the last century. French-speaking Quebec was almost solidly against Canadian participation in Great Britain's imperial wars and sympathetic to the Boers, another minority language group being dominated by British military force. Nonetheless, British and colonial military forces generally acted within the dictates of international and national laws as they existed at the time. Although seemingly inhumane, the policies and measures adopted against the Boers were strictly legal. Military commanders and soldiers worked within the law.

The timeframe involves the third phase of the war in South Africa, roughly from mid-1900 to spring 1902, when the Boers refused to concede defeat and pursued guerrilla warfare against the British in smaller commandos. The Boer military leader Christiaan De Wet adopted classical guerrilla tactics. The Boers attacked where British and other auxiliary troops were weakest, seized supplies, and then disappeared when confronted with stronger columns of flying forces. Eager to bring the war to a quick conclusion and frustrated by Boer actions, British commanders Roberts and Kitchener responded with a number of drastic measures. The existing laws of war and disseminated knowledge about them within British and Canadian forces at the time of the South African War established expected standards of conduct toward civilians and their property. The rules of the game lasted until the gradual escalation of Kitchener's military approach toward irregular opponents. Harsh measures once considered exceptional became routine and systematic. Food and livestock were requisitioned, houses and crops were burned, and Boer families were concentrated into camps under British custody. Canadian troops, even though progressively fewer on the ground during this period, were observers and participants in the uglier side of the South African War with respect to civilians.

The law under which British and Canadian troops, and in fact the Boers as well, fought was based on established usage and custom at the international level. These practices had evolved over several centuries of land warfare on the European continent and abroad. Although national peculiarities always pertained, several attempts to codify common usages and customs in a more formal way were undertaken during the late nineteenth century. A convention for the care and treatment of wounded soldiers in the field was concluded at Geneva in 1864, and a declaration prohibiting explosive projectiles below a certain weight was signed at St. Petersburg in 1868. These written agreements were binding upon all states that signed and ratified, including Great Britain on behalf of itself and the component parts of the British empire.

Delegates from leading European nations subsequently gathered at Brussels in 1874 to draft a comprehensive legal code to govern the conduct of war on land. This admirable effort seemed timely after experiences in the Franco-Prussian War (1870–71), but since states could agree on neither the precise wording nor the topics for consideration, the resulting document represented little more than a statement of general principles. When delegates met again at The Hague in 1899 at the request of the Russian czar, the earlier Brussels draft code was revisited, and a new set of regulations concerning the laws and customs of land warfare was agreed upon. Great Britain ratified the Hague Regulations, issued as an annex to the convention by the larger peace conference, on September 4, 1900, by then already two years into the South African War.

The law of war, as embodied in the 1899 Hague Regulations, dealt tangentially with civilians and their treatment. Although British historian Geoffrey Best has argued that humanity was the guiding impulse behind international efforts to codify the laws of war, the primary purpose of existing codification, at least up to the mid-twentieth century, was to promote a degree of predictability between opposing armed forces.[1] Civilians did not receive formal status and protection under the laws of war until the Geneva Conventions of 1949. The 1899 Hague Regulations instead reflected the concern for armies and their relations with each other and any civilian populations under their control or in their way during military operations. Specific articles defined who was accorded combatant status, the rights and obligations of prisoners of war, accepted means and methods in the conduct of war, the handling of spies, the operation of flags of truce, capitulation, armistices, and occupation of enemy territory. The regulations were not binding in the sense of the 1864 Geneva Convention or the St. Petersburg Declaration. States, which ratified the larger Hague Convention, merely undertook to issue instructions to their military forces in conformity with the regulations. The British government, in particular, viewed the regulations as an ideal standard for its armed forces to aspire to but that could be departed from if and when military necessity demanded. The South African War soon provided ample room for interpretation and unforeseen exceptions.

Great Britain did not fulfil the requirement that the Hague Regulations be known through the armed forces under its control and authority before the end of the South African War and instead relied on an existing manual for guidance. In the absence of a dedicated handbook, reference was made to the *Manual of Military Law,* first published in 1884 and in its fourth edition by 1899.[2] The manual had been prepared and revised under the Parliamentary Counsel by several editors and individual authors for application to imperial and colonial troops falling under purview of the Army Act. Besides detailed coverage of military law in general, the manual included one chapter written by Lord Thring, on the customs of war. The text made specific reference to the expected treatment to be furnished civilians:

> Old men, women and children, wherever found, will be carefully guarded from outrage, unless they take up arms, in which case they subject themselves to the rigid rules of war applicable to combatants and sometimes to still harsher treatment. . . . The general population of the enemy's country who form no part of the armed forces cannot justly be exposed so long as they abstain from acts of hostility, to any description of violence. . . . The first duty of a citizen is to defend his country, but this defence must be conducted according to the customs of war. These customs require that an enemy should be able to distinguish between the armed forces and the general population of the country in order that he may spare the latter, without exposing his troops to be attacked by persons when he might reasonably suppose to be engaged only in peaceful occupations.[3]

Thus, clear limits were delineated between combatants and non-combatants. Civilians who decided to participate in fighting or hostilities in any way lost the minimum protections afforded under the laws of war and faced severe sanctions. The manual cited two main authorities primarily: Emmerich de Vattel's *Law of Nations* and Francis Lieber's code for the federal army during the American Civil War. Vattel, an eighteenth-century legal thinker and writer, argued that in order to be legitimate, war needed to be conducted according to established rules based in natural law. Killing of non-combatants and destruction of private property, although unfortunate consequences arising from resort to force, had to bear some relation to the definite military objectives to be achieved. This idea forms the basis for proportionality within today's law of armed conflict. War was not simply a licence for armies to do what they wanted, particularly concerning civilians. The American jurist Lieber turned Vattel's legalistic and philosophical language into the practical and understandable Union Army general order no. 100, the direct forerunner to Lord Thring's chapter in the British *Manual of Military Law*.

Officers were expected to be familiar with the laws of war and standards of conduct toward civilians. The manual, sold through Her Majesty's Stationery Office, was widely available in its various editions in the military forces of Great Britain and self-governing colonies like Canada. As the most current publication on the subject, the manual provided a basis for instruction and study to pass the written component of an officer's promotion examinations, mandatory since abolition of purchase in 1869. Most British professional military officers and regular non-commissioned officers in South Africa were familiar with the contents of the *Manual of Military Law* and the multitude of regulations it supported. Few Canadian officers and soldiers, on the other hand, were so conversant in the intricacies of military law and laws of war. No system of promotion examinations existed to reward merit and weed out the incompetent, and patronage remained an enduring feature of the late-nineteenth-century Canadian militia. Furthermore, the Canadian government's decision to recruit special service contingents for South Africa brought in many men without previous military experience or training. It is almost certain that most Canadian officers possessed limited knowledge of the Geneva Convention, the Hague Regulations, or the *Manual of Military Law*. Nonetheless, once in the field, all Canadian troops fell under the disciplinary provisions of the British Army Act, read out weekly on parade. They were held to the same standard as any other British imperial or colonial soldiers. The Canadians used common sense, mimicked the tactics of their Boer opponents, and like all good soldiers, obeyed orders from higher authorities.

The actions of the Boers and efforts by British senior commanders to overcome them largely dictated the tenor of the war in South Africa. The British had badly underestimated the strength and resolve of the Boers during the first phase of hostilities. The Boers, unlike the native African peoples whom the British Army fought mostly in the small colonial wars of the late nineteenth century, were white settlers of Dutch descent, tied together by Calvinism and kinship. For them, the struggle was a defence of home and way of life against encroaching British imperial and commercial interests. British imperialists coveted the territories and mineral resources (gold and diamonds) adjoining British possessions. The Boers had earlier bloodied the British, in 1881, and they sought to repeat their success on a larger scale. The barely veiled support of other rival European powers, most particularly impe-rial Germany, provided modern weapons and diplomatic clout to the Boers. Large, organized, conventional formations handed British military forces a series of humiliating defeats and reverses, culminating in the infamous Black Week during December 1899. It was in this context that the first Canadian troops arrived in South Africa and the British anxiously asked for more.

The failures in South Africa also heralded the arrival of a new British mili-tary leadership with the determination and drive to attain victory once and for all. Field Marshal Lord Roberts possessed extensive fighting experience in India and Afghanistan, and his understudy, Major General Lord Kitchener, was fresh from imperial victory in Sudan. They were immensely popular with the British Victorian public as well as with the troops in the field. The two men accepted the daunting task of turning the situation in South Africa around and attacked the problem with greater clarity of strategic thinking than preceding British generals. As reinforcements arrived from home and abroad, Roberts planned to take the offensive into the Boer heartland, with advances on Bloemfontein in the Orange Free State and then Pretoria in the Transvaal. The move was bold as the Boers still invested several besieged British garrisons. Roberts identified the Boer capital cities as the operational centre of gravity and developed his concept of operations accordingly. Cana-dian infantry, field artillery, and dragoons attached to British divisions and brigades actively participated in the advance. Conventionally organized Boer military forces resisted, but they seemed powerless to prevent the relentless progress of Roberts' forces. The Boers abandoned their field artillery and sup-ply wagons in order to flee and regroup. Pretoria was captured on June 5, 1900, and Roberts triumphantly reviewed British and Canadian troops in its streets. Roberts and most soldiers believed that the war was almost over. The hope proved premature.

Unable to match Roberts in strength, the Boers harassed his army's long, vulnerable supply lines and shot at British forces from concealed places before disappearing onto the *veldt*. The tactics derived from both practicality and military necessity. The Boers were notoriously short of supplies, most impor-tantly ammunition. Capture of British convoys – predominantly oxen driven at a speed of three to four kilometres per hour – represented a convenient alternative to a declining logistics base. During these ambushes and firefights, thousands of British and some Canadian soldiers surrendered and entered into Boer captivity as prisoners of war. The Boers generally respected the laws of war, more from religious conviction than any precise knowledge of the Hague Regulations and other legal conventions. Boer combatants elected their officers, called field cornets or commandants, and maintained discipline in different ways from professional armies. The Boers either stripped their prisoners of uniform and equipment before releasing them to walk back almost naked to the nearest point of habitation, or forced them to march along with the rest of the commando unit until food ran short, or transferred them back to the rear. Released or liberated soldiers were quickly re-equipped and put back into formation by the British, even though the Boers made many prisoners sign pledges of no further belligerence in exchange for freedom. Whereas the British *Manual of Military Law* acknowledged the legality of such pledges, Roberts and Kitchener showed more concern in making individual Boers live up to similar assurances of neutrality signed after surrender. It was a common occurrence, the Canadians observed, for individual Boers to return to their farms for some rest and recuperation, particularly at harvest time, before going back on commando. In this respect, the Boers were little more than armed civilians who went in and out of the fight selectively: farmers first and reluctant combatants second. For professional soldiers, being captured or bested in combat by amateurs, no matter how much better experienced and suited to the style of warfare in South Africa, was frustrating and frequently humiliating.

The treatment Boers received from the British and Canadians after surrender often depended on the circumstances of their capture and perceived status under the laws of war. The first problem was recognition as legitimate combatants. Under the Hague Regulations and the customs of war on land, those engaged in fighting were required to wear clearly distinguishable uniforms and insignia as well as be organized into recognizable units under a chain of command. It would be a stretch to say that the Boer farmers in revolt fulfilled the former stipulation, since civilian clothes and even captured British khaki uniforms were far more common. Wearing of an enemy's uniform in combat for other than deceptive purposes was an offence under the laws of war, with harsh penalties up to and including death. The Boers, however, possessed no industrial base to produce their own uniforms or other accoutrements of war expected of an advanced society. Civilians under arms, as suggested by Boer clothing, were technically unlawful combatants under laws of war written explicitly with European armies in mind. Although the British adopted a realistic view in this regard and generally granted combatant status, some British and Canadian soldiers took this ambiguousness as an excuse to kill surrendering Boers out of hand. Kitchener was later accused of issuing verbal orders to this effect, although the claim was never proven. The pretext that the Boers were actually civilians fighting in an illegal manner was used to justify drastic actions or to deny them the protections normally afforded prisoners of war. Determination of status, whether civilian or combatant, was left up to qualified tribunals even under the laws of war at that time.

Civilians conducting hostilities, however, posed a vexing problem for

British and Canadian troops in South Africa. Abuse of the white flag and civilian sniping from houses along the line of march were commonplace. In the first instance, resumption of hostilities after a clear indication of surrender or declared non-belligerence was considered an act of treachery. Persons caught in such activities lost the limited protections afforded civilians under the laws and customs of war, and offences carried numerous sanctions, including death. In one case, mounted infantry from the Strathcona's Horse, a Canadian unit recruited predominantly in western Canada and known by its distinctive Stetson hats, were alleged to have hanged Boers who had abused the white flag by shooting at British soldiers advancing to take their surrender in a farmhouse. The fact that the white flag did not stop other Boers in the nearby vicinity from firing on the British and Canadians only confused the issue from a legal perspective. Soldiers inflamed in the heat of battle frequently forgot the restrictions against killing surrendering enemy, white flag or not. The Canadian soldiers from the Strathcona's Horse probably crossed the line of acceptability because an officer quickly intervened to stop the killings and Roberts later issued reprimands to those involved after a court of inquiry. British conduct against civilians signified a major escalation of the conflict.

Private civilian property became subject to special treatment. On April 27, 1900, Trooper Albert Hilder, a member of the 1st Canadian Mounted Rifles (subsequently renamed the Royal Canadian Dragoons) commanded by Lieutenant Colonel François-Louis Lessard, described military operations prior to the march on Pretoria: "Off back to Bloemfontein. Burning every house and commandeering all the sheep and cattle we could lay our hands on. Also taking all the poultry wanted and looting the houses."[4] That excesses took place cannot be denied. Roberts told the South African Field Force that incidents of wanton destruction of farms and seizure of cattle and livestock without proper authority pervaded the troops, especially among the mounted corps, and he held commanding officers responsible for dealing with offenders severely. The censure was not a prohibition; officers countenanced or ordered actions against civilian property in reprisal for Boer transgressions of the law of war and merely sought to limit private initiative when it got out of bounds of official orders. The work was a regulated activity and not the product of an unruly mob.

Shortly thereafter, Kitchener issued amplifying instructions that required troops be detailed for the purpose, act with proclamation, and issue receipts based on fair and established prices. The small pieces of paper handed to the Boer families who watched their farms and dwellings destroyed and their possessions and livelihood taken away were small recompense, especially when they tried to collect later from the British occupation administration. Disaffected Boer civilians later filed claims for compensation, but no receipts were issued to snipers, those who abused the white flag, or burghers who broke oaths of neutrality. After several weeks of foraging and searches for hidden weapons, the Strathcona's Horse started burning farms on August 29, 1900, near Helvetia. In the midst of a hostile civilian population, obedient and disciplined soldiers fought against an elusive and invisible enemy by throwing his kin and family out into the elements.

What was expedient under Roberts gradually became routine and systematic under Kitchener. Lieutenant E.W.B Morrison, a junior officer with a battery of the Royal Canadian Field Artillery, described a punitive expedition as part of Major General Horace Smith-Dorrien's column near Steilpoort in November 1900:

> During the rest of the trek, which lasted four days, our progress was like the old time forays in the Highlands of Scotland two centuries ago. The country is very like Scotland, and we moved on from valley to valley "lifting" cattle and sheep, burning, looting and turning out the women and children to sit and cry beside the ruins of their once beautiful farmsteads. It was the first touch of Kitchener's iron hand. And we were the knuckles. It was a terrible thing to see, and I don't know that I want to see another trip of the sort, but we could not help approving the policy, though it rather revolted most of us to be the instruments.[5]

Canadians officers and soldiers knew what they were doing under higher direction was inhumane, no matter how legal and necessary from a military perspective. Farms or houses belonging to male inhabitants offering resistance or away on commando, which in some neighbourhoods represented by far the majority, were burned or blown up. Columns of British and Canadian troops destroyed dwellings and crops at the expense of civilians.

The chosen policy was a combination of the changed nature of the war and Kitchener's own personality as a military commander. Although the British now controlled every major town and population centre, the intractable Christiaan De Wet and other Boer leaders continued to fight in smaller commandos. In fact, they stirred up resistance in the Orange Free State (renamed the Orange River Colony by the British) and the Transvaal, and at the same time hatched plans to invade deep into the Cape Colony to strike at the heart of British interests in South Africa and encourage a wider rebellion. The guerrilla phase of the war actually commenced around mid-1900, while Roberts was still in command. De Wet and his band blew up railroads, terrorized weaker town garrisons, and led pursuing British columns on a merry chase around the countryside. Kitchener himself directed efforts to bring De Wet to heel, without much success. As long as Boer military forces remained in the field, peace dangled temptingly out of reach because Boer politicians still saw some hope in a favourable outcome to the struggle. Winning an outright victory over the British was probably beyond reach, but the insurgent Boers wanted some degree of independence preserved in the final settlement to make the struggle worthwhile.

Unlike Roberts, Kitchener considered De Wet as more than just a distraction or a nuisance. The charismatic Boer military commander was a dangerous individual, able to exert enormous influence by his example and possibly even to incite subjugated Boers to renewed rebellion. Everything the British had so dearly achieved during the previous two years would thus be undone. A Canadian logistics clerk observed that the Boers are "hanging on but we are not losing many men. Very little fighting is going on. Their game is about over. De Wet is the slippery one. I doubt if we will ever catch him till he is starved out. They beat us travelling hands down."[6] Kitchener privately shared similar thoughts. A long and protracted low-intensity campaign required commitment and troops from all the "white" colonies of the British empire. During a farewell address before departing South Africa, Roberts told collected troops, "You have in fact acted up to the highest standard of patriotism, and by your conspicuous kindness and humanity toward your enemies, and your forbearance and good behaviour in the towns we have occupied, you have caused the Army of Great Britain to be as highly respected, as it must henceforth be greatly feared, in South Africa."[7] What hypocrisy. This same field marshal issued and reissued numerous orders and proclamations telling British and Canadian troops to live off the land as much as possible through requisitions and to destroy farms belonging to civilians who resisted British power along lines of communication. Displaced Boer civilians in the Orange Free State experienced firsthand British "kindness and humanity." Whatever professed humanitarian impulse still lingered under Roberts evaporated when Kitchener took over operational command in South Africa on November 30, 1900.

Kitchener's overriding concern was to bring a timely end to the war, to which Great Britain and other countries within the British empire such as Canada were beginning to tire. The need for victory took precedence over moral scruples. Kitchener was completely ruthless and undoubtedly epitomized the qualities of a true military realist, translated as heroic within the imperial age in which he lived. Nonetheless, he always worked within the bounds of the law, no matter how loose a reading he may have given it. The characterization of Kitchener in the Australian film *Breaker Morant* is exceedingly unfair and says more about popular Australian sentiment toward the British and the South African War, even a century on, than it does about the man. Myth becomes very hard to disentangle from historical truth. Kitchener can be faulted for many things, but he was extremely legal minded. He dealt almost daily with matters of martial law, trials of Boer leaders, paroles and prisoners of war, and discipline among imperial and colonial troops. Kitchener viewed the law and its sanctions as an essential tool for the successful prosecution of military operations and the political objectives of the war. Officers who surrendered British supply convoys, the last source of Boer provisions, were placed before courts martial; those who overstepped the bounds of propriety by shooting prisoners of war, foreign missionaries, or civilians faced severe punishments from military trial. Kitchener confirmed death sentences handed down on two officers, Harry Morant and Peter Handcock, without the leniency shown by Roberts on previous occasions. The high probability that the men involved actually committed the murders in the field, for which they were charged and convicted, reinforced the soundness of military justice and Kitchener's judgment. Kitchener, an authoritarian, was not the type of commander to ignore crimes and serious infractions of discipline. He rarely tolerated behaviour departing from official policy and acted to the fullest extent of military law and the laws of war against transgressors. Military orders and direction from above gave British and Canadian troops sufficient latitude to plunder and mistreat civilians without killing them directly with a bullet. Civilians were condemned to a slower death through dispossession and starvation.

For Canadian mounted troops, the legal nuances were often lost in the rough and tumble world of guerrilla warfare. Like Kitchener, they gave liberal interpretation to the laws of war. As mentioned previously, requisitioning was an established legal custom resorted to by the British and Canadians, whereby armies could take what they needed in terms of food and other essentials from civilians in occupied territory. Canadian troops had practised widespread requisitioning during the 1885 North-West Rebellion in military operations against Louis Riel and Gabriel Dumont. Foraging parties designated for the purpose were organized under the direction of army supply officers, and receipts were sometimes issued for payment later. The British adopted the view that Boers away on commando forfeited any right to reimbursement and their property could be seized outright. Kitchener cracked down on unauthorized seizure of larger livestock such as horses, cattle, and sheep by issuing orders that any collected had to be turned over to the army's supply park for slaughter. The provost marshal meanwhile was instructed to arrest any soldiers found taking away property from native blacks, increasingly used as auxiliaries and guides by the British against the Boer guerrillas. Kitchener – a realist not a racist – actually tried and executed several soldiers accused of looting against indigenous tribes and populations.

The private property of white Boers, ever so hard to determine the loyal from the rebellious, essentially became fair game. Some Canadian soldiers elevated the act of requisitioning to a fine art, spiriting away fowl, swine, and produce. When persuasion failed, they used force against resisting Boer families. Despite official army orders against looting read only days previously, Trooper George Eyre returned to camp on Christmas Eve "with what he calls 'lapping' consisting of a pig, turkey, and about 10 or 12 lbs of bread and some oranges . . . and from his weary look it appears he had considerable difficulty persuading the old Dutch woman to part with her property."[8] The food was stolen right from the kitchen and dinner table, and civilians went without. What did the old woman and her children eat on Christmas, an especially sacred day for the highly religious Boers? For farming people living on bare subsistence in a country with an inhospitable climate and marginal agricultural returns, the scarcity of food was a matter of life and death, aggravated by the hardships of war. Boer civilians could not simply go down to the corner grocery store. British crop burning and livestock confiscation turned availability of food into a deliberate weapon of war. Requisitioning easily gave way to looting and what soldiers casually called thieving, but Canadian officers frequently looked the other way as long as such activities sustained the fighting unit. Canadian and British mounted troops operated at the expense of the civilian population in order to maintain maximum mobility in operations. The Canadians learned to live off the land like the Boer commandos. The difference was that they did not enjoy the support of a sympathetic populace.

Unable to catch De Wet on his own terms, Kitchener targeted the Boer base of supply, intelligence information, and sympathy, namely the civilian population in the Orange Free State and Transvaal. Charles Clark, a Canadian attached to the Army Service Corps, recorded,

> The British must be prepared for some protracted and tedious police operations before the spirit and armed forces of the enemy are thoroughly crushed. That non-combatants will suffer terribly cannot be denied, but after all the Boers themselves, who made the war, are responsible for that and they can avert such suffering by prompt submission.[9]

The immediate precedent was General William Sherman's March to the Sea from Atlanta, which cut a swath of destruction and retribution across the Confederate southern states during the American Civil War. James Spaight, a contemporary British writer on international law, argued that compared to Sherman, Kitchener was humanitarian in his treatment of Boer civilians.[10] Nonetheless, the effect was the same. Kitchener, like Sherman, took the horror of war directly to the people in rebellion and blamed the guerrillas for the drastic measures forced upon the reluctant British. Roberts wrote to Kitchener from London, "Although the Boers do not appear to be in great numbers, they are formidable for the fact that the majority of the inhabitants are on their side and against us whatever may be their professions of loyalty."[11] In an effort to depopulate the countryside, Kitchener embarked on a scheme of destruction and forcible removal of all Boer civilians to camps. The intent was to leave nothing in the country for the Boer commandos to live upon and nowhere for them to hide.

The Boers' critical vulnerability, as identified by Kitchener, was mobility. Confiscations and seizures targeted horses in particular because a Boer without a horse was a diminished military asset. The British also began construction of a network of blockhouses and barbed wire barriers along the major railways anchored to fortified towns and dividing the provinces into smaller sectors. The blockhouses were built to a standard design and used cheap and widely available corrugated iron. Newly arrived Canadian drafts for the South African Constabulary manned several defended points within sight of each other. Inside the sectors, Kitchener deployed greater numbers of mounted infantry to sweep and drive the Boer guerrillas into open battle or onto the fixed fortifications. Although De Wet managed to escape on several more occasions with smaller and smaller bands of devotees, the condition of the Boer commandos became progressively desperate as deprivation and hunger set in during late 1901. Kitchener set the conditions for success, gained the initiative, and merely outwaited the stamina of the guerrillas. Boer combatants, singly or in small groups, gave up the fight and came to the towns and blockhouses to surrender. Kitchener deported captured Boers to detention centres on distant islands such as Bermuda, St. Helena, and Ceylon (British versions of Guantánamo Bay), though the practice was stopped in December 1901. Concern for the plight of their families in the camps was another significant factor for the erstwhile stubborn guerrillas who finally conceded defeat.

Boer civilians lived and died in squalid conditions inside the camps run by British military authorities. Kitchener contended that the forced relocations were necessary for the Boers' own protection and safety. De Wet, however, challenged British motives and actions in his postwar memoirs:

> Could any one ever have thought before the war that the twentieth century could show such barbarities? No. Any one knows that in war, cruelties more horrible than murder can take place, but that such direct and indirect murder should have been committed against defenceless women and children is a thing which I should have staked my head could never have happened in a war waged by the civilized English nation. And yet it happened.[12]

The British became the aggressors and oppressors. By being removed from the battlefield, women, children, and the old were no longer prey to requisitions, looting, and other unwelcome visitations by British troops. Boer patriarchs told wives and daughters that soldiers only came to the door for the purpose of rape. While unfortunately true in some cases, Kitchener's harsh penalties under military law and the growing absence of women removed temptation. Kitchener even issued proclamations that Boers continuing resistance would be charged for the upkeep of their families in the camps, somewhat ironic given that incarceration was not by choice and the British had taken away their property. Neglect and overcrowding were rampant within the camps. Families accustomed to open countryside with kilometres between each other found themselves literally on top of each other in confined spaces. Many camps were poorly situated because the British considered the situation temporary. Fresh water was a constant problem in South Africa, and British supply of food was irregular and barely met subsistence levels. Mortality rates among the elderly and the young increased substantially as hunger-induced diseases swept through the camps.

Conditions in the camps attracted international attention. Military medical authorities blamed poor hygiene among Boer women for the outbreaks. In other words, the Boers themselves were apparently responsible. The full extent of the tragedy in the concentration camps was not known until a visit of inspection by activist Emily Hobhouse, referred to by Kitchener as "that bloody woman." She and other humanitarian critics launched a public campaign against the treatment of Boer civilians and the military administration in South Africa. Kitchener's military strategy was predicated on time to work, but public outcries against neglect and abuse in the camps undermined support for the war back in Great Britain and the self-governing colonies. The British government barred Hobhouse from visiting South Africa again and embarked on its own public relations effort to discredit her and show that conditions in the camps were not as bad as portrayed. Smuggled photographs of emasculated and starving infants, however, were powerful correctives to the official line. The British Army, Hobhouse decried to parliamentarians and the general public at large, was literally killing babies. Eventually, more than 28,000 civilians – women, children, the elderly, and the sick – died in the camps from disease, neglect, and hunger. The figure was more than twice the number of combat casualties on both sides during the war. Thousands of native Africans also died in the camps from the same causes, a statistic commonly hidden in histories of the war.

For Kitchener, these civilians were merely collateral damage to his strategy to defeat the Boer guerrillas and secure a united South Africa within the British empire. The deaths were not intentional, but he was undoubtedly responsible as the operational military commander. Canadian troops, intimately involved with early implementation of Kitchener's policy of destruction and forcible evacuation, were also indirectly responsible, though there was no conceivable way for them to know the scale of the impending tragedy in the concentration camps. Civilians simply disappeared from the scene in train wagons and cattle cars as the Canadians hunted down the guerrillas and manned defended points. Keith Surridge argues that some landed gentry British officers found Kitchener's policies of farm burning and civilian relocation repugnant and held the rural, honourable Boers in higher esteem than the predominantly urban, working-class soldiers whom they led into battle.[13] The free-spirited Canadians and Australians showed less compunction and loyally performed whatever tasks the British high command ordered. Canadian soldiers, however, were in no sense Kitchener's willing executioners. None are known to have served as guards in the concentration camps. Their field of vision was instead limited to the immediate task at hand and surviving a hard war. Since most Canadian soldiers elected to return home at the end of contracted enlistment terms, the terrible things done in the pursuit of victory became a matter of individual conscience for South African War veterans. The coming end to hostilities saved further contingents of the Canadian Mounted Rifles, recently arrived or on their way to South Africa, from experiencing the tribulations, dangers, and brutality of protracted war. During peace negotiations in May 1902, Kitchener wrote to the War Office, "There is no doubt the Boers admit they are thoroughly beaten, but in guerrilla warfare it is far easier to start than it is to end and this the Boer leaders are now feeling."[14] The Boers had lost their farms, possessions, family members, and independence. What they had not lost was their dignity. Kitchener, no gentleman, could not claim the same in his treatment of Boer civilians during the conflict.

Major General John Frederick Charles Fuller, the noted military historian and outspoken critic of conventional thinking within the British military establishment, described the war in South Africa as the last of the gentlemen's wars. In general, Canadian troops and the opposing Boers respected the existing laws and customs of war. Affairs became markedly worse once the Boers decided to continue resistance and embark on a deliberate campaign of guerrilla warfare. The British response under Kitchener was harsh and uncompromising, aimed at final victory over a stubborn and elusive enemy. The civilian population became the focal point. Under official British direction, Canadians burned houses and crops, seized livestock, and forcibly removed Boer women and children to refugee camps, where thousands died from neglect and disease. Boer commandos in the field were left with no secure source of supply and comfort. Although completely legal under the laws of the day, the actions of Canadian troops following British orders verged on inhumanity. Kitchener's ruthlessness eventually delivered victory, but at what human cost in civilian lives?

British conduct in the South African War set a standard for the rest of the century. Kitchener's methods were emulated and refined by the likes of Heinrich Himmler in Eastern Europe, William Westmoreland in Vietnam, Ariel

Sharon in Lebanon, and Tihomir Blaškić in Bosnia. Today, such actions invite the label of war crimes. Operational commanders and their military subordinates can now face prosecution before the new International Criminal Court if national authorities waive jurisdiction before civil or military tribunals. Members of the Canadian Armed Forces are liable under international law – made part of national law by enabling acts of Parliament, disciplinary provisions of the National Defence Act, and the Canadian Criminal Code – for any illegal acts and atrocities committed against civilians during military operations. All orders issued within the Canadian Armed Forces must conform to the law of armed conflict. While the legal standards are now more clearly defined, Canadians had already lost their innocence in the first war of the last century.

Notes

1 Geoffrey Best, *Humanity in Warfare: The Modern History of the International Law of Armed Conflict* (London: Methuen, 1983).
2 A handbook on the laws and customs of war on land, edited by Professor Thomas Holland, was later published. This annotated reproduction of the 1899 Hague Regulations was as much a product of concerns about British conduct of the war in South Africa as it was simply an outstanding responsibility to a particular international instrument. See Thomas Erskine Holland, *The Laws and Customs of War on Land, as Defined by the Hague Convention of 1899* (London: Harrison and Sons, 1904).
3 Great Britain, War Office, *Manual of Military Law 1899* (London: Her Majesty's Stationery Office, 1899), 290–91.
4 A.G. Morris, ed. *A Canadian Mounted Rifleman at War, 1899–1902: The Reminiscences of A.E. Hilder* (Cape Town: Van Riebeeck Society, 2000), 109.
5 E.W.B. Morrison, *With the Guns in South Africa* (Hamilton: Spectator Printing Company, 1901), 277–78.
6 Herb Mackie to mother, August 28, 1900, Archives of Ontario, Toronto, F775 Mss Misc. Coll. 1900, no. 7, MU 2124.
7 Special Army Order, November 29, 1900, Library and Archives Canada, Ottawa, RG 9, series II A3, reel T-10403, vol. 30.
8 Diary, George Alexander Bowers, Troop 4 Squadron C Strathcona's Horse, December 24, 1900, Glenbow Museum and Archives, Calgary (hereafter Glenbow), Private John S. Robson papers, M7908.
9 Diary, December 29, 1900, Glenbow, Clark collection, M223.
10 J.M. Spaight, *War Rights on Land* (London: Macmillan, 1911), 308–10.
11 Letter, Roberts to Kitchener, January 25, 1901, National Archives, Kew (hereafter NA), Kitchener papers, PRO 30/57/20.
12 Christiaan Rudolf De Wet, *Three Years' War* (New York: Charles Scribner's Sons, 1902), 192–93.
13 Keith Surridge, "'All You Soldiers Are What We Call Pro-Boer': The Military Critique of the South African War, 1899–1902," *History* 82 (1997), 591–94.
14 Letter, Kitchener to John Broderick, May 25, 1902, NA, Kitchener papers, PRO 30/57/22.

Colonial Conquest and the Struggle for the Presence of the Colonial State in German East Africa, 1885–1903

Europe's colonial projects in Africa were driven by a relatively small number of Europeans working with limited resources. Although colonial projects played an ever increasing role in nineteenth-century metropolitan politics, they did not gain high priority among lawmakers when it came to providing the necessary resources for such adventures. Despite their limited resources, colonial projects were ambitious: territories had to be conquered, political and administrative structures had to be implemented, Africans had to be transformed into subjects of colonial rule, and a colonial economy and infrastructure had to be built.

We can draw some conclusions from this shortage of personnel and resources in the early stages of European colonialism in nineteenth-century East Africa. Colonial occupation was a long and arduous process that, both for the colonizers and colonized, often resulted in ambiguous situations and power relations. And it was not irreversible. Early colonial rule faced the problem of establishing the presence of the colonizers in the occupied territories, but the ability of European colonizers to embed African societies in a stable and constant colonial relationship was limited. In this regard, Europeans experienced similar problems to those faced by the founders of precolonial African states. According to Jeffrey Herbst, a weakness of the latter was the lack of resources to enhance their control beyond the limits of the centre.[1] So it was with the Europeans in the first years of their rule: Europeans did not rule over a cohesive colonial territory but over various places that, like islands of colonial rule and control, were scattered over a huge area.

The question of the colonial state's presence is at the core of my argument. I describe the establishment of German colonial rule in Eastern Africa as a struggle for the visibility of the colonial state. In this struggle, collateral damage was not something to be avoided but part of a politics that saw terror as a means of creating colonial order. The notion of terror comprises two dimensions: on the one side, an unbounded and arbitrary violence; and on the other, a symbolic aspect. The aim of terror is not only to destroy the enemy physically but also to drive home a political message. It is politics by means of staged violence.

In 1883, an expedition of Carl Peters became the point of departure for Germany's colonial project in East Africa. Peters negotiated several treaties of protection with African chiefs. These were endorsed by the German emperor, Wilhelm I, who issued an Imperial Protection Bill over the "acquired" territories, and then confirmed by European diplomats at the negotiating tables on which Africa was partitioned, like the cake in a contemporary cartoon. Several more expeditions of Peters' Deutsch Ostafrika Gesselschaft (DOAG, the German East Africa Company) in the following months "acquired" further territories. Some years later, the first stations were founded. Resembling Potemkin villages, the stations were staffed with a handful of DOAG agents who had little experience in colonial endeavours. Most were young Germans who came to Africa in the hope of finding adventure and fortune but had little knowledge about African societies. Their arrogant and ruthless behaviour led to disaster. In 1888, the outrage of Africans turned into open rebellion. The Germans were expelled from their stations, some were taken hostage, and some murdered.[2]

Some months later, the emperor sent Hermann Wissmann with troops and battleships to subdue what Wissmann called the "Arab insurgency," assuming that its leaders were Arab slave traders who feared the loss of their influence and power. In local history this event was called *vita vya kwanza*, or the First War.[3] However, it was the end of the DOAG adventure and the beginning of the German colonial empire in East Africa as a state-driven project. It was the beginning of what appeared to East Africans as the coming of the four apocalyptic horsemen. German battleships bombarded coastal towns. Sudanese and Ngoni mercenaries landed along with German marine soldiers and plundered. The few reports we have from East Africans describe this time as one of absolute lawlessness and great fear. Mosques and houses of wealthy families were plundered, women were raped, and those suspected of being insurgents were executed without any court hearing. Many coastal people fled their towns and hid in the wilderness of the hinterland.[4] The harsh regime of the first months even provoked the criticism of the German consul at Zanzibar, who described Wissmann's regime as a military dictatorship and accused him of not preventing war crimes by his troops against the local population.[5]

The occupation of the coast was followed by several military campaigns serving either to establish colonial rule in the interior or to maintain that rule against rebellious Africans. Between 1890 and 1903, German expeditions conquered most parts of the colony. In some cases, Germans met fierce resistance.

The war against the Hehe state in the southern highlands lasted over eight years, with a severe defeat of German colonial troops in the Battle of Rugaro in 1891. The Germans finally subdued resistance using a scorched earth strategy between 1894 and 1898, in which more than 100,000 Hehe lost their lives. Although the Hehe campaign was somewhat exceptional·in its duration, in the severity with which it was fought, and in its genocidal will of destruction, one should not forget all the smaller campaigns against African societies in the first decades of German colonial rule, which in their basic patterns were quite similar. And the terror did not end with the colonial occupation. When, in 1905 the Maji Maji uprising struck at the very foundations of German colonial rule, the colonial military reacted with the same scorched earth policy it had used during conquest. It took the Germans two years to suppress the rebellion. Africans paid a heavy toll. More than 200,000 lost their lives, dying at the hands of brutalized soldiers or from the hunger and epidemics that followed the destruction of their livelihood.

Space, Time, and German Colonial Rule

The main problem the Germans faced from the beginning was the lack of sufficient personnel and material resources. Eighty-six German officers took part in the occupation of the coast in 1890. At the end of the nineteenth century, the colonial state had a budget of 6 million Reichsmarks. At that time, 515 civil and military officials served in the colony. Toward the end of German colonial rule in East Africa, in 1913, the number of officials serving in the colony had increased to 737.[6]

Insufficient resources meant an insufficient presence of the colonial state and its agents. Until the end of German rule, administrative structures in many areas of the colony remained incomplete. German pressure was strongest at the coast, where most Germans lived and where the colonial infrastructure was most developed. In the interior, by comparison, the deficient character of German colonial rule was quite apparent. Here, colonial rule manifested itself in the expedition, a mixture of precolonial caravans and modern military units, and the station – simultaneously a defence facility, a diplomatic court, an administrative post, and a symbol of colonial rule itself.[7] Two or three officers and a dozen African troops usually occupied a station. They had to exercise control over an area of hundreds or thousands of square kilometres. Outside the station, the presence of the colonial ruler was, therefore, temporary and unstable.

Colonial officials were sometimes aware of the limited influence of the station, as a report from a high-ranking official in 1903 suggests.[8] However, contemporary maps of the colony did not reflect such insights. Here the visualization or representation of political structures created its own reality. What on the map might be an important colonial centre was sometimes not much more than a compound or a small village, as a contemporary observer ironically stated.[9] Lines drawn between points symbolizing administrative stations suggested the existence of an infrastructure. Often these lines represented footpaths rather than roads. Indeed, the stations were not embedded in a developed colonial infrastructure. Communication and transport were based on porters and caravans, which meant that at some stations, it took months to receive a letter with orders or supplies from the coast.

The stations were therefore islands of colonial rule. Germans described the patterns of colonial rule in the interior by using the image of concentric circles of influence and control surrounding the station. In 1914, a report about the introduction of hut taxes in the kingdom of Urundi described the station's influence on local politics: Africans living close to the station were loyal and obedient to colonial rule, while those who lived some days' journey farther away were firm enemies. The District Commissioner (DCO) describes those African peoples living far from the station, and with whom he had no contact as part of nature or the wilderness.[10] In his words, space and the colonial ruler's movement through space determined the influence of the station. Colonial rule in the interior, therefore, was to a certain degree peripatetic or nomadic.[11]

Officials had to travel to establish and maintain colonial authority. Like a traveller the colonial official arrived at a village, exercised his power as a kind of performance, and then left. In some areas of German East Africa, an official paid a visit only every other year. In such cases, the establishment of colonial rule was a circular rather than a linear process. The shortage of resources meant it was impossible to maintain continuous control over the colonized, and colonial rule therefore had to be re-established again and again. German DCOs who had to face sustained resistance or sporadic rebellions among Africans in their districts regarded their insufficient presence as the main reason for turmoil. This was the official reasoning about the roots of the Maji Maji uprising of 1905–07. Reports alleged that the lack of military presence created the opportunity for the uprising. The Africans had almost forgotten the victories won by Wissmann's troops in the very first years of colonial rule.[12] In most areas of the south, the centre of the uprising, German rule had to be re-established, another report noted.[13]

Colonialism's Theatre of Cruelty: Redoubling the Colonizer's Presence

Facing the volatility of their rule, Germans tried to redouble their presence in the consciousness of the colonized.[14] In 1900, for instance, the German DCO of Tabora reported turmoil in his huge district. He had heard only rumours about rebellious activities and assumed that the insufficient military presence was the reason for a generally subversive attitude in the local population. To prevent an outbreak of open rebellion, he took his soldiers and went on a military expedition for some months. Following a zigzag route he tried to reach as many villages as possible, where he attempted to demonstrate the existence of German rule by an exaggerated performance of military power. Or, as he wrote, "where I reminded the natives of German rule by showing the German flag."[15] As the DCO's report suggests, the demonstration of his power was essentially theatrical. The expedition faced no open resistance anywhere and, therefore, no battle had to be fought. Alternatively, the DCO held parades of his troops or manoeuvres: symbolic battles to impress the Africans.

In reports of German DCOs, this peculiar notion of making an impression was widely used when they speculated about the Africans' perception of their rule.[16] Germans tried to impress Africans by spectacular performances of Western technology, by an authoritarian and self-confident appearance, by the splendour of colonial feasts and ceremonies, and, of course, by the exaggerated display of their military power. The often brutal terror that characterized colonial conquest was directly related to such theatrics. The presence of the colonial state and its agents was to be deeply burned into the mind of the overwhelmed African colonial subject.[17] This, Germans hoped, would redouble the presence of the colonizer, even when not actually present. For Georg Richelmann, who belonged to the first generation of German colonial officers in East Africa, the attempt to impress the local African population was a struggle against obliviousness. According to him, colonial rule was threatened by the absence of the colonizer:

In Africa, the peace is not secured if one stays only at a station and goes once in a while on punitive expeditions. No, preventing the natives from rebellions and unrest is necessary. The Negroes are forgetful people. Today punished, tomorrow when the troops are withdrawn they already recover from their fright and they think: oh, the sky is wide and the Tsar is far away! Therefore we have to make clear to them that the Tsar may come every day.[18]

To impress the Africans, the military engagement had to be unambiguous and in a certain sense spectacular. "Setting a warning by example," as these attempts to impress the Africans by overwhelming military violence were called in the reports of German officers, was a political and military as well as a symbolic strategy. Colonial wars were as much spectacles of power for the establishment of colonial rule as they were military operations. This again becomes obvious when Richelmann debates the symbolic dimensions of the military victories of the colonial troops. For him only clear and unambiguous victories were of use because in Africa, "The natives are always following their desire to be on the side of the most powerful. They will side with the victorious; even if he only appears as such."[19] In this notion of the unambiguous victory, war on non-combatants became part of a military and political strategy. In German East Africa, colonial wars were not, as in the well-known words of Clausewitz, the extension of politics by other means, but politics itself became the extension of colonial wars. War was in many cases and aspects the precondition for colonial politics.

In the first moments of colonial rule, this violence was not bound by law or rules. While overwhelming firepower reduced the risk that Europeans would be killed in action, and therefore eased their decision to wage war, the racist disregard of African humanity made it easy for them to sacrifice African blood. This asymmetry in regard for the humanity of Europeans and Africans had its parallels in the Western indifference toward African political structures. Colonial wars were seen not as wars between states but as wars of civilized nations against disorder and inhumane conditions. If Africans lived in states, these states were considered to be ruled by despotic and reckless rulers who had to be held accountable by Europeans.

Where there was no state, or its legitimacy was ignored, the distinction between combatants and non-combatants became a complicated task. The sharp differentiation between civilians and soldiers, as laid down in the Geneva and Hague Conventions of warfare at the end of the nineteenth century, was a product of European history, in which the state had gained a monopoly of legal force. This monopoly was expressed and visible in the uniform of the soldier, which separated him from civilians. Although in many African societies there existed some kind of distinction between warriors and civilians, African warriors seldom wore uniforms. If there was such a distinction, it was not mentioned or was ignored by European colonizers. And this uncertainty produced another remarkable asymmetry in colonial wars. Colonial wars were wars against the whole population of a certain locality, or in other words, total wars, indiscriminately fought against combatants and civilians.

Where no state structures were assumed to exist, the achievement of victory was hard to define. In the Franco-Prussian War of 1870–71, in which some of the later colonial officers had taken part, the German army had entered Paris and the French had surrendered. In East Africa the situation was quite different. Not only was there no capital to be taken (although Germans did their best to invent some),[20] there was no army to surrender and no general or politician to sign a peace treaty. Therefore, German officers discussed at some length what could be regarded as a victory or a defeat for Africans. In this discussion, the political dimension of colonial warfare became an important issue. Victory, cemented by the ceremonial acceptance of German rule by the defeated and humiliated African ruler, was seen as the basis for the establishment of colonial rule.

For German officers, the African ruler was the embodiment, or the *pars pro toto*, of African political systems.[21] It is therefore unsurprising that their violence was often directly pointed at the body of the chief. He was taken hostage, humiliated in front of his subjects, or even killed. When German troops under the command of Hermann Wissmann occupied the Kilimanjaro region in 1891, they forced Chief Manamate to stand beside a Maxim gun while it was fired. According to an officer who described the scene some years later, the chief, an elderly man, collapsed "shrouded in the smokescreen of the Maxim and swore to Wissmann to stay loyal to German rule for the rest of his life."[22] In this scene, the humiliation of the chief was seen as the beginning of a political relationship. A similar scene happened in Ugogo in the centre of the colony in 1892, when a colonial expedition invaded the residence of Chief Massenta, who was then one of the most powerful chiefs of that region. The German commander ordered his soldiers to drag the aged chief out of his home and beat him. After this they forced him to carry a heavy load. Since this happened before the eyes of his subjects, the German officer assumed that this would make the right impression on the Gogo.[23] Similar symbolism was utilized by Tom von Prince, perhaps Germany's most important military leader in East Africa, after his victory against the rebellious Chief Isike of Unyanyembe. Between 1890 and 1893, the Germans had attempted three times to storm the chief's residence. After the second attempt, which the Germans had to call off because of a shortage of ammunition, the prestige of the chief had risen enormously, von Prince wrote in his reports. Therefore, von Prince fought not only to defeat a rebellious chief but also to consign earlier defeats to oblivion. This battle could end only with the death of Isike and his family. In his reports, von Prince states that the murder of the chief made an enormous impression on the population. They came in procession to pay tribute to him. "Now, German prestige," von Prince argued, "has been established and peace has been secured for the conceivable future."[24]

Non-combatant casualties were the product of mingling politics with war and war with economics. Pillaging, for instance, was part of the military economy of early colonial rule. The German political scientist Trutz von Trotha speaks about the politics of the raid for the early colonial state and points out the spasmodic nature of the state's attempt to generate resources from its subjects. Without a developed colonial infrastructure to feed the expeditions and staff them with porters, the Germans counted on gaining ad hoc resources from Africans. Plundering and taking hostages were seen as a political strategy as well because the provision of resources and labour was regarded as a tributary duty of the subjugated. A related African custom was subverted by the Germans and used for their own aims. Waldemar Werther, leader of an expedition of the Anti-Slavery Lottery, learned from chiefs in Usukuma, south of Lake Victoria, that they had found a "magic" to influence the behaviour of colonial rulers. It was to feed them. A well-fed German, the chiefs told him, ensured peace.[25]

Of course, there were many ambiguities in the Germans' unambiguous victories. The colonial troops might be victorious in military engagements with Africans, but usually they had to leave the region after a few days or weeks. The politics of the expedition did not reckon primarily on the future of colonial rule but on the time of the expedition. When in 1895 colonial troops invaded Uhehe for the first time, they destroyed the residence of Mkwawa, the chief of Uhehe. Mkwawa fled with most of his soldiers and had only to wait for the retreat of the Germans, who did not have enough food for their troops to stay longer. The Germans won one of their most impressive victories in Uhehe, but it was of little use. After the retreat of the Germans, Mkwawa rebuilt his residence and the Germans were able to return to Uhehe only a year later.[26]

The terror of the conquest divided the world between victors and vanquished but hardly created a stable relationship between rulers and ruled. Even to Africans, who had never heard of the Hague Convention of Land Warfare, the brutality of German colonial troops was beyond all rationale. A contemporary African singer described the Germans as children with big sticks.[27] Escape was the main reaction of Africans who saw the arrival of colonial troops in their locality. Nevertheless, this often started another circle of violence because many colonial officers regarded such escape as a clear sign of resistance.[28]

The idea of impressing Africans was based on a kind of colonial mimicry in which the Europeans imagined themselves into an African world that was mainly a mirror of their own prejudices and fantasies. If one measures the success of the German strategy by the state of security in the colony, it was a complete failure. Up to 1903, not one year passed without major military campaigns to subdue insurgencies. In some areas, like Uhehe or Unyanyembe, the situation was characterized by a latent state of war lasting for years. Here the Germans could not move without military guard.[29] However, the politics of punitive expeditions was increasingly criticized by officials in the colonial government. In 1903, a draft circular regulating the authority of officers and colonial officials declared the failure of this policy. In a remarkably harsh tone the acting governor, Franz Stuhlmann, condemned the practice of collective punishment of villages or whole areas by colonial troops. The tactic prevented any peaceful economic and political development in the colony, where, as he pointed out, the "natives are the main source of wealth, since there are no natural resources like minerals."[30] The circular demanded a change in German colonial policies toward Africans because, as Stuhlmann argued, with the conquest of Urundi in 1903 the era of conquest had ended. Still, it would take some years before a change in colonial policy was implemented. When, in 1905, the Maji Maji uprising endangered German rule, the military reacted with the same scorched earth policy of the preceding years.

The acting governor faced a basic dilemma in German colonial policy. In the early days of German colonial rule in East Africa, the military dominated the scene. For the officers, colonial policy was essentially conquest and subjugation.[31] The establishment of colonial rule in the interior was more a gathering of trophies of subjugation and military victories than the implementation of a coherent political strategy. The needs of military expeditions for food and porters influenced in great part the pattern of German colonial policy in the interior. Stations were built according to a military point of view. Many were later abandoned because their location was unhealthy or because they were of little use for administrative purposes.

In the 1890s, administrative structures were successively established on the coast, but officers still dominated colonial administration in the hinterland. They showed little inclination to integrate themselves into the bureaucratic apparatus of "assessors," as they contemptuously called the civil servants in Dar es Salaam. Regarding the rather confused responsibilities of the central administration, they were right. In the first years, the commander-in-chief of the colonial troops was located in the Reichsmarineamt (Imperial Naval Bureau), not in the Colonial Department of the Foreign Ministry, which was the senior administrative body for the colonies. In 1896, this was changed and colonial troops came under the command of the Colonial department. The governor formally became the commander-in-chief. What did not change during the colonial era was the differences between promotion of civil servants and of the military. While the success of civil servants was increasingly measured by the level of political stability in their districts or spheres of responsibility, officers achieved merit if they were good soldiers. Large military campaigns counted as a year of war for their pensions, and spectacular victories were honoured with military decorations. Therefore, they had little incentive to avoid war.[32]

To some extent, many officers opposed the colonial system as designed in Berlin or in the government bureaus in Dar es Salaam. Especially in the later years of colonial rule, they were nostalgic for earlier times, when they had not been bound by degrees and laws issued by the bureaucracy. In the final years of the German empire, they tried to preserve their autonomy in the colonial apparatus, and because of the poorly developed infrastructure, they often succeeded. Letters with government directives took weeks or months to reach the DCOs in the interior. Reports, which informed the government about recent developments in the district, had to go the same long route, if they were written at all.

Occasionally it seemed that the DCOs intended to leave their seniors in Dar es Salaam in the dark about the situation in their districts. A compelling example is the invasion of Uhehe in 1896. The commanding officer, Tom von Prince, responded only reluctantly to requests from the newly arrived governor, Eduard von Liebert, to inform him about the latest political developments. Laconically he wrote in a report that he had no time to provide all the requested reports because he was busy with reordering the political system in Uhehe and added that this was a task not for a bureaucrat but for an independent ruler. Von Liebert was left with no choice but to travel to Uhehe to assess the situation for himself.[33]

The politics of the expedition created choreographies rather than political structures. If one looks at how colonial rule was established in many parts of the colony, the importance of symbolic strategies becomes obvious. An expedition's entry into the residence of an African ruler was an intricate moment. It was full of ambiguity, uncertainty, and ceremony. It was at this moment that the colonial order was established and the relationship between the colonizer and the colonized was negotiated. When, for example, the first expedition reached Ujiji in 1893, the German officer sent a delegation to inform the local population of its arrival. Near Ujiji, the expedition halted to wait for a delegation of the town's elites to arrive for negotiations. After the negotiations, the expedition entered the town with a parade of troops, military music, and the flag the forefront. This represented the beginning of colonial rule in Ujiji.[34] Such performances constituted the colonial order as a ceremonial arrangement, in which political ties between the colonizer and the colonized were enacted in role play.

The volatile presence of colonial representatives was related to meagre knowledge about the societies they wanted to subdue. Conquest coincided with exploration, and this had serious consequences for the establishment of colonial rule. The colonial officer seldom had accurate knowledge of the place he was about to enter. He was therefore highly dependent on Africans, whether they were members of his expedition or local people. This opened the door for manipulation of the officer. In some cases, African guides tried to prevent colonial forces from entering specific areas by providing false information. In others, African chiefs tried to provoke conflict between the colonial officer and the chief's neighbouring rival by stating that the latter was a fierce opponent of colonial rule. The accused chief was rarely able to deny the claim because the German officer would usually then aggressively enter his territory, ready to suppress any resistance. The chief often had to choose between fleeing, which was taken by the expedition's officers as a sign of resistance, or openly resisting, which would confirm the accusations.

The Germans did not usually transform the structures of African rule but instead changed its representational patterns. This was case with the introduction of German colonial rule on the Makonde plateau. In 1890, the Germans started negotiations with Machemba, one of the most powerful chiefs of the plateau. Rochus Schmidt, the first DCO of Lindi, describes in his memoirs how he exchanged gifts of cloth in order to establish contacts with Machemba.[35] Machemba tried to keep open as many options as possible. He avoided conflict by constantly negotiating with Germans but more or less openly refused any attempt to establish a German foothold in his territory. After three unsuccessful expeditions to remove him from power, German officials negotiated his acceptance of their sovereignty. Machemba signed the treaty and received the German flag as a sign of his submission. The Germans thought this would be the happy end to their attempts to introduce colonial rule in the region, but for Machemba the treaty remained irrelevant because German troops left his area after the negotiations.[36] About five years later, the Germans sent the *wali* of Sudi from the coast to investigate Machemba's attitude toward colonial rule. The wali reported that Machemba still accepted the sovereignty of the Germans.[37] When, some months later, the commander of the colonial army, Colonel von Trotha, travelled through the colony and visited Machemba, he confirmed the report of the wali. First doubts about Machemba's attitude arose when, some weeks later, another expedition visited him. The expedition's leader paid great attention to the condition of the German flag hoisted in the chief's residence. According to him, the flag had been hoisted only a few hours before his arrival, an assumption based on the flag's sharp folds. He took this as proof of Machemba's dubious attitude. This shows the ways in which, in the reasoning of the German officers, the symbols of colonial rule became synonymous with colonial rule itself.[38] What followed was the increasing deterioration of relations, ending with the flight of Machemba to Portuguese East Africa in 1898.

The Invention of Colonial Warfare

German officers often grounded their arguments for the necessity of the unambiguous victory on the assumption that African warfare was of a special nature. It was believed that unlike European wars, where notions of civilization and humanity set a limit to the violence, African wars were characterized by the unrestrained cruelty of the parties. The Hehe, who had a reputation for mutilating their enemies, were often presented as an example. However, after the German conquest of Uhehe, Ernst Nigmann, the first DCO in Iringa, studied the customs and history of the Hehe and found nothing that confirmed these accusations.[39] Notions of the African way of warfare were thus mainly an invention of German colonial officers, helping to legitimize the use of a scorched earth policy. Only if pillars of smoke rose up from burnt villages, only if the chief saw the destroyed remains of his residence, and only if the villagers lost all their property and livestock, the Germans assumed, would they regard themselves defeated.[40]

In colonial warfare, the distinction between regular and irregular troops had never been very sharp. A colonial expedition was a very complex endeavour, not exclusively dominated by German military structures. An expedition often included women and servants of the *askari* (African soldiers), porters of food and equipment, and irregulars, known in East Africa as *rugaruga*. The German officers may have exercised a harsh discipline over their askari, but they had only little control over the rest of the expedition. We have some reports about incidents in which servants or women of askari travelling with colonial expeditions looted villagers, thus provoking tensions that sometimes ended in open warfare.[41]

The Germans used rugaruga widely as auxiliary troops in their campaigns in Unyamwezi and Usukuma, in the west of the colony, especially for reconnaissance operations and for chasing escaping African warriors. The rugaruga had emerged in the context of the nineteenth-century caravan trade, where they served as mercenaries for coastal traders and African warlords like Mirambo and Nyungu ya Mawe. From the few sources we have about them, it seems that rugaruga were mostly young men who had been uprooted in the political chaos of the time. Some of them were former slaves; others had been porters in various caravans.[42] What attracted some German officers to the rugaruga were their quasi-military habits. Many of them wore a kind of uniform, a red cape, and most of them were, to certain degree, trained in the use of firearms. Some officers compared them to the Prussian territorial reserve units.[43] Others were more sceptical, lamenting their lack of discipline. "They squander a lot of ammunition," an officer wrote, "and demand a lot of money in form of clothes, gifts and food, but escape when the situation on battlefield becomes critical."[44] Despite such reservations, a consensus developed among the Germans that the rugaruga were especially useful because of their knowledge of local conditions and their brutality against the civil population. The same officer, summarizing his experiences with rugaruga in breaking the resistance of Chief Isike of Unyanyembe, remarked,

> The ruga-ruga are of use, if one likes to destroy whole regions. In that they are
> top-notch. If you left them alone in their customary ways of war, the battle

against Sike would already have been won, but the land would have been destroyed and women and children would have been robbed and enslaved.[45]

This was exactly the purpose for which German officers used the rugaruga. The motives of those chiefs who supplied the Germans with rugaruga were as complex as the often labyrinthine local politics. In some places, Germans were seen as powerful allies in conflicts that had little to do with colonial rule, and in this regard took up a role that coastal traders had played some twenty years before. In addition to the political aims of chiefs, the prospect of loot played an important role in the recruitment of rugaruga mercenaries.

Not prevention of war crimes but toleration or even furtherance of them lay at the basis of German colonial politics. This was also the case with their regular troops. The Germans had recruited the core of their colonial army in Sudan and Portuguese East Africa, what is today Mozambique. There are some indications that the German officers, who had no experience in colonial warfare, learned some essentials from their Sudanese mercenaries, who had previously fought under the British in Egypt and Sudan. Some higher-ranking Sudanese and Ngoni mercenaries served as instructors for younger African recruits.[46] This should remind us that the German colonial army (as perhaps other colonial armies) was not a pure European institution characterized and formed exclusively by European military traditions. It was an institution in which different cultures and practices were blended, although it was dominated by Germans.

For some reason, German officers preferred a particular metaphor when they wrote about the askari. They called them "our lansquenets" (from the Thirty Years' War) because the first generations of African recruits were mercenaries. Nevertheless, the lansquenet metaphor developed a life of its own and the officers began to use it to mark the difference between German and African soldiers.[47] Although most German officers might have thought that they were successful in disciplining their African soldiers, they were also convinced that Africans would never meet the standards of the Prussian barrack squares. This concerned not only their military skills but also their moral standards. Despite the harsh military regime under which the askari served, some officers suspected that under the surface of discipline lurked the "wild beast" of Africa.[48]

To secure the loyalty and goodwill of their African soldiers, the German officers had to make compromises. Despite the official anti-slavery policy, many soldiers owned slaves, the majority of them having been captured as prisoners of war. Officers knew about this practice and did little to prevent it. Another compromise was the right of looting. This was a widespread practice among African mercenaries during the military campaigns, and was accepted or tolerated by most German officers, even though some articulated their reservations.[49] If there was a "wild beast," then it was the beast of German militarism. With uniforms the colonial state handed over an enormous power to African mercenaries, which they often misused for their own ends. In some areas they were the only representatives of colonial authority and therefore free to carry out their own interpretation of colonial rule. In the memories of the East Africans, the askari thus became prominent as an embodiment of colonial rule.[50]

Conclusion

War on non-combatants became part of the strategy of the colonial state and its agents, primarily through particular situations and practices rather than official structures and processes. This has to do with the special nature of colonial conquest: in its early stages such structures hardly existed or were only beginning to emerge. The founding of the German colony in East Africa is a good example; just as Germany had no history as a colonial power, East Africa had no history as a German colony. There was little in East Africa that the Germans could count on or that was useful for the development of colonial society. The establishment of colonial rule in 1889 was seen not only as a military conquest but as a fundamental break in the history of that region, or in other words, as the zero hour of history. It was the German philosopher Karl Marx who, some forty years before, had compared history with theatre.[51] For some German colonial officers, colonial history seemed to be a Greek tragedy – full of violence and heroic moments.

In his book *From the Light of War towards the Birth of History*, the French philosopher Michel Foucault states that such a view of history was not uncommon among eighteenth- and nineteenth-century Europeans. In this period, European societies were successively purged of war-like relationships, and war itself became a professional and technological monopoly of the state. A discourse on war as a force of history emerged, and the driving forces of history were seen in hard "facts": physical power or weakness, racial superiority or inferiority, victories or failures. This rather coarse-spun view of history emerged as European societies were being transformed by much more ordinary forces – by economic and political developments and the disciplinary processes of emerging modern societies.[52] I have borrowed much from this notion of a discrepancy between the emergence of the modern state through socio-economic and political change and thinking about violence as a force of history. In fact, colonialism is a literal example of this discourse on war and history put into practice.

This brings me to a central term of my essay: presence. In modern disciplinary societies, the presence of the state is hardly a problem; the state exists not only in its institutions but also, as Foucault reminds us, in the bodies of its subjects, who are tied up in constant disciplinary processes.[53] Or as Deleuze writes in his book about Foucault, the disciplinary power structures of modern states create serial rooms, in which the dispositions of power are inscribed into subjects.[54] However, for the early colonial state presence was a problem. It had no infrastructure on which to rely, and its subjects had not inherited the dispositions of its power structures. In a certain sense, the establishment of colonial rule was this zero hour the German colonizers spoke of, and the unambiguous victory became a powerful theorem in colonial discourse. The unambiguous victory, and in its wake, collateral damage, was thought to create a shared history of the state and its subjects, as had happened in Europe. In the magical moment of the unambiguous victory, it was hoped that a relationship between the colonizer and the colonized would emerge.

When I started to think about how the colonial state in East Africa was built, I found that Germans often discussed colonial rule in terms of a promising future for places to which they never had been and about which they knew nothing. For them, the subjugation of a chief would have inevitable consequences for the attitude of the other toward Germans. German colonial officers were, to employ the terms used by Timothy Brook in his essay, both total warriors and imperialists.[55] They had the military might to do whatever they thought necessary for securing victory. However, as imperialists, they also reasoned or speculated about the consequences of their actions for the establishment of colonial rule. The terror of the unambiguous victory was to a certain degree the result of the "civilizing" mission of colonialism; it was seen as the catharsis on which the colonial order was built.

This brings me back to the question of structures and processes. I favour a perspective on the history of colonial rule that stresses the spasmodic nature of the process. For the first twenty years of German colonial rule, it is hard to describe its establishment as a constant and linear process. The arrival of German troops and the subjugation of a chief did not necessarily mean that colonial rule had been imposed. The founding of a *boma* (military station) was no more than the beginning of the building of a colonial infrastructure. Due to the volatile presence of German colonizers, this process could be, and in many cases was, reversible. Take, for instance, the establishment of colonial rule in Unyamwezi. Germans first arrived in Tabora in 1891. The flag was hoisted and a protection letter issued. After a few days, the German expedition withdrew. In history books we read that 1891 was the year when German rule was established. Far from it. Only two years later, another German expedition reached Tabora, but with few troops. For some years Germans played only a marginal role in local politics. In 1896, Germans troops raided the residence of the most important Nyamwezi chief in the region and killed him. But again the bulk of the troops withdrew after a couple of days. Even seven years later the German position in Unyamwezi remained difficult. This reversibility is the reason why the discourse of the unambiguous victory played an important role for such a long time.

Nor was the colonial state a monolithic institution that produced a coherent political strategy over a long time. The colonial state had the problem not only of transforming Africans into colonial subjects but also of doing so with its European agents. I have here described the structural problems in the administration of the colony, but the difficulty resulted also from the self-image of many colonial officers, who were not bureaucrats but members of the Prussian military, with a tradition of disapproval of bureaucratic regimes. Many officers were therefore reluctant to integrate themselves into a bureaucratic apparatus. But we need also to bear in mind that the colonial project was constructed by Africans as well as Europeans.

When I started my research on German colonialism five years ago, I thought it was no more than a very interesting fragment of the past, but I grew to realize that it contained many parallels to what is happening today in Afghanistan or Iraq. Like the Germans in East Africa, for the Americans and their allies the military conquest was the beginning of an attempt to transform other societies. The Americans today face problems similar to those the Germans confronted 100 years ago. Despite overwhelming military power, they struggle to maintain a continuous presence in the occupied territories that would enable them to set up durable social and political change. U.S. military strategy, reflected in slogans such as "shock and awe," resonates with the German idea of the impressive and unambiguous victory. Implicit is the same aspiration: to replace the hard and long-term process of change with spectacular moments of performing power.

Notes

1 Jeffrey Herbst, *States and Power in Africa: Comparative Lessons in Authority and Control* (Princeton, N.J.: Princeton University Press, 2000).

2 For a detailed description see Carl Gotthilf Büttner, *Die Anfänge der deutschen Kolonialpolitik in Ostafrika: Eine kritische Untersuchung an Hand unveröffentlichter Quellen* (Berlin: Akademie-Verlag, 1959); Jonathon Glassman, *Feasts and Riot: Revelry, Rebellion, and Popular Consciousness on the Swahili Coast, 1856–1888* (Portsmouth, N.H.: Heinemann, 1995); Fritz Ferdinand Müller, *Deutschland – Zanzibar – Ostafrika: Geschichte einer deutschen Kolonialeroberung 1884–1890* (Berlin: Rütten & Loenning, 1959).

3 Anon., "Vita vya kwanza (Der Araberaufstand)," in C. Velten, *Suaheli-Gedichte: Gesammelt und mit einer Übersetzung und Erläuterung versehen* (Sonderdruck aus: Mitteilungen des Seminars für Orientalische Sprachen zu Berlin, 1919).

4 Hemedi bin Abdallah el-Buhiriy, *Utenzi wa vita vya wadachi kutamalaki mrima 1307 A.H. / The German Conquest of the Swahili Coast, 1891 AD* (Nairobi: East African Literature Bureau, 1968).

5 Gustav Michahelles cited in Ann Beck, "Medicine and Society in Tanganyika, 1890–1930," *Transactions of the American Philosophical Society* 45 (1977), 198.

6 Juhani Koponen, *Development for Exploitation: German Colonial Policies in Mainland Tanzania, 1884–1914* (Hamburg: LIT, 1995), 352.

7 See Trutz von Trotha, *Koloniale Herrschaft. Zur soziologischen Theorie der Staatsentstehung am Beispiel des "Schutzgebietes Togo"* (Tübingen: Mohr, 1994).

8 Stuhlmann an Auswärtiges Amt./Kolonialamt (hereafter AA/KA), July 17, 1903, Bundesarchiv Berlin-Dahlem (hereafter BArch) R1001/5499.

9 *Tägliche Rundschau,* February 6, 1892.

10 Stellungnahme zu Einführung von Kopf- und Hüttensteuern (1913–14), Bericht von Langenn-Steinkeller, BArch R1003FC/1150. See also Bericht der Stationen Mwanza und Bukoba, October 1, 1892, BArch R1001/1032; and Ernst Nigmann, *Die Geschichte der Kaiserlichen Schutztruppe für Deutsch-Ostafrika* (Berlin: Mittler, 1911), 78, which also uses the metaphor of circles surrounding the station.

11 In European history, peripatetic rule had a long tradition. European monarchs in the Middle Ages travelled through their empire, moving from city to city or from residence to residence. The most striking example was perhaps the emperors of the Holy Roman Empire in sixteenth and seventeenth century. Surprising for me was Preisendörfer's book on the aesthetics of Prussian monarchy. He states that peripatetic rule was reinvented by European monarchs in the eighteenth and nineteenth centuries. Bruno Preisendörfer, *Staatsbildung als Königskuns: Ästhetik und Herrschaft im preußischen Absolutismus* (Berlin: Akademie-Verlag, 2000).

12 Bericht Booth an AA/KA, January 25, 1906, BArch R1001/726. For a similar statement see Merkers Bericht über Vorkommnisse von September 7–15, 1905, in Kilwa, Bundesarchiv Freiburg Abteilung Militärarchiv (hereafter BArch/M), RM121/438, Kilwa, November 16, 1905; Denkschrift des Gouverneurs von Götzen über die Ursachen des Aufstandes in Deutsch-Ostafrika 1905, December 26, 1905, BArch/M RM5/6063.

13 Denkschrift über den Verlauf des Aufstandes in Deutsch-Ostafrika, Dar es Salaam, August 31, 1906, BArch R1001/726.

14 This notion of redoubling of presence is highly influenced by the writings of Jacques Derrida, especially by his comments on Antoine Artaud, a French surrealist. Artaud was an actor and director and theorized what he called the "theatre of cruelty." It was an attempt to think about the borders between theatre and everyday life. Derrida made his theories a starting point to reflect about the process of representation. See Jacques Derrida, *Die Schrift und die Differenz* (Frankfurt am Main: Suhrkamp, 1989).

15 Bericht über einen eventuellen Waniamwezi-Aufstand, zufolge Befehls des stellvertretenden Gouverneurs, Major von Estorff, Tabora, March 30, 1901, BArch R1001/1030.

16 See, for instance, Reisebericht Schnees an Kolonialamt, April 26, 1913, BArch R1001/237/1.

17 This psychological notion of the use of military power was present in many theories on colonial warfare. See, for instance, Hermann von Wissmann, *Afrika: Schilderungen und Ratschläge zur Vorbereitung für den Aufenthalt und den Dienst in den Deutschen Schutzgebieten* (Berlin: Mittler & Sohn, 1903).

18 Georg Richelmann, "Die Besiegung der Feinde vom Rufiji bis zum Urumba," in *Hermann von Wissmann – Deutschlands größter Afrikaner: Sein Leben und Wirken unter Benutzung des Nachlasses dargestellt*, ed. Conradin von Perbandt, Georg Richelmann, and Rochus Schmidt (Berlin: Schall, 1906), 247.

19 Georg Richelmann, "Die Schaffung der Wissmanntruppe," in *Hermann von Wissmann*, ed. Perbandt, Richelmann, and Schmidt, 200.

20 See, for instance, the changing German perspectives on Mkwawa's Hehe empire. When Germans fought their first encounter with Hehe, they described them as "bands of robbers," thus denying the "stateness" of the Hehe. This view changed when Germans were defeated by the Hehe in the Battle of Rugaro in 1891. Then Germans elevated the Hehe to a nation and Iringa, the residence of the Hehe chief Mkwawa, to its capital. Bericht des Hauptmanns von Prince an das Gouvernement Dar es Salaam, November 4, 1896, BArch R1001/1039; Über einen Zug nach der Landschaft Uhehe und die Begründung einer Station in Kuirenga, Bericht des Hauptmanns von Prince, Lager östlich von Kiringa, September 20, 1896, *Deutsches Kolonialblatt* (1895), 773–74; Heinrich Fonck, "Bericht über meinen Marsch Mpwapwa-Ugogo-Ussandaue-Irangi-Burungi-Ugogo-Mpwapwa," *Mitteilungen von Forschungsreisenden und Gelehrten aus den deutschen Schutzgebieten* (hereafter *MFGDS*) 7, 5 (1894), 295; Heinrich Fonck, *Deutsch-Ostafrika: Eine Schilderung nach 10 Wanderjahren* (Berlin: Voss, 1907), 28; Richard Kiepert, "Hauptmann Prince's und Lieutenant Stadlbaur's Reisen im Wakimbulande," *MFGDS* 11, 1 (1898), 89; Ernst Nigmann, *Die Wahehe: Ihre Geschichte, Kult-, Rechts-, Kriegs- und Jagd-Gebräuche* (Berlin: Mittler, 1908), 1–3; Nigmann, *Die Geschichte der Kaiserlichen Schutztruppe für Deutsch-Ostafrika*, 32, 45–47; Erich Schultz-Ewerth and Leonhard Adam, eds., *Das Eingeborenenrecht* (Stuttgart: Strecker & Schroeder, 1929), 43.

21 See, for instance, the ethnographic writings of colonial officers published in the *MFGDS*: H. von Elpons, "Uhehe," *MFGDS* 9 (1896), 75–77; Bernhard von Kalben, "Über die Rechtsverhältnisse der Eingeborenen in der Umgebung von Bukoba," *MFGDS* 1 (1896), 37–40; Karl Kannenberg, "Durch die Marénga Makali," *MFGDS* 13, 1 (1900), 3–17; Tom von Prince, "Geschichte der Magwangwara nach Erzählung des Arabers Raschid bin Masud und des Fusi, Bruder des vor drei Jahren verstorbenen Sultans der Magwangwara Mharuli," *MFGDS* 7, 3 (1894), 213–22.

22 Werner Steuber, "Die Unterwerfung des Kilima-Ndjaro-Gebiets," in *Hermann von Wissmann*, ed. Perbandt, Richelmann, and Schmidt, 372.

23 Von der Expedition des Lieutenants Herrmann, *Deutsches Kolonialblatt* (1892), 260.

24 Prince an das Gouvernement von Deutsch-Ostafrika, Tabora, January 28, 1893, BArch R1001/1030; Bericht des Leutnants Prince über die Niederwerfung und Vernichtung des Häuptlings Sike, Tabora, January 2, 1893, *Deutsches Kolonialblatt* (1893), 198.

25 C. Waldemar Werther, *Die mittleren Hochländer des nördlichen Deutsch-Ost-Afrika: Wissenschaftliche Ergebnisse der Irangi-Expedition, 1896–1897 nebst kurzer Reisebeschreibung* (Berlin: H. Paetel, 1898), 32.

26 Uhehe, Bericht Prince an das Gouvernement Dar es Salaam, *Deutsches Kolonialblatt* (1897), 653.

27 Hans Koritschoner, "Some East African Native Songs," *Tanganyika Notes and Records* 4 (1937), 51–64.

28 Sigl an Soden, Tabora, August 31, 1891, BArch R1001/274; Bericht über die Ereignisse im Bezirk während des Monats Januar, February 1, 1895, BArch R1001/1036; Über einen Zug durch das Wakondegebiet, Bericht des Kapitän Berndt, Langenburg, February 9, 1896, *Deutsches Kolonialblatt* (1896), 372; Bericht Ramsays aus Ujiji, August 1, 1896, *Deutsches Kolonialblatt* (1896), 770; Gustav Adolf Graf von Götzen, *Durch Afrika von Ost nach West: Resultate und Begebenheiten einer Reise von der Deutsch-Ostafrikanischen Küste bis zur Kongomündung in den Jahren 1893/94* (Berlin: D. Reimer, 1899), 141; Wilhelm Langheld, *Zwanzig Jahre in deutschen Kolonien* (Berlin: Wilhelm Weicher, 1909), 135; C. Waldemar Werther, *Zum Victoria Nyanza: Eine Anti-Sklaverei-Expedition und Forschungsreise* (Berlin: H. Paetel, 1894), 47.

29 Düna-Zeitung, Riga, October 3, 1892, reprinted in Ausführungskommission des Deutschen Antisklavereikomites, *Die Akten der Ausführungskommission des Deutschen Antisklavereikomites betreffend Das v. Wissmann-Dampferunternehmen* (Koblenz: Deutsches Antisklavereikommitee, 1893), 461.

30 Stuhlmann an Auswärtiges Amt, Kolonialabteilung, Dar es Salaam, July 17, 1903, Entwurf für eine Runderlass, n.d., BArch R1001/5499. This circular, which I think is one of the most important documents for the understanding of early patterns of colonial rule, resulted in a draft for a decree that postulated the future lines of colonial politics. See Entwurf für einen Runderlass, Dar es Salaam, n.d., BArch R1001/5499; Steubel (AA/KA) an GovDar, March 3, 1903, BArch R1001/5499.

31 See Wissmann's "Abschluss-Bericht über die Eroberung der Küste," cited in Nigmann, *Schutztruppe*, 25; Michahelles cited in Beck, "Medicine and Society," 8, and Langheld, *Zwanzig Jahre*, 124

32 Nigmann, *Wahehe*, 155; Tom von Prince, *Gegen Araber und Wahehe: Erinnerungen aus meiner afrikanischen Leutnantszeit 1890–1895* (Berlin: Mittler & Sohn, 1914), 209.

33 Über einen Zug nach der Landschaft Uhehe und die Begründung einer Station in Kuirenga, Bericht Prince, Lager östlich von Kiringa, September 20, 1896, *Deutsches Kolonialblatt* (1896), 773; Eduard Liebert, *Neunzig Tage im Zelt: Meine Reise nach Uhehe Juni bis Sept. 1897* (Berlin: Mittler & Sohn, 1898), 9.

34 Bericht Sigls vom September 30, 1893, *Deutsches Kolonialblatt* (1894), 10.

35 Rochus Schmidt, *Geschichte des Araberaufstandes in Ost-Afrika: Seine Entstehung, seine Niederwerfung und seine Folgen* (Frankfurt am Main: Trowitzsch, 1892), 223; Rochus Schmidt, *Kolonialpioniere: Persönliche Erinnerungen aus kolonialer Frühzeit* (Berlin: Safari-Verlag, 1938), 227.

36 Station und Bezirk Lindi, *Deutsches Kolonialblatt* (1891), 262; Norbert Aas, *Koloniale Entwicklung im Bezirksamt Lindi (Deutsch-Ostafrika): Deutsche Erwartungen und regionale Wirklichkeit* (Bayreuth: Bumerang, 1989), 79; Schmidt, *Kolonialpioniere*, 223.

37 Über die Verhältnisse im Hinterland von Lindi (Brief des Wali Abdallah bin Mohammed aus Sudi an das Governement in Daressalaam), December 14, 1896, *Deutsches Kolonialblatt* (1896), 167.

38 Bericht über einen Besuch bei Sultan Machemba, April 18, 1896 (Everbeck), BArch R1001/277.

39 Nigmann, *Wahehe*, 65.

40 Georg Maercker, *Unsere Schutztruppe in Ostafrika* (Berlin: Siegismund, 1893), 201.

41 August Schynse and Karl Hespers, *Mit Stanley und Emin Pascha durch Deutsch Ost-Africa: Reise-Tagebuch* (Köln: Bachem, 1890), 68; Max Weiß, *Die Völk-*

erstämme im Norden Deutsch-Ostafrikas (Berlin: Carl Marschner, 1910), 265; Werther, *Victoria Nyanza*, 165.

42 R.G. Abrahams, "The Political Organization of Nyamweziland," *Cambridge Studies in Social Anthropology* 10 (1967), 38; Ralph A. Austen, *Northwestern Tanzania under German and British Rule: Colonial Policy and Tribal Politics, 1889–1939* (New Haven, Conn.: Yale University Press, 1968), 18; R.W. Beachey, *The Slave Trade of Eastern Africa* (London: Rex Collings, 1976), 14; Norman R. Bennett, *Mirambo of Tanzania, 1840?–1884* (New York: Oxford University Press, 1971), 38–40; Aylward Shorter, "Nyungu-ya-Mawe and the 'Empire of the Ruga-Ruga,'" *Journal of African History* 9 (1968), 236, 240.

43 Berichte Leues an Auswärtiges Amt, Kolonialabteilung, February 17, 1896, BArch R1001/1030.

44 Schwesinger an Soden, Tabora, November 26, 1892, BArch R1001/1030.

45 Ibid.

46 Ramsay an Kaiserlichen Gouverneur Soden, Lindi, July 19, 1891, Tanzania National Archive (hereafter TNA) G2/2; Gouvernement Dar es Salaam an Auswärtiges Amt, Kolonialabteilung, Dar es Salaam, November 28, 1892, TNA G2/3; Verfügung des Gouvernements Dar es Salaam, May 26, 1896, TNA G2/4; Bericht des Gouvernements Dar es Salaam, Finanzabteilung, September 2, 1896, TNA G2/4; Nigmann, *Schutztruppe*, 73.

47 Wilhelm Föllmer, "Die Schutz- und Polizeitruppe in Deutsch-Ostafrika," *Die Deutschen Kolonien* 9, 13 (1913), 71; Friedrich Fülleborn, *Das Deutsche Njassa- und Ruvumagebiet: Land und Leute* (Berlin: Reimer, 1906), 8; Theodor Tafel, "Von der Schutztruppe in Ostafrika," *Deutsche Kolonialzeitung* 31, 28 (1914), 467; Werther, *Victoria Nyanza*, 114.

48 Artur Heye, *Vitani: Kriegs- und Jagderlebnisse in Ostafrika, 1914–1916* (Leipzig: Grunow, 1922), 16.

49 Kommandobefehl no. 4, April 30, 1913, BArch/M RM2/1844; Jan Georg Deutsch, "Slavery under German Colonial Rule in East Africa, c. 1860–1914" (Habilitationsschrift, Humboldt-Universität zu Berlin, 2000), 212.

50 Katrin Bromber, "Ein Lied auf die hohen Herrn: Die deutsche Kolonialherrschaft in der historiographischen Swahiliverskunst der Jahrhundertwende," in *Alles unter Kontrolle: Disziplinierungsprozesse im kolonialen Tanzania (1850–1960)*, ed. Albert Wirz (Köln: Köppe, 2003), 78–80; W.K.O. Busse, "Aus dem Leben von Asyuike Malango," *Zeitschrift für Eingeborenensprachen* 35 (1950), 201; J. Czekanowski, ed., *Forschungen im Nil-Kongo-Gebiet* (Leipzig: Klinkhardt & Bierman, 1917), 270; Simbo Janira, *Kleiner Grosser Schwarzer Mann: Lebenserinnerungen eines Buschnegers* (Eisenach: Erich Röth, 1956), 118; Charles Pike, "History and Imagination: Swahili Literature and Resistance to German Language Imperialism in Tanzania, 1885–1910," *International Journal of African Historical Studies* 19 (1986), 218.

51 Karl Marx, "Der achtzehnte Brumaire des Louis Bonaparte," in *Ausgewählte Schriften in zwei Bänden*, ed. Karl Marx and Friedrich Engels (Berlin: Dietz, 1989), 267.

52 Michel Foucault, *Vom Licht des Krieges zur Geburt der Geschichte* (Berlin: Merve, 1986), 8ff.

53 Michel Foucault, *Dispositive der Macht: Über Sexualität, Wissen und Wahrheit* (Berlin: Merve, 1978), 82–90.

54 Gilles Deleuze, *Foucault* (Frankfurt am Main: Suhrkamp, 1992), 42.

55 See Timothy Brook's chapter in this volume.

Part 3
Collateral Damage and the Culture of Imperialism

Progress and Collateral Damage

> The joy of killing! The joy of seeing killing done! These are traits
> of the human race at large. We white people are merely modi-
> fied Thugs; Thugs fretting under the restraints of a not very
> thick skin of civilization. . . . Still we have made some progress –
> microscopic, and in truth scarcely worth mentioning, and cer-
> tainly nothing to be proud of – still, it is progress: we no longer
> take pleasure in slaughtering or burning helpless men.
>
> – Mark Twain, *More Tramps Abroad*, 1897

Collateral damage, the euphemism denoting the inadvertent killing of
civilians as a by-product of a military action, needs to be considered his-
torically within frameworks that extend beyond the boundaries of military
engagement. For the killing of a civilian to constitute "mere" collateral damage, the death must be of a civilian other than one of "our" own. The death of
the latter would, in "our" minds, constitute murder, terrorism, a war crime,
and so forth. So, if we should perpetrate the act of killing, and the dead individual is not one of our own and a victim of "friendly fire," then the corpse
belongs to the other and can be viewed euphemistically, thereby effectively
being deprived of humanity. Consequently, collateral damage is as much
about the way in which we define difference – often (but not exclusively)
around the nation state – as it is about the actual act of killing.

One can find many examples of the connection between collateral damage
and the depriving of victims of their humanity in ongoing events in Iraq.
Patrick Cockburn, for example, wrote in May 2004:

> Saad Mohammed was one of a large but unknown number of Iraqis shot down
> by U.S. troops over the past year. There seems to have been no rational reason
> why he had been killed. But the high toll of Iraqi civilians shot down after

ambushes or at checkpoints has given Iraqis the sense that, at bottom, American soldiers regard them as an inferior people whose lives are not worth very much.[1]

Saad Mohammed had become collateral damage; he was not killed because he might have been considered a danger to somebody (i.e., killed because he was one of the enemy, or for a strategic reason). His death was a by-product of the assumption that such deaths will occur in war, that there will be loss of life that should not receive the same kind of scrutiny as when it occurs to one of "our" soldiers or civilians. Cockburn gets to the heart of the matter in attributing the cause to American regard for Iraqis as "inferior people." Such people correspond to those who have been or are exploited for their labour, or discriminated against, or who have been infected (physically and sometimes ideologically), their lives becoming forfeit as they are believed to represent a danger to the rest of society.

The notion of collateral damage therefore needs to be considered beyond the boundaries of military engagement, it seems to me, because this line of thinking draws clearly from realms that have little direct or necessary relation to the rules of war. In particular (while there are no doubt other sources worthy of consideration), collateral damage draws on discourses that emerged in the context of colonialism. I am thinking here especially of those relating to colonized or unfree labour and to the containment of disease. In the minds of those considered citizens, who must be served by and protected from lesser mortals and their diseases, the slave moving out of servitude and the virus migrating to a new host are often closely related.[2]

As such, the response to slave uprising or anti-colonial insurgency, as well as to the quarantining of those infected by disease, bears strong similarity to thinking about collateral damage. Whether or not the latter draws directly on the former, and it is probable that it did, it is clear there is nothing new or unique about the phenomenon of collateral damage, if it is considered part of a necessary process of containment beyond a specific target of engagement. The manner in which Europeans and white Americans thought about the indiscriminate killing of those associated, even if only in marginally, with a slave or colonial uprising (as seen in the Denmark Vesey "conspiracy," the Nat Turner uprising, and many others like those in Demerara and Jamaica), or in response to the so-called Indian Mutiny of 1857, corresponds to the ways that civilian deaths are considered in collateral damage discourse. Such deaths are unfortunate but may be unavoidable if the insurgency, disease, or enemy is to be effectively destroyed.

Further, the malleable boundaries of what we consider "civilization," encompassed, for example, within the Geneva Conventions, modulate the conventions of collateral damage and associated discourses. For example, many journalists and their readers were at least at first willing to accept that the torture and death of prisoners in Guantánamo Bay might be legitimate, as these were supposedly in response to the terror that American leaders linked, appropriately or otherwise, to the events of 9/11. The extension of these practices to Iraq, a country with which Americans have identified themselves, and for whose citizens they have proposed the establishment of democracy, is considered unacceptable. Equivalent acts, therefore, may represent something akin to collateral damage in the case of the military base located on Cuban soil but murder or torture at Abu Ghraib and other prisons in Iraq or other CIA-approved locations around the world.

The intention of this essay, then, is not to talk about war and about particular cases of collateral damage but about theories within the disciplines of economics and anthropology that, alongside the notion of collateral damage, emerged in the fertile soil of colonialism. I will begin by focusing on the work of the economist Henry George, who in some ways created a type of progressivism through an assault on Malthusian notions of poverty and helped to forge a space for the notion that humanity might be doing more than simply dancing with death; that a felicific calculus might replace a dismal science that had made levels of civilian deaths something that could be calibrated in accordance with land-per-capita ratios.

But if George's economics opened up space for a progressive colonialism (and anti-colonialism), emerging strains within anthropology, especially in the colonial setting, might develop a progressivism of their own (tied to modernization) that would bring casualties also. If empire is tied to economic growth and uplift, mantras that would come to replace Malthusian and mercantilist assumptions of limits, then those who got in the way of such cultural, economic, or political progress would need to be removed or re-educated, becoming a different kind of damage from the starving peasants who had gone before.

The second part of this chapter focuses on two men whose work was shaped by different anthropological sensibilities and whose conflict came to a head in the interrogation at Scotland Yard of one man by the other. These sensibilities had different implications for the notion of collateral damage, one man (Basil Thomson) coming to represent British efforts in the First World War, the other (Sir Roger Casement) first representing the victims of colonial and capitalist oppression in Leopold's Congo Free State and Putumayo, and then challenging the legitimacy of "the horror" itself. Even the death of Sir Roger Casement, largely as a consequence of the persistence of Thomson and his associates, speaks to the issue of collateral damage. In the face of potential opposition from the U.S. government, it became necessary to demonize Casement, as sexually depraved and a homosexual, in order to legitimize his execution.

When considering collateral damage we are inclined to ask if the notion is a reflection of a new awareness that certain forms of killing are wrong so that they now need to be hidden in euphemism, when before they had been considered acceptable. Or is the tendency of humanity to create euphemisms for immoral acts a reflection of the unceasing ability of people to find new ways to undertake and justify evil? Henry George, one imagines, would have embraced the former position; Sir Roger Casement, consular official and casualty of war and imperialism, would no doubt have seen things differently.

Startling the Civilized World

This gentleman, who has hardly passed middle age, and whose theories of political economy have startled the whole civilized world, have given a charm to what was hitherto regarded as a "dismal science," and have held out hopes of a bright future to millions of suffering men who have for centuries been offered as a sacrifice to a heartless philosophy – this Henry George was in his youth a common sailor, and subsequently an ordinary printer.

If this is not triumphant democracy, what is?[3]

One of the central texts in the study of poverty in American history is, of course, Henry George's *Progress and Poverty*.[4] Published in 1879, this work would become one of the best-selling books of the late nineteenth century, following behind the Bible, Harriet Beecher Stowe's *Uncle Tom's Cabin*, and Edward Bellamy's *Looking Backward* (which drew heavily on George's ideas in the establishment of its Utopia), but few others. And considering that *Progress and Poverty* was a work of economics, and not the easiest read by any means, its popularity is really quite stunning.

This was a seminal text in the emergence of New Liberalism on both sides of the Atlantic. In *Atlantic Crossings*, Daniel T. Rodgers has noted that Henry George's writings made an important contribution to the transatlantic intellectual exchange and "tangibly affirmed the New World's radical promise."[5] This is how Rodgers summarizes George's impact:

In the transatlantic radical world of the 1880s, the biggest splash of all had been made by the American radical economist Henry George. His influence on Australasian politics was formative; his five tours of Great Britain and Ireland took the islands by storm. The Fabian Society was jolted out of its initial gauzy spiritualism by George's lectures on land monopoly. In the mid-1880s, as George and his labor allies seemed to be closing in on electoral victory in New York City, even Marx's London circle was sure that the initiative had passed to the

Americans. . . . When Sidney Webb wrote in 1889 that "the present English popular Socialist movement may be said to date entirely from the circulation here of *Progress and Poverty*," it was only a modest exaggeration.[6]

Clearly, George's impact has long been acknowledged. Contemporary social theorists on both sides of the Atlantic, from J.A. Hobson to John Dewey, paid homage to George, while intellectual historians from George Geiger in the 1930s to Daniel Aaron in the 1950s and Alan Trachtenberg in the 1980s stressed his contribution to social politics in this Progressive Age.[7]

But the book's influence would extend beyond the Atlantic milieu. Amrita Lal Roy, who came to live in New York City for three years in 1885, immediately saw the significance of Henry George's work. For Roy, it was not derived from its adaptation of republican ideology to the predicament of industrialization and an ongoing "incorporation of America" – as Alan Trachtenberg would later describe it. Rather, its significance lay in its consideration of the global predicament of poverty. This was how *Progress and Poverty* had "startled the whole civilized world," and this was how it would hold out "hopes of a bright future to millions of suffering men who have for centuries been offered as a sacrifice to a heartless philosophy." This text, whose genealogy can be traced back to India (since George had first witnessed extreme poverty on his trip as a sailor to India), would return there in Amrita Lal Roy's carpetbag and receive considerable coverage in his published travelogue.[8] It would also make its way back to India via other more circuitous routes, through the influence of the Irish Land League among Indian nationalists and through Count Tolstoy's correspondence.[9] George continued a long correspondence with Tolstoy, who came to believe that the American "had formulated the next article in the programme of the progressist [sic] Liberals of the world." No direct link between George and Mohandas K. Gandhi was made (George died before the latter's success in South Africa brought him worldwide acclaim), but the fact that Gandhi listed Tolstoy among his most important influences suggests that George's ideas filtered down into the pool of social theory that Gandhi would tap liberally.[10] In addition, George greatly influenced the English socialist H.M. Hyndman, and he in turn contributed to the emergence of the "drain theory" associated at the end of the century with Dadabhai Naoroji and Romesh Chunder Dutt. Naoroji's *Poverty and Un-British Rule in India*, published in 1901, and Dutt's *Famines in India*, published a year earlier, resembled in many ways George's earlier critique of British colonial rule in India. It is likely, though, that George himself drew, either directly or indirectly, on Naoroji's earliest essay on the subject, entitled "The Poverty of India," which was published at the time he was writing *Progress and Poverty*.[11]

One of *Progress and Poverty*'s most important contributions lay in its assault on Malthusianism, which George believed was one of the greatest stumbling blocks in the way of combating poverty. Thomas Malthus' *An Essay on Population* had persuaded many liberally inclined intellectuals to rethink their commitment to policies of amelioration such as the English poor laws. Lynn Hollen Lees has summarized the ideas underlying Malthus' theory thus:

> The shift in public opinion about charity was accelerated by growing awareness of classical economic theory and the linkage between poverty and poor laws in the writings of Thomas Malthus. If, as Malthus argued, population tended to increase faster than the means of subsistence, workers were inevitably condemned to lives of privation. Wars, diseases, and famines operated to check population growth and therefore could lessen pressure on resources and arrest declines in wages. In contrast public benevolence to the poor, such as relief offered through the poor laws, eventually made conditions worse because it encouraged the poor to have more children and helped them to stay alive. In other words, the poor laws "may be said therefore in some measure to create the poor which they maintain."[12]

Drawing on the work of Gertrude Himmelfarb, Lees notes that *An Essay on Population* "decisively shaped" social attitudes and policies in Britain for half a century. "The book went through multiple editions," she writes,

> inspired dozens of critiques and commentaries, and became one of the defining texts of its generation as its view of political economy supplanted that of Adam Smith. Malthusianism and the hostility to the poor laws it fostered set the intellectual tone for debate on the poor laws well into the 1840s. Although not everyone accepted the policies Malthus recommended, his view of the futility of poor relief had to be confronted, as did his notion that the poor laws undermined the independence and self-respect of the destitute. Such ideas became staple arguments among would-be reformers in the period between 1800 and 1830.[13]

By taking on Malthus in *Progress and Poverty*, George cast off his dismal shadow and facilitated the leap from classical economic liberalism to progressive liberalism on both sides of the Atlantic. Founded on George's populist and almost anarchist inclinations, *Progress and Poverty* could chart a new way of considering the relationship between the individual and society, providing an alternative to Marxian socialism that seemed less threatening to capitalism than the German-inspired doctrines. In this it was certainly not unique; many other liberal theoreticians were endeavouring to move beyond utilitarianism in similar ways, but the popularity of *Progress and Poverty* legitimated alternative approaches to configuring the state that would become commonplace during the Progressive Era.

Culture and Anarchy

The "tramp" comes with the locomotive, and almshouses and prisons are as surely the marks of "material progress" as are costly dwellings, rich warehouses, and magnificent churches. Upon streets lighted with gas patrolled by uniformed policemen, beggars wait for the passer-by, and in the shadow of college, and library, and museum, are gathering the more hideous Huns and fiercer Vandals of whom Macaulay prophesied.[14]

In the chapter of *Progress and Poverty* entitled "Inferences from Facts," George endeavoured to show how the philosophy of Malthus had been developed from certain misconceived inferences about the fact of Indian poverty. India had become the testing ground for Malthus' *Essay on Population* because historians like Henry Thomas Buckle, in his *History of Civilization in England*, had endeavoured to make the history of India conform to Malthusian theory. But lands of great potential like India and China had been turned into wastelands of poverty and famine, George asserted, not because of overpopulation, as Malthus had claimed, but because of particularly harsh social conditions. These oppressive social conditions had had a long history, George thought:

In both countries great natural resources are wholly neglected. This arises from no innate deficiency in the people, for the Hindoo, as comparative philology has shown, is of our own blood, and China possessed a high degree of civilization and the rudiments of the most important modern inventions when our ancestors were wandering savages. It arises from the form which the social organization has in both countries taken, which has shackled productive power and robbed industry of its reward.

In India from time immemorial, the working classes have been ground down by exactions and oppressions into a condition of helpless and hopeless degradation. For ages and ages the cultivator of the soil has esteemed himself happy if, of his produce, the extortion of the strong hand left him enough to support life and furnish seed; capital could nowhere be safely accumulated or to any considerable extent be used to assist production; all wealth that could be wrung from the people was in possession of princes who were little better than robber chiefs quartered over the country, or in that of their farmers or favorites, and was wasted in useless or worse than useless luxury, while religion, sunken into an elaborate and terrible superstition, tyrannized over the mind as physical force did over the bodies of men. Under these conditions, the only arts that could advance were those that ministered to the ostentation and luxury of the great. The elephants of the rajah blazed with gold of exquisite workmanship, and the umbrellas that symbolized his regal power glittered with gems; but the plow of the *ryot* was only a sharpened stick. The ladies of the rajah's harem wrapped themselves in muslins so fine as to take the name of woven wind, but the tools of the artisan were of the poorest and rudest description and commerce could only be carried on, as it were, by stealth.

Is it not clear that this tyranny and insecurity have produced the want and starvation of India; and not . . . the pressure of population upon subsistence that has produced the want, and the want the tyranny?[15]

But if things were bad under the rajahs they were to become immeasurably worse under British colonial rule. "To this merciless rapacity," George wrote, "which would have produced want and famine were the population but one to a square mile and the land a Garden of Eden, succeeded, in the first era of British rule in India, as merciless a rapacity, backed by a far more irresistible power."[16]

George then turned to the authority of Thomas Macaulay's essay on Clive of India, which had described the "enormous fortunes . . . rapidly accumulated at Calcutta, while millions of human beings were reduced to the extremity of wretchedness." Indians, Macaulay had averred, "have been accustomed to live under tyranny, but never under tyranny like this."[17] If Macaulay only touched on the horrors of East India Company rule, Edmund Burke's "vivid eloquence" painted a more complete picture, with "whole districts surrendered to the unrestrained cupidity of the worst of human kind, poverty-stricken peasants fiendishly tortured to compel them to give up their little hoards, and once populous tracts turned into deserts."[18]

While George noted that this "lawless license of early English rule" had been restrained and had given way to "the just principles of English law," nevertheless, "with increasing frequency famine has succeeded famine, raging with greater intensity over wider areas." George asked rhetorically,

Is not this a demonstration of the Malthusian theory? . . . Does it not show, as Malthus contended, that, to shut up the sluices by which superabundant population is carried off, is but to compel nature to open new ones, and that unless the sources of human increase are checked by prudential regulation, the alternative of war is famine? This has been the orthodox interpretation.[19]

But George disagreed with orthodoxy. The reasons for the famines lay in the nature of English colonialism, regardless how ordered and fair colonial rule was intended to be:

The millions of India have bowed their necks beneath the yokes of many conquerors, but worst of all is the steady, grinding weight of English domination – a weight which is literally crushing millions out of existence, and, as shown by

English writers, is inevitably tending to a most frightful and widespread catastrophe. Other conquerors have lived in the land, and, though bad and tyrannous in their rule, have understood and been understood by the people; but India now is like a great estate owned by an absentee and alien landlord. A most expensive military and civil establishment is kept up, managed and officered by Englishmen who regard India as but a place of temporary exile; and an enormous sum . . . is raised from [an impoverished] population . . . is drained away to England in the shape of remittances, pensions, home charges of the government, etc. – a tribute for which there is no return.[20]

And as with all absentee landlords, the English had squeezed the population relentlessly, creating a class of landed proprietors, who had become "hereditary tax-gatherers," and who "rack-rent the cultivators most mercilessly." In other areas rent was taken by the state in the form of a land tax that drove the *ryots* "into the claws of money lenders, who are, if possible, more rapacious than the *zemindars*." "We do not care for the people of India," he wrote, quoting Florence Nightingale. "The saddest sight to be seen in the East – nay, probably in the world – is the peasants of our Eastern Empire." And the causes of the terrible famines lay in taxation, and the slavery that resulted from English law, producing in "the most fertile country in the world, a grinding, chronic, semi-starvation in many places where what is called famine does not exist."[21]

Then, after turning to the authority of the English socialist H.M. Hyndman, George ended his section on India with a flourish:

In India now, as in India in past times, it is only the most superficial view that can attribute want and starvation to pressure of population upon the ability of the land to produce subsistence. Could the cultivators retain their little capital – could they be released from the drain which, even in non-famine years, reduces great masses of them to a scale of living not merely below what is deemed necessary for the sepoys, but what English humanity gives to the prisoners in the jails – reviving industry, assuming more productive forms, would undoubtedly suffice to keep a much greater population. There are still in India great areas uncultivated, vast mineral resources untouched, and it is certain that the population of India does not reach, as within historical times it never has reached, the real limit of the soil to furnish subsistence, or even the point where this power begins to decline with the increasing drafts made upon it. The real cause of want in India has been, and yet is, the rapacity of man, not the niggardliness of nature.[22]

Ending thus his analysis of India, George turned his attention to China and Ireland, where the same arguments were reinforced. Lest he be in any way misunderstood, he wanted to make clear his difference with Malthusianism:

I do not mean merely to say that India or China could, with a more highly developed civilization, maintain a greater population, for to this any Malthusian would agree. The Malthusian doctrine does not deny that an advance in the productive arts would permit a great population to find subsistence. But the Malthusian theory affirms – and this is the essence – that, whatever be the capacity for production, the natural tendency of population is to come up with it, and, in the endeavor to press beyond it, to produce, to use the phrase of Malthus, that degree of vice and misery which is necessary to prevent further increase; so that as productive power is increased, population will correspondingly increase, and in a little time produce the same results as before.[23]

What George had to say instead was "that everywhere the vice and misery attributed to over-population can be traced to the warfare, tyranny, and oppression which prevent knowledge from being utilized and deny the security essential to production." This fact was obvious "with regard to India and China." It was clear also in the case of the potato famine in Ireland.

George's critique of Malthus would end with a passage on Ireland, cementing a bond that would become very strong over the ensuing years, as the Irish Land League adopted many of his ideas and invited him on several occasions to make lecture tours in Ireland. The words are powerful indeed. "I know of nothing," he wrote,

better calculated to make the blood boil than the cold accounts of grasping, grinding tyranny to which the Irish people have been subjected, and to which, and not to any inability of the land to support its population, Irish pauperism and Irish famine are to be attributed; and were it not for the enervating effect which the history of the world proves to be everywhere the result of abject poverty, it would be difficult to resist something like a feeling of contempt for a race who, stung by such wrongs, have only occasionally murdered a landlord![24]

Yet while he would end with the Irish, it was India that had borne the weight of the critique.

This emphasis on India is important because George's work is generally considered only in light of the American context in which it was written, namely the aftermath of the economic slump of 1873. But while this recession was occurring in the United States, India was witnessing a widespread and horrendous famine, providing the backdrop for George's assault on Malthus. For, just as Malthus had been drawn on to assuage guilt about the famine in

Ireland thirty years earlier, he was once again being deployed to defend British inaction by colonial officials who "worshipped political economy as a sort of fetish" and "famine as a salutary cure for over-population."[25] George's argument was not just part of an academic dispute about a distant peasantry; it was a pressing argument asserted in the face of resurgent elites on both sides of the Atlantic.[26]

What we find in *Progress and Poverty*, then, is that the British empire and India had been placed front and centre in the establishment of a new progressive economic theory. For the dichotomy of poverty and progress to take hold over the reader's imagination, an understanding of the conditions of the poor in India was required. Without George's grappling with India there could be no refutation of Malthus; and without that there could be no new and coherent progressive economic system. Without the stark descriptions of British land practices in India there would be no easily proven, widely accepted example (especially once the Slave Power had been vanquished) to show the dangers of rent and monopoly; and without that there would be no justification for the state to introduce its "single tax," thereby transgressing laissez-faire convention for the benefit of capitalism.

The success of George's work gave impetus to the more liberal imperialists who began to take hold in the colonial office between 1880 and the First World War. Many of these were the intellectual descendants of the Philosophic Radicals and Utilitarians who had begun to make inroads into the corridors of power as early as the 1840s, as Eric Stokes has noted, but they were now committed to state intervention in accordance with the ideas of T.H. Green and the precepts of New Liberalism.[27] As such, ideas about the "white man's burden" and social "uplift," dominant in the 1890s, were antidotes to the notion that the poverty stricken should be left to starve. Though, of course, in many instances such intervention, particularly when it was required to control outbreaks of social and other diseases could easily lead down the same road of sacrificing people for the benefit of the larger society.

Ironically, then, while George's ideas would be deployed by the anti-colonialist in Ireland and India and would gain widespread adherents in Australia and New Zealand (among other places), thereby representing a thorn in the side for many a colonial administrator, it was in this deployment of India and the Indian peasant that George's main contribution would lie – colonial discontents would in this way become a foundation stone for a new progressive imperialism.

Pagans were conceivable primarily as incomplete or imperfect forms, rather than as "peoples" of a comprehensibly distinct kind.[28]

Basil Thomson (later Sir Basil) played a crucial role in the development of British policing, bringing to his job as head of the Special Branch of Scotland Yard the kind of familiarity with ethnography shared by S.M. Edwardes in Bombay and, in a more amateur fashion, by William McAdoo in New York City.[29] But Thomson's application of this mindset to policing would take an altogether new direction from the two police commissioners. While Edwardes and McAdoo placed great store in the cementing and policing of boundaries between different ethnic groups, Thomson believed that such groups were an inevitable casualty of the expansion of European civilization, and that the major purpose of colonialism was to ensure the power vacuum arising from the "decay of custom" was managed as effectively as possible.

Like both McAdoo and Edwardes, Thomson paid a good deal of attention in his study to the different customs and proclivities of the peoples he encountered. These people, however, were markedly different from those encountered in New York City and Bombay. Son of the Archbishop of York, Basil Home Thomson had received his imperial baptism and subsequent colonial experience in the South Seas, most especially in Fiji. He lived for ten years among the Fijians, as he later recalled, "first as Stipendiary Magistrate in various parts of the group [of islands], then as Commissioner of the Native Lands Court, and finally as Acting Head of the Native Department." From 1900 to 1901 he also served as prime minister of Tonga, negotiating the establishment of the protectorate there with the local chiefs. Then, in 1903, he was appointed to a commission formed "to investigate the causes of the decrease of the natives." For this work he gathered considerable "anthropological information," from which he published the well-respected study, *The Fijians: A Study of the Decay of Custom*, in 1908.[30]

Thomson had cut his teeth in imperial administration under the watchful gaze of Sir Arthur Gordon, who had become the first governor of Fiji with the Deed of Cession in 1874. Gordon wanted to ensure "the continued existence of the Fijian race" and believed that this "was dependent on the preservation of their traditions against the corrupting influences of the planter community."[31] His policy, therefore, was "to insulate Fijian tradition against the disintegrative effects of a market in land and labour. He resolved to return all lands alienated prior to Cession to customary owners and to stop Fijians from being recruited for plantation work in favor of indentured labourers from India."[32] This had two obvious repercussions. First, it entailed inventing certain traditions of land ownership among the Fijians. The Great Council of Chiefs convened to formalize land tenure, "initially stressed the diversity and fluidity of Fijian concepts of land tenure." It was only Gordon's threat of alienation of property in perpetuity that took care of the Fijians' "confusion." Second, it cemented these customs in a way that made them unlikely to change according to fluctuating circumstances. A new orthodoxy was cultivated, which "relied on a codification of social units – lineage, clan, and tribe were neatly defined and marshaled into a segmentary system – a system far more bounded and less fluid than the precolonial counterpart."[33] It was made more static still by the introduction of large numbers of Indian indentured labourers, whose alien customs could be seen as threatening to the newly "invented" native traditions.

As a commissioner in the Native Lands Court, Basil Thomson undertook an anthropology almost necessarily inflected, not to say infected, by this approach to the Fijian communities. What Thomson observed during his time in Fiji was "the decay of custom," something that he took for granted as existing in coherent and unchanging form prior to the arrival of Europeans. But this gave him an altogether different perspective from other policing theorists, Edwardes and McAdoo, who tended to see discrete cultural essences surviving within the city and shaping the way it needed to be policed. In Thomson's case these communities were discrete in origin, perhaps, but, shifting toward a modernization perspective, he believed they would not remain so as European influences spread. Extrapolating from the assumptions of this alternative anthropological perspective would lead in new directions with regard to the manner in which people would be policed.

Let us examine, briefly, Thomson's views about decay. He began his book thus:

> The present population of the globe is believed to be about fifteen hundred millions, of which seven hundred millions are nominally progressive and eight hundred millions are stagnant under the law of custom. It is difficult to choose terms that even approach scientific accuracy in these generalizations, for, as Mr. H.G. Wells has remarked, if we use the word "civilized" the London "hooligan" and the "Bowery tough" immediately occur to us; if the terms "stagnant" or "progressive," how are the Parsee gentleman and the Sussex farm labourer to be classed? Nor can terms "white" and "coloured" be used, for there are Chinese many shades whiter than the Portuguese. But as long as the meaning is clear the scientific accuracy of terms is unimportant, and so for convenience we will call all races of European descent "civilized," and races living under the law of custom "uncivilized."[34]

In some respects, this is a more liberal and inclusive definition (however problematic) than the essentialisms frequently deployed at the time. Clearly, the notion that Europeans do not live "under the law of custom," while others do, is open to question. But there is no barrier that prevents the "uncivilized" from becoming "civilized," except custom itself. Get rid of this (ignoring that it is actually being imagined and invented and so is not unchanging) and "civilization" will be attained. In a way, then, this is a liberal and progressive perspective, one that even those who are being "uplifted" or are "uplifting" themselves might readily embrace.[35]

The question, or the problem, such a perspective raises struck Thomson immediately: "What part is to be taken in the world's affairs by the eight hundred millions of uncivilized men who happen for the moment to be politically inferior to the other seven hundred millions?" He continued:

> For centuries they have been sleeping. Under the law of custom, which no man dares to disobey, progress was impossible. The law of custom was the law of our own forefathers until the infusion of new blood and new customs shook them out of the groove and set them to choosing between the old and the new, and then to making new laws to meet new needs. This happened so long ago that if it were not for a few ceremonial survivals we might well doubt whether our forefathers were ever so held in bondage.[36]

Migration and interaction of peoples brought people out of their isolated stagnation and set them on the road to "civilization." And if this had happened to Europeans themselves, it would surely happen given the global reach and influence of European societies. He writes:

> In the sense that no race now exists which is not in some degree touched by the influence of Western civilization, the present decade may be said to be a fresh starting-point in the history of mankind. Whithersoever we turn, the laws of custom, which have governed the uncivilized races for countless generations, are breaking down; the old isolation which kept their blood pure is vanishing before railway and steamship communication which imports alien labourers to work for European settlers; and ethnologists of the future, having no pure race left to examine, will have to fall back upon hearsay evidence in studying the history of human institutions.[37]

Pretty radical ideas. Thomson here recognized an ongoing "mongrelization" that had been taking place for centuries among European and Asians, and which was now going to spread throughout the Pacific and, one might infer, Africa too.

Notions of racial inequalities associated with Social Darwinism were also brought into question. There is nothing intrinsically or innately different between the Fijian and the Londoner, only their experience and those of their "forefathers." Nor is racial antipathy an inevitable sentiment that arises from racial interactions. "The colour line," Thomson notes, having read W.E.B. Du Bois, "deep-seated as it is in the Southern States just now . . . may be nothing more than a passing phase of sentiment, a subconscious instinct of self-preservation in a race which feels that its old predominance is threatened by equality with its former servants."[38] Thomson would certainly worry if it were anything more than this: "If this race contempt were a primitive instinct with the white race the future of mankind would be lurid indeed, for it is impossible to believe that one half of humanity can be kept for ever inferior to the other without deluging the world with blood. But it is not a primitive instinct." He then concludes the passage with phrases that would not be out of place in Du Bois' *The Souls of Black Folk*.[39]

But differences between the "civilized" and "uncivilized" were significant nonetheless, for the decay of custom "may be fraught with momentous consequences for the civilized races."[40] The most obvious problem may arise from the spread of disease. However, Thomson remained confident that though the interaction between Europeans and indigenous populations might lead to the decimation of the latter, by and large these populations would not disappear altogether. As soon as they rejected their customs, which would become clearly inadequate in the face of the new diseases, they could adopt modern medical practices and civilization generally and thereby save themselves.

However, there was, Thomson thought, a problem evident in the process of decay. Customs were built on power, and however arbitrary they might seem to the observer they were there for a reason. They were functional to the particular society. As such, once they lost their hold over people and were replaced by the values of the "civilized" society, there would be a breakdown in social order, in large part because the new, civilized values were based on reason and not on force. Freed from the restraint of custom, a people could lapse into a situation of moral chaos. Nowhere was this clearer, Thomson believed, than in the case of sexual morality, to which he devoted a whole chapter. Fijians, for example, conformed to sexual customs of which few civilized Christians would approve. Yet the introduction of Christianity would not a moral community create:

> Sexual licence, formerly prevented, was now only forbidden. The missionaries' endeavours to inculcate "family life" on the English plan produced a surprising result. The *mbure-ni-sa* was gradually deserted by all but the old men; the youths went to sleep in their parents' houses, and, when the novel idea of

unmarried men sleeping in the same house with women had been digested, the other houses of the village were open to them. Association of the sexes and emancipation from parental control did the rest.[41]

The extent of the problem was considerable, forcing Thomson to resort to the liberal use of Latin to get around the obscenities necessary to describe some of the sexual activity of the Fijians in their communities. (This familiarity with and ability to write about obscene acts may have come in useful in his dealings with Sir Roger Casement eight years later.)

Clearly, in this situation, missionary uplift was insufficient. While *The Fijians* did not provide a proscription that dealt with cultural decay, as a commission report it certainly made an appeal for the strong hand of the imperial protectorate to guide the natives of these islands. This was a difficult enterprise, as Thomson's closing words in the volume indicate:

> As Sir Henry Maine said of the native policy of the government of India, those responsible for guiding native races in Fiji, as elsewhere, are "like men bound to make their watches keep true time in two longitudes at once. Nevertheless the paradoxical explanation must be accepted. If they are too slow, there will be no improvement; if they are too fast, there will be no security."[42]

The desire to help provide this much-needed security may have led Thomson into his next profession, that of Scotland Yard detective. In the ensuing Great War he would play a pivotal role, heading up the Yard's Special Branch, ensuring that the British empire was not pulled down by nationalism and patriotism tied to the decaying cultures of India and Ireland. Which must mean we need to turn to the Casement case.

Colonialism's Cultures

It is far better to make Casement ridiculous than a martyr.[43]

This will be necessarily sketchy, but then what isn't sketchy in the saga of Sir Roger Casement, about whom so much is conjecture? Whatever the cause, and it has been attributed to anything from idealism to lust for the native body,[44] Casement did not share Thomson's sanguine view of the decay of custom and the casualties it brought. Having been a labour recruiter for a railway company in the Congo Free State in the early 1890s, Casement became increasingly unhappy about "the horror" of empire. At first, he could maintain loyalty to the British empire (sharing Thomson's view that British imperialism was somehow better than other versions) and attribute the cruelties associated with the rubber plantations to the fact that they were run by Belgians. But once he became acquainted with the conditions of labourers in the Putumayo district of the Amazon, which were fostered largely by the British government, he became sceptical about the claims of the British empire (particularly when he found that Sir Edward Grey in the Foreign Office was less responsive to his dispatches even than William Howard Taft in the White House).[45] This scepticism was fuelled by his growing romanticism with regard to Irish culture, and then turned to outright hostility when the army mutiny occurred in Ireland and the Ulster loyalists essentially, in his view, hijacked the Liberal government in 1911.[46]

Casement's connections with Thomson are interesting. One would want to have been a fly on the wall in the sweltering heat of July 1911, when they both attended the Universal Races Congress at the University of London.[47] Of course, just about every notable anthropologist and sociologist of race was present at the Congress, and so they may not have fallen into conversation. Moreover, Casement's position of hostility was then still evolving, so the starkness of their differences would not have been as overt as it would become over the next few years. It is unlikely, though, that Casement would have shared Thomson's recently expressed views on the progressive impulse underlying imperial expansion. But with the majority of scholars present, most notably W.E.B. Du Bois, largely sharing Thomson's perspective, Casement would possibly have kept his dissent to himself.[48]

What a difference five years made! When Thomson interrogated Casement in Scotland Yard, after the latter had arrived in Ireland in a German submarine and been picked up on the Irish coast, their differences would have been most clear. While Casement would perhaps have insisted that he wanted to halt plans for the Easter Rising rather than provoke it – he realized that German help would not be forthcoming – he nonetheless claimed that Ireland's rights could not be subsumed under those of the empire. The duty of empire was to protect its subject peoples, and if it failed to carry out this duty, it was the right of those peoples to do as the Americans had done more than a hundred years previously. The very defence that Casement wanted used on his behalf, but which his counsel seems to have neglected, spoke to this issue. Casement had landed in Ireland. His crime, if he had committed any, needed to be judged by a jury of his peers, not in an English court. Moreover, he claimed that in supporting Ireland he was protecting his people on behalf of his king; that he was in the service of the United Kingdom, not England, against a government that since 1911 had been threatening to use armed force "against the liberties secured . . . by the Constitution and by the Parliament of Great Britain and Ireland."[49]

I do not want to discuss at length the question of whether the diaries used to undercut support for a reprieve of Casement's death sentence were forgeries. Suffice it to say that the case for forgery has never really been made in its entirety, involving as it would an intimate look at the workings of British intelligence and the creativity, in particular, of Basil Thomson. It is enough to know that Thomson lied on several occasions, producing a number of conflicting stories about how he came into possession of the diaries, and that British intelligence had Casement's writings in their possession for many months while they were desperately tracking his activities in the United States and across Europe, to deduce that something was rotten in the state of Denmark – where Casement claimed British Intelligence tried to have him killed. The British government desperately needed to discredit Casement long before he was finally arrested, as British Intelligence believed that the successful prosecution of the war would hinge largely on thwarting Irish and Indian nationalist efforts in the United States.[50] While Thomson would never take credit for arranging for a forgery of the Casement diaries, he did celebrate other acts of deception and dirty tricks that helped promote the British war effort. His own familiarity with the kinds of sexual acts described in the so-called Black Diaries, which he "witnessed" in Fiji, his ability to provide a believable account of a European working with native informants, and then his own arrest and conviction a few years after the war for indecent exposure in Hyde Park are facts that haven't been given sufficient weight in the discussion of the Casement diaries.[51]

Important to our discussion of collateral damage, though, is the way that Casement hovered on the line between being considered someone who could not be and someone who should be executed. Woodrow Wilson, who in spite of his claims to neutrality had firmly placed the United States behind the British, was nonetheless in a position whereby he needed to protest the death sentence to assuage his Irish-American constituents. (It was certainly concern about the American reaction that had prevented the British from executing Brooklyn-born Eamon de Valera in the aftermath of the Easter Rising.[52]) The leaking of excerpts of the diary took care of any resistance from the American officials, who were only too happy to see the "moral degenerate" hanged.[53]

Once again, as in cases of collateral damage or of famine victims and victims of capitalist excess in the rubber plantations of the Congo and Putumayo, it is not the death alone that is troubling. It is also the manner in which the victim is defined so that his or her death may be made palatable. At his death, Sir Roger Casement had been reduced to the level of those whose horrific experiences he had trudged through thick jungle to unearth.

Can Collateral Damage Speak?

I am not Hamlet, nor was meant to be.[54]

Eliot's Prufrock is far too genteel to be mistaken for collateral damage; and he certainly speaks, even if he doesn't say very much of anything. But if, playing games of association as we must, we turn to Hamlet's "attendant lords," Rosencrantz and Guildenstern, we may recognize in Tom Stoppard's characters the literary embodiment of collateral damage. Here we have two figures who are constantly waiting in the wings to be called onto the stage, knowing all the while that they are caught up in some political intrigue that is larger than they are and that will inevitably kill them, but never being able to do anything about it. And while, from their perspective, the play was very much about them, they will have managed only "to move a scene or two" in the history books.

The category of collateral damage and the people whom it encompasses take up a similar liminal or marginal position to that inhabited by Rosencrantz and Guildenstern. Were they agents or victims, then the story would be about them; they would be the winners or losers. If the former, then they (or at least their descendants) could take solace in the temporary favour that history has given them; if the latter, then they might become the martyrs upon whose deeds future challenges to hegemony may be built. But collateral damage is the spillage from this narrative of good and evil.

How like the category of subaltern, then, is collateral damage? As soon as it speaks, it is prone to disappear.[55] Indeed, the term becomes the sign for the unknown and unknowable, beyond the reaches of the impotent historian. These dead – what did they think of the turmoil swirling around their heads? Did it give meaning to their lives in some way? Did they identify with one side or another because of their race, their nationality, their class, or their gender? Or were they just bystanders, observing political theatre beyond their concern? These things we cannot know, and if we did the category might become evacuated as we located allies and enemies among them. What we do know is that, like Rosencrantz and Guildenstern, they are dead.

Notes

1 Patrick Cockburn, "Disgrace: A Year on from 'Mission Accomplished,' an Army in Disgrace, a Policy in Tatters and the Real Prospect of Defeat," in *The Independent*, May 3, 2004.

2 See, for example, Alan M. Kraut, *Silent Travelers: Germs, Genes, and the "Immigrant Menace"* (Baltimore: Johns Hopkins Press, 1994).

3 Amrita Lal Roy, *Reminiscences: English and American,* part 1, *Three Years among the Americans* (Calcutta: Roy Publishing House, 1888), 64.

4   Henry George, *Progress and Poverty: An Inquiry into Causes of Industrial Depressions, and of Increase of Want with Increase of Wealth. The Remedy* (1879; reprint, New York: Walter J. Black, 1942).

5   Daniel T. Rodgers, *Atlantic Crossings: Social Politics in a Progressive Age* (Cambridge, Mass.: Harvard University Press, 1998), 36.

6   Ibid., 70.

7   George Raymond Geiger, *The Philosophy of Henry George* (New York: Macmillan, 1933); Daniel Aaron, *Men of Good Hope* (New York: Oxford University Press, 1951); and Alan Trachtenberg, *The Incorporation of America: Culture and Society in the Gilded Age* (New York: Hill and Wang, 1982). "No one, Hobson believed, exercised so much influence on English radicalism in the 'eighties and 'nineties as Henry George." *Men of Good Hope*, 79. See also the comments of George Bernard Shaw, on ibid., 78.

8   Amrita Lal Roy's essay on British India, "English Rule in India," *The North American* 142 (1888), 356–70, appeared in the same issue of the journal as one of George's essays on Ireland. A.L. Roy does not mention meeting George, however.

9   For the impact of George on the Irish Land League, see Geiger, *The Philosophy of Henry George*, 56–62.

10 Henry George Jr., *Life of Henry George* (New York: Doubleday, Page, 1904), 514; see also Robert V. Andelson, "Introduction," in *Critics of Henry George*, ed. Robert V. Andelson (Rutherford, N.J.: Farleigh Dickinson University Press, 1979), 15. For Tolstoy's influence on Gandhi, see his bibliography in *An Autobiography; or the Story of My Experiments with Truth* (Ahmedabad: Navajivan Publishing House, 1948).

11 For the connections between Hyndman and Naoroji and Dutt, as well as Florence Nightingale, on whom George drew also, see Mike Davis, *Late Victorian Holocausts: El Niño Famines and the Making of the Third World* (London: Verso, 2001), 54–59.

12 Lynn Hollen Lees, *The Solidarities of Strangers: The English Poor Laws and the People* (Cambridge: Cambridge University Press, 1998), 91.

13 Ibid.; "Malthus' giant shadow" extended across the Atlantic, though in altered guise (ibid., 92–93). See also Gertrude Himmelfarb, *Poverty and Compassion: The Moral Imagination of the Late Victorians* (New York: Random House, 1991). In the United States, Malthus' impact may well have been most noticeable in the continuing influence of republicanism and the growing belief that an expanding frontier was essential as a means to enable the poor to avoid becoming trapped as their European counterparts were – a kind of displacement that meant Americans would not confront the philosophy directly until after the Civil War but rather would become deeply concerned about the impact of the frontier being closed. See Edmund Morgan, *American Slavery, American Freedom* (New York: Norton, 1975). To some extent republicanism could represent a refutation of Malthusianism in its own right, so that Henry George's work can be seen as an elaboration of republicanism, once it became necessary to consider the implications of a closing frontier. Republicanism could be seen as a contradiction of the moralistic aspects of Malthus' doctrine, for it was clearly the case in republican theory that the urban poor could rise out of this station if opportunities were presented to them, whereas Malthus believed that there was some moral failing on the part of the poor, a kind of "culture of poverty" holding them back. George's observation of the experience of the Irish in the United States, many of whom had come to the New World as a result of the potato

famine, seemed to confirm republicanism, not Malthus' more dismal assessment of them.

14 George, *Progress and Poverty*, 6

15 Ibid., 97. George here cites a lengthy passage from Rev. William Tennant's "Indian Recreations" (1804) to illustrate his point.

16 Ibid.

17 Macaulay quoted in ibid., 97–98.

18 Burke paraphrased in ibid., 98.

19 Ibid.

20 Ibid., 98–99

21 Ibid., 99–100. The words of Florence Nightingale are from "The People of India," *Nineteenth Century* (August 1878).

22 George, *Progress and Poverty*, 101.

23 Ibid., 102–03.

24 Ibid., 106.

25 Salisbury, quoted in Mike Davis, *Late Victorian Holocausts*, 32.

26 Ibid., 25–59.

27 Eric Stokes, *The Utilitarians and India* (Delhi: Oxford University Press, 1989); Francis G. Hutchins, *The Illusion of Permanence* (Princeton, N.J.: Princeton University Press, 1967).

28 Nicholas Thomas, *Colonialism's Culture: Anthropology, Travel, and Government* (Cambridge: Polity Press, 1994).

29 McAdoo is the focus of my essay, "Uneasy Streets: Police, Corruption, and Imperial Progressives in Bombay, London and New York City," in *Corrupt Histories*, ed. Emmanuel Krieke and William Chester Jordan (Rochester, N.Y.: University of Rochester Press, 2004).

30 Basil Home Thomson, *The Fijians: A Study of the Decay of Custom* (London: Heinemann, 1908), v.

31 Margaret Jolly, " 'Postcolonial' Politics – Continuities and Discontinuities," in *Remembrance of Pacific Pasts*, ed. Robert Borofsky (Honolulu: University of Hawai'i Press, 2000), 348.

32 Ibid.

33 Ibid., 348–49.

34 Thomson, *The Fijians*, vii.

35 It is interesting to note in this regard that Herbert Aptheker, in his 1975 introduction to a new edition of W.E.B. Du Bois' *The Negro* (1915), cites Basil Thomson as one of the influences on W.E.B. Du Bois when he is writing. It is unlikely that Du Bois could have known what kind of work Thomson was then undertaking at Scotland Yard.

36 Thomson, *The Fijians*, vi.

37 Ibid., viii–ix

38 Ibid., xvi.

39 Both W.E.B. Du Bois and Booker T. Washington received mention in Thomson's text as examples of "negroes of the highest attainments." An article by Thomson would later be published in Du Bois' *The Crisis*.

40 Thomson, *The Fijians*, xii.

41 Ibid., 236–37. *Mbure-ni-sa* is a segregated residence for bachelors.

42 Ibid., 390.

43 Cecil Arthur Spring Rice, British ambassador to the United States, quoted in Her-

bert O. Mackey, *Roger Casement: The Truth about the Forged Diaries* (Dublin: C.J. Fallon, 1966), 26.

44 See Colm Toibin, "The Tragedy of Roger Casement," *New York Review of Books*, May 27, 2004, 53–57.

45 Peter Singleton-Gates and Maurice Girodias, *The Black Diaries: An Account of Roger Casement's Life and Times* (Paris: Olympia Press, 1959); Roger Sawyer, *Casement, the Flawed Hero* (Boston: Routledge and Kegan Paul, 1984); Brian Inglis, *Roger Casement* (New York: Harcourt Brace Jovanovich, 1974); Herbert O. Mackey, ed., *The Crime against Europe: The Writings and Poetry of Roger Casement* (Dublin: C.J. Fallon, 1966); Basil Thomson, *Queer People* (London: Hodder and Stoughton, 1922); and *My Experiences at Scotland Yard* (Garden City, N.Y.: Doubleday, Page, 1923).

46 George Dangerfield, *The Strange Death of Liberal England* (New York: Capricorn Books, 1961).

47 G. Spiller, ed., *Papers on Inter-Racial Problems: Communicated to the First Universal Races Congress held at the University of London, July 26–29, 1911* (London: P.S. King and Son, 1911).

48 See Robert Gregg and Madhavi Kale, "*The Negro* and *The Dark Princess*: Two Legacies of the Universal Races Congress," *Radical History Review* 92 (2005), 133–52; and Robert Gregg, "Afterword" in W.E.B. Du Bois, *The Negro* (Philadelphia: University of Pennsylvania Press, 2001).

49 George H. Knott, *The Trial of Sir Roger Casement* (London: William Hodge, 1926), 150. Casement at his sentencing declared, "I for one was determined that Ireland was much more to me than 'Empire,' and that if charity begins at home so must loyalty" (203).

50 Hugh Cleland Hoy, *40 O.B. or How the War was Won* (London: Hutchinson, 1932).

51 Parts of this are mentioned in Mackey, *Roger Casement*, 20, 32, and Joseph Maloney, *The Forged Casement Diaries* (Dublin and Cork: The Talbot Press, 1936), 209–10, but these authors do not consider Thomson's background in anthropology and other aspects of his work for intelligence at Scotland Yard.

52 Owen Dudley Edwards, *Eamon de Valera* (Washington, D.C.: CUA Press, 1997), 58.

53 Thus when Joseph Tumulty, the president's private secretary, approached Wilson about the matter he responded, "It would be inexcusable for me to touch this. It would invite serious international embarrassment." Mackey, *Roger Casement*, 31.

54 T.S. Eliot, "The Love Song of J. Alfred Prufrock," *Prufrock and Other Observations* (London: The Egoist, 1917).

55 Gayatri Chakravorty Spivak, "Can the Subaltern Speak?" in *Marxism and the Interpretation of Culture*, ed. Cary Nelson and Lawrence Grossberg (Urbana: University of Illinois Press, 1988), 271–313.

"Elegant and Dignified Military Operations in the Present Age"

The Imperfect Invisibility of Collateral Damage in Late-Nineteenth-Century Metropolitan Illustrated Magazines

This chapter discusses some evidence of how overseas imperialism looked to imperialists at home as the nineteenth century turned into the twentieth. In the pages of up-market general-interest illustrated weekly magazines in London and Paris, imperialism looked like wholesome, though dangerous, fun.[1] On very rare occasions, however, representations of collateral damage found in these prosperous journals poisoned the wholesomeness or destabilized the fun. This essay examines some things that these non-standard images can tell us or force us to ask, but first it concentrates on the conventions, and on the huge majority of representations, to which such images are exceptions. I focus on English media, and particularly on pictures published in the *Illustrated London News* (*ILN*), but one can find confirmation in any of the journals surveyed of the fact that these magazines published thousands of pictures of imperial conflicts while very seldom illustrating the impact of imperialist violence on the lives of subject peoples.[2]

Journalistic pictures of the haphazard, unjust, cruel, and uncivilized ("barbaric") dimensions of imperial military activity were very rare for many reasons. The production of such representations would be incompatible with some of the fundamental assumptions that made nineteenth-century French and British imperialism seem like a good idea to the British and French. These indispensable assumptions are first, that the military is competent; second, that imperial military activity brings an increase of happiness to the subjected peoples; and third, that the peoples incorporated into the empire have until then been uncivilized. With the idea of civilization come the satellite concepts of "civil" and "civilian"; thus until civilization had been brought, it was impossible to suppose that any casualties could be civilian, and in the absence of a distinction between civil society and the state, there could to imperial eyes be no identifiable boundary to their opponents' armies, no clearly distinguishable non-combatants.[3]

As part of a larger project, I have conducted a systematic five-year sampling of four of the leading illustrated weekly magazines in England and France in the second half of the nineteenth century – the *Illustrated London News*, *L'Illustration*, *The Graphic*, and *Le Monde illustré* – and have for this essay done a more focused trawl through some periods that were especially newsworthy in terms of imperial military activity. Although by 1900 the heyday of such magazines was perhaps over, they continued to have a particular cultural authority. One of their crucial representational functions was to establish the specifically metropolitan dimension of the events and personalities they reported. Partly for this reason, since a metropolis cannot be a metropolis without its *coloniae*, these magazines figured colonial and imperial powers and adventures very fully among their subjects, and took considerable care to inscribe a colonial-imperial readership within their covers. Thus colonial wars were a favourite subject matter; they had held this place of honour since the genre emerged in the early 1840s, first in London and then in Paris.

The visual resources for representation of the work of war had largely become standardized by the end of the century, in terms both of the genres that were mobilized and of the repertoire of topics normally deployed in representing the cycle of a campaign. This does not signify that the meanings of such representations had become entirely conventional: in at least one of the pictures I show here (of an execution, Figure 6, below), there seems to be some anxiety about the legitimacy of the action represented and some possibility of an identification other than with the firing squad, given the large contingent of mounted officers set high up in the image to give needed authority to the executioners.

A set of images within a series would start with pictures of the outrages, or the locations of the outrages, or the perpetrators of the outrages, or the victims of the outrages, any of which had made military intervention a necessity. Then there would be pictures of the generals appointed to lead the expeditionary force, and, when relevant, pictures of the expeditionary troops embarking from a French or British port. "Library pictures" of the port of arrival, of the principal topographical features of the area to be invaded or terrorized, and of the villainous ruler or insurrectionist to be brought low would also feature (Figures 1 and 2).

Then, at a decent interval, there would be a combination of further officers' portraits, genre images of camp life, pictures of battles and skirmishes in the hills, savannah, or jungle (Figures 3 and 4). Next, there might sometimes

Figure 1: "The Zulu War in South Africa: Cetewayo, the Zulu King. Drawn from life in June 1877, by the late Mr. Edward Tilt, during his visit to Zulu-land," wood engraving, 268 x 215 mm. *ILN*, February 22, 1879, 141, Goldsmith's Library, University of London, author photo.

appear genre images of hospitalized or convalescent soldiers, often attended by trim-looking nurses. On punitive expeditions, texts might refer to the work of burning and demolition, but after 1880 images seldom encompassed such actions or effects, and neither the haphazard impact of military violence nor its miserable aftermath had any place in this conventionalized suite of imagery (Figures 3 through 6).

The ideological functions of such a flow of images are various. Some are

Figure 2: "The War in Afghanistan / Lieutenant-General Donald Martin Stewart, C.B., commanding the expedition to Candahar," wood engraving, 200 x 174 mm; "Fort of Kapiyanga, Entrance to Khoorum Pass," wood engraving, 126 x 213 mm. *ILN*, January 11, 1879, 36, Goldsmith's Library, University of London, author photo.

Figure 3: "The Indian Frontier Rising: Gurkhas Descending a Pass in the Upper Mohmand Country under Fire," signed R. Caton Woodville, half-tone screen from wash drawing, 300 x 224 mm. *ILN*, September 25, 1897, 405, Goldsmith's Library, University of London, author photo.

obvious: representations of power, domination, glory, heroism, and magnanimity glamorize imperial adventurism, bring its epic allure into metropolitan libraries and drawing rooms. Some are not so obvious. Much of the imagery represents the balance of forces in the clash of battle as roughly equal:

Figure 4: "The Indian Frontier Rising. From sketches by Lieut-Colonel C. Pulley, Gurkha Rifles with the Tirah Field Force," half-tone screen from wash drawing, 162 x 234 mm; "The 'Khan Sahib' Has His Hair Cut with the Clippers," half-tone screen from wash drawing, 166 x 235 mm. *ILN*, November 6, 1897, 638, Goldsmith's Library, University of London, author photo.

Figure 5: "The Advance in the Soudan / Making Dum-Dum Bullets at Damarli, near Berber. Drawn by Wal Paget from a photograph by Major C.W. Cockburn," half-tone screen from wash drawing, 150 x 228 mm. *The Graphic*, April 23, 1898, 500, Goldsmith's Library, University of London, author photo. Dum-dum bullets were soon to be outlawed in an early Hague Convention.

plucky Brits or Frenchmen battle zealous Pathans or Berbers; manliness is fairly distributed, even if cleanliness is not.

I have seen thousands of such pictures, and among this profusion there are perhaps only a couple of dozen that involve any representation of the fact that the British or the French military cause the death of non-combatants and blight the lives of the families whose lands they conquer or punish. And there

Figure 6: "The Afghan War: Execution of a Ghazi, or Mohammedan Fanatic, at the Peshawur gate, Jellalabad. From a sketch by our special artist," worked up by W. Overend, wood engraving, 265 x 215 mm. *ILN*, February 8, 1879, 117, Goldsmith's Library, University of London, author photo.

are fewer than a dozen images that make such episodes in any sense their subject. As it happens, most of these images are from London's journals, rather than from Paris. But the set is too small to draw any general conclusions about the relative slaughter-blindness of the French or the British bourgeoisie. In any case, the evidence is overwhelmingly that in neither country were civilian casualties welcome at the imperial feast.

Before discussing my handful of exceptional images, it is worth considering the process of origination, filtering, and mediation that was completed when they were printed on the pages of the *Illustrated London News* or *The Graphic*.[4] Newspapers would send artists as well as war correspondents to accompany imperial expeditions in the South African veldt, Sudan, the Northwest frontier, Madagascar, or Indochina. These men would sketch what interested them, and then try to get their sketches back to London or Paris to be turned into newspaper pictures; alongside this picture supply, the magazines were also sent sketches and photos by serving soldiers or sailors and by freelance journalists.

The delays between event and illustration for this sort of material were long. Pictures could not be sent by telegram: real pieces of paper had to be transported from encampment or fleet to the metropolis, arriving weeks or months after the telegraphic announcement of the mere events to be represented had first been made. After the sketch arrived, it still had to be turned into a magazine picture. In 1880, that meant in the great majority of cases that it had to be redrawn by an artist, who worked it up into something much more like a finished watercolour or drawing than a notational sketch. This "artwork" had then to be transferred onto a block of wood, either by redrawing or, more likely in 1880, by using an end-grain woodblock as the support for a photographic print. Then came the wood engraving, the process by which the picture on the block was carved by hand into a relief printing surface.

By 1900, very few sketches or photographs were being turned into wood engravings, but the tradition of editorial reinterpretation of the reportorial images provided by correspondents to the magazine was still strong.[5] Many, if not most, photographs would be translated into wash drawings with firmer tonal variation and clearer outlines, but still showing clearly their derivation from a photograph, before being turned into a half-tone printing block. Many correspondents' sketches were simply reinterpreted, either as new drawings or, more frequently, as wash drawings, by a London- or Paris-based artist, whose signature could well be more prominent than that of the far-flung sketch provider. Sometimes, more often in England than in France, the war artist's original sketch would be photographed and presented as "the original sketch"; but in general the rule of multiple mediations between the work of the artist and the picture in the magazine held sway right through the period of the Boer War.

The question of the relationship between texts and images in these magazines is complex. During the period under discussion, the English media in particular were developing a practice of giving an extended discursive caption for each picture as well as a brief title. The caption might give the circumstances of the picture's making, explain what was represented, or connect the picture to some ongoing debate or story. As well as such captions, the magazines also carried extended blocks of text, still vestigially subject to a convention that had been very powerful until the mid-1880s, that texts and images should be presented in separate parts of the journal, offered as distinct and separate modes of representation with distinct conventions and satisfactions to offer. Both the discursive captions and the relevant editorial texts tended to reduce the novelty of news stories. The discursive captions were supplementary to the image, rather than to any particular story, and tended to embroider the picture's anecdotal context rather than stressing its journalistic impact. It was in the interest of the magazines to reduce, in their editorial texts, the urgency and the glamour of the "news" aspect of their news coverage, both texts and images, since they could not compete with the daily press on immediacy. Pictures in general interest weekly illustrated magazines, that is to say, could not be promoted primarily as hot news, as part of the primary stream of information about the conflict in question.[6] As the products of a process of filtration, organization, and construction, they had to be given the status of summative representations, aiming to achieve a different sort of truth from that available in the daily press. They rendered vivid, clear, and memorable reported events that had a few days, or in the case of imperial conflicts a few weeks, earlier seemed disjointed and confusing. As such they are always implicitly monumental.

The constraints of production and the enthusiasms, reticences, and rhetorics entailed in the wider cultural role of these journals must have tended to ensure that images of collateral damage and civilian casualties would, if ever contemplated, have been left on the drawing board or rejected in the editorial office. I have so far left the problem of censorship aside. Where there is military authority, there is censorship. War correspondents had their dispatches read by a military censor, war artists had their sketches vetted, and even where this did not lead to actual refusals to transmit, it must certainly have led to more or less well-internalized self-censorship. While it was easy to send home pictures of the enemy's mistakes or brutalities, it was difficult, to say the least, to send home pictures of atrocities or collateral damage inflicted by our own boys. British military censors, French military censors, Boer military censors, Russian, Turkish, Chinese, Japanese, or American military censors controlled access and transmission routes, and were happy to use that power.[7] But back home in England or France, there was in this period no censorship as such, and no legal inhibitions on the publication of texts or pictures beyond the normal bars on obscenity, blasphemy, libel, and treason. Inhibitions that operated at the front had no legal force in terms of editorial decisions in London or Paris. The stock-in-trade of the military genre was so well established that pictures could have been concocted at home from narrative reports in the matter of atrocities, as they regularly were for other sorts of news story, especially where there were plenty of "local colour" pictures on file. Military censorship thus cannot explain the persistent scarcity of pictures of even the generic effects of imperial military activity resulting in displaced populations or destroyed villages.

Self-censorship takes many forms. The war artist who does not draw a certain sort of picture because he knows that the military censor would never pass it and might cease to bestow favours is self-censoring. But self-censorship also takes place in relation to what the magazine's editors think that their readers are prepared to look at. Sometimes, in special circumstances, these magazines may articulate their concern for their readers' sensibilities. More often, one is left to infer the existence of a reticence, a reluctance, a protectiveness of the delicacy of their bourgeois family public.

This reticence was always contextual and conditional, not determined by the abstract terribleness of the thing to be shown; nor were these artists and their editors unprepared to show the horrible in such a way as would maximize its impact. I have found a handful of pictures in which civilian deaths, in civilian accidents, are shown in "full frontal" detail and a handful of pictures of the aftermath of battle that focus on the dead.[8] Among them is a grimly exultant French picture of British deaths in battle in the Transvaal in 1900. Since this essay concludes with a discussion of the representation of collateral damage in the Anglo-Boer War, it is perhaps worth a specific comment here. The picture represents a trench full of dead British soldiers, killed in a battle between Britain's imperial army and the army of another "white" nation state (Figure 7).

Late in January 1900, the British, attempting to relieve the siege of Ladysmith, lost a bloody battle at Spion Kop. Heroic retreats, grace under fire and desperate courage figured in London illustrated magazines' pictures of the battle, but the central facts of reckless leadership, slaughter, and defeat were largely absent. Not so in France. "La guerre au Transvaal. – Champ de bataille de Spionkop. – Une tranchée de cadavres anglais. – (Photographie Van Holpen)" is the front-page picture from *Le Monde illustré* nine weeks after the battle, on March 31, 1900. The French wished the British no luck at all in the Boer War, so as well as its primary impact in terms of a universalizing human sympathy, the image has a secondary force as Schadenfreude. Since universalizing human sympathy was so rarely deployed in relation to the effects of military violence, we may suppose that it was licensed in this case by its political dimension, given that the French might be pleased to see a trench full of dead Brits.

There are other images in which casualties are represented – of our wounded boys or our dead heroes – as a way of signifying the courage and honour of those who survive, as well as images of the enemy's dead fighters as

Figure 7: "La guerre au Transvaal. – Champ de bataille de Spionkop. – Une tranchée de cadavres anglais. – (Photographie Van Holpen)," worked up and engraved by H. Dochy, wood engraving, 295 x 245 mm. *Le Monde illustré*, March 31, 1900, 209, British Library, author photo.

a sign of the cost of war and the folly of resistance. From time to time, such pictures exceed this conventional set of representational tasks and let one imagine the deadness of the dead, or understand their sheer numbers as a slaughter; but such pictures, like the Spion Kop front page, do not raise the question of collateral damage. They represent war's product in an unusually direct way, but they do not mention its by-product.

This part of the essay, on images of the British Army blowing up or burning down what one normally takes to be non-military targets, has three aspects to the discussion. The first deals with some remarkable pictures of actions taken by imperialists against cultures and populations clearly excluded from "us"; the second with pictures of military actions against holy places; and the third, visual representations of the conduct of British imperial forces toward civilian populations in the long terminal phase of the Boer War, focusing on one particular image, in which the invisibility of collateral damage is evidently imperfect (Figure 13).

Figure 8: "The Zulu War: Isandlwana Revisited – Fetching away the Wagons, May 21. From a sketch by our special artist, Mr. Melton Prior," worked up by W. Overend, wood engraving, 315 x 480 mm. *ILN*, July 12, 1879, 44–45, Goldsmith's Library, University of London, author photo. This print was published without text on its reverse: it was intended to be pulled out and pinned up.

To start, I want to discuss a handful of images of British actions against "native" villages, both in South Africa in 1879 and later in Kashmir. In late 1878, the British government considered it necessary to invade independent Zululand to punish its king, Cetewayo, for actions he had taken to protect his acknowledged treaty rights against the Boers in the Transvaal.[9] The expedition was arrogantly mismanaged, and a force of British and "native contingent" troops, around 1,000 men in all, was surrounded and killed at Isandlwana. Through most of the rest of 1879 the British pursued their revenge on Cetewayo and his army. They burned Zulu settlements (generically known as kraals) and fought with Cetewayo's *impis*, finally burning his largest settlement, Ulundi, and capturing the king.[10]

The debacle at Isandlwana made sensational news. Thus, when the British forces returned to the battlefield to collect the wagons left there, the *ILN* gave the scene its centrefold, to memorialize this half-year-old calamity (Figure 8). The picture is strikingly composed as a grand-manner landscape. In the middle ground, groups of soldiers pick their way through skeletons of oxen and soldiers and the detritus of a sacked encampment to retrieve the wagons; behind this scene rears a kop, a south African *mesa*, which gives an authentic topography to this scene. However, in the context of this essay, God is in the details. In the foreground, the *ILN*'s readers are shown representative figures viewing both the middle ground and the detritus on the earth at their feet: a jumbled still life with skulls and the possessions of the soldiers who had lost their lives in the defeat. One notices in particular the long-handled hairbrush and album of *carte de visite* photographs, locating the loss of life within a particular class culture (that of the *ILN*'s target readers) and inscribing in the scene a link between metropolitan material and visual culture and the imperial experience that the image itself produces and reproduces.

The wagons being fetched away had belonged to the military force that had been overwhelmed; as this contingent of troops, irregulars, and native scouts contemplates the work of repossession, one of the justifying strands of this encounter between civilization and savagery seems to be that the Zulus have no use for the wagons, any more than for the portmanteaus, the photographs, or the hairbrushes. They have no use for our material culture, and this fact justifies and normalizes our extirpation of theirs.

In the background can be seen four sources of flame and smoke. The text that accompanies this piece does not mention them specifically, but other texts linked to pictures on the same theme do: these are Zulu kraals, and they have been burned by the advancing imperial army. Material goods are being looted, livestock butchered, and the houses burned out everywhere across the veldt, as far as the eye can see. In images such as these the burning of homesteads is not represented as collateral damage: the photo album and the hairbrushes tell us that this is a struggle between incompatible cultures, and since culture is a totalizing concept, collaterality is inconceivable.

This unambiguous but many-layered image and the dozen other images that show kraal burning or looting during the campaign of 1879 have a remarkable sequel (Figure 9). This is a facsimile-style wood engraving combining four sketches by the *ILN*'s special artist, Melton Prior. The collaging will almost certainly have been done by an anonymous staff artist, charged with redrawing a range of sketching styles and finishes to standardize them to the

ILN's house style. At the top, Prior depicts himself, twice, being thrown from his horse: the first time in a landscape in which smoke from burning kraals can be seen, by now almost as much of a topographical cliché as the flat-top hills. In the centre-left picture he is disturbed by an over-anxious "native" scout while attempting to sketch a skirmish, and in the largest image, he and another journalist set fire to a kraal while Africans look on. Some of them are clearly "native scouts," but some appear to be locals watching the destruction of their homes, incensed but powerless. Like the other three sketches, this image has a title inscribed at its foot: "Special artists setting fire to a kraal," and the page title refers the reader to a text on page 366. The text runs thus:

> The performance of an incendiary act, doubtless by order of the general in command, at one of the enemy's kraals or villages, might perhaps have been left to the hands of soldiers; but it was thought expedient, in this instance, that the Europeans present should set an example to the native troops. African warfare is not very nice; and there is a saying we have heard among officers who have served at the cape, that "a kaffir war is the snob of all wars." However needful it may be, the burning of huts and the driving away of cattle to inflict distress on a hostile population cannot be regarded as the most elegant and dignified of military operations in the present age.[11]

This comment throws into question the authority under which the burnings were carried out, carrying the implication that the higher the authority the more problematic. It is a remark full of contradictions, succeeding in being both humanitarian and racist. It communicates a distinct lack of enthusiasm for this form of "pacification," as well as the feeling that such action is beneath the dignity of the British Army.

Neither of these attitudes was often voiced; neither of them seems to have inflected many visual representations of the actions of European armies or the experiences of local populations. That the *ILN* printed Melton Prior's remarks suggests that to some extent his distaste at this sort of action was shared. So does the fact that it chose make this sketch the largest in the collaged image: its emphatic inclusion indicates clearly that the decision to publish both text and image was a collective and a deliberate one. It shows that the processes of filtering and consensus that are entailed in the making and publishing of a magazine illustration such as this can sometimes leave a trace of controversy, rather than of consensus. In this case, there is evidently a specific debate about whether war against the Zulu armies should be accompanied by war against Zulu settlements. But there is also, perhaps, another struggle, over the representational role of the illustrated magazine in relation to the imperial project. In this image and its understated text we see a trace of the failure of consensus

Figure 9: "Our Special Artist's Adventures in Zululand," wood engraving, 215 x 312 mm. *ILN*, October 18, 1879, 368, Goldsmith's Library, University of London, author photo.

that for a moment disrupted the measured and controlled surface of the magazine, giving its readers a glimpse of the fact that every monument to civilization is also a monument to barbarism.[12]

That the campaign of 1879 induced a crisis in representation and a change of policy in this section of the British press is suggested by the fact that though pictures of torched kraals are recurrent motifs in the 1879 imagery, even occurring on blank-on-the-back, pull-out-and-keep pictures, such scenes almost never figure in representations of imperial military actions from the 1880s onward, though certainly these were not the last dwellings that Tommy Atkins torched.[13]

Figure 10: "The Indian Frontier Rising: The Burning of a Native Village outside the British Camp at Bagh. From a sketch by our special artist, Mr. Melton Prior," worked up by H. Seppings Wright, half-tone screen from wash drawing, 312 x 450 mm. *ILN*, January 8, 1898, 52–53, Goldsmith's Library, University of London, author photo.

Almost never. We meet pictures of a burning village again, after a twenty-year gap, in a curious episode on the northwest frontier of India (Figure 10). The episode occurred in the course of a punitive expedition called the Malakand Field Force. It was pictured in a double-page spread in the *ILN* and in a very similar scene, one of four, on a page in *The Graphic*.[14]

In the autumn of 1897, a British army was sent to extinguish an uprising in Kashmir. While encamped outside Bagh, this force came under attack from opportunist snipers, using the cover of darkness. The local authorities in the surrounding villages were warned that if the firing continued, their villages would be burned (this at the onset of winter in the Himalayan foothills). The sniping continued. The villages were burned. There was, in the early morning after the fires had been set, a temperature inversion in the valley where the action had been taken. This meant that the smoke rising from the burning buildings was trapped at the level of the valley rim, which provided a spectacle exotic and interesting enough to overcome the tendency of the *ILN* (and *The Graphic*) not to report the results of pacification actions against the general population.

The publication of both these pictures of action against imperfect military targets is accompanied by two specific justifications, one military and the other spectacular: the work had to be done, and the visual result was amazing. Both reports have the smoke in the background, the positions held by the Indian Army in the foreground. The double-page spread in the *ILN* puts two British officers, once of them with field glasses, in the foreground; the middle ground is taken up by a neat and regular military encampment, evidently occupied by native troops, with the occasional officer visible. The picture's formal disposition carries a clear political implication: the population of the empire faces two alternatives: supervision by the occupying power, or ruthless and extensive destruction. That this message is not aimed at the subject populations of the empire but at their metropolitan overlords and -ladies makes it no less significant.

The punitive arson of 1897, while troublesome for the fantasy of elegant and dignified military operations, is not represented as collateral damage. In both the Zulu and the Malakand instances, non-combatant casualties are implied though not specified. We are thus certainly permitted to imagine the consequences, in terms of cold and hunger, for those Kashmiris whose homes and resources have been destroyed. Although it may have been harder to imagine the half-clothed African savages actually needing a material culture (as suggested by their failure to loot), it is indicated that their lives will be poorer and more uncomfortable for the kraal torchings. However, in both cases such consequences are intended, are indeed the whole point. The overarching assumption governing such actions is that the warriors and the general population are indistinguishable, that the population as a whole is at war. In the case of the Malakand Field Force in Kashmir, this assumption was in conflict with another about the influence of the village leaders, which suggests that a civil authority was recognized and that its power over the local military might be effective. It turned out not to be. Just as the Zulus' inability to loot like civilized people had cast them as savages and made them available for coaxial reprisals, so the inability of the local headmen to control the military could trigger the gestalt switch that erased the distinction, in the minds of soldiers and of the illustrated magazines' readers alike, between military casualties and civilian ones. In the circumstances, the discourse that categorizes the

Pathans as "tribesmen" rather than as "imperial subjects" triumphs, and a desert is made to produce peace.[15]

As I have indicated, such images of the direct impact of military action on civilian populations were rare, and became rarer as late-nineteenth-century imperialism hit its stride. But the fact that imperialism is a struggle to extinguish not merely armies but cultures remained a central theme of the way these journals represented empire. For the most part, these culture-extinction representations take the form of pictures of the monuments and achievements of civilization. However, from time to time the veil is twitched aside and imperial civilization's resort to barbarism is laid bare in representations of imperial actions not against defenceless populations or the material culture of subject populations but in violence against the material supports of the symbolic resources of the peoples to be subjected or punished. Such images are very rare indeed. I have found only two absolutely clear and frontal visual representations of such "civilizing" iconoclasm. Both are contrived pictures that clarify and distil the events they represent. The first comes from another British punitive expedition, this time against Ashanti populations in what is now Ghana, in 1895 (Figure 11).

As the 1895 British expedition against the Ashanti progressed, it came upon a local shrine in which skeletal human remains, principally skulls, were arranged round the base of the trees in a sacred grove. As part of its punitive progress, the British force used high explosive to demolish the trees and their votive calvaries. The text that accompanies this shocking picture, published back in London four months after the event, is highly technocratic in its rhetoric:

> An incident in the destruction of one of the sacred groves of Ashanti is here depicted. The trees in the grove were blown down by the engineers in the following fashion. Five holes were bored into a tree and were charged with guncotton. The bugles then sounded the alarm, and the men having withdrawn to a safe distance, the charges were exploded by means of electricity. The great tree then fell, cut through as cleanly as though by a knife.[16]

Together with the lack of living humans in the image, the impersonal verbs and the combination of historical and technical language act to represent the violence as surgical rather than as barbaric. Modern technology (nitrocellulose and electricity) triumphs both over nature and over old and cruel superstitions. Because this African glade is a place of sacrifice and of skulls, reference to Golgotha and the story of the crucifixion would have been inescapable; thus this display of technological power could be mapped directly onto the process of bringing Christianity to a heathen world, and a scientific supernatural evoked. In terms of the preoccupations of this essay, the precision, method, and modernity of the processes of destruction neutralize the vandalism of the

Figure 11: "The Ashanti Expedition: The Fall of a Fetish. Drawn by our special artist, Mr. H.C. Seppings Wright," half-tone screen from wash drawing, 316 x 230 mm. *ILN*, March 14, 1896, 333, Goldsmith's Library, University of London, author photo.

action, focusing the imputation of barbarity on that which is destroyed. There are no civilians here, no "merely" religious beliefs. Sacred groves with "primitive fetishes" are the enemy; electro-detonated dynamite is the weapon; Christianity, and its transcendence of Golgotha, is the victory.

We may also observe the logic that legitimized such actions at work in circumstances less easy to parse in terms of us and them, modern and primitive. A picture published in the *ILN* on December 1, 1900, offers such an instance (Figure 12). Entitled "Getting at the Root of the Evil: The Destruction of a Chinese Temple on the Bank of the Pei-Ho," this is a double-page spread: the sort of picture that is available to cut out and keep (though, with regular pagination and text printed on the verso, the magazine does not present the image as being specifically *intended* for pinning up), and that is certainly offered as bearing the admiration and enthusiasm of the magazine's editors.

Figure 12: "With the Allied Forces in China / Getting at the Root of the Evil: The Destruction of a Chinese Temple on the Bank of the Pei-Ho. From a sketch by Mr. John Schönberg, our special artist in China," worked up by Forestier, half-tone screen from wash drawing, 316 x 462 mm. *ILN*, December 1, 1900, 812–13, Goldsmith's Library, University of London, author photo.

It is impossible to know what first readers would have made of this image, or of the image of the dynamiting of the sacred Ashanti grove. But it is at least possible that the Chinese report was more problematic, if not more disturbing, than the African. In the Chinese case, the destruction is not of something frightful and unfamiliar, of something easy to categorize as savage and benighted. It is more difficult to imagine the destruction as a cleansing. By 1900, the British had long regarded Chinese architecture as beautiful, and both Chinese sculpture and Chinese landscape painting, of which the branches and trunks of pine trees are a constitutive motif, as having exquisite qualities. It had also been normal to accept Chinese religious practices as embodying ancient and legitimate traditions holding real stores of wisdom, even though their eclipse by Christianity would in the long term be both inevitable and desirable.

This tradition of respect for Chinese culture was placed in abeyance at the very end of the nineteenth century by the fact that some Chinese factions, some of them with specific religious affiliations, had recently offered Western businessmen, missionaries, and diplomatic legations xenophobic violence, including the violence of an armed siege of the Westerners' diplomatic compounds in Beijing.

The temple burning was a response to that siege, which was easy to represent as a violation of all the normal rules governing warfare and the relation between states, thus licensing retaliatory actions beyond military engagements.[17] Despite the "back story," this representation of the military's spoliation of symbolic cultural resources had to be justified and legitimated, with a specific textual spin on the image. The caption refers to Chinese religious practices as "the evil," and encourages the fantasy that destroying the temple will destroy the tradition and the practice. The more plausible motives for this incendiarism – revenge, punishment, cultural humiliation – are suppressed, and that most us/them of rhetorics, the battle between good and evil, is invoked. However, since the *ILN* is not a religious tract but a general interest weekly magazine, this apocalyptic tone has to be domesticated, anchored. In the Ashanti case, the clash of cultural principles had been normalized by emptying the human dimension from the image, representing it as a clash between atavism and science.

In contrast to the picture of the Ashanti sacred grove, the picture of the burning of the Chinese temple is very well staffed: seven British soldiers, including an officer (nearest to us), and one Chinese man watch the blaze, while another soldier finds a place from which to spectate, and a solitary soldier scavenges a sculptured head, like a hot potato, from the ruin. These idlers evoke a bonfire scene and thus reassure the viewer by domesticating the destructive savagery; the means are different, but the end, the normalization of violent cultural intolerance, is the same as that achieved by the technical and historicizing rhetoric in the dynamiting of the Ashanti shrine.

In all the images discussed so far, the violence depicted produced, or was understood to have produced, intended effects. In these representations, the issue of whether the targets of the violence have been "civilian" or otherwise has been largely irrelevant; none of the damage inflicted has been represented as collateral. The images and their associated texts may raise in their readers' minds the idea that there could be more than one way of fighting a war or extirpating a troublesome culture, more than one axis of military action, but nothing has been depicted as beside the target, beyond sanctioned intentions. Damage to targets less than obviously military has been represented as coaxial, not collateral.

―――――――

The final section of this essay deals with actions in which these two mechanisms – the denial of the caesura between civil and military, and the masking of collateral by coaxial – functioned much less effectively but were nevertheless necessary ingredients in both the conduct of war and the processes of its representation for metropolitan consumption.

The Boers were a "white" group, whose aspirations to develop a nation state in southern Africa independent of the British Cape Colony had been irritating but not intolerable before the discovery of gold and diamonds in large quantities in the emergent republics. However, in 1899 British interference in the internal affairs of the Transvaal and the Orange Free State was followed by ultimatums and the outbreak of hostilities. The war went very badly at first for the imperial forces, and even after various sieges had been lifted and the Boers' field armies dispersed, the British found it extremely difficult to keep control of the countryside. The war mutated in and after the first quarter of 1900. What had been expected to be a conflict between armies in the field turned into one in which civilian populations became directly involved, first as the Boers laid siege to Ladysmith and Mafeking, and then as the British developed a strategy for defeating the Boer irregular forces, working in small bands called Kommandos, by depopulating the countryside in which they operated. The Boer population was driven from its farms and concentrated in large camps away from the fighting. The abandoned farmsteads might be used as shelter or strongpoints by the Boer guerrillas, so they were often dynamited once the Boer families had been moved away.

The policy of concentrating the Boer population in barbed wire internment camps was a military success but a political and public-relations disaster. The camps were not adequately prepared or serviced, and tens of thousands of Boer women and children died during late 1900 and 1901. International opinion focused on the concentration camps as a clearly atrocious policy, and a strong coalition emerged in the United Kingdom during 1900, bringing together pacifists, humanitarians, internationalists, anti-imperialists and feminists.

The imperial military in South Africa had decided to win the war against the Boers by turning it from a war between armies into one between an army and a population. Given that the Boers were a white, Protestant, Indo-European-speaking, nation-forming political and ethnic community, the decision to project onto them the technologies that work when civilization meets barbarism took a certain amount of ideological, as well as military, work. In the *ILN* and *The Graphic*, as elsewhere, the Kommandos and their families were represented as cunning but stupid, backward, treacherous, dishonourable; that is, representation worked to move them out of the category of "us," where in the early months of the war they had resided, into the category of "them."

This work did not perfectly succeed. Though none of the few pictures of the concentration camps present them as anything other than well organized, well run and well meaning, both the *ILN* and *The Graphic* carried a regular trickle of representations of farms being sacked by the imperial military, families evicted, and farmsteads burned or dynamited. The representations began as early as May 1900, when the scorched earth policy of the imperial generals, faced with the Boers' adoption of a war of movement and dispersal, was already being developed, though the bureaucratization of the concentration camp system had not yet been put into place. Usually the captions of such pictures asserted that the imperial forces had been fired on under a flag of truce from the farmhouse under demolition. But such pictures also usually made perfectly legible the fact that the imperial troops looted the properties and that civilians (women, children) bore the brunt of the violence against their homes. There is a steady stream of images of the British soldier as a looter, all of them amused, tolerant, boys-will-be-boys-ish, though from time to time there is an implied reproof in that troops carrying sewing machines and euphoniums will not find it easy to march far or fast enough.

Usually, one can be confident that this "sympathy for the enemy" reading of the iconographic clues is not in the minds of the picture's originators or producers at the magazine. Lieutenant Hennessy's sketch "A Punishment for the Abuse of a White Flag" (*ILN*, September 29, 1900, 445), worked up by the military artist R. Caton Woodville, is a case in point. It shows mounted troopers driving the farm's cattle, and its one-note representation makes an earlier, and superficially rather similar picture (Figure 13) all the more striking.

Figure 13, "Just Retribution: Burning the House and Confiscating the Goods of a Boer Who Fired upon Our Troops under the White Flag," has been printed as a double-page spread: the *ILN* has decided that its readers should pay maximum attention to the representation. And the caption writers have done their best to make our encounter with the scene capable of only one interpretation. Justice is invoked, and the idea that by firing on our boys under a flag of truce, the Boers have put themselves outside the pale of civilization is suggested; "confiscating" also gives somewhat more legitimacy than "looting" would. But one wonders whether that caption had been in the mind of our old friend Melton Prior when he made the sketch on which Caton Woodville's picture is based. One wonders, too, whether the editorial team at

Figure 13: "Just Retribution: Burning the House and Confiscating the Goods of a Boer Who Fired upon Our Troops under the White Flag. From a sketch by our special artist, Mr. Melton Prior," worked up by R. Caton Woodville, half-tone screen from wash drawing, 312 x 480 mm. *ILN*, May 26, 1900, supplement 4–5, Goldsmith's Library, University of London, author photo.

the *ILN* was so unanimously supportive of the way the war was being conducted as is the rhetoric of the caption. The most obvious problem with a settled meaning for this picture is in the figure of the young woman – presumably the elder daughter in the household – shaking her fist at the troops. She is the most still, the most stable element of the picture, with all the conventional signs for innocence and appeal; thus she is both compositionally and semiotically at odds both with her gesture and with her position as "the enemy." This disjunction forces us to imagine ourselves into her situation, whereas a demonized, dynamic, enraged body would have forced its signifying charge melodramatically upon us. There are other compositional and semiotic problems. The carriage being hauled away to the right is an object that would call forth the strongest of identifications with the *ILN*'s readers: upholstered seat, carriage lamp, and folded hood combine to suggest strongly that this is collateral damage against "us" rather than "them": the rupture of a recognizably middle-class existence. And the confrontation (if it is that) between the woman of the house (a daughter behind her) and a black man over the dressing table adds an absolutely relevant racist dimension to this troubled image: Black is laying hands on the bedroom property of White. This implied conflict is amplified by the mattresses that connect the anecdote in the middle ground with the confrontation in the foreground: the rifle that crosses the mattresses toward the enraged elder daughter of the house is itself suggestive, a suggestion reinforced by the unfortunate shape of the saddle the trooper carries on his other arm. These two central figures stare aggressively at one another; this exchange is not, it turns out, a matter of justice, but a personal and furious encounter in which "retribution" is undercut by savage desires and unspeakable deeds. In this picture, the binomial operations on which the success of representing collateral damage as "coaxial damage," of denying civilian casualties by denying the existence of civilians, collapse.

But we have seen how they have tended to collapse whenever such representations have been attempted. Refusal to depict was the only effective way of dealing with the problem of how to picture collateral damage, as the aftermath of the representation of the 1879 Zulu war showed. After the repeated representations of kraal burning had been subverted by Melton Prior's representation of himself as an arsonist, making the *ILN*'s readers complicit with the action, the visual reporting of collateral damage took a long holiday. The self-censoring practice was disturbed only when religion could be called in to justify the violence (collateral redemption, I suppose you would call it); or when, as at Bagh, the destruction of culture resulted in a natural spectacle. The Boer War could not be contained in this way. The military effort was too great, the international attention too intense and contestatory, but above all, the enemy was too like us. After the Boer sieges had first done so, international outrage at the calamity of the concentration camps put the problem of collateral damage at centre stage in the representation of the war. Mostly, the *ILN* dealt with the challenge by insisting that the damage was not collateral but coaxial. But increasingly, it and *The Graphic* also did so by a practice of "othering" the Boers, representing them as white trash: violent, ignorant, denatured, incapable of civilization and thus incapable of being civilians.

Melton Prior's 1879 picture of the artist burning the kraals came at the end of a sustained sequence of pictures of such arsons as subjects or as backgrounds; his 1900 picture comes at the beginning of such another sequence, which, as it develops, finds it easier to cast the Boers as "other," to deny them civilized/civilian status, and to represent the dynamiting of their farms and the slaughter of their cattle as coaxial, rather than collateral damage.

That is a neatly symmetrical and cyclical juxtaposition, but things were actually by no means so neat. Warfare had changed. Already at the sieges of Ladysmith and Mafeking, the use of big guns taken from ships and hauled over hundreds of miles of veldt, firing high-explosive shells at ranges up to ten kilometres with only approximate accuracy, had brought the tactics and indiscriminate carnage of the shore bombardment into continental warfare. Media had changed and were changing ever faster: the general interest weekly illustrated periodicals had lost their monopolistic dominance as the market fragmented, and illustration became cheap and easy enough for mid- and downmarket periodicals, both dailies and weeklies, to use. The moving pictures date from 1896 and the first telegraphically transmitted photograph from 1904.

Perhaps most significantly, the Western world was running out of supplies of easily identifiable "others" not yet incorporated within existing empires or nation states. Melton Prior was making pictures for a vastly different audience in 1879 from the one he addressed in 1900. The conflict with the Boer republics utterly disrupted the obscene fantasy of elegant and dignified warfare. All of these factors would make the twentieth century a very different environment for collateral damage than the last quarter of the nineteenth had been. Compared to the early twentieth century, with its emerging and inevitable power to inflict collateral damage, to report its infliction, and to connect that infliction directly with geopolitical struggles, the last decades of the nineteenth century may seem like a golden age of collateral damage. But it is possible to see, from the pages of the *Illustrated London News*, that the worm was already in the bud.

Notes

1 This essay does not seek to make a contribution to the debate over the causes or impact of nineteenth-century European imperialism, or to bring evidence that could help to identify the (many) interests served by imperialist policies and practices. Recent work in English on the French case includes Alice Conklin, *A Mission to Civilize: The Republican Idea of Empire in France and West Africa, 1895–1930* (Stanford, Calif.: Stanford University Press, 1997) and Tony Chafer and Amanda Sackur, eds., *Promoting the Colonial Idea: Propaganda and Visions of Empire in France* (Basingstoke: Palgrave, 2002). In the case of British imperialism, the historiography is dense and the controversies tense. Core theses of P.J. Cain and A.G. Hopkins' recent and agenda-setting synthesis, *British Imperialism: Innovation and Expansion 1688–1914* (London and New York: Longman, 1993), are, first, that British imperialism is to be explained in large part by reference to the interests and actions of "gentlemanly capitalism," whose political base was situated in the established elites residing for the most part in southeast England; and, second, that imperialism was a crucial tool for nation building within the British Isles. Both of these ideas seem to me to offer a more-than-illustrational significance for the upmarket illustrated papers, with their "gentlemanly" tone and clientele and their endlessly re-enacted insistence on the cultural and anecdotal links between colony and metropolis.

2 An important recent discussion of the rhetoric of imperialism in the *Illustrated London News* (hereafter *ILN*) is Peter Sinnema, *Dynamics of the Pictured Page: Representing the Nation in the Illustrated London News* (Aldershot: Ashgate, 1998), though it concentrates on textual rhetorics. Other relevant works include Paul Hogarth, *The Artist as Reporter* (London: Studio Vista, 1967); Pat Hodgson, *The War Illustrators* (London: Osprey, 1977); and Peter Johnson, *Front Line Artists* (London: Cassell, 1978).

3 Catherine Hall, *Civilising Subjects: Colony and Metropole in the English Imagination, 1830–1867* (Chicago: University of Chicago Press, 2002).

4 The surveys at note 2 are useful. See also Philip Beam, *Winslow Homer's Magazine Engravings* (New York: Harper and Row, 1979); Melton Prior, *Campaigns of a War Correspondent* (London: Edward Arnold, 1912); Jane Carruthers, *Melton Prior: War Artist in Southern Africa 1895 to 1900* (Houghton, S.A.: Brenthurst Press, 1987); Richard Caton Woodville, *Random Recollections* (London: Eveleigh Nash, 1914).

5 Tom Gretton, "Signs for Labour Value in Printed Pictures after the Photomechanical Revolution: Mainstream Changes and Extreme Cases around 1900," *Oxford Art Journal* 28, 3 (2005), 371–90, esp. 376.

6 The title of Leonard de Vries' two uncritical compilations, *History as Hot News 1842–1865: The World of the Early Victorians as Seen through the Eyes of 'The Illustrated London News'* (London; John Murray, 1967), and *History as Hot News, 1865–1897: The Late Nineteenth-Century World as Seen through the Eyes of 'The Illustrated London News' and 'The Graphic'* (London: John Murray, 1973), notwithstanding.

7 Jacqueline Beaumont, "The British Press and Censorship during the South African War 1899–1902," *South African Historical Journal* 41 (2000), 267–89.

8 For example: "The Site of the Bazaar Immediately after the Disaster. From a Photograph by Benque, Paris," *The Graphic*, March 15, 1897, supplement, 3; "Les cadavres transportés à la gare de Dax," *L'Illustration*, November 21, 1900, 328. One striking picture of enemy casualties in an imperial war is "The Advance in the Soudan: After the Battle of the Atbara. In the Enemy's Position from a Photograph by R.X. Webster," *The Graphic*, May 28, 1898, 661.

9 The king's name is now more usually given as Cetshwayo. The spelling I use was common in the *ILN* and elsewhere at the time.

10 Zulu military units were called *impis*, now more usually rendered as "*iMpi.*" They were raised through something like conscription and in this context an impi probably had a complement of around 1,000 men.

11 *Illustrated London News*, October 18, 1879, 366.

12 Here, I quote Walter Benjamin in his essay on Eduard Fuchs: "There is no monument of civilisation that is not at the same time a monument of barbarism."

13 Such pin-up representations include "The Zulu War: The Burning of Ulundi. From a Sketch by our Special Artist, Mr. Melton Prior," *ILN*, August 23, 1879, 184 and 185.

14 There is a famous contemporary account of this punitive expedition from the pen of a young journalist embedded with the force: *The Story of the Malakand Field Force: An Episode of Frontier War* (London: Longmans, 1898), by Winston Churchill.

15 Here I quote Tacitus, putting the words "They make a desert, and call it peace" into the mouth of Calgacus, a leader in the British resistance to the Roman conquest in the first century CE. He is of course critiquing the self-image of the imperialists.

16 *ILN*, March 14, 1896, 333.

17 The punitive action by the international powers in the aftermath of the siege was described by a contemporary in *The Nation*, February 15, 1906, as "a carnival of loot," but it also included, inevitably, burning, molestation, rape, and murder.

9 Timothy Brook

The Deliverer's Dilemma

Japan's Invasion of China, 1937–38

Takada Mitsusaburō was a young civilian who worked for the Japanese army in China from January to June 1938. His life before January is unknown and what happened to him after June a mystery. The only sources from which we can reconstruct his life are two classified reports that happen to survive in the archives of the Japanese Self-Defense Force in Tokyo. Two official documents are hardly sufficient to recreate a life, and Takada's will not emerge here in its full complexity. Yet they contain just enough to suggest the complexity of his response to the civilian damage that war and occupation cause. It is rare in war to find the aggressor reacting to the damage he causes when he comes as a deliverer other than to deny it, and rarer still to watch him grapple with the deliverer's dilemma: that the measures by which an invasion succeeds in the short run are exactly what undermine the possibility of sustaining it in the long run.

In the summer of 1937, Japan invaded China at Beijing and then at Shanghai. The invasion was launched on the thinnest of pretexts. Its goal was to break the Chinese government's refusal to enter into agreements with Japan that would have allowed the latter to shape Chinese economic and foreign policies to its interests. The invasion at Beijing was relatively swift and bloodless; the invasion at Shanghai was just the opposite. The Chinese army resisted staunchly for three months, then was overwhelmed and forced to withdraw across the Yangtze Delta to the national capital of Nanjing (Nanking). The Japanese army went in hot pursuit, determined to destroy China's capacity to resist and force its government to terms. In the middle of December, the Japanese army entered the capital, committing a wave of aggression against the defeated soldiers and civilians that soon became known as the Rape of Nanking.

As the army ground its way across the Yangtze Delta, the Japanese army sent civilian agents in behind the army to re-establish order in the occupied areas. As many as 200 young men fanned out across the delta in "pacification teams" of three to six members. Takada was one of these. Their assignment was to return China to normality. They were to clean up the debris, recruit collaborators into local administrations, revive the economy, and get tax revenues flowing again.[1] It was a superhuman task, for the invasion had been an enormous disaster for the civilian population across whose landscape the army had advanced. The tactics the army was willing to use showed no serious distinction between military and civilian targets, or rather, the targeting of civilians was understood to be part of the process of forcing the Chinese government to capitulate. The aerial bombing of civilian targets, search-and-destroy operations, reprisals, and arbitrary executions were not unprecedented in the history of modern war, but they were unmatched in scale. It was the great misfortune of the residents of the Yangtze Delta to find themselves at the moment when the practice of modern warfare was shifting "from armed forces to civilians, who were not only its victims, but increasingly the object of military or military-political operations," as Eric Hobsbawm has put it.[2] The conduct of the Japanese army may not have reached the point at which, in the language of the Nuremberg judgment, "rules, regulations, assurances and treaties all alike are of no moment" and its leaders "freed from the restraining influence of international law" to wage war "in the most barbarous way,"[3] but it came close, and for the first time in what soon turned into the Second World War. For those who lived on the Yangtze Delta, the winter of 1937–38 was one of extraordinary suffering and loss, the full scale of which may never be calculated.[4]

Takada's six months in Danyang, the county toward the western end of the delta to which he was assigned, gave him an unobstructed view of the civilian damage that war could impose. The reality he had to deal with when he got to Danyang made a mockery of Japan's official rhetoric of delivering China from Western imperialism and promoting East Asian revival on the basis of co-prosperity. He could not sweep the damage he saw under the thin rug such ideology provided; indeed, the only way to be effective in reversing that damage was to acknowledge not just its scale but its impact. The conditions under which he, as a pacification agent, was charged with delivering the people of Danyang were the very conditions that the Japanese army had imposed. Some locals were willing to make an accommodation with Japanese power, having little choice to do anything else, but none to embrace the cause of alliance and co-prosperity that the bearers of Japan's *mission civilitrice* were intent on delivering. Takada would try earnestly to act in the best interests of the people of Danyang, and he would fail.

Danyang county does not loom large in anyone's history of the Japanese invasion, yet the Yangtze Delta and the winter of 1937–38 are significant, not just for Chinese history but for world history. The attack on Shanghai might have remained what the Japanese originally called it, an "incident," just as an earlier attack in 1932 had been. But the push westward into the hinterland beyond Shanghai during the winter of 1937–38 was the aggression that started that vast war and the first wave of the civilian suffering for which the Second World War is infamous. This is the place and time when the Second World War began.

The protection of civilians against such aggression had been established in international law at the Fourth Hague Convention of 1907. This was the first time when states at war were enjoined to ensure that inhabitants in a war zone "remain under the protection and governance of the principles of the law of nations, derived from the usages established among civilized peoples, from the laws of humanity, and from the dictates of the public conscience." The protection of civilians in war zones thus became an explicit responsibility of war commanders.[5] Commanders who could not show that they had made every effort to concentrate on military targets and keep damage to non-military personnel and infrastructure to a minimum could henceforth be charged with war crimes. The London Charter, which governed the International Military Tribunal at Nuremberg, further enlarged the legal protection of civilians by specifying that "murder, ill-treatment or deportation to slave labour or for any other purpose of civilian populations" belonged within the category of "war crimes." The charter also introduced the concept of "crimes against humanity," defined as "murder, extermination, enslavement, deportation, and other inhumane acts committed against any civilian population."[6] The mistreatment of civilians, regardless of by whom or where they were harmed, would be prosecuted.

The categories of "war crimes" and "crimes against humanity" were imported directly into the Charter of the International Military Tribunal for the Far East in Tokyo. With respect to the protection of civilians during wartime, however, this charter went beyond Nuremburg. Count 55, the last in the indictment, made criminal the failure to "take adequate steps to secure the observance" of the laws of war and prevent the commission of war crimes. The failure to *prevent* the commission of war crimes, and not just their commission, became a "legal duty." Japanese leaders may not have ordered their soldiers to behave as atrociously as they did, but the absence of such an order could no longer stand as a defence against a war crimes charge.[7] The innovation, written into the Statute of Rome governing the International Criminal Court, has forever changed the legal threshold for crimes committed against civilians.

———

The city of Danyang, which was seat of the county of the same name, is eighty kilometres east of Nanjing at the junction of the main canal, road, and rail lines in the region. Being on the rail line between Shanghai and Nanjing positioned Danyang for economic prosperity in peacetime, but it put the city directly in the path of the invading army in time of war.[8] The population of 60,000 was already dwindling by the time the first Japanese plane bombed the city on November 27. The first attack hit the gasworks in the city centre, starting a fire that burned for three days. A second aerial attack two days later destroyed the neighbourhoods around the south and east gates: the directions from which the infantry would attack. Seventy-two people were killed in these attacks. On December 3, twenty days after the fall of Shanghai, the Japanese entered the nearly deserted city of Danyang. Their arrival finished the work of making the city uninhabitable. A few bold scavengers sneaked back in through breaks in the city wall during December to scrounge whatever was still worth taking, but no one dared share the city with the Japanese garrison. The garrison commander did not even bother to place it under martial law.

The pacification team of five arrived early in January, with Takada Mitsus-aburō as head. Takada had been a civilian employee of the South Manchurian Railway Company, the largest Japanese development corporation in China, before being seconded to the Japanese army's Special Service Department to work on postconflict reconstruction. All we know about him comes from the excerpts from his monthly work diaries that were included in two reports that the central Pacification Office in Shanghai wrote for circulation back to Tokyo at the vice-ministerial level.[9]

The first item that appears in the first of these two reports is dated January 9, 1938. It notes that Takada was visited that morning by the anxious head of the Danyang Peace Maintenance Committee (PMC). This was a Chinese agency that the Japanese garrison commander had cobbled together in December to handle local affairs. The head of the PMC reported that 200 to 300 "bandits" had raided the committee's compound inside the city the previous night. Two employees had been injured, one seriously. The raiders stole their clothes and managed to carry off half of the 6,000 kilograms of salt that the Japanese garrison commander had given to the PMC to sell to pay for its operating costs. Takada inspected the compound, then went to talk to the shanty people living by the gap in the wall through which the raiders had come. They named a bandit leader and told Takada what village he came from. By the time the Japanese soldiers got there, the band had fled. (They returned the next night to collect the rest of the salt; this time, four PMC employees were shot and killed.)

Takada was dismayed by his PMC's inability to organize its own defence. He told the members of the committee that people looked to them "to build a new heaven on earth with the support of the Japanese army" and that the committee should do "everything in its power to give assistance to these poor people." The PMC members must have been astonished to hear a Japanese scolding them to do their duty in a situation that the Japanese had created and in which everyone took survival and self-interest to be their first concerns. What Takada calls his "lecture" must have contributed to his subsequent poor relationship with the PMC, which he regarded as a worthless bunch of incompetents. "Completely lacking in administrative talent" was how he describes the head of the PMC, a former soldier turned soy sauce and lumber merchant from a smaller county town. But the PMC was caught in an impossible position between the new masters it served and the old social order in which it had no basis of legitimate authority. One of Takada's chief responsibilities in the coming months would be to dissolve the Peace Maintenance Committee and find more capable men to form the Danyang Self-Government Committee (SGC).

Takada estimated that 2,000 people were waiting at the city gates to re-enter. Another 4,000 to 8,000 were camped just beyond the city and could be expected to show up as soon as it was reopened.[10] "Since the garrison was shorthanded, what was there to do," Takada asks, "but settle on the policy of allowing ordinary residents back in?" The one condition was that they register at one of the team's reception centres. In the meantime, he had to feed and house them. He got control of the 1,800 kilograms of rice that the garrison commander had confiscated and given the PMC, but that amount would not last long. Takada dispatched two of his team, each with eight bodyguards, into the countryside to buy more rice, but that netted them barely 200 kilograms. In the end, he had to leave the task of finding food to the refugees themselves; he had nothing more to give them. If food was a serious problem, housing was even worse. Takada estimated that four-fifths of the buildings inside the city's wall were destroyed, a percentage that puts Danyang at the high end of urban destruction in the Yangtze Delta. Again, he had no means to rebuild the city; it would be up to the residents to bring in building supplies and put their homes back together.

Takada turns his estimate that four-fifths of the city's physical fabric was destroyed around to propose that four-fifths of the buildings in the countryside had escaped devastation. That estimate would prove to be far too optimistic, as he would discover in person over the next month as he undertook the exceptional project of touring the entire county. He ended up making no fewer than three tours through rural Danyang. These tours showed him at first hand what the task of pacification put him up against. By looking at what he saw and how he struggled to come to terms with it, we get a rare glimpse of invasion from the invader's perspective but not the invader's point of view.

The first tour began on the morning of January 21, when he and three of the other four members of the team headed out of the city in a northwesterly direction. The four took an interpreter, a military police officer, and a military escort of 150 soldiers. The agents were hoping to talk to rural residents, but everyone fled at the sight of their contingent. The first town they reached, Baitu, had been completely gutted and abandoned. Japanese troops had been stationed there early in December and had destroyed the place when they departed. The group proceeded to the next village, Dengxiang.[11] A Japanese army unit passing through early in December had burned 143 houses; what they had not burned was locked and abandoned. Eventually soldiers found three villagers in hiding. They were brought trembling to Takada, who in his work diary registers surprise at their terror. They had to point out to him that the Japanese who had last come to Dengxiang had burned a blind man alive and bayonetted an elderly man and his adult son. Takada's comments on this incident seem to suggest that he supposed such incidents were abnormal and that most Chinese should have nothing to fear when Japanese soldiers showed up. The team passed the night at Dengxiang, the lieutenant in charge of the military escort cautioning his soldiers to exercise "self-control." Takada concludes his account of the day by observing that the visit showed the villagers that Japanese soldiers were not so terrible after all. At this early stage in his education as a military imperialist, Takada could regard the suffering of civilians as regrettable rather than inherent to the project of which he was a part.

The next town on their itinerary, Baoyan, had been previously been burned in reprisal when two Japanese corpses were discovered in a neighbouring hamlet. One hundred and eighty-five houses had been destroyed and over twenty people executed. Some houses were still in good repair and well stocked, however, and the population did not entirely evaporate when the team arrived, since a Japanese commander had already set up an SGC in the town to begin the work of building a base of collaboration. Takada's assessment of Baoyan is tinged with the same naïveté he showed regarding Dengxiang. "Although you couldn't say that their feelings toward Japan were extremely good," he concedes, "when we set off, many of the residents bade us a warm farewell." Was Takada unaware that the people of Baoyan wanted to get the Japanese out of their village, and that what he took as a sign of friendship was really a gesture of appeasement? A more experienced agent might have seen it more cynically, but Takada looked with the hopeful eyes of the benevolent imperialist who believed he could transmute the violence of invasion into a mutually beneficial co-operation between invader and invaded.

The team passed through a few more places that day, and some villagers came out to greet them. By the end of the second day, Takada is writing more cannily that they were "putting on the outward appearance of friendliness." They ended the day in the relatively unscathed town of Jiuli, where the inhabitants gave them a warm welcome. Takada had the wit to ask why. The villagers declared that they preferred Japanese troops to Chinese, since the latter were more rapacious. Takada takes this response at face value, as it serves his need to project a future for Japan as the bringer of a stable order for China. Despite the warmth of the welcome, the villagers of Jiuli nonetheless politely suggested that their resources were too meagre to put up the entire delegation, and would they mind spending the night outside the village? Takada takes the hint and has his men to find shelter in abandoned buildings rather than billet in people's homes. The correct sentiments had been expressed, the right arrangements made, and a politic accommodation reached on both sides. Takada was learning the politics of collaboration.

At the town of Yanling the following morning, the team found shops reopened and recovery well advanced. Yanling had an SGC, and its head came out to greet Takada and tell him everything he wanted to hear: that the people of the town had warm feelings for the Japanese, and that they hoped the day when China and Japan became close allies would arrive as soon as possible. A bandit raid a month earlier and a shortage of salt may have had something to do with the SGC head's desire for closer ties with his new patrons. When the team departed for the final leg of the journey back to Danyang city that afternoon, the SGC got a crowd out to wave Japanese flags in farewell. Yanling was keeping up appearances, though appearances would change when the Communists took over the town later in the occupation.

Back in Danyang city, Takada drew the conclusions he needed to draw from his first tour: that destruction in the countryside had been less than in the city, that there was a shortage of tools and oxen but that otherwise the prospects for agricultural production seemed good. The people's attitude to Japan was positive, and only real obstacle was the free hand that bandits had to prey on the people. The answer to this problem, he insisted, was more propaganda work of the sort the team had done on the tour, though that had amounted to little more than putting up posters and handing out caramels to children. So the tour had been a great success, he declared to his superiors in Shanghai. It had calmed all fears about the Japanese. He was confident that war-damaged Danyang was on the road to recovery and Sino-Japanese co-operation.

It would prove a hasty judgment. Four days later, roughly the same group of soldiers accompanied all five pacification agents on a second tour, heading east from the city. This time Takada arranged for the pacification team to lead the way, placing the soldiers half a kilometre to their rear to give their approach a less militarized face. The itinerary took them to the town of Fangxian, where they were greeted by members and employees of the town

SGC, all waving Japanese flags. Those willing to listen to their message to trust in Japan received tobacco; the children got candies. The fighting had missed Fangxian, so the shops were operating and the markets well stocked with local produce. During the day the creeks were busy with boat traffic and the markets bustled with trade, but banditry was a nightly problem. The SGC handed over a few old pistols and hunting rifles it had confiscated as tokens of submission. The Japanese conducted their own search for weapons but found none. Fangxian was ready to accept the new order without protest. The next town on their itinerary, Menghe, which had similarly escaped destruction, also staged a flag-waving welcome. The team stayed the night, then headed south the following morning.

Beyond Menghe, the scene changed. The Japanese found themselves in a depopulated landscape of burned-out houses and ruined villages, where the few survivors scuttled from sight as soon as they came into view. The way south to Benniu was a wasteland. After posting notices declaring Japan's good intentions, the agents abandoned their planned itinerary and headed directly over to the railway line. Their arrival at the line set off a panic, as the bandit gangs that roamed the countryside at night gave surviving locals nowhere to flee. There were no warm welcomes or waving flags here. Takada decided to cut the inspection tour short. The following morning, the team traced its way back to Danyang along the roads that followed the creeks through this part of the county, pasting posters in the ruined villages as they went. All Takada could write at the close of this entry in the team work diary was that "we all returned safely." The tour did not seem to offer any more positive lesson.

A third tour was mounted four days later to cover the places the second tour had missed. The team would go to the railway towns of Lingkou, Lücheng, and Benniu, work its way across the south end of the county to Erling in the southwest corner, then return north to Danyang city. Several days of rain before they set out turned the roads to mud, but they set out anyway, slogging their way to Lingkou. What had been a good-sized railway town they found a shambles of burned buildings. At most twenty families were living in the ruins. The agents paused long enough to put up propaganda materials, then continued down the line to Lücheng. Advancing Japanese troops who had found their way blocked here in late November by a destroyed bridge had rounded up sixteen people and shot them in a nearby field as punishment. One of the executed was a pregnant woman. Every building in the area had been burned. The team postered what was left of Lücheng and then went on to Benniu. Benniu too was decimated, with fewer than three dozen of its original 400 homes still standing. The few refugees living in the charred ruins under the leadership of a fledgling SGC accepted tobacco and candies, gestures that enabled Takada to declare Benniu to be pro-Japanese.

The next day, the team went from village to village across the southern end of the county, everywhere finding the same devastation, the same fear and flight at their arrival. The agents tried to explain Japan's good intentions but got positive responses only in places where some kind of SGC existed to organize such responses. The team ended their day in Erling, where a nine-member SGC preparatory committee was operating. The SGC told the pacification team that the only looting they had suffered had been at the hands of retreating Chinese soldiers on November 20. The team stayed the night and returned to Danyang the following morning.

Takada summed up his tours with this observation: "I believe that these three military tours improved the people's attitude toward the Japanese army and achieved really big results." Was this declaration intended to satisfy the expectations of the Pacification Bureau back in Shanghai to which he had to report, or was it an expression of his hope that he might still play a positive role in China? Was he taken in by the charades that the PMCs and SGCs had arranged for his arrival, or was he simply trying to make the best of a difficult situation? Takada is a hard subject to read from the brief entries in the work diary: repeatedly hopeful, often jejune, alternately perceptive and mistaken. How aware was he of the contradictory position he maintained in the Japanese occupation? On the one hand, he was charged with the task of moving Danyang from military to civilian rule and of transforming an area devastated by war into a stable unit of civil administration, and must have wanted to hope that he could achieve this worthy goal. On the other hand, he was ultimately answerable to the Japanese army to bring his county under control, by whatever means this might require. Takada was a civilian who desired to normalize a military situation and revert to civilian methods of rule, but whose duty it was to enhance the viability of Japan's military occupation.

That contradiction inhered in the goals that Japan declared its invasion to be in the service of, anchored to the claim that Japan had invaded China not to conquer it but to rescue it from its bondage to Western imperialism and warlord misrule. Takada's comments in the work diary indicate that he accepted this claim of counter-imperialism. He begins to approach the problems of such a claim when he registers the contrary responses of Chinese people to his approaches. Those who fear or reject him he chooses to characterize as acting on the basis of misunderstanding, even though their actions derive from their suffering through military conflict. Those who welcome him and wave flags in his honour he is content to view as genuinely pro-Japanese, as though there were no calculation on the Chinese side of the bargain – indeed, as though there were no bargain at all. So Takada held to the idea that Chinese people wanted only security and prosperity. He was confident, or expressed himself to be so, that the Chinese could be induced to set aside their objections and support what Japan claimed was their deliverance.

Other than easing some of the war damage Danyang civilians had suffered, Takada could do little to alter the situation in which he found himself. Food remained short, morale low, administration crippled. He worked at building a Self-Government Committee, but in March had to report to his superiors that the SGC was still "in the process of consolidation." It would take until May to oust the PMC soy sauce merchant who still wanted to run the county. That done, Takada could turn to the task of mobilizing popular support for Japan. His work diary declares the next step to be organizing mass movements to persuade the local people of Japan's noble goal of co-operation among the nations of East Asia. He got the SGC to organize a public meeting on May 25 to celebrate Japan's substantial victory over the Chinese army in the Battle of Xuzhou, north of the Yangtze. He reports that 500 people attended and that the event had a big effect on "the masses."

That was the public side of the victory. Privately Takada worried that the collapse of the Chinese forces at Xuzhou would mean a huge influx of defeated soldiers slipping southward across the Yangtze and into his jurisdiction. As it was, the Japanese soldiers garrisoned inside Danyang did not dare venture more than a kilometre beyond the city wall, even in broad daylight. The prospect of thousands of soldiers-turned-guerrillas filtering into the county was alarming, given the lack of military capacity to deal with this threat. His fears proved exaggerated. The guerrilla resistance did not grow to that strength, and indeed was never able to break Japan's hold on the Yangtze Delta. Still, his anxiety suggests how vulnerable he felt and how far he was from completing the task of pacification.

Takada left his post as team leader on June 20. The work diary does not say why he departed. It does note, however, that his replacement, Morozumi Shōichi, immediately launched a review of all policies and personnel. Morozumi's clean sweep suggests that Takada had been removed for failing to produce results. The majority of pacification agents ended their terms demoralized and unable to advance their careers, and Takada was probably one of them.[12]

Morozumi would have no easier time of it. Five weeks after taking up his post, he called the chairs of the rural SGC branch committees to a meeting to press them to mount a more effective response to the growing insurgency. The chair of the Erling branch committee turned the tables on his new boss. He presented Morozumi with six demands for concrete action: Why were armed garrisons not being stationed in the rural towns? Why were salt offices not being set up in these towns to deal with smuggling, which was a lucrative business for the guerrillas and a significant loss for the local administrators?

When would the branch committees receive more funding to pay for the work they had to do? Why was there no financial assistance to revive primary schools in the rural towns? Why were the branch committees not getting first-aid kits so that they might offer basic treatment for the ill and injured? And why weren't the poor being organized into road gangs to give them employment and get the roads back in repair?

Here were six concrete proposals from a minor official at the bottom of the occupation state to deal with some of consequences of waging war in a civilian zone: release of predatory violence, loss of economic resources and livelihood, collapse of regular administration, injury and ill health, and destruction of schools and roads. The concept of collateral damage is usually extended only to civilian casualties, but these losses are part of the suffering that war causes. These proposals were designed to restore local administration to a minimum level of operation and compensate for the utter disappearance of public services and economic livelihood that invasion had caused. Not only that but they came from the conquered, whose demand for action might just have been intended to shame their conqueror into doing something.

Morozumi responded lamely by noting "the current situation" and tabling these proposals for future discussion.[13] The Japanese could neither deliver the security necessary to carry out such ameliorative measures nor raise the funds to rebuild the administration they had destroyed so long as the countryside lay beyond their capacity to tax. The reality of occupation meant that the fiction of co-operation would elude both sides.

Takada Mitsusaburō's experiences in Danyang provide a perspective that is rare in the records of war: the perspective of the invader on the damage his army has done. His inability to reverse the effects of his army's invasion on civilian life are brought into high relief by the persona who creeps out of his work diary, the enlightened servant of his nation who wants to do his best for the people in his care. Takada was not projecting this image for public consumption, since the work diary was for internal reference only and the reports based on it were classified documents. Takada may have needed to please superiors, and yet I doubt that this consideration shaped the record. He was more concerned with letting his superiors know exactly how things stood in Danyang so that the measures guiding the work of pacification could be improved than with passing off his failures as successes.

The person who emerges from the work diary excerpts is neither a warrior nor a war criminal. Takada saw himself as a deliverer, not as an advocate of war or an agent of military conquest. He desired to replace military rule with civil administration and did everything he could to bring about this difficult transformation. But whatever he achieved by way of delivering the Chinese from the disorder, maladministration, and trauma that war had caused was in the service of installing a regime at the local level to support Japan's policies as an imperial power in China, policies that had produced just the problems he had to solve. Takada's realization that the very terms of his appointment contradicted the goal of normalization must have been discouraging for him. They placed him in the classic contradiction of imperialism: having to espouse an ideology of deliverance while enacting a reality of oppression. No agent of foreign imperialism, however well meaning or hard working, however innocent or reluctant, could bridge the gap that civilian suffering opened between invader and invaded, for it was that suffering – the collateral damage the invasion caused, as much if not more than the actual military defeat – that kept resistance to the invader alive.

Nothing that happened in Danyang ever came before the International Military Tribunal for the Far East as evidence of war crimes or crimes against humanity. Danyang was not a major centre, and the damage it suffered was no worse than the casualties and destruction the Japanese army had imposed elsewhere on the Yangtze Delta. It was simply one place among many that the army attacked, one more semi-anonymous casualty of the Second World War. It is the ordinariness of the case that makes it a good window onto the suffering that war causes, for this is the norm of what happened to civilians in this war that could only be lost. That one young Japanese thought he could "build a new heaven on earth" neither prolonged the war nor hastened its collapse, but it did throw him into the same circle of suffering by forcing him to see the impossibility of squaring occupation with deliverance, or violence with justice.

Notes

1 The pacification process is reconstructed in my *Collaboration: Japanese Agents and Local Elites in Wartime China* (Cambridge, Mass.: Harvard University Press, 2005), ch. 2.

2 Eric Hobsbawm, "War and Peace in the 20th Century," *London Review of Books*, February 21, 2002, 16.

3 United Nations War Crimes Commission, *History of the United Nations War Crimes Commission and the Development of the Laws of War* (London: His Majesty's Stationery Office, 1948), 222.

4 After the war, the Chinese government organized surveys of casualties and property damage to support its claims for justice and reparation against Japan. These surveys, some of which are held in the China Number Two Historical Archives in Nanjing, have not been adequately analyzed, but the categories the investigators used reflect what people at the time understood as the cost of war. I note six: civil-

ian deaths, the destruction of housing, the destruction and looting of factories, the killing and requisitioning of agricultural draught animals, the disruption of transportation infrastructure, and the burning and looting of such cultural property as libraries and museums. On the destruction of cultural monuments, see Robert Bevan, *The Destruction of Memory: Architecture and Cultural Warfare* (London: Reaktion, 2005).

5   U.N. War Crimes Commission, *History*, 25–26. The Tokyo judgment notes Japan's obligations under the Fourth Hague Convention; International Military Tribunal for the Far East, "Judgment," reprinted in *The Tokyo War Crimes Trial*, ed. B. John Pritchard and Sonia Zaide (New York: Garland, 1981), 48456.

6   U.N. War Crimes Commission, *History*, 191, 193.

7   Count 55 was included in the Tokyo indictment to provide grounds to try those who ordered or led the occupation of the Yangtze Delta in the fall and winter of 1937, which climaxed with the capture of the national capital and the Rape of Nanking; see Timothy Brook, "The Tokyo Trial and the Rape of Nanking," *Journal of Asian Studies* 60, 3 (2001), 682, 684, 690. On the role of the Rape of Nanking in shaping the indictment, see my *Documents on the Rape of Nanking* (Ann Arbor: University of Michigan Press, 1999), 18.

8   According to Eric Hobsbawm, one of the factors accounting for why "the suffering of civilians is not proportionate to the scope or intensity of military operations" in modern warfare is because war in the twentieth century targeted commercially networked areas integrated into larger systems of communication and dependent on supplies and services from elsewhere ("War and Peace in the 20th Century," 16). Danyang was certainly vulnerable on these grounds.

9   The first report is "*Tanyō senbuhan kōsaku gaikyō*" (State of work of the Danyang pacification team), April (Shanghai: Mantetsu Shanhai jimusho, 1938); the second is "*Senbu kōsaku gaikyō: Tanyō han, kan 2*" (State of pacification work: Danyang team, vol. 2), April 30 (Shanghai: Mantetsu Shanhai jimusho, 1940). Both survive in the archives of the Self-Defense Research Institute, Tokyo, and are reprinted in Inoue Hisashi's collection, *Kachū senbu kōsaku shiryō* (Materials in pacification work in central China) (Tokyo: Fuji shuppan, 1989). Additional information on Japanese atrocities in Danyang has been taken from Ji Junsheng, "Zhenjiang diqu lunxian qianhou" (Before and after the occupation of the Zhenjiang region), reprinted in Zhang Yibo, *Zhenjiang lunxian ji* (A record of Zhenjiang under occupation) (Beijing: Renmin chubanshe, 1999), 81–83.

10   Additional information on the refugee situation has been taken from "*Naka Shina senryō chiiki nai fukkimin narabi nanmin shūjō ni kansuru sho kōsaku*" (Work relating to returnees and refugee accommodation within the occupied region of central China), February 21 (Shanghai: Mantetsu Shanhai jimusho, 1938), reprinted in Inoue, *Kachū senbu kōsaku shiryō*, 37–38. Takada provides no statistics of civilian or military casualties in Danyang. His sole reference to physical suffering is a report that 250 people received medical treatment at the pacification team's clinic in the second half of January, and that another 70 had to be treated at a Japanese military field hospital.

11   Takada gets the name wrong: someone must have told him that if he takes a certain road he will *jin* ("enter") Dengxiang village, so he calls it "Jindengxiang."

12   Brook, *Collaboration*, 235–36.

13   Inoue, *Kachū senbu kōsaku shiryō*, 260–61.

10 Smita Tewari Jassal

Criminals, Heroes, Martyrs

A Backward Caste Remembers the Colonial Past

C olonial rule in the Indian subcontinent was characterized by sporadic and intermittent struggles that were invariably suppressed in diverse ways by the colonial state. The nature of these conflicts and the manner of their suppression richly illustrate the ways in which the term "collateral damage" can have multiple, layered meanings. In contemporary military parlance, the concept's rather limited association with use of high-technology weapon systems in inflicting civilian casualties obscures the history of massive political and legal forces that were periodically deployed to suppress rebellions during colonial rule and the political, ideological, and legal frameworks that facilitated such control.

The concern of this essay is with ways in which data about collateral damage and civilian casualties during colonial rule are currently being utilized to fashion holistic and inclusive interpretations of people's pasts. I investigate how collective memory reconstructs the links between individual and group acts of defiance and the punitive measures that the state inflicted on vast masses of people. Much like the use of weapons systems that affect large civilian populations and lead to collateral damage, the colonial state's resort to measures that marginalized entire social groups and damaged livelihoods is foregrounded. I examine ways in which established narratives are interrogated and refashioned and alternative narratives articulated in opposition to existing state and national discourses.

Although I highlight contemporary uses and interpretations of the past, this exercise also illuminates how the concept of collateral damage should be understood in the broadest possible historical terms. These processes are of special interest in the case of subaltern and marginalized social groups, which see their contributions as either excluded from dominant historical discourses or inadequately represented within established national narratives of struggles for independence.

By focusing on ways in which information is processed, interpreted, transmitted, disseminated, and narrativized to "reconstruct" and rewrite the group's own social history, we can understand how alternative histories are refashioned from the vantage point of the present. The focus here on the range of river-faring castes illustrates one such retelling from the perspective of the castes today. As such narratives represent the dialogue the castes hold with the past – with their own history – wherein selections from the past are used to fashion new traditions or histories, they are deeply reflective of the current concerns of caste groups.[1] Given the nature of such endeavours, it is worth investigating the extent to which they follow the pattern of *puranic* writings, particularly caste *puranas*, the written and oral traditions of the castes, which, in narrating the history of castes, have tended to blur distinctions between history and myth.

Contemporary caste narratives are informed by a new logic that seeks to address the continuing distance of castes from the sources of political power, their increasing economic marginalization, their limited access to productive resources, and the growing superfluousness of caste-based skills and occupational specializations. Interestingly, a striking feature of this logic is the reasoning that colonial legislation, introduced largely to suppress the "rebelliousness" and "volatility" of people in the wake of the 1857 Mutiny, remains largely responsible for the persistent marginalization of the range of river-faring sub-castes along the Ganga (Ganges) River, thus constituting collateral damage on a vast scale.[2] The causes of chronic economic, political, and cultural backwardness and the cultural silencing that accompanied these processes are some of the themes addressed in caste narratives.

Mallah caste narratives, for instance, attribute the marginalized status and distance of the caste from centres of power to the role of its members in the Mutiny. This distinct brand of rebellious spirit is seen as having caused the Mallah to be labelled criminal and subjected to stringent and punitive colonial laws. These laws are seen to have progressively deprived them of a secure livelihood derived from traditional rights in fisheries and rivers and on the riverbanks.[3]

The narratives also focus on a search for heroes to restore dignity and self-worth and to act as a rallying point for disparate sub-castes in the interests of an overarching Nishad river dweller identity, the caste group of which the Mallah form a part. In order to claim a place for itself in the story of the nation's heroes and martyrs, this group of castes had to make common cause with a range of tribal and lower caste rebellions and struggles for freedom from colonial oppression. Such alignments have been used to strengthen regional political coalitions with a range of marginalized castes and tribes, thus broadening the Mallah/Nishad political base. In recent years, the strategy of making common cause with tribes and castes lower in the social scale has prepared some Mallah/Nishad groups to make demands for Most Backward Caste (MBC) status and encouraged others to agitate for inclusion in the Scheduled Tribe or Scheduled Caste (ST/SC) category, which enables access through affirmative action to government employment and higher education.

Collateral Damage in Accounts of Heroes, Martyrs, Criminals

> A society that does not have a knowledge or memory of its history and heroes is exactly like the son who does not know his father or his parentage and therefore lacks confidence and pride.[4]

No account of subaltern heroes or martyrs from the colonial past is complete without data on collateral damage. In official historical accounts, participants in the Non-Cooperation Movement and a range of nationalist struggles, especially if they also happened to belong to the subaltern castes and classes, were often described as "criminal elements."[5] The activities of these individuals, whether picketing, sabotage of government property, or other forms of political protest against the symbols of colonial authority such as police headquarters, were seldom differentiated from the actions of common criminals and hoodlums. In response to violent political actions, protesters were charged with criminality and imprisoned.

Although the postcolonial Indian state was constitutionally committed to redressing inequalities and building a casteless and egalitarian nation-state, it took over the terminology and categories of the colonizers. Terms such as *criminal* and *backward* for groups that had hitherto suffered a range of social disabilities continued to be used to identify those eligible for affirmative action. Moreover, in the postcolonial state's understanding of history, the space for heroes was, and continues to be, appropriated by upper caste, Western-educated, intellectual elites. As people's histories and identities thus remain eclipsed within the nation's master narrative, efforts are underway to correct these partial understandings, which rely both on relatively unknown or unexplored sources of data and on the established evidence.

In thus identifying with a range of caste and tribal groups and establishing points of commonality, the sense of isolation ensuing from a lifestyle on the margins, as well as distance from sources of economic and political power, might be bridged. By adopting other struggles and causes as their own, a more inclusive stance is promoted by the caste intelligentsia, which also helps to balance out the pressures of an exclusivist, caste-based north Indian identity politics. In adopting tribal heroes, and making common cause with tribal revolts, political ground is prepared for seeking Scheduled Tribe status and the accompanying political concessions and privileges. Mallah remembrance of the quintessential martyr, Jubba Sahni, exemplifies efforts to reclaim and assert the caste's own space within the narrative of the Nation.

The colonial state labelled certain sections, or sub-castes, of Mallah as "criminal tribes" by in 1871, a move that has generated many unusual and creative caste responses in recent years. During the course of fieldwork in eastern Uttar Pradesh (United Provinces) and Bihar villages, I found it unsettling at first that at a general level, there was little awareness of the history of this labelling. Closer and prolonged investigation, however, revealed a tendency toward denial, theorized by Stanley Cohen as the reluctance to acknowledge historical reality or the effort to ascribe altogether different meanings to it.[6]

By suggesting that the label *criminal* was the price paid for resisting the colonial regime, the Mallah stake their own claim in the nation's anti-colonial master narrative while simultaneously rejecting identification with the label assigned by the colonial state. Both denial and loss of memory about the caste's criminal past, as well as the effort to imbue it with a different meaning, are reflected in the Mallah response to history. Caste retellings of the Mutiny rely on the evidence of collateral damage to retrieve an alternative narrative that both subverts and empowers.

In this context, the colonial state's charge of criminality does not carry the intended slur but becomes almost a badge of honour, as Shahid Amin has shown, worn by the most daring of revolutionaries and rebels.[7] Moreover, subaltern puranic myths are replete with celebratory cults of "criminal" gods who protect and bestow boons upon their "demon" devotees.[8] Thus, in subaltern consciousness, *criminal* was sometimes another term for *heroic* and *brave*. The term could be just as easily applied to the subaltern hero. The search for new heroes and martyrs is a device not just to retrieve but to fashion a new historical narrative. In this sense, too, the search refutes colonial interpretations as it seeks to reclaim respectability for the group within the existing power configuration.

The search for heroes begins with the sometimes nameless and faceless individuals whose participation in the Mutiny remains unrecorded. Attempts to reconstruct and retrieve these stories from the scanty evidence is a challenging exercise for the Mallah leadership. Fieldwork informants on the banks of the Ganga repeatedly and imaginatively expressed the idea that the Mallah boatmen had contributed to the uprising. Typical of this kind of eclipsed hero are Bhima and Maiku Mallah, bodyguards of the upper caste mutineer and folk hero Kunwar Singh Bhojpur, the *zamindar* of Gaya district in Bihar, who, along with his men, fought against the British forces in Arrah, Patna, Banda, and Kanpur before reaching Awadh in April 1858. Crossing the Ganga at Sheopur Ghat, sixteen kilometres from Ballia, he was injured, lost his arm, and then succumbed to his injuries three days later. According to Shivprasad Chaudhary of Ara, Bhima ferried the mutineers of 1857 across the river, among them Kunwar Singh, who was shot while trying to cross. While Kunwar Singh is eulogized in the region, the heroic role of the Mallah boatman, who also lost his life in the process, remains unacknowledged. According to Tilakdhari Nishad, BSP (Bahujan Samaj Party) leader and an office holder in the Jaunpur Naukaghat Association,

> In 1857 during the first war of independence, Nishads made a tremendous contribution, today forgotten. Revolutionaries such as Nanaji and Topeji requested our community for cooperation [sic]. They used to sink the boats of the British and bring their weapons to the revolutionaries. Since that time, the British declared our Samaj [community] as jerayampesha [criminal]. Despite Independence, our name has not been struck off that list. Our people died for this country's freedom, yet there is no recognition of this fact. Our community's role is forgotten. We are looked at with hatred. I wish that since our community has made such a contribution, it should flourish and our name be struck off the Criminal Tribe list.[9]

Criminality, Collateral Damage, and Issues of Livelihood

The narrative of the heroic boatmen during the Mutiny has entered the folklore of the region. In caste consciousness we find that the Mutiny story remains incomplete unless the saga of colonial onslaught against customary and occupational rights of the Mallah in fisheries and forests and on riverbanks is also told, thus underlining the collateral damage suffered by the caste.

When the East India Company introduced a contract system into river faring, whereby contracts for plying boats on the waters were auctioned to the highest bidders, it provoked one of the chief causes of Mallah resentment against the British. By 1857, when the unrest spread, the Mallah appear to have been quick to rebel. A version of the same incident in the pages of a caste journal makes the quantum leap from describing the event to showing its connection to the deprivations suffered by the caste as a result of the crackdown by the colonial state:

> The patriotic caste was declared criminal and their basic rights were snatched away through four Acts by the Privy Council of London which attacked the basic rights of the Nishads – rights connected to forest, waters and mountains. These were the Northern Indian Ferries Act, Northern India Mining Act, Northern India Fisheries Act and the Northern India Forest Act, which meant that their hereditary survival rights were taken away.[10]

The journal *Nishad Jyoti* asserts that after Independence, too, these former rights were not restored, and on the advice of Sardar Patel to Dr. Ambedkar, they were declared Denotified Tribes.[11] The Mallah were not included in the Scheduled Tribes list and even other river-faring castes such as Kewat, Dheewar, Chain, Bathwa, and Majhi were not included.[12] The economic marginalization and political injustice that continues to haunt the Mallah sixty years after Independence is thus traced to its heroism during the uprising of 1857.

In recent times, the narrative about criminality has identified the Criminal Tribes Act of 1871 as the first in a series of successive acts that eroded the security of the caste's livelihood. Successive acts inherited from the colonial state (the All India Fisheries Act, the Indian Forest Acts, and the Mineral and Metals Act) were adopted by the postcolonial state with minor alterations. In the Mallah narrative, these acts contain the seeds of their continuing marginalization.

The Criminal Tribes Act was passed to provide for the registration, surveillance, and control of certain tribes. The category "criminal tribe" could be extended to any gang or group of persons "addicted to the commission of non-bailable offences." In the United Provinces alone, 2.8 million people were identified as members of criminal tribes. The act's provisions also empowered officials to resettle criminal tribes or to remove them to reformatory settlements.[13] Underlying the legislation were certain assumptions about "readily identifiable dangerous castes with criminal tendencies." It was believed that members of such castes were destined to commit crimes because their castes not only condoned such activity but also provided the network that facilitated and sustained it over long periods. Elsewhere, I have shown that this single act served several ends for the colonial state, including the suppression of innumerable revolts and rebellions.[14] With the continuous process of marginalization over the course of a century, the Mallah are conscious, even bitter, about the heavy price they have had to pay for their militant stance in the Mutiny.

With the Northern India Ferries Act of 1874, transportation of goods and people, or crossing the river by means of any kind of bridge, steamer, or boat, became liable to state taxation. Once river transportation and commuting by bridges became a source of revenue, it was in the interest of the state to auction off the rights to the highest bidder. The colonial state also began to make a distinction between public and private ferries and stipulated where these would ply their trade. The state could now appoint those who would be in charge of the public ferries, collecting tolls, planning routes, and deciding which would be discontinued.

The system that soon evolved was of thrice-yearly public auctions. The maintenance and construction of different kinds of bridges and the plying of barges, steamers, and boats for crossing rivers became the responsibility of the leaseholder or *thekedar*, the highest bidder in the auction, whose tender was approved only because of his presumed ability to make the down payment and maintain the facilities stipulated in the contract. While the *thekedar* would appoint some Mallah for plying the boats and barges, they were never in the running for the auctions. As recently as 2003, Jawahar Lal Nishad of Varanasi, who has struggled to participate in such auctions in eastern Uttar Pradesh, expressed the way in which the system disadvantages him and described the drawbacks that continue even now:

> Since colonial times, only wealthy *zamindars* could participate in the auctions since they were in a position to make the down payments. *Ghats* and river sites of transportation and toll collection were managed by influential *zamindars* and petty functionaries appointed by them to collect the tolls. Under the Zamindari Abolition Act, the state took over all ferry *ghats*, ponds, and other water bodies and began to auction them. These came into the hands of the *zila parishad*, fishing departments, and Fish Farming Development agencies and could be auctioned off by any of these bodies. Even the minimal income which could be generated from these, slipped out of our hands and became a source of state revenues.[15]

Ironically, the systemic injustice that Jawahar Lal Nishad speaks of, which has so blatantly marginalized the Mallah from their own caste-based occupational specialization and skills, is embodied in none other than Upadhaya, a powerful and wealthy upper caste contractor from Gorakhpur. More than forty *ghats* in eastern Uttar Pradesh have been under his control since the 1950s, giving the lie to the idea that river faring, as a polluting occupation, is unsuitable for Brahmins. Contracting for river rights has evolved into an upper caste monopoly, as the public auctions and tender system favours those who are financially in a position to make huge down payments. Thus it comes as no surprise that upper caste dominance, a feature of east Uttar Pradesh agrarian relations, is repeated even in the realm of riparian rights and resources.

In an October 31, 1936, *sammelan* (conference) in Bateshwar, Agra district, it was proposed that the Ferries Act be amended so that the poor Mallah were not deprived of their livelihood.[16] The proposal was ignored by the British. Citing the minutes of this conference, the Mallah political intelligentsia argues today that the legislation that has dealt the severest blow to the livelihood of the caste has its origins in the colonial state. The post-Independence state merely took them over and refined so that upper caste dominance would not be threatened. Loopholes ensured that access to productive resources would remain in the hands of the upper castes and classes.

Martyrdom and Collateral Damage

This section explores the continuing and extraordinary appeal of martyrs for the caste and the conditions under which martyr narratives are claimed and perpetuated. The reclamation of caste martyrs and heroes serves two purposes. It counters colonial typologies of certain castes as "criminal" and "backward" which were taken over unquestioningly by the postcolonial state. And more significantly, it refutes post-Independence paradigms wherein the space for heroes was appropriated by an upper caste, Western-educated intellectual elite that led the masses to victory in anti-colonial struggles and claimed the glory reserved for the first nation builders. The post-Independence state further denied Mallah heroes their rightful place and honour, and this appears to be a central impetus for Mallah reinterpretation. Caste literature reveals a range of martyrs, each of whom serves to awaken social and political pride and to nurture a sense of collective identity (Tables 1 to 3).

Table 1
Historical Martyrs

Martyr	Place	Date of martyrdom
Baba (Shaheed) Tilka Majhi	Bhagalpur	1784
Siddho Majhi	–	1857
Samadhan Majhi – Satichaura, Kanpur	–	September 6, 1857
Lochan Mallah – Satichaura, Kanpur	–	September 6, 1857
Maiku Mallah, bodyguard of Kunwar Singh Bhojpur	–	1857
Bhima Mallah, bodyguard of Kunwar Singh Bhojpur	–	1857
Shankar and Bhawani Laxmibai's topchi	–	1857
Kunjbehari Kewat, son of Mahadev	Deshwan village, Gorakhpur district	February 24, 1922
Vipat Kewat and 17 others	Chauri Chaura	
Jubba Sahni	Captured at Meenapur-Muzaffarpur	1942

Source: *Who's Who of Indian Martyrs*, 3 volumes. Ed. P.N. Chopra (New Delhi: Ministry of Education and Social Welfare, 1969-73).

The example of Baba (Shaheed) Tilka Majhi, who carried out a guerrilla war against the British in the 1780s, is typical of the kind of hero whose narrative of resistance and struggle continues to impart pride and confidence to caste members. The narrative also bridges differences among sub-caste, regional, and tribal identities to bring together a range of disparate groups on the basis of their common low caste, tribal, and water-based occupational

Table 2
Mallah Martyrs, Quit India Movement, 1942

	Birthdate	Birthplace	Martyrdom
Kumar Mallah	1917	Maryadpur village, Mau district	Police firing, Madhuban, 1942
Soren Majhi	–	Santhal pargana, Shinghat village	Arrested and jailed, Rajmahal jail, died in custody March 25, 1944
Diwali Machhua, Dheewar caste	–	Sabzibaag village, Patna district	Police firing, Krishnaghat, Patna, August 26, 1942
Vidyapati Gond	1918	Mailki village, Ballia district	Police firing, Bairiya thana, 1942
Ramjanm Gond	–	Milki Tewari village, Ballia district	Police firing while participating in a demonstration on Bairiya thana, August 18, 1942
Laxman Gond	–	Sasaram, Shahabad district	Police firing, August 14, 1942, died August 16, 1942
Kobinda Koli	1920	Pune	Police firing near Garitaal, August 11, 1942

Source: Lalta Prasad Nishad, "Nayak v Itihaas Vihin Smaj ki Dasha" (Conditions of a society without visionaries and histories) *Nishad Jyoti* (Ghazipur, May 2002), 18.

affiliation as fishers. The narrative emphasizes the nature of the heroic struggle in which the British surrounded the Tilapore forest where Tilka Majhi
operated, and the bravery of his men, which enabled them to hold the enemy
at bay for several weeks. In popular memory, the revolt is remembered by the
sakhua leaves that were used to carry messages from village to village. Finally
caught in 1784, tied to the tail of a horse, and dragged all the way to the col-
lector's residence at Bhagalpur, Tilka Majhi achieved martyrdom and his lac-
erated body was hung from a banyan tree. A statue of this heroic leader was
erected on the spot after Independence, in what has since come to be known
as Tilka Majhi Square. Tilka's legendary sacrifice holds deep appeal. In a similar vein, collateral damage suffered by the caste during the first War of Independence makes the case for the trope of martyrdom.[17]

The inspirational heroes whose lives and deeds impart pride to the com-
munity and are most frequently mentioned in the pages of *Nishad Jyoti* are
Maharaj Kaalu Dheewar, Samadhan Nishad, Avantibai Lodhi, Mahadev
Kewat, Birsa Munda, Tilka Majhi, and Jubba Sahni.[18] The striking feature of

Table 3
Commemorations and Days of Observance

Commemoration	Day of observance
Maharaj Guhraj Jayanti	Chaitr Shukla Panchami
Vyas Pooja	Ashasrdh Poornima
Eklayva Smriti Divas	Ashardh Poornima
Samadhan Nishad Kranti Diwas	September 6
Gorakhnath Jayanti	Baisakh Poornima
Matsya Jayanti	Chaitr Tritiya
Mahadev Kewat Kranti Diwas	February 5
Rani Avantibai Lodhi Jayanti	August 16
Rani Avantibai Lodhi Balidaan Diwas	March 20
Swami Brahmanand Nirvan Diwas	September 13
Veerangana Durgawati Ballidaan Diwas	June 24
Bhagwan Birsa Munda Shaheedi Diwas	June 4
Sagarpujan Gangapujan	Naarikel Poornima, Shravan Poornima

Source: Lotan Ram Nishad, *Nishad Jyoti,* special issue on revolutionary ideas (Ghazipur), 25.

this collection of martyrs is the high proportion of tribal heroes. By making common cause with local, tribal, and folk heroes such as Birsa Munda, the Nishads identify with the struggles and rebellions of Kols, Mundas, and Gonds, thereby extending their pool of heroes. British suppression of rebellions by these people has been well documented, and by aligning themselves with these movements and their heroes, the Mallah greatly enrich their own repertoire. The names do not imply that the Mallah were without heroes but that they remain faceless and unsung precisely because of their subaltern position. In this regard, it is fitting to note the dismissive words of H.H. Risley, a senior member of the Indian Civil Service and a colonial anthropologist and ethnologist, about the Santhal rebellion: "A people whose only means of recording facts consists of tying knots in strings, and who have no bards to hand down a national epic by oral tradition, can hardly be expected to preserve the memory of their past long enough or accurately enough for their accounts of it to possess any historical value."[19]

Yet the resistance of the subalterns has been an important feature of the colonial past, and sharing a geographical and cultural universe appears necessary in order to disseminate and co-opt the lore of local heroes. Geographical proximity to Bhagalpur and other districts out of which the Santhal *parganas* (administrative units) were carved out has kept alive the collective memory of the Santhal rebellions among lower castes in vast areas of Bihar.

Estimates of non-combatant deaths amount to anything from 15,000 to 20,000. The great numbers of insurgents who died during suppression of the revolt of 1854–55 make it a heroic struggle in popular memory, second only to the Mutiny. K.S. Singh refers to another revolt in the same region, describing the suppression by troops and the 1917 trial in which four Mahato, Majhi, and Munda peasants were sentenced to death and hanged and 977 people out of the 1,118 tried were convicted.[20]

Further research would be required to understand the nature of collective memory and how it has been transmitted and kept alive. Unlike lengthy descriptions of events, which may be diluted with factual and chronological errors in the process of dissemination, data about numbers of casualties and figures of collateral damage are more likely to be remembered. It is possible, however, that the overarching Nishad identity sought so assiduously and cultivated from the early twentieth century onward has served at least one very significant function. Over the course of a century, linking groups on the basis of hereditary occupational specialization has collapsed differences not only among the entire range of fishing and river-faring sub-castes but also among several tribal groups occupying common geographical and ecological niches. In this sense, caste-based solidarities are the precursors of wider class mobilizations.

Attendance at caste *sabhas* and *sammelans* and the mobility this requires has brought forth an astounding awareness of and familiarity with struggles that might have otherwise remained regionally specific. These conventions have also been a valuable venue for accessing data to support a critique of the disempowering clauses within colonial legislation that have diminished the livelihood security of the Mallah, based as it was on their customary rights to rivers, forests, and riverbanks. The networks established at these sammelans were very likely the source of information about insurgencies during colonial times that involved the looting of over thirty *zamindari* tanks (used for water supply and fishing) in the Jungle Mahals district, a process whereby Santhals asserted their communal fishing rights. The agrarian nature of the Santhal and Munda rebellions, prompted by an onslaught against the customary rights of the people, is readily understood. In popular consciousness, their suppression and the resulting collateral damage flows into a single narrative, in terms of both casualties and livelihoods. What emerges as significant is the retelling itself, rather than an accurate chronology. Through retellings, people preserve cultural memory and attempt to reverse the cultural silencing of the marginalized.

Jubba Sahni: The Quintessential Martyr

The Mallah vision of social justice and empowerment is best articulated in the many narratives of the martyr Jubba Sahni (1906–44). What is important is that the story belongs to the caste and brings glory to it, and the embellishments it undergoes along the way refurbish the image of the caste. It is a tale of martyrdom, and by virtue of Jubba's involvement in the nationalist movement and proximity to its leadership, the story also shares in the glory of the nationalist discourse. Perhaps because more is known of his life than of the faceless boatmen of the Mutiny period, he is the hero/martyr who receives the most attention within the pages of the *Nishad Jyoti*. Jubba's closeness to the nationalist leadership, especially to Jawaharlal Nehru, is established with an account of the warm embrace with which the former greeted him:

> In 1932, Jubba was injured in his left hip by the police while picketing against drunkenness at the spirit dealership at Muzaffarpur's Dharamshala Square. Soon after, Jawaharlal Nehru visited Muzaffarpur. From within the crowd, Nehru singled out and embraced Jubba and addressed him as brother. Since then he was referred to as Jubba bhai. From 1932 to 1942 within the national struggle, he delivered secret mail to and fro.

Jubba's imprisonment and hanging make him the quintessential martyr, worthy to be counted among nationalist heroes. The narrative establishes a connection between the humiliation and insults he suffered at the hands of the British officer while working as a loader in a sugarcane factory and the rage that led to his final violent act:

> In 1942, under the supervision of brave Jubba, many offices and mail centres were set on fire and destroyed. Finally under the leadership of Jubba on 15 August, 1942, a massive demonstration with the Quit India slogan set out for the Meenapur thana and confronted Mr. Waller [a British officer]. The latter retaliated by opening fire on the satyagrahis. Along with his friends, crazed Jubba leapt up and disarmed him. The crowd was outraged and set the British officer on fire in the courtyard. The furniture of the thana was utilized as fuel in this deed.
>
> Along with 54 others, Jubba Sahni was arrested and sent to Muzaffarpur, where under the sub-judge, he took upon himself sole responsibility for setting Mr. Waller on fire. While the others received life imprisonment, Jubba was sentenced to death by hanging.[21]

This account counters the charge of looting government property, attributed in the official discourse to deprived subaltern classes. S. Henningham cites a government report suggesting that initially the lower castes did not take part in the movement but joined in its later stages when they hoped to benefit from the looting.[22] The narrative emphasizes that despite grinding poverty, the subaltern rebels attacked government property precisely because it represented the *sarkar*, the government.[23]

A 1997 article concludes a eulogistic account of Jubba Sahni by listing his name along with Khudiram Bose, Bhagat Singh, Chandrashekhar Azad, Ram Prasad Bismil, Subhaschandra Bose, Maharani Laxmibai, and others and urging that his statue be erected and martyrdom day celebrated.[24] It blames the government for its two-faced policies, whereby a low-born martyr has not received the recognition he is due.

Through retelling the narrative of Jubba Sahni the Mallah enter many levels of the prevailing discourse and seek to smoothen and clean up the tale. By using the surname Sahni instead of the court's pejorative use of "Mallah," the narrative dignifies and elevates him. The narrative confirms that subalterns were very much a part of the movement. Establishing proximity to upper caste heroes is an attempt to claim greater cohesiveness with the elite leadership. Attacks on government property are configured as acts of protest and rebellion against the colonial state rather than as looting for the sake of material benefit. The narrative posits the existence of a whole range of nameless lower caste heroes, who remain forgotten because of collective amnesia. It points to a vibrant, enthusiastic, and rebellious subaltern consciousness, which was as, if not more, important than the elite contribution to the Quit India Movement.

In caste retellings, in addition to the retrieval of heroes, evidence of collateral damage serves a significant purpose. The collateral damage suffered by caste members through violence in the First War of Independence in 1857, followed by the slur of criminality through legislation that subjected them to humiliating surveillance and control, is juxtaposed against the non-violence of Gandhi's national struggle for independence. The caste discourse is therefore pitted against both colonial narratives and postcolonial state narratives of heroes and leaders – the builders of the nation. Such discourse buttresses a politics of identity through which local histories and narratives challenge and subvert established, though restricted, understanding of national history and heroes. In addition, the sense of pride and belonging that these accounts foster is of special importance in uniting various sub-castes under the banner of Nishad, which now more than ever is necessary for political action and mobilization.

Narrative Structures and Traditions

With increasing literacy has come a lower caste preoccupation with writing the history of the people. Propelled by concerns of collective identity, the narratives fill important gaps in historical knowledge about collectivities. Interwoven with contemporary concerns, they supplement origin myths and folklore by providing a repertoire of caste-specific histories from the perspective of those "culturally silenced." However, popular historical narratives echo the concerns deeply embedded within the folk and collective consciousness and at a symbolic level, tend to parallel the hero motifs and themes of puranic literature.

In caste puranas, the written and oral traditions of castes, narratives are specific to the caste and often in opposition to Brahminical traditions. Puranic folk heroes symbolically enact the constant struggle of the lower against the higher castes. Eklavya, the folk hero of the Mallah and a lower caste character from the *Mahabharata*, for instance, sought and was denied training in archery from an upper caste teacher, Drona. The story is told to emphasize the exclusion of lower castes from knowledge and skills. It especially underlines the treachery of Brahmins in demanding Eklavya's right thumb in return for transmitting knowledge. The popularity of the tale among the Mallah and the lessons it holds for the caste are underlined at the annual celebration of Eklavya Jayanti. The tragedy of the folk hero, Eklavya, also resonates with the stories of Maiku and Bhima Mallah, the daring boatmen of the Mutiny, as well as countless others whose contributions have been eclipsed by elitist nationalist narratives.

Equally popular is the story of Shambook, a lower caste sage who was supposedly killed because of his attempt to impart knowledge of the Vedas to tribals. Here the motif of withholding knowledge from lower castes recurs.

Whereas the emphasis in the stories of Eklavya and Shambook is on exclusion and disempowerment, the Satyanarain Katha is a puranic tale in which the hero reclaims and re-establishes his superiority. Its narration is supposed to bestow merit and is to be accompanied by the performance of ritual and collective prayer. The tale is about a Mallah who on finding a small coin is startled to hear a voice emanating from a tree, urging him to purchase small items for a ritual offering and instructions on how to conduct a collective prayer. The Mallah, following the mysterious instructions, carries out the prayer ritual and at its conclusion, offers *prasad* (sweets) to the congregation. However, a Brahmin refuses to accept the sweets because of the perceived pollution of the Mallah. He is struck by calamities and in desperation turns to prayer. This time the voice from the tree castigates him for rejecting the food offering from the righteous Mallah and advises him to carry out the entire ritual in accordance with instructions from the Mallah. On doing this, the Brahmin's fortunes are restored.

As puranic tales are invariably about the extraordinary exploits of heroes, their familiar structure provides a convenient and effective mode of transmission for new tales as well. Through these narratives, the Mallah retrieve a space for protest and resistance to contest the dominant and hegemonic structures of both past and contemporary society.

Conclusion

As people's histories have remained largely eclipsed within the master narrative of the Indian nation, efforts are underway to correct this partial understanding. Alternative Nishad narratives of lower caste heroes emphasize resistance and agency and are therefore both empowering and inspirational. They represent a political strategy that seeks to challenge existing power structures and modes of dependence and domination. By providing alternatives to cultural stereotypes, the narratives open up the possibility of charting new frameworks for relationships among subaltern groups as well as between them and the Indian state.

Tropes of heroes and martyrs emerge as necessary in reclaiming agency and in evolving appropriate metaphors to challenge the colonial charge of criminality made against the caste. The colonial state's arguments about character traits such as "vagrancy," "lawlessness," and associated "criminal tendencies" are here inverted to present an image of the caste as heroic, brave, and patriotic and therefore to be feared even by the colonizing power, with its powerful machinery for exercising control.

This essay has argued for an understanding of collateral damage not just in the realm of civilian casualties but also as including collective punishments meted out to an entire social group by the colonial state. Thus, all members of the Mallah caste were designated as criminal, not just those who fought against the British. The long-term effects of the colonial laws that reinforced the punitive approach of the colonial state toward the caste further marginalized its members from their sources of livelihood. The cumulative effect of these state measures therefore needs to be understood as scarcely different in degree from the civilian casualties accruing from the deployment of military technologies in the context of contemporary wars. Historicizing our understanding of collateral damage is a necessary step in tracing the evolution of the concept and in recovering the layered meanings of the term in different contexts.

Notes

1 Romila Thapar, *Narratives and the Making of History: Two Lectures* (New Delhi: Oxford University Press, 2000).

2 Shahid Amin, *Event, Metaphor, Memory: Chauri Chaura 1922–1992* (New Delhi: Oxford University Press, 1995).

3 Smita T. Jassal, "Caste and the Colonial State: Mallahs in the Census," *Contributions to Indian Sociology* n.s. 35, 3 (2001), 319–54.

4 Lalta Prasad Nishad, "Nayak v Itihaas Vihin Smaj ki Dasha" (Conditions of a society without visionaries and histories) *Nishad Jyoti* (Ghazipur), May 2002, 9, 18.

5 S. Henningham, "Quit India in Bihar and the Eastern United Provinces: The Dual Revolt," in *Subaltern Studies II*, ed. R. Guha (New Delhi: Oxford University Press, 1983).

6 Stanley Cohen, *States of Denial: Knowing about Atrocities and Suffering* (Cambridge: Polity Press, 2001), 8.

7 Amin, *Event, Metaphor, Memory.*

8 Alf Hiltebeitel, *Criminal Gods and Demon Devotees: Essays on the Guardians of Popular Hinduism* (Albany: State University of New York, 1989).

9 Sheoprasad Choudhary, interview with author, Ara, April 17, 1997.

10 Lautanram Nishad, "Rozi Roti Nyaya v Samman ke liye Aarakshan Avashyak" (Affirmative action necessary for livelihoods, justice, and respect), *Nishad Jyoti* (Ghazipur), August 2002, 5.

11 Vallabhbhai Patel, known as Sardar Patel, was a major figure in the Indian nationalist movement, a former president of the Indian National Congress, and after independence, deputy prime minister. Dr. Ambedkar was a pioneering scholar of Untouchable origins and activist leader in the struggle against discrimination. He played in major role in framing the Indian Constitution.

12 *Nishad Jyoti* (Ghazipur), August 2002, 5–7.

13 Sanjay Nigam, "Disciplining and Policing the Criminals by Birth: Part I, The Making of a Colonial Stereotype – the Criminal Tribes and Castes of North India," *Indian Economic and Social History Review* 27, 2 (1990), 131–64.

14 Jassal, "Caste and the Colonial State."

15 Jawahar Lal Nishad, interview with author, Varanasi, April 10, 2003.

16 *Nishad Jyoti* (Ghazipur), May 2003.

17 Lalta Prashad Nishad, "Nayak v Itihaas Vihin Smaj ki Dasha."

18 *Nishad Jyoti* (Ghazipur, May 2002), 18–23.

19 H.H. Risley, *Tribes and Castes of Bengal*, vol. 2 (Calcutta: Government Press, 1891).

20 Ranajit Samaddar, "Territory and People: The Disciplining of Historical Memory," in *Texts of Power: Emerging Disciplines in Colonial Bengal*, ed. Partha Chatterjee (Calcutta: Samya, 1996).

21 Umashanker Sahni, "Swatantrata Sangram ke Amar Shaheed Jubba Shani: Ek Mahan Deshbhakt" (Jubba Sahni: A martyr of the freedom struggle, a great patriot), *Nishad Jagaran* (Patna), August 1994, 6.

22 Henningham, "Quit India in Bihar and the Eastern United Provinces," 151.

23 Ibid.

24 Mayanand Mahaldar, "Azadi Ke Deewane: Amar Shaheed Jubba Sahni" (Crazy for Freedom: The Immortal Martyr Jubba Sahni), *Nishad Jagaran* (Patna), February–March 1997, 6.

Part 4
Sexual Violence and War

11 Marlene Epp

Sexual Violence in War

Mennonite Refugees during the Second World War

The exposé in 2004 of the abuse of Iraqi prisoners by American forces in Iraq once again brought to our attention an age-old historical pattern whereby the violence of war is imbued symbolically and literally with sexuality and gender. While the media accounts that I heard and read at the time did not clearly spell out all aspects of the sex-related abuse that occurred at the Abu Ghraib Prison, there appear to have been multiple levels of sexualized violence at work. Men abusing men, Marines sexually cavorting with each other and with prisoners, and other activities, almost all of which combine sex and violence with the goal of humiliating and degrading the weaker individual, whether he or she is prisoner or "comrade." Indeed, Myra Mendible recently argued that humiliation, as a "gendered emotion" and a "strategy of postmodern war," is "one of the most persuasive of disciplinary tactics."[1] And humiliation was certainly at work at Abu Ghraib. The now historic photo of Lynndie England proudly holding a trodden-down prisoner by a leash showed another, more atypical, demonstration of gendered wartime violence: an American woman abusing an Iraqi Muslim man, or as Barbara Ehrenreich observed, "female sexual sadism in action."[2] The abuse underway was clearly gendered, from the perspective of both males and females. What unsettled me was that the world was surprised or shocked by these revelations.

The behaviour exhibited at the Abu Ghraib Prison revealed a mentality toward the enemy that young soldiers are trained to develop and that is required to motivate them to perform the horrific acts they are instructed to do in wartime. A film about boot camp that I show to my undergraduate students in Peace and Conflict Studies at the University of Waterloo, *Anybody's Son Will Do*, depicts this ethos quite graphically. Trainees and their supervisors use motivating images and language that mix hatred of the enemy, humiliation of each other, and sexually demeaning attitudes toward women, including their own girlfriends.[3] There is, of course, a growing body of literature that describes and analyzes the intersection of gender and militarism and, to a lesser extent, the ways in which maleness and femaleness overlap with the actions and discourses of peacemaking as well.[4] That scholars and others have begun a critical and thought-provoking discussion about wartime violence as gendered and sexualized is encouraging. The accounts from Abu Ghraib were perhaps most disturbing because, contrary to what is considered normative gender behaviour, the most highly profiled victor and violator was a woman. The entry of women into combat units of the military will undoubtedly present new questions and conclusions about the perpetrators of wartime sexual violence, highlighting the at times contested notion that women, too, can humiliate and kill. Yet despite the need to expand our thinking about gender on the issue, it is important to recognize that women and girls are numerically by far the majority of victims of gender-based violence; in fact, one United Nations document describes it as having "reached epidemic proportions."[5] If one includes victims and survivors of sexual violence within the tabulation of wartime collateral damage (though this is a misnomer), then female damages are indeed huge.

The most pervasive form of sexualized violence during wartime, and probably the most well documented, is the rape of women by military personnel of the opposing forces, though rape, sexual exploitation, and other related forms of violence occur in many other wartime and conflict circumstances as well. Women in flight as refugees of war are raped by border guards, sea pirates, refugee camp officials, and others who hold power over escape and security; for example, oral histories of the so-called boat people who escaped Southeast Asia in the late 1970s include numerous accounts of rape and sexual terrorism by notorious pirates.[6] Girls and women are coerced into providing sexual services to armies on both sides of a conflict; well documented are the brothels established by the Japanese military in the Second World War, which saw up to 200,000 women forced into prostitution.[7] The pattern continues in the early twenty-first century as girls (and boys) as young as six years old are abducted and used as soldiers and sex slaves by rebel militias in conflicts that rage in such countries as Uganda, Sudan, Sierra Leone, and the Democratic Republic of the Congo.[8] Female political prisoners frequently experience rape as part of their torture, evident especially under the dictatorial regimes of Central and South America during the 1970s and 1980s.[9] Furthermore, we now know that "even" United Nations peacekeepers, expected to be a protective presence for civilian populations, have exploited prostitutes and enacted sexual violence in the course of their duty.[10] As well, domestic violence frequently escalates during and in the aftermath of wars, since the gendered nature of militarism inevitably heightens male power and aggression, both personally and systemically.[11] Deborah Harrison's research on Canadian military wives, for instance, reveals the violence within military homes that results from a mentality of "control" that is necessary for "combat readiness." Madeline Morris' study of rape by U.S. military personnel also reveals the connections between the culture of militarism and the potential for rape, whether in peace or wartime.[12]

Susan Brownmiller's groundbreaking 1975 study on rape was one of the first exposés to name rape as a "common act of war."[13] By now, we can draw up a long list of global and localized conflicts in which rape was, if not a key component of military strategy, then certainly a gendered by-product of victory and loss. When Japanese forces captured the Chinese city of Nanjing (Nanking) in 1937, 20,000 women were raped in the first month of occupation: hence the designation of the invasion as the Rape of Nanking. As many as a million women were raped when the Soviet army entered German-occupied territory in Eastern Europe toward the end of the Second World War. Hardly explored at all is the rape of Jewish women during the Holocaust; one Holocaust educator told me that racial purity laws made it an offence for German soldiers to rape Jews but it happened nevertheless, and the women were killed afterward. More than 200,000 Bengali women were raped by Pakistani solders in the 1971 Bangladeshi War of Independence. During the Vietnam War, countless Vietnamese women were raped by American soldiers, but these incidents have for the most part been silenced. The listing, past and present, could go on.

While one can point to a long history of sexual violence in war, the dramatic increase in the number of civilian casualties – among other collateral damages – in wars of the later twentieth and early twenty-first centuries, has heightened the use of sex as a weapon of war. The number of civilian deaths during war has risen from 50 per cent of all casualties during the Second World War to a staggering 90 per cent in the early twenty-first century, and the majority of those civilian victims are women and children.[14] Civil conflicts, in particular, heighten the potential for sexual violence in the form of rape of civilian women, use of women and girls as sex slaves, and sexual torture of female prisoners, as noted above. Recent conflicts have brought this to world attention in disturbing (at times pornographic) ways. In the 1990–91 war against Kuwait, Iraqi troops reportedly raped about 3,200 women.[15] Shortly thereafter, 20,000 to 50,000 women were raped in sixteen notorious "rape camps" operated by Serbian nationalist extremists during the conflict in Bosnia-Herzegovina that consumed the republics of the former Yugoslavia in the early 1990s.[16] Adding to the horror that might lead one to conclude the 1990s were the decade of war on women, during the genocidal war in Rwanda in 1994, during which approximately 800,000 people were slaughtered, it is estimated that 250,000 to 500,000 Tutsi women were raped by Hutu extremists.[17] Most recently, in 2006, the media focused on the Democratic Republic of the Congo, where 4 million people have died in violent conflict involving foreign armies and internal militia, and in which an estimated 50,000 to several hundred thousand women and girls have been raped since 1998.[18]

Analysts of wartime rape have increasingly identified the incidence of such violence not as an aberrant by-product of warfare but as a key component of military strategy and soldier training. We are increasingly recognizing – though historical gendered power relations mean that this has been true since the beginning of time – that "women's bodies are . . . part of the battlefield."[19] The historical tendency has been to portray sexual violence against women in war within a descriptive yet anaesthetizing framework of "lootpillageandrape" – to use the telling word collapse of Cynthia Enloe[20] – but the mass rapes committed in Bosnia and Rwanda in the early 1990s, especially, caused scholars, activists, policy makers, and others to look more carefully at how rape functions for nations, communities, and women in the midst of conflict. Zainab Salbi, founder of Women for Women International, an NGO that assists women in war-torn regions, summed up this function by stating that "rape is used to achieve political and social goals, from the destruction of the social fabric of the society, to avenging historical acts, to political propaganda."[21] This leads to the obvious conclusion that the victims and survivors of sexual violence during war are not collateral damage as usually understood, but in fact direct targets as civilians alongside soldiers and military sites.

My own limited expertise on this topic arises from my research on wartime rape as remembered by Mennonite refugees from the Soviet Union and Eastern Europe during the Second World War. My interest occurred in the context of a larger study on the displacement of Mennonites from southern Ukraine during the war and followed their eventual migration to Canada and Paraguay.[22] The Mennonites, a culturally German, ethnoreligious group with ancestral origins in the Netherlands and Prussia, represented almost 10 per cent of the close to 1.5 million ethnic Germans living in the Soviet Union at the outset of the Second World War. Most Mennonites lived in the part of Ukraine under German occupation from August 1941 to September 1943. By the time the German army arrived, the Mennonite population of Ukraine had been altered dramatically as Communist authorities forced the deportation of thousands of German-speaking colonists to labour camps in the east and north of the country. In particular, a noticeable gender imbalance occurred in Mennonite communities as a result of several waves of arrests and disappearances, mainly of adult men, beginning in the late 1920s and culminating in the Stalinist purges of 1936–38. As ethnic Germans, the Mennonites were perceived as potential collaborators and so more deportations occurred after war with Germany broke out. It was mainly adult men who were taken and not returned, so that by the time the German forces occupied southwest Ukraine in 1941, the Mennonite population was composed almost exclusively of women, children, and the elderly. In most Mennonite villages, about 50 per cent of households were without a father, and in some villages there was only a handful of men between the ages of sixteen and sixty.

When the Germans retreated two years later, they took with them the remaining population of Mennonites – about 35,000 – and at the same time conscripted any men left over the age of sixteen into the German army. When the war ended, this remnant of Mennonite refugees was scattered across Eastern Europe and Germany; some remained near the Eastern Front, while others trekked farther west and north, and still others went to Austria and Yugoslavia. The Mennonite refugee population now included, in addition to those who had left the Soviet Union, Mennonites displaced from their homes in Poland, Prussia, and Danzig. After the war, over 20,000 Mennonites were dead or missing or were repatriated back to the Soviet Union, while the remaining 12,000 or so (most of whom had travelled farther west) migrated to Canada and South America in the late 1940s and early '50s.

In the context of this study of gender and migration, I learned about the mass rapes experienced by German women when the Soviet army advanced into the territories of Eastern Europe in the winter of 1944–45. Although the majority of Mennonite refugees were Soviet born, they were viewed as, and saw themselves as, ethnic Germans. In fact, once they were in German-occupied territory, most of those who had fled their homes in Ukraine went to great efforts to hide their ability to speak Russian in order to avoid repatriation. As such, Mennonite refugees experienced the ending of the war much like citizens of the Reich; for women, this meant fearing the possibility of becoming victims of rape. The Soviet advance into Eastern Europe resulted in the displacement of 15 million Germans from their homes and a violent rampage against civilians, including widespread rape of German women by Red Army soldiers. Statistics on the number of rapes during this assault vary from 20,000 to 2 million; one of the challenges of documenting casualties of rape is, of course, that numbers can vary dramatically depending on whether one counts numbers of women raped or number of rapes, since most women are violated more than once in wartime campaigns of sexual violence.[23] As a recent example of this, a 2004 account documented the story of Athanasie Mukarwego, a Tutsi woman who was raped by more than 500 men over a three-month period during the genocide in Rwanda in 1994.[24] One Congolese woman, who died from her injuries, was raped by seventeen men, while women who were imprisoned in the notorious rape camps in Bosnia were also assaulted repeatedly over weeks and months.[25] Thus, the number of rapes committed in a particular conflict can appreciably exceed the number of women raped.

With regard to my own research, recollections about the mass rapes of the

Second World War, as experienced by Mennonite refugees, were obtained through oral interviews, written memoirs, and assorted other pieces of documentation.[26] While I have no statistics to offer on the number of Mennonite women who were raped, various sources confirm that "many" experienced wartime sexual violence in this manner. A number of observations and questions emerged in my own study that, I believe, parallel and can be applied to comparable scenarios in different wars and historical eras.

First, notwithstanding the significant media, public, and academic attention given to wartime rape in the past decade, in prior global and civil conflicts, sexual violence was generally a taboo subject. In my own research, I was interested to know, given the unmentionable nature of the topic, how people would talk about rape and its impact. The limited Mennonite historical literature that examines these events tends to deal with rape cursorily and then quickly move on. For instance one account, in describing the impact on Mennonites of the Soviet advance into Germany, summarizes the matter in two sentences: "Women and even children had been raped (hundreds, perhaps even thousands; we do not know; it is a subject too painful to talk about). Men and women were forced to watch as their mothers and sisters were abused."[27] In a 1949 letter to a friend, a postwar Mennonite immigrant woman in Canada wrote, "We . . . reached Brandenburg before the Russians overtook us. How they tormented us! Words cannot describe how horrible that was." Another woman brought closure to the topic by saying, "I cannot describe this time adequately to you, it was too terrible."[28] By declaring a topic "too painful" to discuss, both victims and their communities, as well as chroniclers of their history, absolve themselves of analyzing the gendered nature of wartime violence and militarism more generally. What became most interesting to me was the prevalence of using third-person language to discuss sexual violence, whether orally or in writing, rather than acknowledging it as personal experience. In accounts of extreme violence, which include rape, women frequently detach themselves from their narration, giving the impression that the teller of the story was invisible. While the context makes it obvious that a woman was present, her narrative will often provide third-person details of another's fate without revealing any about her own. In 1951, a recent Mennonite immigrant to Canada described in lurid detail the brutal attack by Soviet soldiers on a group of women. Although the narrator herself fits the profile of the women who were victims, she tells the episode apart from herself; yet she switches abruptly from "they" to "we" when she moves on to the more benign subject of food rations.[29] Because of the shame and humiliation that surrounded the experience of rape, women protected their own fragile memories and emotions by more objectively describing the experience of others.

Researchers examining the experiences of refugee women in other contexts and periods have found similar patterns of denial and depersonalization in accounts of sexual violence. Ruth Harris, in her study of the First World War testimonies of French women, also observed a rhetorical style in which as little as possible was said about the assault itself.[30] In an oral history project with women refugees from Cambodia during the late 1970s, interviewers found that although the women normally had no difficulty telling them that something did or did not happen, "none of the women admitted to having been raped," even though rape was acknowledged as a frequent occurrence in refugee camps. One interviewer noted, "When the question of rape came up, they all essentially became mute and started doing something else without looking at me or anyone else."[31] A Croatian journalist also described the "wall of silence" evident to those investigating reports of rape in Bosnia in the mid-1990s.[32] Following the political, media, and activist attention to mass rapes in several global regions in the late twentieth century, the wall of silence gradually began to diminish, as war crimes investigators, human rights groups, and women themselves were increasingly compelled to tell the stories of rape. So while Mennonite women raped during the Second World War repressed or hid their experiences, today "women in so many cultures . . . feel empowered enough to report when they have been raped," a development that Cynthia Enloe says is "one of the success stories of the second wave of the women's movement."[33] It should not be inferred from this, however, that the shame and guilt that caused Mennonite women to subjugate or redirect their stories has also diminished. In today's world, women who are coming forward with their stories, first because they are asked and second because they seek justice, are nevertheless consumed with shame over what has happened to their bodies, experiencing a sense of dishonour that is reinforced by the way in which they are often stigmatized by their families and communities. Alexandra Stiglmayer, in chronicling the mass rapes in Bosnia-Herzegovina, noted that even while women wanted to tell their stories to journalists and others, it was extremely difficult because "rape is that terrible, humiliating, almost unutterable 'it.'"[34]

A second observation I propose is that rape can be understood as a gendered form of wartime death. While victims of rape do not count as civilian deaths, for many survivors, death would have been the preferred outcome of their experience. For Mennonite refugees and other German women, many suicides preceded the threat of rape or followed rape.[35] It has even been suggested that some rape victims were driven to kill themselves after experiencing rejection by their own menfolk.[36] One Mennonite woman, a child during the war, recalled this scenario in eastern Germany: "The worst thing was molesting women and girls. My mother hid me under coal and she herself had to suffer. The grandparents had a very big house right beside a fresh water lake. . . . Women and girls just ran into the lake, drowning themselves. Bodies were just coming to the shore."[37] In other cases, survivors expressed the wish that they had in fact died, or reflected that they continued to have physical life even after dying emotionally and psychologically. One Mennonite woman who knew she would be "mistreated" if captured by the Russians said she "would rather die than fall into their hands," although she escaped rape in the end.[38] Another wrote in her memoir that after her three friends were raped, "There were days that [they] didn't care to go on with their lives."[39] Historians of this era have described how German women carried cyanide capsules with them at all times, so they would be prepared when presented with the choice between rape and death.

Many women in today's conflicts are able to rebuild their lives in a spirit of hope with the help of human rights and humanitarian organizations as well as supportive family members, but others exist – just barely – in a state of continuous pain and ongoing health problems as a result of brutal sexual attacks, unable to support themselves economically and ostracized by their families. Combined with this is the stigma, for many women in the world today, of contracting HIV/AIDS, of bearing children conceived from rape, or of living with the consequences of severe mutilation of their internal organs. For this group, physical death may well have been preferable to the emotional and social death that followed the violence inflicted on them. As one Rwandan woman who almost committed suicide said, "I did not want to cope with living."[40] These women also need to be categorized in any tabulation of civilian casualties of war.

A third observation, which may be obvious, is that rape is a particularly pernicious weapon of war because it is difficult to document (perhaps less so now than in the past) and because victims are shamed by the experience and do not want to talk about it. The death of a soldier is heroic, but the rape of a civilian is inglorious for the individual, for her family, and for her community, however that is defined. The humiliation, and indeed guilt – as if the victim were somehow culpable – is ongoing. Certainly for the group of highly moral and religious Mennonite refugees that I studied, sexual violation was something to be kept hidden, a source of life-time guilt intertwined with issues of fallen morality and community condemnation. Culpability was even greater when women became pregnant as a result of rape, which was a frequent occurrence.

Especially striking in sources that I examined was the limited differentiation between unmarried mothers who became pregnant in consensual relations during wartime and rape survivors who bore children; each was perceived as a "fallen woman," regardless of the circumstances of conception. Indeed, the unique exigencies and circumstances of war meant that after experiencing successive rapes, or threats of rape, women sometimes sought out a protector, usually in the form of an army officer, for whom she provided sex in return for a limited kind of safety. Described by one scholar as "instrumental sex,"[41] such scenarios saw a woman submit to sexual acts in order to avoid other forms of violence against her and her children, to obtain food for her family, or to obtain assistance in crossing tightly guarded borders. One Mennonite woman who did housework for Soviet officers in the Russian zone following the war said, "It was better . . . if you had a friend, then the others would leave you alone."[42] In another account, the author recalls a conversation with her sister about a group of Mennonite women who were repatriated to Soviet labour camps during the war: "As I got re-acquainted with these women I heard them talking about their children. Later I asked my sister how come all these sons have their mothers' last names? Did they not have fathers? The color rose in [her] face, she came and stood close in front of me and said with a raised and forceful voice I had never heard from her, ' . . . Think about it! What do you think kept these women alive? They did what they had to do. Yes, those children had fathers, but they never knew them.' "[43] In such cases, the difference between rape and prostitution is slight, suggests one historian of rape in the Second World War.[44] Greater international awareness of the prevalence and brutality of sexual violence in conflict has, some analysts suggest, brought a shock value to wartime rape that obscures the continuum of violence and exploitation that women in those settings experience. As a 2002 report by the United Nations Development Fund for Women (UNIFEM) states, "Women are physically and economically forced or left with little choice but to become sex workers or to exchange sex for food, shelter, safe passage or other needs; their bodies become part of a barter system, a form of exchange that buys the necessities of life."[45]

Another observation is that wartime sexual violence reinforces traditional gender roles that may have been upset by the exigencies of war. For the Mennonite women refugees of my study, traditional gender roles within families and communities had been radically upset by the loss of adult men to the community. Already in the 1930s, the women in Mennonite villages in Ukraine had become primary income earners for their families and, with the exile of most church ministers and other men who held official positions of authority, had taken on leadership roles – albeit informal and unsanctioned – to maintain, in particular, the religious life of their households and community. During their years as refugees in flight, women had taken on responsibility for negotiating with (and bribing) army and border officials, for controlling unruly horse teams and fixing broken wagons, and for ensuring, as best they could, that their families were safe, fed, and warm. In the absence of adult men, who would normally be expected to undertake the heavy physical tasks and take leadership in family decision making, women were compelled to take on roles traditionally allocated to both genders. Yet the fear and reality of rape reinforced a gender hierarchy in which women were vulnerable in the face of male violence and also dependent on male protection. Whatever sense of female autonomy or shift in gender roles that had occurred in these female-headed families was brutally shaken by rape's display of masculine power over them. In this particular community, it could be that rape also reinforced gendered characteristics of obedience and submission by women, traits that were already idealized in Mennonite culture. Apart from the particularities of the Mennonite historical experience, wartime rape has the overall societal function, as Ruth Seifert concludes, to "regulate unequal power relations between the sexes: it serves to maintain a cultural order between the sexes or – when this order becomes fragile – to restore it."[46]

If wartime sexual violence reinforces traditional gender hierarchies through the exertion of male power on the part of the victors, it can also weaken the masculine self-identity of other men. In particular, rape as a weapon of war serves to empower the perpetrator and to make weak the man who has been unable to protect. Humiliating the enemy, a psychological weapon so crucial to the success of military victory, is achieved most intensely when a man is unable to protect his wife, daughters, sisters, or other female relatives from sexual assault by opposing militia. Or even more so, when he is compelled to watch or participate, as painful accounts from Democratic Republic of the Congo and elsewhere reveal. In such settings, where rape is so public and so shameful for men whose masculinity and family honour is at stake, the pain and ostracism felt by women is sometimes overshadowed by the shaken social position of their menfolk. For instance, in prewar Congolese law, rape was considered a crime of honour against the husband and so, while some men fled out of shame over their inability to protect their women, others rejected wives and daughters who were raped.[47] Chroniclers of the situation in Bosnia observed that in many households, husbands just didn't want to know what had happened to their wives.

For Mennonite men who were eyewitnesses to wartime rape or whose family members were victims of rape, their memories occur in the context of their own vulnerability. During the civil war that brought vengeful violence to Mennonite settlements in Ukraine following the First World War, traditionally pacifist Mennonite men established a controversial arms-bearing self-defence league, motivated mainly by a masculinist desire to protect their womenfolk, who were being raped by soldiers and bandits. During the Second World War, one Mennonite man, forcibly conscripted into the German army, described to me a situation in which he had hidden in a hayloft and thereby saved himself from capture by Soviet soldiers but simultaneously had been unable to protect German women who were being raped nearby; later he learned that his younger sister had also been sexually assaulted. The overriding emotion in his memory was horror and shame that in order to protect himself, he could offer no protection or aid to the women. His recollections fit with Susan Brownmiller's observation that to the extent that rape restores the victor's masculinity, husbands and fathers of rape victims have their masculinity humiliated and taken away.[48]

The emasculation of the defeated male through the rape of women in his family and community/nation also has the purpose of threatening national and/or ethnic identity, which brings me to my final observation.[49] Strategic campaigns of mass wartime rape, as well as random attacks, have a genocidal purpose, in that impregnating the enemy's women is believed to result in offspring with the perpetrators' ethnic identity. Analysts of the conflict in the former Yugoslavia in the early 1990s, for example, noted that rape was used as a "weapon for ethnic cleansing" and that attacks on women specifically represented an attempt to exterminate the enemy by virtue of eliminating ethnic identity.[50] The mass rapes of women in Rwanda shortly thereafter were similarly given political motivation, though explicit media propaganda, with the call to eliminate Tutsi ethnicity by impregnating women with Hutu babies.

My own research, as well as others, revealed clearly that wartime rape is not solely an individualized act of violence against a woman but has strong political intent and ramifications. The limited historical accounts by Mennonite historians on the rapes of the Second World War highlight issues of national identity more than the physical and emotional impact of sexual violence on women. To the extent that they even acknowledged the presence of rape victims within their own community, Mennonite accounts focused on racializing and demonizing the Soviet soldiers, who were described as "unshaven, dirty and putrid ... cruel Asiatic people, yellow-skinned, broad-faced with high cheekbones."[51] Such racist characterizations served both to reflect and to reinforce anti-Soviet sentiments among Soviet-born Mennonites. For their part, Germans have drawn on the mass wartime rapes as a symbol of national identity for a defeated and victimized people.[52] The converse side of this interpretation was revealed to me when, delivering a paper on this topic in Ukraine a number of years ago, I was soundly trounced by one Ukrainian scholar for my German bias and depiction of the Soviet army as the sole perpetrators of rape in the Second World War. It was an important lesson for me. Similarly, interpretive approaches that placed issues of ethnonationalism at the centre were pervasive in analyses of the mass rapes that occurred in the civil wars in Bosnia-Herzegovina.[53] In all these cases, readings of wartime sexual violence emphasized issues of national symbolism and identity over the outcomes for individual victims and survivors. While helping to illuminate the complexity of cause and effect in civil conflicts particularly, emphasizing group identity over against personal trauma can also verge on the propagandistic.

Wartime sexual violence is not an easy topic to discuss for scholars, survivors, or the general public. Yet one hopes that with more historical analysis and contemporary exposés, rape and other forms of sexualized violence during wartime will eventually be viewed as an integral part of war weaponry, along with bombs and landmines. And that survivors will be numbered among lists of civilian casualties, alongside the dead and injured.

Notes

1 Myra Mendible, "Dominance and Submission in Postmodern War Imagery," *Peace Review: A Journal of Social Justice* 17, 1 (2005), 55.
2 Barbara Ehrenreich, "A Uterus Is No Substitute for a Conscience: What Abu Ghraib Taught Me," *Z-Net*, May 21, 2004, www.zmag.org.
3 Paul Cowan, director, *Anybody's Son Will Do* (National Film Board of Canada, 1983). There is a growing body of literature that explores the gendered aspects of military training and militarism. See for instance: Ingeborg Breines, Robert Connell, and Ingrid Eide, eds., *Male Roles, Masculinities and Violence: A Culture of Peace Perspective* (Paris: Unesco Publishing, 2000); Cynthia Cockburn and Dubravka Zarkov, eds., *The Postwar Moment: Militaries, Masculinities and International Peacekeeping, Bosnia and the Netherlands* (London: Lawrence and Wishart, 2002); Paul R. Higate, ed., *Military Masculinities: Identity and the State* (Westport, Conn.: Präger, 2003).
4 Cynthia Enloe's books and articles explore gender and militarism from a variety of vantage points. See, for instance, her most recent book, *Maneuvers: The International Politics of Militarizing Women's Lives* (Berkeley: University of California Press, 2000). See also Wenona Giles and Jennifer Hyndman, eds., *Sites of Violence: Gender and Conflict Zones* (Berkeley: University of California Press, 2004); Nicole Ann Dombrowski, ed., *Women and War in the Twentieth Century: Enlisted with or without Consent* (New York: Routledge, 2004); Caroline O.N. Moser and Fiona C. Clark, eds., *Victims, Perpetrators or Actors? Gender, Armed Conflict and Political Violence* (London: Zed Books, 2001); Anne Llewellyn Barstow, ed., *War's Dirty Secret: Rape, Prostitution, and Other Crimes against Women* (Cleveland: The Pilgrim Press, 2000); Lois Ann Lorentzen and Jennifer Turpin, eds., *The Women and War Reader* (New York: New York University Press, 1998); Jean Bethke Elshtain and Sheila Tobias, eds., *Women, Militarism, and War: Essays in History, Politics, and Social Theory* (Totowa, N.J.: Rowman and Littlefield, 1990); Margaret Randolph Higonnet et al., eds., *Behind the Lines: Gender and the Two World Wars* (New Haven, Conn.: Yale University Press, 1987); Betty A. Reardon, *Sexism and the War System* (New York: Teachers College Press, 1985).
5 Elisabeth Rehn and Ellen Johnson Sirleaf, *Women, War, Peace: The Independent Experts' Assessment on the Impact of Armed Conflict on Women and Women's Role in Peace-Building*, Progress of the World's Women 2002, vol. 1 (New York: UNIFEM, 2002), www.unifem.org.
6 See essays in Ellen Cole, Oliva M. Espin, and Esther D. Rothblum, eds., *Refugee Women and Their Mental Health: Shattered Societies, Shattered Lives*, (Binghamton, N.Y.: The Haworth Press, 1992).

7 See, for instance, George Hicks, *The Comfort Women: Japan's Brutal Regime of Enforced Prostitution during the Second World War* (New York: W.W. Norton, 1995); Yoshiaki Yoshimi, *Comfort Women: Sexual Slavery in the Japanese Military during World War II* (New York: Columbia University Press, 2000).

8 See, for instance, Stephanie Nolen, "Uganda's Child Soldiers," *Globe and Mail* (Toronto), January 25, 2003, www.stephanienolen.com/dispatches.

9 For a brief summary of the Chilean situation, see Enloe, *Maneuvers*, 129–32. See also Inger Agger, "Sexual Torture of Political Prisoners: An Overview," *Journal of Traumatic Stress* 2, 3 (1989), 305–18.

10 See, for instance, Paul Higate and Marsha Henry, "Engendering (In)security in Peace Support Operations," *Security Dialogue* 35, 4 (2004), 481–98; Enloe, *Maneuvers*, especially ch. 3.

11 Jennifer Turpin, "Many Faces: Women Confronting War," in *The Women and War Reader*, ed. Lorentzen and Turpin, 7. See also Rehn and Sirleaf, *Women, War, Peace.*

12 Deborah Harrison, "Violence in the Military Community," in *Military Masculinities*, ed. Higate, 71–90; Madeline Morris, "By Force of Arms: Rape, War, and Military Culture," *Duke Law Journal* 45, 4 (1996), 651–781.

13 Susan Brownmiller, *Against Our Will: Men, Women, and Rape* (New York: Simon and Schuster, 1975).

14 Turpin, "Many Faces: Women Confronting War," 4.

15 Cynthia Enloe, *The Morning After: Sexual Politics at the End of the Cold War* (Berkeley: University of California Press, 1993).

16 Ruth Seifert, "War and Rape: A Preliminary Analysis," in *Mass Rape: The War against Women in Bosnia-Herzegovina*, ed. Alexandra Stiglmayer (Lincoln: University of Nebraska Press, 1994), 55.

17 Zainab Salbi, *The Other Side of War: Women's Stories of Survival and Hope* (Washington, D.C.: National Geographic Society, 2006), 220.

18 Wendy Lehman, "CPT [Christian Peacemaker Teams] Delegation to Democratic Republic of the Congo Report, October 18–November 4, 2006," www.cpt.org.

19 Salbi, *The Other Side of War*, 16.

20 Enloe, *Maneuvers*, 108.

21 Salbi, *The Other Side of War*, 16.

22 The study was published as *Women without Men: Mennonite Refugees of the Second World War* (Toronto: University of Toronto Press, 2000); the following article grew out of my doctoral research project: "The Memory of Violence: Soviet and East European Mennonite Refugees and Rape in the Second World War," *Journal of Women's History* 9, 1 (1997), 58–87.

23 For discussion of these statistics, see, for instance, Annemarie Troeger, "German Women's Memories of World War II," in *Behind the Lines*, ed. Higonnet et al., 285–89; Barbara Johr, "Die Ereignisse in Zahlen," in *BeFreier und Befreite: Krieg, Vergewaltigungen, Kinder*, ed. Helke Sander and Barbara Johr (Munich: Verlag Antje Kunstmann, 1992).

24 Stephanie Nolen, "Don't Talk to Me about Justice: Rwanda 10 Years After," *Globe and Mail* (Toronto), April 3, 2004, F6–7.

25 Lehman, "CPT Delegation to Democratic Republic of the Congo Report"; Alexandra Stiglmayer, "The Rapes in Bosnia-Herzegovina," in *Mass Rape*, ed. Stiglmayer, 82–169.

26 The memory sources that were useful to my study were oral interviews, several

done in 1951 with recent Mennonite immigrants to Canada, and more done with the same population in the early 1990s; published and unpublished autobiographies and memoirs; and semi-autobiographical historical fiction. A more detailed discussion on my methodology is in the "Introduction" to *Women without Men*, 3–16.

27 George K. Epp, "Mennonite Immigration to Canada after World War II," *Journal of Mennonite Studies* 5 (1987), 117–18.

28 Letter dated February 6, 1949, cited in C.P. Toews, Heinrich Friesen, and Arnold Dyck, *The Kuban Settlement*, trans. Herbert Giesbrecht (Winnipeg: CMBC Publications, 1989), 90; and Recollections of Anna Heide Retzlaff, in Agatha Loewen Schmidt, *Gnadenfeld, Molotschna, 1835–1943* (Kitchener, Ont.: Author, 1989), 72.

29 Mary Fast, interview by Cornelius Krahn, c. 1951, Mennonite Library and Archives, Bethel College, North Newton, Kansas.

30 Ruth Harris, "The 'Child of the Barbarian': Rape, Race and Nationalism in France during the First World War," *Past & Present*, 141 (November 1993), 178–79.

31 See Patricia K. Robin Herbst, "From Helpless Victim to Empowered Survivor: Oral History as a Treatment for Survivors of Torture," in *Refugee Women and Their Mental Health*, ed. Cole, Espin, and Rothblum, 144.

32 Slavenka Drakulic, "Women Hide behind a Wall of Silence," *The Nation*, March 1, 1993, 270.

33 Enloe, *Maneuvers*, 133.

34 Stiglmayer, "The Rapes in Bosnia-Herzegovina," 83.

35 See, for instance, Cornelius Ryan, *The Last Battle* (New York: Simon and Schuster, 1966); Norman M. Naimark, *The Russians in Germany: A History of the Soviet Zone of Occupation, 1945–1949* (Cambridge, Mass.: The Belknap Press of Harvard University Press, 1995); Gerhard Lohrenz, *The Odyssey of the Bergen Family* (Winnipeg: Author, 1978), 92–93.

36 Stuart Liebman and Annette Michelson, "After the Fall: Women in the House of the Hangmen," *October* 72 (spring 1995), 5–14.

37 Interview no. 25. During the early 1990s, I interviewed Mennonites who had immigrated to Canada and Paraguay after the war. To maintain anonymity, I identify specific interviews by number.

38 Katie Friesen, *Into the Unknown* (Steinbach, Man.: Author, 1986), 83.

39 Margaret L. Dick, *From Breslau to America* (Wichita: Author, 1992), 71.

40 Salbi, *The Other Side of War*, 227. Salbi's book includes numerous stories of the outcomes of wartime rape. Surprisingly, there is limited discussion in literature on contemporary conflicts about suicide as a response to sexual violence.

41 Anita Grossmann, "A Question of Silence: The Rape of German Women by Occupation Soldiers," *October* 72 (spring 1995), 54–55.

42 Interview no. 28.

43 Justina D. Neufeld, *A Family Torn Apart* (Kitchener, Ont.: Pandora Press, 2003), 216.

44 Annemarie Troeger, "Between Rape and Prostitution: Survival Strategies and Chances of Emancipation for Berlin Women after World War II," in *Women in Culture and Politics: A Century of Change*, ed. Judith Friedlander, Blanche Cook, Alice Kessler-Harris, and Carroll Smith-Rosenberg (Bloomington: Indiana University Press, 1986).

45 Rehn and Sirleaf, *Women, War, Peace*.

46 Seifert, "War and Rape," 57.

47 Salbi, *The Other Side of War*, 62–63.

48 Brownmiller, *Against Our Will*, 31–40. Amy Friedman also argues that the rape of refugee women heightens male vulnerability in their communities and further-more, increases the likelihood of domestic violence as a way of re-establishing au-thority; See "Rape and Domestic Violence: The Experience of Refugee Women," in *Refugee Women and Their Mental Health*, ed. Cole, Espin, and Rothblum, 65–78.

49 Ruth Harris describes the "psychological emasculation," to the point of suicide, experienced by a First World War French infantryman whose wife and two daugh-ters were raped. This masculine impotence, she argues, was adopted to mean an overall threat to French national identity. See "The 'Child of the Barbarian': Rape, Race and Nationalism in France during the First World War," *Past & Present* 141 (November 1993), 170–206.

50 See Stiglmayer, *Mass Rape*.

51 Lohrenz, *Odyssey of the Bergen Family*, 127.

52 Grossmann, "A Question of Silence."

53 See for instance, Stiglmayer, *Mass Rape*; Cynthia Enloe, "All the Men Are in the Militias, All the Women Are Victims: The Politics of Masculinity and Femininity in Nationalist Wars," in *The Women and War Reader*, ed. Lorentzen and Turpin, 50–62.

Part 5
Bombing and Civilian Casualties

12 Sven Lindqvist

Translation by Linda Rugg

The War against Women and Children

> Bombers will never learn to respect the laws of today, as long as
> the crimes of yesterday are excused or even extolled.

The bombing of the German civilian population during the Second World War is a sore spot in the British conscience. Every year new books are published in defence of the destruction of German cities. This essay discusses in detail two recent examples: Mark Connelly's *Reaching for the Stars: A New History of Bomber Command in World War II* and Robin Neillands' *The Bomber War: Arthur Harris and the Allied Bomber Offensive 1939–1945.*[1] My criticism of these works is based on the version of history more fully presented in my *A History of Bombing.*[2]

On many points Connelly is critical of the bombing offensive. He questions both its effectiveness and the authorities' attempt to conceal what they were actually doing. He wants to shift the burden of guilt from the main accused, Arthur "Bomber" Harris, to the War Cabinet, which made the decisions, and to the British people, who could not have missed what was going on. But in the final analysis there is no guilt, he argues: the collective punishment of German women and children was justified, since other Germans had committed much worse crimes.

Connelly's defence of the bombing of civilians is often indirect; it emerges in his evaluations of what others have said and written. Neillands speaks in his own name and explains that the bombing of civilians was militarily effective or at least a military necessity, and therefore also morally and legally defensible. Besides, the Germans were the ones who started it. And if anyone was guilty, it was not Arthur Harris. Let us examine these assertions one by one.

Was the Bombing of Civilians Militarily Effective?

From the moment of its birth, the airplane came loaded with exaggerated notions of its military worth. The prophets of aerial warfare – Giulio Douhet in Italy, Hugh Trenchard in Great Britain, Billy Mitchell in the United States – believed that airforces would soon render armies and navies superfluous. The war of the future would not be decided on the fronts but by bombing women, children, and elderly until the enemy's will to continue was broken. Victory without troops, without battles on the ground – that was what Neillands calls the "Bomber Dream."

This dream has never been realized. "Bombing has *never* destroyed civilian morale in any meaningful way" writes Neillands (30). Not in Spain, not in London during the Blitz, not in Germany, not in Vietnam, Iraq, or Serbia. The effect has in many cases been precisely the opposite; the air attacks have increased the people's will to resist.

This is a point that Neillands is very clear about already at the beginning of his book. But again and again he loses sight of it and argues as if, despite everything, it were possible to realize the Bomber Dream of winning the war from the air.

During the spring of 1942, the newly appointed head of Bomber Command, Arthur Harris, ordered the first night raids against the city centres of Lübeck and Rostock. Of these attacks Neillands writes, "Area bombing was the only feasible method of attack – and a highly effective one" (114). But what was so effective about making 15,000 people in Lübeck homeless? It had no military worth. Nor could the bombs wipe out the people's will to resist.

Harris was not the only one who failed to crush resistance by bombing. Neillands reminds us, "Until 1999 history does not record an example of a war won by air power" (204). But already in the next chapter Neillands has again forgotten this insight and uses the Bomber Dream to justify the firestorm of Hamburg in the summer of 1943, where approximately 50,000 civilians were killed in a single night: "It was by any standard a horrific event – hard to justify, terrible to contemplate in later, peaceful years. And yet at the time, in the context of total war, it may almost have achieved its purpose." "Perhaps if Harris had been able to repeat the process and devastate another German city as completely as Hamburg within the next few days something decisive might have been achieved, but Harris did not have the force for that" (242ff).

Poor Harris! But no commander ever had all the resources he could desire for the realization of his dreams. The trick is to win given the limits of available means. And note how abstractly the aim is described: "something decisive might have been achieved." What? By whom? In what way? The Allies had made it clear that the only thing they would accept was unconditional surrender. Germany's rulers had everything to lose by surrendering. Those Germans who had something to gain had been rendered powerless. Bombing them would not increase their influence.

In November 1943, Harris had only another six months to win the war from the air, before the invasion of Normandy. He had orders to attack the German oil industry but instead he devoted himself to destroying Berlin, neighbourhood by neighbourhood. And once again Neillands allows himself to be seduced by the Bomber Dream: "Given the dramatic effects of bombing Hiroshima and Nagasaki less than two years later it is hard to maintain the argument that Harris' idea was totally flawed. . . . Had he been given full support Harris might have been able to prove his point" (277–78). Neillands forgets that not even the total destruction of Tokyo and of all of the other large cities of Japan achieved the result Harris was hoping to attain with his attacks on Berlin.

The closer D-Day came and the more resources Harris received, the more convinced he became that with just a little increase in resources and more independence to use them as he wanted, he could bring about a German defeat. The Germans would rise up against their Nazi rulers and demand peace.

Was Harris right? Neillands asks this question in chapter 13 and answers it himself: "[The] people of Japan were battered into surrender by two [nuclear] attacks and we have no reason to suppose that similar devastation on Germany, though achieved with 'conventional' weapons, would have been any less effective. . . . Had the Japanese elected to fight on, the Americans would have destroyed their country, city by city – and unlike Air Chief Marshall Harris, they had the means to do it" (300–01).

This argument is grossly misleading. The Americans had already destroyed Japan city by city. This had not sufficed because the Allies demanded unconditional surrender and the Japanese could not think of surrendering without guarantees for the emperor. The Japanese knew they had lost when the Soviet Union entered the war. They already knew they had lost when Germany surrendered. Even earlier than that they knew they had lost when their navy was defeated. The American navy had the country in a stranglehold. Neither food nor fuel for transport could be imported. The primary thing delaying the peace was America's demand for unconditional surrender. As soon as the Japanese had received a guarantee for the emperor's immunity, they surrendered.

Neillands does not manage to prove that the bombing of civilians was ever militarily effective. It caused terrible destruction and enormous pain but never achieved its intended aims. This became more and more obvious the longer the bombing war continued.

Both Connelly and Neillands correctly point out that the bombing of German cities, even if it did not achieve the intended goal of forcing Germany to surrender, still produced side effects of military importance. The Germans were forced to allot a large portion of their scarce resources in the form of artillery, fighter planes, and labour to defend their cities and to keep them functioning after bombardment.

But neither author discusses the price of these side effects. Bomber Command consumed a third of Great Britain's war costs. This enormous investment cannot be considered justified by military side effects achieved. It seems likely that the British navy, army, and tactical airforce, all of which were competing for the same scarce resources, would have been able to use them with better military results.

Was the Bombing of Civilians a Military Necessity?

Even acts of war that are not militarily effective can, in certain circumstances, be militarily and politically necessary. When Churchill decided in May 1940 to begin bombing Germany, he was not so unrealistic that he hoped the strategy would bring about a German defeat. Instead he wanted to ease the impact of the defeat of the English and French armies on the Western Front. Bombers were the only weapons with which he could reclaim the initiative and go on the offensive against the enemy.

In order to avoid a forced peace with Hitler, in order to be able to continue fighting at all, it was necessary to use bombers. And the bombers again and again proved unable to find and hit the military targets they had been sent out to bomb. Military inefficiency combined with heavy losses of bombers and their crews made it necessary for Bomber Command to switch from daylight precision bombing to bombing entire cities by night. This is Neillands' second line of defence in his attempt to rescue Bomber Command.

What were the alternatives? As long as Great Britain fought alone against Nazi Germany there were scarcely any. And for that period, Neillands' argument holds.

But by spring of 1942 the situation was completely changed. Germany and Japan had attacked the two superpowers, the Soviet Union and the United States, and forced them into the war on the side of the British. The national emergency that had justified the British bombing of civilians no longer existed. So why didn't they stop? The American strategy was precision bombing of military and industrial complexes. Why didn't Bomber Command follow the American example?

During the years Great Britain stood alone, it invested a great deal in the production of heavy bombers. If the planes were not to be used, this investment would seem like a waste of resources. And in the beginning, the American precision bombing proved to be just as ineffective and prone to heavy losses as the British attempts had been. The Americans had not counted on the cloud cover over Europe or the effectiveness of the German air defence. If the British had followed the American model it would have led to a waste of the bombers and crews they had worked so hard to put in place. And so, according to Neillands, it was a military necessity to continue with the bombing of civilians.

Once again: what were the alternatives? The Americans focused on producing a long-distance fighter that could follow and protect the bombers all the way to the target. The British airforce commanders were uninterested in these plans and even worked against them, probably because the Bomber Dream made precision bombing unappealing. While waiting for the new long-distance fighter, the Americans for the time being bombed targets within the range of their existing fighters. Deeper into German territory, only particularly important targets considered worthy of heavy losses were bombed.

I agree with Neillands that the residential raids were militarily and politically necessary in 1940–41, despite their ineffectiveness. But from 1942 on he can no longer show that they were necessary.

Was the Bombing of Civilians Morally Defensible?

The moral rehabilitation of the British bombing of civilians is a primary concern for both Connelly and Neillands. But Neillands does not seem to be aware that there is already a great deal of literature published on the ethics of wartime bombing. See, for example, Stephen Garrett's *Ethics and Air Power in World War II: The British Bombing of German Cities*, with its extensive bibliography.[3] Neither of the two authors bothers to organize his arguments into a coherent line of reasoning or even to ensure that their respective positions have an internal consistency. Here I will comment on those moral arguments strewn through the two books that, in my opinion, seem most important.

The British Had Their Backs against the Wall

The British bombing of Germany was "hideous because it was designed to be" (3). This Connelly admits candidly. It proves "how vicious a people can be when they feel that their backs are collectively pushed up against the wall" (3). The British nation found itself in a desperate situation, "like a penned animal" (48). Today's critics can not understand how desperate the atmosphere was in 1940–41 (162).

Connelly returns again and again to the crisis in Britain as the decisive argument for bombing women and children. But only 0.5 per cent of the bombs dropped over Germany were dropped in 1940–41, when the British really had their backs against the wall. Soon Great Britain had not only its empire on its side but also the two superpowers, the Soviet Union and the United States. It was in 1942, when the emergency was already over, that residential bombing began in earnest. Eighty per cent of the bombs dropped on Germany fell during the last ten months of the war. Then it was the Germans who had their backs against the wall.

If Some Means of Conducting War Are Immoral, Others Must Be Moral

The conclusion does not follow. If one says that chemical and biological warfare are immoral, it does not mean that all other means of waging war are therefore approved. It means only that some types of warfare are even more abominable than others. Neillands agrees with this, for he continues, "That said, there are actions which are clearly beyond the pale – even in the context of war" (32). The question is, which actions?

When RAF commander Charles Portal, in a letter written in the fall of 1941, suggested an intensification of the area bombing of cities, which according to his calculation would kill nearly a million German civilians and seriously injure another million, he was, according to Connelly, "not a vicious man, but [a] shrewd one" (48) and according to Neillands "a decent man" (186). His proposal to arrange "a kind of aereal Auschwitz simply indicates how the war had eroded, and would continue to erode, the morality with which Britain had entered the war three years before" (186).

His colleagues and superiors reproached him for the suggestion because it emphasized an aspect of the bombing war that conflicted with Churchill's express assurances that British bombing was not intended to terrorize the civilian population. The attempt of the politicians to conceal and deny the bombing of civilians indicates their sense of guilt, or at least of shame. Neillands writes: "The allied commanders were reluctant to face this or at least admit publicly that their attacks killed civilians – civilians working in German industry, but civilians nevertheless" (186).

And what about the *children*, then? Were they also working in industry? Neillands forgets that the bombs were aimed not only at working people but also at infants and schoolchildren, pregnant women, the old, sick, and disabled, and their female attendants, not to mention invalids from the war and from previous wars. Two-thirds of the civilian victims of bombing are estimated to have belonged to groups that did not in any way contribute to the war effort. This was probably precisely the reason why commanders and politicians wanted to conceal what the bomb attacks were all about. Yes, even today Neillands' wording glosses over and hides the fact that the British bombers devoted the bulk of their powers to intentionally killing civilians, the majority of whom did not contribute to war even indirectly.

Moral Prohibitions Are Not Absolute

The killing of prisoners or women and children lies "beyond the pale," writes Neillands (386–87). But such moral restrictions are not absolute. Whether something should be considered an atrocity often depends on timing. The killing of a prisoner of war in the heat of battle is something entirely different than murdering him a day later. It may be unavoidable that women and children are killed during an attack of a village, but it would be murder to kill them once the village is taken.

The bomber crews can perhaps claim that they bombed women and children during "the heat of battle," even if they were several thousand metres above their victims at the time. But all the technicians and bureaucrats who sat, day after day, planning the bombing of German women and children can hardly blame the heat of battle for their actions. They sat safe in their offices and acted in cold calculation.

It may be unavoidable that women and children die during the bombing of a city. But it is especially unavoidable if the bombers are aiming at their homes. In this way it is possible to keep on intentionally killing women and children for several years, but according to Neillands this becomes murder only if the bombing of the city continues once it is taken. What strange morality! The intentional killing of civilians is always murder.

In a Total War All Targets Are Legitimate

Harris often expressed his notion that "to be certain of destroying anything, it was necessary to destroy everything."

"This is a perfectly sound argument," writes Neillands (396). "In a city, in a time of total war, everything is a valid target." Everything, then, contributes to the enemy's ability to wage war, even bars, restaurants, and marketplaces, and of course private homes: "When Bomber Command hit a city, the aim was to leave behind a non-productive ruin. That was a harsh policy, but a realistic one."

It turned out that this harsh policy was *not* so realistic, as Neillands himself has demonstrated. The destruction did not lead to its intended result. And even if the bombing of civilians had been successful, one could not argue that therefore any target was legitimate.

If the term "legitimate military target" is extended to include even marketplaces and residential areas, it becomes meaningless. If anything is a valid military target, conducting air attacks only on military targets is no longer a limitation. As soon as a war is defined as "total," anything can be attacked. And the criterion for establishing whether a war is "total" is that everything is attacked. This moral tautology allows anything. In the end, the destruction of humanity becomes a legitimate military privilege.

"[T]he bomber, when deployed strategically, is fundamentally a *terror* weapon, and that fact has to be faced and not fudged," writes Neillands. "It should be clear that the bomber always was a 'terror weapon' . . . It was the effect of bombing on *civilians* that gave the bomber threat its greatest potency. Inspiring terror, causing massive destruction and killing civilians, *was what the strategic bomber was for*" (390).

If Neillands' characterization of strategic bombing is correct, it certainly provides no defence for strategic bombing. It is wrong to invest in a weapon that can be used only by war criminals to commit war crimes.

Was the Bombing of Civilians a War Crime?

Connelly avoids legal issues. Neillands discusses the status of bombers in international law without any reference to the extensive literature on the subject. He seems completely unaware of the prohibition against attacking children and the elderly that was first formulated in Baghdad during the tenth century and rediscovered in seventeenth-century Europe. Even in a just war, according to "the father of international law," Hugo Grotius, "one must take care, as far as is possible, to prevent the death of innocent persons, even by accident." Children and the aged must always be spared, and women as well, as long as they do not take the place of men in battle.

Seventeen states, among them Great Britain, signed the St. Petersburg Declaration of 1868, which states, "The only legitimate object which states should endeavour to accomplish during war is to weaken the military forces of the enemy." To weaken the enemy's civilian population or its morale is therefore not a legitimate object.

The Fourth Hague Convention of 1907, signed by Great Britain as well, prohibited "bombardment, by whatever means, of towns, villages, dwellings or buildings which are undefended." The phrase "by whatever means" was added precisely to cover any conceivable future bombardment from the air, a phenomenon that in 1907 had not yet occurred.

Instead, Neillands maintains, there was no legal prohibition against the bombing of civilians. The only attempt to ban the bombing of civilians that Neillands knows of is the one made at the Hague in 1922–23. He correctly states that the rules discussed there were never more than drafts (28). But he does not say why the discussions were fruitless.

There were two major opposing plans. The British wanted to limit bombing to "military objectives," a phrase that even during the First World War had proven to be so flexible that it provided scarcely any shelter. The Americans wanted air attacks to be permitted only in "the combat area," which was defined as the area where land troops were engaged. In other words, the Americans wanted to permit only tactical and not strategic bombing.

The Japanese and later the Germans, too, supported the American plan, while the French backed the British. The compromise finally agreed upon by the commission ran as follows: "Where a military objective is so situated that it cannot be bombarded without the indiscriminate bombardment of the civilian population, it cannot be bombarded at all." The United States and Japan were prepared to sign the new wording, but although it was based on the central concept of the British plan, Great Britain and France refused to sign. For a half-century, the British continued to resist this paragraph until another one very much like it was finally included in the 1977 Additional Protocols to the Geneva Conventions for the defence of civilians, which is valid international law today. So it was primarily due to resistance from Great Britain that the Hague rules of 1923 remained in draft form.

But the Fourth Hague Convention of 1907, which Neillands has apparently never heard of, was still valid. The 1935 edition of the British standard work on international law, Oppenheim's *International Law*, lays it out: "There ought, therefore, to be no doubt that International Law protects non-combatants from indiscriminate bombardment from the air, and that recourse to such bombardment constitutes a war crime."[4]

It cannot be expressed more clearly than that.

The creation of a new service branch, Bomber Command, whose primary task was to break the enemy's will to fight through the bombing of women, children, and the elderly in civilian residential areas, was of course a war crime. The responsibility for these crimes falls on Arthur Harris as the commander of that service branch but also on other military and political decision makers, including Winston Churchill.

The Notion That Certain Means of Warfare Could Be Criminal Did Not Emerge until after the Second World War

Neillands writes: "Only after the Second World War did the notion arise that, quite apart from the obvious atrocities, some *methods* of fighting wars, some operational tactics, might amount to criminality – a charge increasingly directed since the war at RAF Bomber Command" (32).

This is one of the most astonishing statements made in a book full of surprises. Neillands is clearly ignorant of the entire discussion, ongoing in Europe since the seventeenth century, of how various means of waging war can or cannot be reconciled with the laws of war.

Moreover, already on the following page he claims the opposite: "When Britain went to war it was accepted that if the RAF could not attack a target without putting civilian lives at risk, that target should not be attacked at all" (33). And in a later chapter he says that the British admitted that "the willful bombing of civilians was contrary to the principles of international law" (186). So in fact even for the British, and even before the end of the Second World War, there was an international law prohibiting certain methods of waging war, among them the intentional bombing of civilians.

When a Technology Exists, It Is Impossible to Avoid Using It

Neillands writes: "The invention of the Minié bullet enabled soldiers to kill more soldiers, the invention of strategic bombers allowed commanders to kill civilians." That this should happen was unavoidable: "[T]he bomber, once created, was going to be used" (390).

But it is not a given that a military invention has to be used simply because it exists. Gas weapons were invented and used during the First World War, were forbidden in 1925, and were not used during the Second World War. Biological weapons were not used either, though they had been invented. Since the invention of nuclear weapons, they have been used only twice. Fortunately, there is no law of nature that says that they will be used again.

Nor was there a law of nature that forced the British to use bombers in the way they did. Bombers could have been engaged as tactical weapons in cooperation with the army and navy. In that role they would have had more military impact than in the terror bombing of women, children, and the elderly. And in that role they could have bombed without committing a war crime.

The Laws of War Do Not Apply in Wartime

"The simple defense against the charge levelled against the aircrew who destroyed Dresden is that *there was a war on*. It was the *war* that killed the citizens of Dresden," writes Neillands (359).

War crimes, of course, can not be justified by the fact that a war was on when the crime was committed. When are the laws of war supposed to apply, if not in wartime?

And it is not primarily the crews who stand accused, but the decision makers. Arthur Harris and his superiors knew as well as Neillands and I that certain actions are not permitted even in wartime. They lie, as the British say, "beyond the pale." The German commanders on trial in Nuremberg could not blame such actions on the fact that "there was a war on." Nor can British generals and politicians avoid the moral and legal responsibility for the bombing of Dresden and other German cities.

Harris and Portal both wanted the public to know that the German civilian population and their homes were the bombers' main targets. But the government's spokesmen always said that targets were military and industrial. Connelly, who is a specialist in the history of propaganda, has gone through press reports and other media coverage at the different stages of bombing. He comes to the conclusion that the British public must have understood what the bombing war was about and approved of it while it was going on:

> All along the British people knew deep down what this policy actually meant and were glad of it. What they did not want to do was think about the real details of the implications. They shied away from the savage in them. After the war they would try to deny it altogether (64).

> [They were] vicariously glad to be causing intense misery to their enemies, but pretend[ed] that it was part of a simple policy of hitting vital industry (73).

The readers of the popular press were informed that "Germany was going to have its guts ripped out. But some," Connelly states, "managed to think that it was going to be done by bombing factories alone" (103). Berlin, the press wrote, would be turned into the same kind of smoking ruin as Hamburg. "The feigning of ignorance about bombing policy by British people after the war seems more and more like a confidence trick" (111).

Connelly criticizes the British people but not those who committed the crimes the people pretended not to know about. In November 1943, he notes, a journal as highbrow as the *Spectator* excuses "the loss of civilian life" by saying that "it is a consequence which the Germans have made inevitable by compelling us to strike at the centres of their strength as they have struck at ours" (112). Connelly allows this kind of opinion to stand unanalyzed, probably because it resembles his own. But how did residential areas become German "centres of strength"? How did the Germans manage to "force" the British to focus their bombing on residential areas? How had the Germans made this consequence "inevitable"? And if the British had to avenge the German bombing of England, would it not have sufficed to strike at the Germans twice or three times as hard? Was it really necessary to hit the German civilian population with 315 times the tonnage that they had used against the British?

Connelly does not ask such questions. His criticism is directed instead at Churchill, whose victory speech of May 13, 1945, did not even mention Bomber Command, which after all had received a third of the resources Great Britain had poured into the war and had suffered a very substantial part of the casualties. Why did Churchill, precisely at the moment of victory, begin to be ashamed of a policy that he himself had initiated and supported throughout the war? One reason could be that Germany now lay within reach of the press and their cameras (141). It was one thing to order the destruction of distant, unknown cities but quite a different one to have the results served up at your breakfast table.

While the Germans worked to rebuild their country, the British managed to forget who had destroyed it. When the official history of Bomber Command came out in 1961, the public was shocked at the government's lies and at the bombing offensive's intentional targeting of German civilians (148–51). The British people were robbed of their belief that 500,000 civilians had by pure accident become victims of the raids. The myth was revealed.

Who Started Bombing Civilians?

"They started it!" is an argument that belongs on the playground. Neillands is clear on that point (392). Still he cannot stop himself from making tiny, almost unnoticeable adjustments of the truth in order to show that it was not the British who started it. The "wind sown" by the enemy in Warsaw, Rotterdam, London, and Coventry was "reaped as a whirlwind" in Hamburg and Dresden (60, 278, 353, 357, 392). For Connelly, too, this is an oft-repeated mantra (28–29, 125–26, 162).

The Germans had no strategic airforce. Their airforce was designed to support infantry and armoured divisions on the battlefield. When a city – Warsaw, for example – was attacked and refused to surrender, it became a battlefield and was consequently bombed. If the surrender came too late to stop the bombers, as in the case of Rotterdam, the city could be bombed even though it had surrendered.

That Germany invaded neutral Belgium in the first place, thus turning Rotterdam into a battlefield, was a violation of international law. But both Connelly and Neillands point to the German bombing of Rotterdam on May 14, 1940, as the reason that the British began their strategic bombing offensive against Germany on May 15. They do not mention that Churchill had already made the decision to bomb Germany on May 11, three days before Rotterdam.

At other times, Neillands characterizes the British bomber offensive against Germany as an answer to the Blitz on London and other English cities. But when the Blitz began on September 7, 1940, the British had already been bombing German cities for nearly four months without attacks in response from Germany. Thus it is easier to see the Blitz as a response to British bombing than the other way around.

Of the Blitz Neillands says that "even if aimed at legitimate military and economic targets, like the London docks and railway stations or naval bases like Portsmouth and Plymouth, it inevitably caused severe casualties among the civilian population" (43). The same is of course true of the earlier British attacks on similar targets in Germany. Neither Connelly nor Neillands mentions this. But could it not be said that the British reaped the whirlwind of the Blitz from the wind they themselves had sown over Germany?

J.M. Spaight, the British Air Ministry expert on international law, was clear on the point that the Blitz was revenge for several months of British bombing of Germany. He was proud that it was the British who had taken the initiative in the bombing war. The entire third chapter of his book, *Bombing Vindicated*, deals with "the splendid decision" to begin bombing Germany.[5] But in Connelly's argument Spaight voices the opposite opinion: "Germans had started the bombing war and so had no right of appeal against it" (125). Spaight's true opinion is attributed instead to the Duke of Bedford, who can be dismissed as a Nazi sympathizer.

In Neillands' book, the German attack on Coventry of November 14, 1940, is presented as the prelude to and cause of the bombing war: "The high ideals with which the RAF and the British government had entered the war were being rapidly eroded by the realities of the conflict; enemy morale was now a prime target, and the way to attack it was to bomb the enemy out of house and home" (47).

According to Neillands, area bombing constituted a response to Coventry, beginning with an attack on Mannheim on December 16, 1940. Most of the bombs struck residential areas, killing 115 people. A train station, a hospital, and a school were destroyed. "City bombing was now an accepted policy carried out by both sides without any attempt to disguise the fact by naming military targets within the urban conurbation" (48).

But once again Neillands' chronology is backwards. Already on June 20, 1940, Bomber Command had received orders to bomb industrial targets, including the surrounding workers' homes. In September of the same year, Charles Portal proposed area bombing in twenty to thirty Germany cities. In October, he took over as commander of the airforce and his proposal was approved. On October 30, Bomber Command received the order to firebomb twenty to thirty German cities. The German bombing of Coventry in the middle of November cannot reasonably be cited as the reason for a proposal put forward in September or a decision taken at the end of October.

The undermining of British idealism that Neillands sometimes wants to attribute to the Blitz of London, sometimes to the attack on Coventry, he finally grounds in the period between the wars – with the German bombing of Guernica, the Italian bombing of Ethiopia, the Japanese bombing of China (391). The strange thing about this theory is that Neillands names only the enemy nations of the Second World War, and particularly the nation that engaged in tactical rather than strategic bombing. He does not mention the Spanish bombing of civilians in Morocco, the French attacks on Syria and Vietnam, the South African bombing of Southwest Africa, or the American bombing of Nicaragua. Above all, he does not name the truly great bombing power that held entire countries under occupation through the use of punitive bombing expeditions against rebellious villages: the British.

The British airforce survived as an independent branch of service during the period between the world wars by bombing rebels in India, Afghanistan, Aden, Iraq, Palestine, Egypt, and Somaliland. There, in the colonies, the laws of war did not apply. There it was an old custom to punish the people by burning their villages. It was there that Arthur Harris invented his method of burning villages from the air. It was there that his closest colleagues gained their military experience. And there, too, his immediate commander, Portal, had learned how to bomb.

Both between the wars and during the Second World War it was above all the British who bombed civilians. The best example for Neillands' thesis that bombing morale had already began to decline during the interwar years is provided not by the German but by the British airforce.

The British began the bombing war against civilians. The British were always one step ahead in the escalation of the bombing war. The culmination was not achieved until the last six months of the war. Eighty per cent of the bombs dropped on Germany fell during the war's last ten months, on an already beaten and as good as defenceless Germany. Why? What was that supposed to achieve?

On the final pages of Neillands' book a new answer to that question vaguely begins to take shape. The bombing war against children and the elderly, especially its dreadful conclusion during the last months of the war, was perhaps not necessary to achieve victory. Instead it had a pedagogical aim. It was intended to teach the Germans a lesson for the future. Ever since the middle of the nineteenth century, Germans had waged war in other countries, not in their homeland. During the Second World War, their battles were fought primarily in Russia, North Africa, and France. Only the heavy bombers brought the war home to the German people and forced them to lose their desire for war. "If the price of European peace and a final freedom from chronic German militarism was the physical destruction of Germany, many may argue that the price was well worth paying" (400).

But was there not a nation even better than Germany at avoiding wars at home and waging them in other countries? Was there not a nation that had built up a worldwide empire, extending over a third of the world's population, through global warfare? This was a people that had not experienced a battle at home since 1066. According to Neillands' reasoning, the physical destruction of Great Britain would be both desirable and necessary to the achievement of world peace and the end of British imperialism.

In fact the British empire dissolved without anyone having to bomb Great Britain into ruins. Economic necessity, political pressure, and military defeats proved entirely sufficient for the dissolution of the empire and for slaking the British thirst for conducting wars in other countries. The same forces would have influenced Germany to move in more peaceful directions. Is it so certain, then, that the German civilian population needed that last 80 per cent of bombing to learn to love peace?

The Bombs Are Still Falling

Most of the German civilians who were killed in the bombing war would be dead today anyway. So why care?

It does not ease the guilt of the Germans, in any case. In the first place, while the bombing war was on, the Germans murdered about 6 million Jews and about 5 million other *Untermenschen* – gypsies and Jehovah's Witnesses, the handicapped and the homosexual, Communists and Social Democrats, Poles, Ukrainians, and Russians. The half million lives claimed by the Allied bomber offensive against Germany disappears in the margin of error surrounding the German crimes.

In the second place, the Germans' victims were almost completely defenceless. There were, to be sure, uprisings in the ghettos and camps, but these were exceptions and were all put down with the harshest brutality. The Bomber Command's greatest victories – Hamburg and Dresden – were won over cities that either were or had been rendered almost defenceless. But these were exceptions. Up to the conclusion of the war, Germany's cities defended themselves energetically; the graves of 56,000 British airmen testify to that fact. Perhaps the most important contribution made by Bomber Command to the war was forcing the Germans to allocate so many resources to the defence of their cities.

And in the third place, the British had no plans for a conquest that would require the killing of Germans to make room for British settlement. Even though Harris claimed that the object was to obliterate "German cities and their inhabitants as such," the aim of the British was never to exterminate the Germans, only to force their surrender. The air attacks against Germany stopped as soon as the German armed forces had surrendered.

The German war crimes, on the other hand, were committed for the most part after the surrender of their opponents. More than 2 million Soviet prisoners of war were murdered after they had surrendered. Millions of Russians were left to starve once the German occupying forces had appropriated their food and sent it to Germany. The German bureaucracy planned to starve another 20 million people in order to make room for German settlement in Poland and Ukraine after the war.

As part of this process, the Jewish people, the primary objects of Nazi hate, were to be completely wiped out. Hundreds of thousands of Jews from areas where no German settlement was planned at all were driven into Auschwitz and other extermination camps to be murdered. It is obvious that the Holocaust represents a crime of an entirely different order from all the other war crimes committed during the Second World War. Thus when Neillands speaks of the British plans for the bombing war against Germany as an "aerial Auschwitz," it is just an extravagant expression. Neither he nor anyone else would dream of seriously equating these two crimes.

As a unique crime, the Holocaust has also received unique publicity. Several big trials, countless research projects, mountains of books and articles, films and television series, memorials, and museums have documented extensively how the Germans' victims were put to death, and the perpetrators have been branded. No one aside from a handful of neo-Nazis tries to defend today what happened in Auschwitz.

Perhaps that is precisely why Auschwitz has remained unique. History has not repeated itself.

The bombing war against the German civilian population, on the other hand, was just one war crime among many. Further, it was the particular war crime of the victors and for that reason was never brought to trial. Certainly the bombing of women and children has been researched, but the results have done little to change the propaganda image that was forged during the war. The British, unlike the Germans, have never been forced to admit their war crimes and look their victims in the eye. Museums, films, and television series have continued to glorify the bombing war and represent the bombers as heroes. Even today, books are published – Connelly's and Neillands' are just two examples – that with questionable reasoning and pseudo-arguments attempt to defend the perpetrators.

Perhaps that is precisely why the British bombing of women and children in Germany has not remained unique. On the contrary, it opened the door for the American bombing of the Japanese, which was even more horrifying than what the German civilian population experienced. During five years of bombing, 200 square kilometres of German urban territory was destroyed. In Japan, 460 square kilometres was levelled in a half year.

Once the sixty-six largest Japanese cities had been burned, the atomic weapons used against Hiroshima and Nagasaki seemed to be the next logical step. About 100,000 people, the great majority of them civilians, were killed immediately. Just as many went on to die a lingering death due to radiation sickness.

And once the atom bomb had received the political seal of approval, it was taken as a given that it would be the point of departure for military planning in the future. In 1947, the first American atomic war plan, code-named "Broiler," was drawn up. In the event of a Soviet invasion of Western Europe, twenty-four Soviet cities were to be destroyed with thirty-four atom bombs. In the 1948 plan, the number of cities had been upped to seventy, and by the year following 100 Soviet cities were to be destroyed, with a cumulative explosive effect of more than 800 Hiroshima bombs. There was not even pretence that these targets were military.

Four years after Hiroshima, when new injuries from radiation were still being discovered every day, four years after the firestorms in the Japanese cities, which still lay in ashes – four years later, 800 new Hiroshimas were already being planned.

The Soviet cities targeted by the U.S. atomic bombs had already been destroyed by the Germans and had scarcely managed to rebuild. The German cities that the United States was now supposed to defend were still in ruins after the British bombings only four years earlier. Back then the Americans had thought themselves too good to bomb civilians, at least in Europe. Now hundreds of Soviet cities were to be destroyed.

But these were just plans, one could argue. By keeping attacks at bay through terror threats, these plans actually worked to preserve the peace.

They preserved the peace for some but not for all. French bombs continued to drop over Syria and Algeria, over Madagascar and Indochina. British bombs kept falling over Malaya, Aden, and Kenya. Even the smaller European colonial powers tried to prolong the dissolution of their empires with bombs.

During the Korean War of 1950–51, battles swept back and forth so that the entire peninsula became a target for American bombers. Both the northern and southern parts of the country were completely destroyed.

For the destruction of Japan's cities, the United States had used 14,000 tons of napalm. In Korea, 32,000 tons were used. The culmination was reached in Vietnam. There, between 1963 and 1971, the United States dropped more than 373,000 tons of napalm, and a new, more effective kind. The military result was, as usual, disappointing. The bombs could prolong the war but not alter the outcome. On April 30, 1975, the Saigon regime fell.

During the Second World War more than 70 per cent of American bombs were aimed at individual targets and only 30 per cent at entire areas. In Indochina, area bombing made up 85 per cent. In Germany and Japan, twenty-six kilograms of bombs were dropped per hectare of enemy territory. In Indochina, the figure was 190 kilograms. Auschwitz was not allowed to continue decade after decade in ever more technically perfect forms. But the bombing war against women and children continued after the Second World

War as if nothing had happened. During the entire postwar period, the United States and the European colonial powers resisted attempts by the International Red Cross to renew and strengthen protection for civilian populations under the laws of war. The British were against rules that "restrict[ed] freedom to carry out operations, particularly bombing." They also worked hard to remove the term "war crime" or any other wording that would indicate that an infraction of the convention would be criminal and could lead to a trial.

Not until the end of the Korean and Vietnam wars and the independence of most of the Third World colonies would the leading Western powers reluctantly join 120 other countries in signing the 1977 Additional Protocols to the Geneva Conventions, which reinforced the protection of civilians and extended to all parts of the world, all political systems, and both external and internal conflicts. The most relevant article (48) states: "In order to ensure respect for and protection of the civilian population, the Parties to the conflict shall at all times distinguish between the civilian population and combatants and between civilian objects and military objectives and accordingly shall direct their operations only against military objectives."

The article states a norm that shall apply to all wars. It applies when Russia bombs Chechnya as well as when the United States and Great Britain bomb Iraq or when NATO bombs Kosovo. Whatever noble intentions the bomber might have, even if a democracy is bombing a dictatorship, even if it is a question of punishing separatists or terrorists, even if one bombs in the name of human rights or in order to prevent "ethnic cleansing" or to keep villainous regimes at bay, it is still a war crime to bomb women, children, and the elderly. It is also a crime to bomb structures that are necessary to the survival of civilians, such as water reservoirs and water-purifying plants.

But when was the last time you saw an international bombing mission examined from the perspective of international law? Who, outside the circle of experts, has any idea that there is an absolute prohibition against dropping bombs where they can strike at the civilian population? Hardly any provision of international law is as little known as this one. And since no one knows the law and no one is ever held responsible for breaking it, no one bothers to obey it.

The bombs are still falling. The war against women and children continues. It will keep on as long as we avoid coming to terms with the crimes of the past. Bombers will never learn to respect the laws of today as long as the crimes of yesterday are excused or even extolled.

Notes

1   Mark Connelly, *Reaching for the Stars: A New History of Bomber Command in World War II* (London and New York: I.B. Tauris, 2001), Robin Neillands, *The Bomber War: Arthur Harris and the Allied Bomber Offensive 1939–1945* (London: John Murray, 2001).
2   Sven Lindqvist, *A History of Bombing* (New York: New Press, 2001).
3   Stephen A. Garrett, *Ethics and Air Power in World War II: The British Bombing of German Cities* (New York: St. Martin's Press, 1993).
4   Lassa Oppenheim, *International Law: A Treatise*, 5th ed., ed. H. Lauterpacht (London and New York: Longmans, Green 1935), §214.
5   J.M. Spaight, *Bombing Vindicated* (London: G. Bles, 1944).

13 Marc W. Herold

"Unworthy" Afghan Bodies

"Smarter" U.S. Weapons Kill More Innocents

> Karzai is not president, B-52 is president.
> – Common saying in Kabul, February 2003[1]

"It's sort of the immaculate conception to warfare," was how Professor of Strategy Col. (ret. U.S. Marine) Mackubin Owens of the U.S. Naval War College in Newport, Rhode Island, described the U.S. military campaign in Afghanistan in November 2001.

A striking fact about recent U.S. bombing campaigns is that as the U.S. bombs got smarter, civilian casualties increased through human decision. This truth of "surgical precision" has been carefully concealed by the Pentagon, its numerous boosters in the U.S. corporate media, and defence intellectuals such as William Arkin.[2] Taking the most reasonable estimates of civilian casualties caused directly by bombing during the most recent three air campaigns – 3,200 for the 1991 Gulf War, 1,200 for the Yugoslavia campaign, and approximately 3,000 for the Afghan campaign – I construct an index of civilian casualties: civilians killed per 10,000 tons of bombs dropped.[3] This index is then compared with the share of precision-guided munitions (PGMs) in total numbers of bombs dropped (Table 1).

The result is very clear. The greater the share of precision weapons employed, the higher the rate of civilian casualties. *I emphasize that this result establishes correlation, not causality.* The finding is not explained away either by much higher tonnage dropped or by a higher level of urbanization in Afghanistan (or Serbia).

For months in 2002, the mainstream corporate press headlined stories about the four Canadian soldiers killed by U.S. F-16 warplanes near Kandahar in a friendly fire incident in April of that year. Yards of newspaper print

Table 1
Intensity of Civilian Casualties in Four Recent Military Campaigns

Military campaign	Civilians killed per 10,000 tons of bombs dropped	PGMs as proportion of total bombs (units) dropped (%)	Total tonnage dropped	Rate of urbaniza-tion, 2000 (%)
Iraq, 1991	397[a]	¯6	88,000	77
Yugoslavia, 1999	923[b]	29	13,000	48
Afghanistan, October 7 to December 10, 2001	1,832–2,104[c]	60	14,000	22
Iraq, March 20 to April 5, 2003	1,971	>90	6,350	77

a The Iraqi figure of more than 3,000 civilian impact deaths in 1991 (397 × 8.8) is based on Beth Daponte, "Global Crisis over Iraq: Changing the Rules of War," *Le Monde Diplomatique* (March 2003), http://mondediplo.com. According to a *Business Week* story, Beth Osborne Daponte, a demographer in the Commerce Department assigned to do work for the Pentagon, estimated in 1992 that 40,000 Iraqi soldiers died along with 13,000 civilians. Much of that destruction happened after Saddam Hussein had abandoned Kuwait.

b Three different estimates exist for civilians killed in the Kosovo air war: Human Rights Watch has reported ca. 500, http://www.hrw.org/legacy/reports/2000/nato/. Fred Kaplan reports 1,200 in "Bombs Killing More Civilians Than Expected," *Boston Globe* (May 30, 1999). Yugoslav sources estimated some 2,000–2,600 civilians had been killed, as per General Vladimir Lazarevic, who claimed that NATO airstrikes against Yugoslavia killed some 2,000 people, half of whom were children. Further discussion is in my article at http://cursor.org/stories/civpertons.htm

c Based on a two-month aerial campaign that caused 2,565–2,945 civilian impact deaths.

Source: Civilian casualty database, http://pubpages.unh.edu/¯mwherold

columns explored the relevant and irrelevant minutiae. No such concern was ever shown for Afghan families, such as those of Abdul, Nasreen, Nazirullah, or Qamber, killed by "stray" U.S. bombs in Kabul during that frightful October 2001 of U.S. bombing. They were "abstract collateral damage," not real people (Table 2).[4]

Nazirullah will never forget that night of October 17–18, when U.S. war-planes flew over Kabul, seeking to strike Taliban forces in the capital. Nor will his relative, Abdullah, twenty-seven, who said as he searched in the rubble of his home, "I have lost my mother, my brother, my brother's wife, my grand-mother, and my sister. I have lost all hope; they were my hope. ... This is inhuman and unjust. Those people who did this will suffer a worse fate."[5]

Abdul and Nasreen, residents of Macroyan, were struck on October 18 by

Table 2
Effect of and Response to Three U.S. Bombing Incidents, Afghanistan

Surviving family members	Location	Report	Date	Details	Response
Kamila, Abdul, Shakila, Nasreen	Old Soviet-built, six-storey Macroyan housing complex	"Stray" bombs kill two	October 17, 2001	• Hit complex, killing eight-year-old girl, Nazila, and a boy • Two other children wounded in the head	No U.S. apology, no U.S. assistance offered
Nazirullah, Abdullah	Qalaye Zaman Khan neighbourhood	"Stray" bombs kill five to eight	October 18, 2001	• Killed five family members • Nazirullah's wife "has gone crazy" • Six homes destroyed • Woman passing by killed by a second bomb	A 35-person U.S. unofficial delegation gave Nazirullah's family a pair of trousers, a ball, and a pair of gloves
Qamber Begum	Wazir Abad district	"Stray" bombs kill four	October 26, 2001	• Destroyed Qamber's home, his father-in-law's house (killing his mother-in-law) and one other home • Qamber's two sisters, Saya, aged six, and Rayhan, aged eleven, also killed	No U.S. apology, no U.S. assistance offered

Source: Civilian casualty database, http://pubpages.unh.edu/~mwherold

U.S. warplanes. "Despite the Americans having modern air technology, they caused tremendous damage to this block. If we are hit by a small earthquake or even heavy rain, it will fall down," said Abdul. Nasreen added, "I lost my son in the bombing, my hearing is [now] bad, and two of my children, Naseer and Zareena, suffered head injuries. Now I just want the Americans to leave us alone, because everything is destroyed."[6]

A U.S. bomb landed on Wazir Abad early on October 26, 2001, and destroyed three houses. Two young sisters, aged six and eleven, died in the rubble of their mud-brick home. A neighbour, a widow herself, said two bombs were dropped. The second partially destroyed her house. She said, "I had to force the door open to get out and then I heard shouting and screaming next. They managed to get the mother and father out but both girls were dead."[7]

They were just Afghans. The bodies of their dearest kin are "unworthy bodies," unlike the four Canadian soldiers.

The three attacks cited above killed eleven to fourteen innocent Afghan civilians, or about four to five on average per attack. This fact is important insofar as it illustrates the nature of the U.S. military campaign: many individual bombing attacks, each of which killed relatively few Afghan civilians. There were no Dresdens, Tokyos, or Amiriyahs.[8] Figure 1 illustrates the weekly distribution of civilian deaths caused by U.S. attacks. The vertical axis shows the totals of civilians killed while the horizontal axis is a weekly timeline, from October 2001 to March 2003. Two tabulations exist – a high count and a low count (see Table 3).

Table 3
Civilian Casualties in Afghanistan

	Low count	High count
October 2001	931	1,148
November 2001	961	1,073
December 1–10, 2001	489	540
No date available	186	186
Total, October 7 to December 10, 2001	2,567	2,947

Source: Civilian casualty database, http://pubpages.unh.edu/~mwherold

By early 2003, reports from Afghanistan noted that "the nuclear nightmare" had started.[9] My estimates indicate that two to three times more depleted uranium was left in Afghanistan than in Iraq during the first Gulf War.[10] In the U.S. campaign against Afghanistan, the two primary delivery agents firing depleted uranium munitions have been the F-15E "Strike Eagle" and the A-10 "Warthog."

Ever since the first Gulf War, the U.S. military has increasingly used radioactive depleted uranium (DU) munitions.[11] Against Iraq in 1991, they proved very effective at penetrating enemy armour (tanks). More recently in the Afghan campaign a new generation of uranium weapons is suspected to have been used extensively for targeting underground facilities and caves. Table 4 summarizes estimated usage of radioactive DU in three of America's recent wars. Dai Williams, an independent researcher on the use and effects of DU munitions, estimates that 50 to 70 per cent of a warhead's weight (minus guidance system weight) comprises DU.

DU burns intensely and is very hard. As the shell hits its target, it burns and releases uranium oxide. This aerosol contains particles of DU 0.5 to 5

Figure 1
Weekly Casualty Count of Afghan Civilians Killed in U.S. Bombing and Special Forces Attacks, October 2001 to March 2003

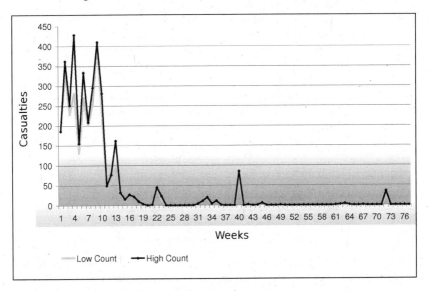

Source: Civilian casualty database, http://pubpages.unh.edu/~mwherold

microns in size that, once they are in the air, can be carried by the wind and inhaled or ingested. DU is both radioactive and toxic. Once in the lungs, one such particle is equivalent to having one chest X-ray per hour for life. Because it is impossible to remove, the victim is gradually irradiated. There are extensive reports from southern Iraq about a large increase of stillbirths, birth defects, leukemia, and other cancers in children born since 1991.

On October 20, 2002, Dr. Asaf Durakovic, professor of nuclear medicine at Georgetown University and discoverer of Gulf War syndrome, reported preliminary test results on sick civilians from southern Afghanistan to a military medicine conference in Qatar. Specimens contained 100 times the normal level of uranium contamination.[12] Curiously this was undepleted, not depleted, uranium. If this contamination came from the suspected U.S. guided weapons, he said in an interview on Al-Jazeera television in November 2002, U.S. forces may have used more uranium weapons in Afghanistan than they had in the Gulf War and the Balkans.[13] Thousands of DU bombs were dropped upon Afghanistan. The high-temperature explosions associated with large bombs generate very high conversion rates to deadly uranium oxide particles. Since far more bombs were dropped at so-called hard targets in Afghanistan than in Iraq, we can expect far greater contamination. The high temperatures of the Afghan summer and winds cause even greater dispersion.

Table 4
Use of Depleted Uranium in Recent Military Campaigns

	Munitions known or suspected of containing uranium	Delivery agent of DU-laced munitions	Total tons of DU delivered
Iraq, 1991	30 mm, 105 mm, and 120 mm cannon shells	Abrams tank and A-10 Warthog	320–750[a]
Balkans, 1999	30 mm cannon shells, bunker-busting bombs, and missiles (GBU-15, 24, 27, 28, 31)	A-10 Warthog, B-2, F-15E, BGM-109 Tomahawk, and AGM-86D CALCM (prototype) cruise missiles	10–200
Afghanistan, 2001	25 and 30 mm shells, bunker-busting bombs, and missiles (GBU-28, 15, 24, 27, 31 and 37, AGM-130C)	F-15E, B-2, A-10, AC-130H Spooky, BGM-109 Tomahawk, and AGM-86D CALCM cruise missiles	500–600[b]

a The U.S. Department of Defense estimates that 315 tons of DU were deposited in the Gulf War battlefields, www.ngwrc.org/Dulink/du_Map.htm
b This estimate is based on an assortment of A-10 firing (15 missions per month, each mission 1,500 rounds), 200 GBU-24 bombs being dropped, 50 GBU-28 and GBU-37 bombs being dropped, and the use of a variety of other DU-containing weapons (AC-130s, AGM-130, etc.).
Source: http://cursor.org/stories/uranium.htm and references there.

Why the High Level of Civilian Casualties? Killing Deliberately "by Mistake"

[Afghan fighters] won't give up no matter how many bombs you drop. They're not right in the head. Obviously, they don't think the way normal people think.[14]

We just sit in the dark, watching the sky, waiting to die.[15]

On July 22, 2002, Secretary Rumsfeld proclaimed, "We can take some comfort in the knowledge that this war has seen fewer tragic losses of civilian life than perhaps any war in modern history. We can also take pride in the fact that coalition forces have gone to extraordinary lengths not only to avoid civilian deaths but to save civilian lives."[16]

With the proliferation and increasing political importance of mass media during the post-Vietnam era – a dramatic collapse of time and space in our postmodern world – the need for the state to manage public opinion grows. We saw this very well with the Afghan intervention when, in October 2001, the Bush regime appointed a senior public relations expert to the high post of undersecretary to manage the presentation of the U.S. aggression. We also saw it in both the extreme measures taken to keep images and written accounts of civilian casualties away from the U.S. public and the endless repetition of sanitized phrases to describe the war – "collateral damage," "precision weaponry," "smart bombs," and so forth.

The Pentagon and its corporate media cheerleaders describe "war without death," a "vision of combat as bloodless and antiseptic" as admirably stated by Patrick Sloyan.[17] Pepe Escobar of the *Asia Times* provided a cogent summary in late October 2001:

> The smart, high-IQ bombs of the Pentagon may not find Osama bin Laden and the evildoers of Al-Qaeda, but they are finding houses a mile away from their targets, U.N. mine-clearing staff, shepherds and their families, a whole village, a Red Cross compound, a school, a bus, the bazaars of Kandahar, a hospital in Herat, a Mercedes bus in Kandahar. It is a sterling record – but of course this cannot be independently verified. One of these days the Pentagon may even "inadvertently" drop a bomb on Al Jazeera's office in Kabul – and remain mute about it. Or accuse an accusing voice of lying. . . . So the major public relations lesson is this: if you are rich and powerful and Western, you can bomb whatever you like, the way you like, for as long as you like. And you disclose information – if any – about it the way you like. If you are poor and miserable and Islamic, you shut up and get bombed. Don't make any attempt to say anything about it, because your information cannot be independently verified.[18]

A perfect example of the U.S. corporate media's "being in bed" with the Pentagon is provided by the *Washington Post*'s Vernon Loeb, answering a call-in question on March 21, 2003:

> I believe the U.S. military when it says it is attempting to minimize civilian casualties. It is also a fact that U.S. precision strike capabilities will kill far fewer civilians than the old carpet-bombing techniques employing dumb bombs. . . . Innocent civilians will almost undoubtedly be killed, when intelligence is faulty, when smart bombs malfunction, and when human beings make mistakes as they inevitably will. We've seen multiple examples of this in Afghanistan. I think the number of civilians killed by mistake in that conflict numbers in the hundreds, probably not more than 1,000.[19]

Now what is revealing about Loeb's response is his use of the bad old carpet bombing imagery to which he counterposes the perfection of the new precision bombing. Second, Loeb says nothing about the U.S. politico-military elite's decision to drop powerful bombs in civilian-rich neighbourhoods but instead points to "mistakes" that caused at most 10 per cent of the 3,000 plus impact deaths in Afghanistan. Third, Loeb is apparently ignorant that the measure of bombing's lethality to civilians is best captured by civilians killed per tons of bombs dropped, and not by comparisons to yesteryear's carpet bombing.

Mike Toner, reporter with the *Atlanta Journal-Constitution*, notes, "Military officials maintain that the Afghan bombing inflicted less collateral damage for its size than any other air war in history."[20] Eric Schmitt and James Dao sang hosannas in the *New York Times* to the new smart bombs ("pinpoint air power"), going so far as to declare that "Afghanistan will be remembered as the smart-bomb war."[21] In a series of columns in the *Washington Post*, William Arkin continues along a path trodden earlier when he praises the smart bombs used in the first Gulf War, repeating the mantra.[22]

A more candid statement about bombing Afghanistan can sometimes be found by listening to the pilots involved, rather than to the packaged, sanitized accounts from Pentagon spokespeople and their courtiers, the media defence intellectuals. "Major Jake" of the 419th Air Force Fighter Wing, flying an F-16 out of the Al-Jabar base in Kuwait Arabia during the Afghan campaign, provided a revealing statement published in Lockheed Martin's magazine, *Code One*:

> We couldn't find the target area. . . . My wingman dropped a bomb to mark a target area, but it wasn't the target area that the GFAC [ground-based person who locates target] wanted. An F-14 came through. We trailed it. He dropped and missed, too. Basically, all the fighters were not seeing what the GFAC wanted us to see. The terrain had lots of mountains and high ridges and valleys and it all looked the same. . . . We were in the northeast portion of Afghanistan near the borders with Uzbekistan and Pakistan. We worked with a second GFAC. . . . This time, we found the GFAC's target area, but then clouds began rolling in. The GFAC asked us to drop through the clouds on a heading over the friendlies, a very dicey maneuver even when we have everything lined up. We made sure we were looking in the right target area. I flew in trail of my flight lead. He dropped the first bomb. *It fell short about 700 meters*. It didn't fall in the friendly lines but short enough that we decided not to drop again.[23]

High levels of Afghan civilian casualties have been caused less by mechanical or human errors, malfunction, or faulty intelligence and more by the decision of U.S. political and military planners to use powerful bombs in "civilian-rich" areas where perceived military targets are located.[24] The United States, of course, is not alone in doing such; Russia bombs Chechnya, and Israel bombs Gaza. Pavel Felgenhauer correctly opines that we "are sinking into a mire of brutality" as internationally accepted laws and conventions are ignored.[25] Whether intended or not, murderous collective punishment is a crime against humanity. Felgenhauer continues, "Each time the U.S. military commits a war crime in Afghanistan, it claims it was: first a 'mistake'; second that it is sorry it happened; and third that the terrorists are themselves to blame, since they use civilians as human shields."

Proximity to what the U.S. planners defined as military targets caused at least 3,000 Afghan civilian impact deaths,[26] or in U.S. terms of pain equivalence – civilian casualties as a proportion of national population – *42,000 deaths; that is, fifteen World Trade Centers*. On February 13, 2001, Peshawar's daily newspaper, *The Frontier Post,* got it more right than all the U.S. media war pundits and apologists put together, headlining a brief article, "Proximity to Taliban was Fatal!": "The bomb craters are like enormous footsteps a few hundred yards apart, marching in the direction of a Taliban radio transmitter. Along the way, four men die . . . a fatal proximity to a site considered militarily useful to Afghanistan's Taliban or Osama."

Hundreds of individual stories exist, as yet mostly untold, of how proximity to what U.S. war planners deemed a military "target" is at the heart of so many innocent Afghan civilian deaths.[27] Ghulam and Rabia Hazrat lived on the outskirts of Kabul, near a Taliban military base. One day, a U.S. missile landed in the family's courtyard and the neighbourhood was showered with cluster bombs. Mrs. Hazrat remembers, "There was no warning. I was in the kitchen making dough when I heard a big explosion. I came out and saw a big cloud of dust and saw my children lying on the ground. Two of them were dead and two died later in the hospital."[28]

Abdul and Shakila Amiri lost their daughter, Nazila, in that American air strike on the morning of October 17.[29] Nazila was playing with her younger brother and sister close to their home in Kabul's Macroyan apartment complex when it was hit by a type of "smart" bomb glorified on the pages of glossy magazines hawked from newsstands and seen on television across the United States. Nazila was crushed to death by a concrete block. She was not mentioned on U.S. television news.

Along with the U.S. military planners' decision to bomb perceived military targets in civilian-rich urban areas, the use of weapons with great destructive blast and fragmentation power necessarily results in heavy civilian casualties. The weapon of choice during the first three weeks of the air campaign was the 500-pound bomb, which has a lethal blast range of twenty metres; later, the 2,000-pound became the weapon of choice, with a lethal blast range of thirty-four metres (Table 5). The Navy's favourite has been the 1,000-pound Mark 83 bomb. In order to be safe from a 2,000-pound bomb, a person needs be almost half a kilometre away. The JDAM (joint direct attack munition) technology consists of a $21,000 kit produced by Boeing that transforms 1,000- and 2,000-pound conventional "dumb" bombs into "smart" bombs, which rely on the global positioning system. When global positioning updates are available, the JDAM-outfitted bomb can strike within thirteen metres of its target. When updates are not available due to jamming or other problems, it can still hit within thirty metres.[30] The B1-B bombers flying out of Diego Garcia in the Indian Ocean can carry twenty-four to thirty Mark 84 2,000-pound JDAM bombs. Each bomb is four and a quarter metres long and will destroy military targets within a twelve-metre radius from the point of impact. A 1,000-pound Mark 83 bomb falls more than thirteen metres off target 50 per cent of the time under ideal weather conditions and creates a lethal blast of some twenty-six metres.

A single B-52 bomber carries forty CBU-87 cluster bombs with a total of 8,080 bomblets. Theoretically, assuming an admitted danger radius of seventy-six metres, one B-52 could carpet bomb over 147 million square metres – equal to 27,500 football fields. Thus, the twenty-eight B-52s that reportedly dropped 470 tons of explosives on Iraqi ground forces on January 30, 1991, could have obliterated 4,140 square kilometres, an area the size of Connecticut. On New Year's Day of 2002, Eric Falt, UNIC (United Nations Information Centres) director, disclosed that such cluster bombs – like the CBU-87 – had been dropped on at least 103 cities in Afghanistan.[31] On October 26, 2001, the United Nations publicly denounced the use of cluster bombs by the United States, which had indiscriminately killed civilians in the city of Herat.[32] The U.S. policy of mixing yellow cluster bomb drops with yellow food aid drops aggravated the carnage.[33]

Table 6 reconstructs from official sources the types and amounts of munitions dropped on Serbia/Kosovo and Afghanistan. These figures err on the conservative side. For example, in the Kosovo NATO campaign, British planes dropped over 1,000 munitions, but only 40 per cent are reported to have reached their target. Many accounts of the NATO campaign report that only 50 per cent of munitions dropped hit their targets, whereas for the Afghan campaign the figure often mentioned for bombs that went astray is 25 per cent of those dropped.

Official Pentagon data report that 10 per cent of the precision-guided munitions dropped in Afghanistan missed their target.[34] I will assume that 25 per cent of the gravity bombs also missed their targets (the Navy admitted that 25 per cent of the 5,500 bombs it dropped between October 7 and April 4, or 1,375 bombs, missed their intended targets), or in other words that 2,200

Table 5
Weapons Systems Used in Afghan Aerial War Theatre

	Officially reported CEP[a] accuracy range	Maximum fragmentation range (ft)[b]	Blast shrapnel range	Effective casualty radius[c]	Lethal blast range[d]	Crater on impact	Price per unit ($)	Manufacturers
Mark 82 500-lb. Paveway II bomb	9 m	3,180	–	About 60 m radius	About 20 m radius	12 ft. (4 m)	19,000	Texas Instruments and Raytheon
Mark 83 1,000-lb. JDAM bomb	13 [–30] m, 39 ft. in tests	3,200	600 ft. radius	–	About 26 m	35 ft. wide	25,000	Boeing Corp. and Lockheed Martin
CBU-87 1,000-lb. cluster bomb	n/a	n/a	500	Disperses 202 bomblets, each with 300 steel fragments	100 ft., each bomblet	200 x 400 m footprint	12,400	Alliant Techsystems Inc.
Mark 84 2,000-lb. JDAM bomb	13 [–30] m, 39 ft. in tests	3,880	~1,000 ft. radius (250 m)[e]	Safety at least 400 m from impact site	110 ft. (34 m)	50 ft. wide x 36 ft. deep	25,000	Boeing Corp. and Lockheed Martin

a CEP, or circular error probability, means that 50 per cent of the time bomb falls outside this range.
b Measurements in this table are supplied in the form used in original sources.
c 50 per cent of exposed persons will die.
d 100 per cent mortality within this range.
e "National Defense with Vernon Loeb and Dana Priest," *Washington Post Live Online*, March 21, 2003, www.washingtonpost.com/wp-srv/liveonline/.

Source: http://cursor.org/stories/civpertons.htm

Table 6

Bomb Misses in Three U.S. Campaigns

	Units dropped/missed				Percentage dropped/missed		
Precision-guided munitions (PGMS)	Gravity bombs	Total dropped	Total missed	PGMS out of total dropped	PGMS missed	Gravity missed	Total bombs missed
Iraq 1991[a]	12,730	209,655	222,385	158,514	5.7	10	75	71
Kosovo	6,775	16,839	23,614	9,918	28.7	22	49	42
Afghanistan	13,200	8,800	22,000	3,500	60	10	25	16

a   In Iraq, campaign a total of 88,500 tons was dropped, of which 6,250 tons were PGMS (or 7.4 per cent of total tonnage), but reportedly 75 per cent of the damage done to "strategic targets" during the first Gulf War was attributed to PGMS ("National Defense with Vernon Loeb and Dana Priest," *Washington Post Live Online*, March 21, 2003, www.washingtonpost.com/wp-srv/liveonline/). B-52Gs dropped 25,700 tons of gravity bombs during the Iraq conflict.

gravity bombs fell astray. In both the Iraq and Yugoslavian air campaigns, fewer than half of the bombs hit intended targets. A conservative estimate of bombs missing their intended targets in the Afghan campaign is thus 3,500. This figure provides further strong support for my estimate of 3,100 to 3,600 innocent Afghan civilians dying from U.S. projectiles. The overall miss rate amounts to approximately 16 per cent (3,500 out of 22,000). A serious technical problem arises here in evaluating the officially reported "hit rates": what is the assumed size of the "target box"? If it is fifty metres, then a building adjacent to the targeted one can be hit, and the attack still register as a hit.

What can be said about the JDAM bomb technology is that it has reduced both the cost of hitting a target and the number of planes dispatched to take out a target: "A JDAM gives a single jet the ability to do the job that required 10 planes or more just a few years ago."[35]

This is quite different from the picture the public is spoon fed by the U.S. military, defence "intellectuals," and the compliant U.S. corporate media, which recite the refrain that JDAM technology was developed to reduce civilian casualties. JDAM technology was developed simply because it is a more cost-effective form of aerial bombing. One might recall a statement of then U.S. Undersecretary of State Alexis Johnson in 1975, discussing the covert bombing of Laos that killed some 750,000 civilians: "[The Laos operation] is something of which we can be proud as Americans. It has involved virtually no American casualties. What we are getting for our money there . . . is, I think, to use the old phrase, very cost effective."[36]

No inference should be drawn here about modern aerial warfare being more "humane" in the sense of reverting back to the wars of the nineteenth century, wherein most of those who died were combatants. As documented below, the air war in Afghanistan has been the costliest of four recent air wars in terms of civilians killed per tonnage dropped.[37] On the other hand, the daily intensity of the bombing, as measured in missions per day, has been far lower than in previous wars: the average missions per day were 1,500 for the Gulf War, 500 for Serbia, and only about 80 for Afghanistan.[38] In El Salvador during the 1980s, the U.S. and Salvadoran militaries unleashed a rain of terror by bombing.[39]

Stephen Budiansky has pointed out that the Afghan air campaign reflects an abandonment of the traditional theory of strategic bombing dominant from the First World War and through the nuclear age, which stressed that air attacks should target the enemy's vital centres and in so doing undermine his will to fight.[40] The core notion was that a population's resolve would be sapped if enough government, urban, and civilian infrastructure was destroyed. But facts showed that rather than sapping resolve, such bombing strengthened resilience, seen most clearly in the Indochinese air campaigns. Beginning with the Gulf War, a new view emerged that stressed hitting enemy *military forces directly*, assisted with the use of precision weaponry, and *before* launching a ground war. The bombing campaigns around Mazar, Kunduz, and Khanabad exemplify this approach. But the distinction between the newer thinking about air war and the older classical doctrine of strategic bombing (best exemplified in Dresden and Tokyo) should not be overdrawn. U.S. strategic bombers delivered millions of tons of ordnance on the Ho Chi Minh trails in Laos and Cambodia in the late 1960s and '70s as part of a campaign of interdiction that resulted in very heavy civilian casualties and long-lasting environmental hazards.

In the Afghan air campaign, an initial bombing campaign of a more traditionally strategic nature – bombing airfields, attacking radar sites, and the like – during the first two weeks of October shifted toward having bombers act as mobile, quick-reaction artillery, hitting the enemy.[41] The planes were increasingly being guided by Special Forces units on the ground. Small, eight-man units of Special Forces were helicoptered into northern Afghanistan as of October 19. The new, real-time strike operations designed to attack moving targets within five minutes of identifying them was inaugurated in late October.[42]

As Table 7 indicates, the past seven major U.S. bombing campaigns fall into three clusters in terms of resulting civilian deaths. The first Gulf War has the lowest ratio of civilians killed per tonnage dropped, though I am not suggesting it was a clean air war.[43] This is followed by the Vietnam and Serbian bombing campaigns, and a third group comprising Cambodia, Laos, and Afghanistan with over 2,000 civilians killed for every 10,000 tons of bombs dropped.

The Afghan air war has been particularly destructive in terms of civilian impact deaths compared with previous aerial bombing campaigns. In an article in the *Boston Globe* on May 30, 1999, Fred Kaplan argued that the so-called "kill ratio" in Serbia was about the same as in the Vietnam Rolling Thunder campaign – about one civilian killed for every ten tons of bombs dropped – whereas in the Gulf War, it was reportedly half that, though this seems to be a serious underestimate.[44] The index is, of course, at best suggestive since civilian casualties will reflect type of ordnance used, local demographic factors, topography, emplacement of military facilities, and so forth. After surveying innumerable reports on civilian impact deaths caused by bombing, I estimate the following numbers: Cambodia, 100,000; Iraq, 3,000; Serbia, 1,200; and Afghanistan, 3,000. These translate into respective kill ratios (civilians killed per 10,000 tons of bombs) of 2,565 in Afghanistan; 1,852 in Cambodia; 522 in Serbia; and 341 in the first Iraq war.

Some have sought to question my argument about the lethality of the U.S. Afghan bombing campaign. First, they point to the enormous decline in the percentage of bomb misses, falling from 71 per cent in Iraq in 1991 to 16 per

Table 7
U.S. Bombing Campaigns and Resulting Civilian Deaths

Bombed region	Date	Tonnage dropped	Reported civilian deaths	Civilians killed per 10,000 tons of bombs
Vietnam, Rolling Thunder campaign	1964–67	650,000	52,000[a]	800
Laos[b]	1965–73	2,000,000	350,000–500,000	1,750–2,500
Cambodia, Arclight campaign	1969–73	540,000	50,000–150,000	926–2,778
Christmas bombing of Hanoi–Haiphong	1972	20,000	1,600	800
Iraq	1991	88,000	2,500–3,500	284–397
NATO bombing of Yugoslavia (Serbia)	1999	13,000	500–1,200–2,000	385–923–1,538
U.S. Afghan air campaign	October to December 2001	14,000	2,565–2,945	1,832–2,104

a North Vietnamese.
b The U.S. bombing of Laos involved a planeload of bombs being dropped on the tiny country every eight minutes for nine years. See also Simon Jenkins, "Bombs That Turn Leaders into Butchers," *The Times*, January 17, 2001.
Source: See Table 1.

cent in Afghanistan. Such decline in no way undermines my argument since *I am not saying that bombing has become less precise*. Neither am I saying that had the older weaponry still been in use, fewer or equal casualties would have resulted. Second, they argue that the relevant number to use is the absolute number of killed civilians, not the ratio of civilians per bomb tonnage. The reason advanced is that comparison between campaigns is flawed insofar as mix of bombs, local terrain, chosen targets, and so forth vary and confuse the comparisons. Again, the critique misses my main argument and that is, that the bombing decisions made – with a rate of PGMs rising from 6 per cent of total bombs dropped in the first Iraq war to 60 per cent in the Afghan intervention – and the types of bombs employed have resulted in *greater loss of civilian lives*. U.S. planners could have chosen to bomb Al Qaeda and/or Taliban facilities in remote desert or mountain areas, or in the hills of the Shomali Plain (which they did carpet bomb) – as they had bombed the Iraqi Republican Guard in the Gulf War, but instead *chose to drop bombs on perceived military targets in civilian-rich areas*. Why? Because except for in the Shomali Plain and around Kunduz, the Taliban chose not to concentrate their forces, understanding that doing so would be suicidal given U.S. mastery of the skies.

By way of concluding here, the U.S. air war upon Afghanistan is best described as being of low bombing intensity though with elevated civilian casualty intensity, precisely the opposite of the air war carried out in Iraq more than a decade ago. The American bombing was carried out from altitudes beyond the reach of Taliban anti-aircraft fire and relied heavily on sophisticated targeting technology, but this technology could not prevent the inevitable killing of thousands of innocent Afghan civilians.

The effects of technology, as anyone familiar with the process of economic development knows, are heavily determined by social context. To talk about PGMs outside of context is rather meaningless.

I am not arguing that in a strict sense U.S. military planners intentionally targeted civilians. This was not a strategic bombing campaign.[45] But I believe it has been a case of *second-degree intentionality*.[46] A 1,000-pound JDAM bomb dropped on a residence or a tank parked in a residential area will necessarily kill people in proximity. And all the more so since most of the U.S. bombing attacks were carried out at night, when people were in their homes. Moreover, most Afghan homes, whether in urban neighbourhoods or mountain or plains villages, are made out of mud bricks. To this should be added the many instances in which U.S. bombs simply landed way off target. Sean Moorhouse, a de-mining expert working with the United Nations World Food Programme, compared the target coordinates provided by the U.S. military with where the bombs fell and concluded that "the accuracy of the U.S. figures is pretty doubtful," differing by as much as four miles on occasion.[47]

Afghan civilians in proximity to alleged military installations will die, and must die, as collateral damage of U.S. air attacks aiming to destroy these installations in order to make future military operations from the sky or on the ground less likely to result in U.S. military casualties. The military facilities of the Taliban were inherited mostly from the Soviet-supported government of the 1980s, which had concentrated its military infrastructure in cities; these could be better defended against the rural insurgency of the *mujahideen*. This reality is compounded insofar as the Taliban maintained dispersed facilities: smaller units spread out. U.S. military strategists and their bombers thus engaged in a very widespread bombing. Such intense urban bombing causes high levels of civilian casualties. From the point of view of U.S. policy makers and their mainstream media boosters, the "cost" of a dead Afghan civilian is zero as long as these civilian deaths can be hidden from the view of the general U.S. public. In this, the U.S. corporate media has done the Pentagon's bidding – with a few notable exceptions (like Barry Bearak and Carlotta Gall of the *New York Times*, John Donnelly of the *Boston Globe*, Doug Struck of the *Washington Post*, Philip Smucker of the *Christian Science Monitor*). The "benefits" of saving future lives of U.S. military personnel are enormous, given the U.S. public's post-Vietnam aversion to returning body bags. In effect, the U.S. military has made a trade-off: dead Afghan civilians today versus possible U.S. military casualties in the future, reflecting a monstrous different valuation of lives.[48]

The absolute imperative to avoid U.S. military casualties meant flying high up in the sky, increasing the probability of killing civilians: "Better stand clear and fire away. Given this implicit decision, the slaughter of innocent people, as a statistical eventuality is not an accident but a priority – in which Afghan civilian casualties are substituted for American military casualties."[49]

The documented Afghan civilians killed were not participating in war-making activities, and therefore had not forfeited their right to immunity from attack.[50] In effect, as an astute scholar has noted, I am turning Michael Walzer's notion of "due care" upside down; that is, far from acknowledging a positive responsibility to protect innocent Afghans from the misery of war, U.S. military strategists chose to impose levels of harm on innocent Afghan civilians to reduce present and possible future dangers to U.S. forces.[51]

The types of weapons used by the United States – whether deadly cluster bombs, the daisy cutters used for the first time on troops, or the extensive employment of munitions with depleted uranium – further reveal the low value put on Afghan lives by the U.S. political and military elite. Much that was bombable in Afghanistan – schools, houses, factories, bridges, hospitals, power plants and lines, infrastructure – had already been destroyed in twenty-two years of civil war. New bombs just made more dust. Figure 2 points out

Figure 2
Human Costs of the U.S. Air Campaign

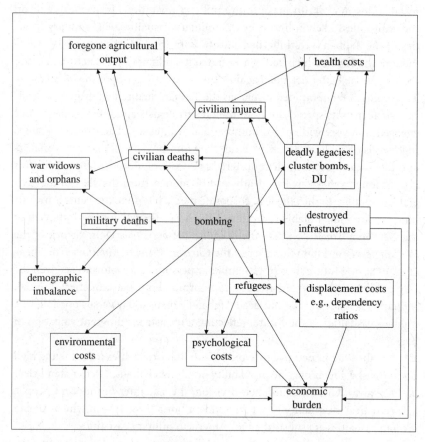

some of the connected deadly legacies of the U.S. air war on Afghanistan, many of which I have addressed in separate essays elsewhere.

An examination of twenty weeks of U.S. bombing of Afghanistan reveals the danger of everyday life in Afghanistan under U.S. bombs. During the U.S. bombing campaign of 2001 it was life threatening

- to be having breakfast with your children in Kabul
- to be praying at a mosque in Jalalabad
- to be kicking a gourd in a playground in Kandahar
- to be asleep with your groom of six weeks in Kabul
- to be sitting at home, sewing, in the Shomali Plain, Koko Gul
- to be fleeing to Pakistan
- to be a patient in a hospital
- to be driving a truck carrying fuel oil or fruits
- to be farming with your father in Helmand

- to be walking home from school in Kandahar
- to be shopping in Kandahar's central bazaar
- to be attending a funeral
- to be protecting a United Nations warehouse at night
- to be preparing for a wedding
- to be sleeping next to your broken-down truck in Zabol
- to be living near a radio station
- to be a goat in Pakistan
- to be getting water at a pump in Kabul
- to be waiting for a bus
- to be collecting firewood
- to be driving to a Sufi shrine
- to be living in a mountain village like Karam or Kama Ado or Shah Aga, or in a desert village like Chowkar Kariz . . .

and to be following hundreds of other routines of everyday life.

Under the rules of the International Criminal Court, which came into being in July 2002, the United States could have been charged for war crimes involving breach of international humanitarian law for its bombing of Afghanistan in 2001–02. The United States did launch attacks on populated, civilian areas such as Kandahar and Kabul without warning; did use indiscriminate weapon systems such as cluster bombs and weapons made of depleted uranium; did attack Afghan infrastructure; did directly bomb electricity supplies (causing death of civilians due to power outages and failed water supply), including not only Afghanistan's largest hydroelectric plant at Kajakai but also smaller units, for example near Kabul and Jalalabad. The bombing campaign also took a very heavy toll on urban infrastructure, destroying buildings,[52] airports, clinics, communication systems, water and electricity supplies, and fuel storage depots, cratering innumerable roads, and destroying public transportation.[53] As of late October 2001, Afghan fuel trucks had become a favoured target.

Looking at the twenty weeks of U.S. bombing of Afghanistan reveals the following human costs of this attack:

- 3,100–3,600 civilians killed directly by bombs and missiles
- 4,000–6,500 civilians injured, many requiring prostheses
- 8,000–10,000 dead Taliban and allies
- 19,000–43,000 Afghan refugees dying of hunger, disease, and cold in camps
- an additional estimated 5,000 war widows and thousands of orphans
- destroyed animals and livestock
- 49,000 BLU-97 cluster bomblets in at least 103 cities and villages, more deadly than land mines
- long-term health effects from using munitions containing depleted uranium

- an infrastructure further destroyed: bridges, power plants, water supplies, roads, communication systems, hundreds of incinerated trucks, burned fuel storage facilities, and so forth
- environmental costs (in addition to aforementioned unexploded ordnance) that cause loss of agricultural land and human injuries, including massive forest fires in Tora Bora, dead wildlife, altered migratory patterns, a resurgence of locusts, and so on
- and the psychological costs of being bombed: post-traumatic stress disorders, anxiety, irritability, loss of appetite, depression, and "a real feeling of loss – loss of body, loss of money, loss of friends and family," according to Dr. Ghulam Rasool, a psychiatrist treating Afghan refugees in Quetta.[54]

A World Health Organization report in November estimated that mental illness is serious for one in five Afghans as a result of twenty-three years of war.[55] A recent account detailed the forms of mental disorders:

> A 4 year-old boy named Hasib grimaces like an animal and repeatedly butts his head on the floor. A young man named Fawad says his father startles awake, terrified, in the middle of every night. A man, Mohammad, averts his eyes from the rubble of his village; when he looks, he is overwhelmed by a flashback vision of dismembered bodies.

Conclusion: An Immaculate Deception

We can't simply bomb a just world into shape.[56]

Nida Ahmad was interviewed by Craig Nelson of the *Sydney Morning Herald* in Kandahar in February 2002. Ahmad, a thirty-four-year-old shopkeeper, said of the U.S. attack three months before, "My father was killed there. The Americans saw he was wearing a turban and kneeling on the ground praying, so they bombed him."[57]

As the tricolour flags on the antennae of U.S. pick-up trucks have faded and become ragged in these years after 9/11, greater clarity is slowly emerging over the human costs of the U.S. air and ground campaigns. Let this be a caution to further military adventurism. When we begin seeing ourselves more as citizens of the world than as defenders of a nation, we may move toward equal valuations of life across space. We might then begin to question past and future uses of air power to achieve military-political ends and understand how such bombing campaigns flow directly from a differential valuation of life. In this sense, the bombing of Afghanistan is no different from that of Guernica or Dresden. Guernica and Dresden went down in history because we – Euro-Americans – were the ones who died. Who knows about the Spanish bombing of Chechaouen, the French bombing of the neighbourhoods of

Damascus on October 18, 1925, the killing 89,000 to 100,000 simple people in Madagascar in 1948, and so forth?[58] The bombing and killing of average Afghans is the reflection of the carnage perpetrated in Manhattan on 9/11. In both tragedies, thousands of innocents perished.

Too many Americans who consider themselves informed are incapable of grasping the political complexities in the Middle East and Central Asia.[59] Ignorance in America is alive and well. Bush and the Pentagon liked it that way. For reasons I have elaborated elsewhere, the U.S. mainstream corporate media have resisted portraying the carnage caused by U.S. bombs in Afghanistan.[60] In late October 2001, CNN chair Walter Isaacson said that a focus in news reporting on Afghan civilian casualties would be "perverse."[61] Anthony Lloyd, the *London Times* foreign correspondent of the year, wrote, "Seldom in a modern conflict have the facts been so manipulated as in Afghanistan."[62] Paraphrasing the U.S. Marine colonel, an immaculate deception has been perpetrated on the U.S. public.

The "others" see it differently. Let me end by mentioning one "other," Mahtab, twenty, an Afghan refugee living in a squatter camp in Peshawar, who spoke to Barry Bearak of the *New York Times*:

> But it was the bombing that made her leave Kabul on Oct. 18. Her house was hit during a raid and her mother-in-law was killed by shrapnel, she said. "It pierced her heart."
>
> She is angry at America, and when she is told that the United States is trying to minimize civilian casualties, she answered with a list of neighborhoods where innocents have been killed: Khuja Bughra, Maidan Hawai and others. Her patience wore away quickly at this subject.
>
> "It is easier to understand if it is you being bombed," she said.[63]

Notes

1 Mentioned in "U.S. Adds Hekmatyar in Wanted Men Posters," *Pakistan News Service*, February 3, 2003, http://e-ariana.com/ariana/eariana.nsf/.

2 I borrow the term *surgical precision* from Peter Spang Goodrich, "The Surgical Precision Myth: After the Bomb Explodes – (CCDP) Cumulative Collateral Damage Probability," (Providence, R.I.: Department of Management, Providence College, June 11, 2003), www.psgoodrich.com/war/surgical/. A shorter version was published as "Dead Aim Still Deadly," *Bulletin of Atomic Scientists* 59, 4 (2003), 18–19. The selling of the Afghan war to the American public is examined in my "War as an 'Edsel': The Marketing and Consumption of Modern American Wars," April 9, 2005, http://pubpages.unh.edu/~mwherold/.

3 A number of other estimates exist for civilian deaths in Afghanistan. I have summarized and critically assessed them in my article, "Counting the Dead," *The*

Guardian, August 8, 2002, www.guardian.co.uk/.

4 A scholar who has researched Cambodians killed by U.S. bombs, Ben Kiernan of Yale University's Genocide Studies Program, wrote " 'Collateral Damage' Means Real People," *Bangkok Post*, October 20, 2002, posted at www.yale.edu/gsp/publications/collateral_damage.html.

5 "At Least Six Dead as U.S. Bombs Hit Afghan Homes: Witnesses," *Agence-France Presse*, October 18, 2001.

6 Rahhimullah Samandar, "Painful Legacy of U.S. Airstrikes," Institute for War & Peace Reporting, September 6, 2002, www.iwpr.net/.

7 "Girls Killed As U.S. Bomb Strikes Village, Red Cross Stores Razed," *Agence-France Press*, Kabul, October 26, 2001.

8 The Amiriyah bomb shelter in Baghdad was hit by a 2,000-pound U.S. smart (laser-guided) missile in 1991, killing 408 Iraqi civilians. See Scott Peterson, " 'Smarter' Bombs Still Hit Civilians," *Christian Science Monitor*, October 22, 2002, www.csmonitor.com.

9 Davey Garland, "Afghanistan: The Nuclear Nightmare Starts," *Coastal Post*, January 3, 2003, www.coastalpost.com.

10 See my essay "Uranium Wars: The Pentagon Steps Up Its Use of Radioactive Munitions," November 13, 2002, www.cursor.org/stories/uranium.htm.

11 Bernard Rostker, "Development of DU Munitions," in Department of Defense, *Environmental Exposure Report, Depleted Uranium in the Gulf (II)* (Washington, D.C.: Department of Defense, 2000), www.gulflink.osd.mil/du_ii/du_ii_tabe.htm

12 In an Internet communication by Dai Williams, dated November 18, 2002 at: http://www.casi.org.uk/discuss/2002/msg02087.html.

13 "U.S. Used More DU Weapons in Afghanistan than in Persian Gulf War: Dracovic," *Tehran Times*, November 9, 2002; and "U.S. Asked Not to Use DU Arms against Baghdad," *The Frontier Post*, November 11, 2002.

14 Spoken by Sgt. Paul Dominguez of Hillside, New Jersey, somewhere in Afghanistan, quoted by Barry Bearak in the *New York Times*, March 12, 2002, and cited in Richard Reeves, "Why We Are in Afghanistan," March 15, 2002, http://www.richardreeves.com/column_archive.html.

15 Jamal Uddin, vegetable seller in Kabul, quoted in Associated Press, October 10, 2001.

16 Tom Shanker, "Rumsfeld Calls Civilian Deaths Relatively Low," *New York Times*, July 22, 2002.

17 Patrick J. Sloyan, "War without Death: The Pentagon Promotes a Vision of Combat as Bloodless and Antiseptic," *San Francisco Chronicle*, November 17, 2002, www.sfgate.com/.

18 Pepe Escobar, "This Report Cannot Be Independently Verified," *Asia Times*, October 25, 2001, www.atimes.com/c-asia/CJ24Ag04.html.

19 "National Defense with Vernon Loeb and Dana Priest," *Washington Post Live Online*, March 21, 2003, www.washingtonpost.com/wp-srv/liveonline/.

20 Mike Toner, "Warfare Tests New Technology," *Atlanta Journal and Constitution*, September 2, 2002. An account that makes little mention of the human cost of the U.S. punitive operation and instead interprets it as a "masterpiece of military creativity and finesse" is Michael E. O'Hanlon, "A Flawed Masterpiece," *Foreign Affairs* (May-June 2002), 47–63.

21 Eric Schmitt and James Dao, "Use of Pinpoint Air Power Comes of Age in New War," *New York Times*, December 24, 2001; and Eric Schmitt, "Improved U.S. Ac-

curacy Claimed in Afghan Air War," *New York Times*, April 9, 2002.

22 William M. Arkin, "Smart Bombs, Dumb Targeting," *Bulletin of Atomic Scientists* 56, 3 (2000), 46–53; "Checking on Civilian Casualties," *Washington Post*, April 9, 2002.

23 "Enduring Freedom Debrief: F-16 Operations over Afghanistan – 419th Fighter Wing," *Code One* 17, 3 (2002), emphasis added.

24 In a strange critique of my work, Jeffrey C. Isaac claims I ignore the fact that "why the U.S. has bombed these areas is simply because that is where the targeted facilities are located. But Herold strangely chooses to ignore this possibility." Jeffrey C. Issac, "Civilian Casualties in Afghanistan: The Limits of Marc Herold's 'Comprehensive Accounting,'" *OpenDemocracy*, March 14, 2002, www.opendemocracy.net.

25 Pavel Felgenhauer, "Sinking in Mire of Brutality," *Moscow Times*, July 25, 2002, 9.

26 By "impact death" I mean death caused at the moment of explosion of the bomb or missile. This seriously underestimates the actual number of deaths as it omits all those injured who later die. My estimates indicate that for every impact death, about two people were injured. Others report much higher figures.

27 Hundreds of these individuals' stories are collected in my electronic memorial, "Afghan Victim Memorial Project," http://pubpages.unh.edu/~mwherold/.

28 Carlotta Gall, "Shattered Afghan Families Demand U.S. Compensation," *New York Times*, April 8, 2002.

29 For details on the Amiris, see Kelly Campbell, "Six Months On. Part II, The Victims," *ARROW Briefing* 13, March 11, 2002, http://www.j-n-v.org/AW_briefings/ARROW_briefing013.htm

30 Loren Thompson, *What Works?* vol. 8, *The Joint Direct Attack Munition: Making Acquisition Reform a Reality* (Arlington, Va.: Lexington Institute, 1999).

31 "Cluster Bombs Dropped in 103 Afghan Cities: U.N.," PakistanNews.com, January 1, 2002.

32 "U.N. Slams Use of Cluster Bombs as 8 Die," *News International*, October 26, 2001, www.commondreams.org/headlines01/1026-06.htm.

33 Hamish McDonald, "Death Comes in a Little Yellow Package," *Sydney Morning Herald*, December 17, 2001.

34 Data partially presented in "Officials: U.S. Bombing in Afghanistan Could Be Most Accurate Ever," *Associated Press*, April 10, 2002, www.foxnews.com.

35 Scott Canon, "Missouri Product Puts U.S. on Target," *Kansas City Star*, March 12, 2002.

36 Between 1965 and 1973, the U.S. dropped more than 2 million tons of bombs on Laos, more than were dropped on Germany and Japan during the Second World War (see Testimony before the U.S. Armed Services Committee, Hearings on Fiscal Year 1972 Authorizations, July 22, 1971, 4289).

37 The point has been made in conjunction with the (questionable) figures adduced by Arkin for the Kosovo air war, that *only* 500 civilians were killed in 78 days of NATO bombing, making it incomparably "cleaner" than Allied bombing of Germany during the Second World War or "the horrors of Vietnam." This argument fails to recognize that, first, the Kosovo air campaign involved a low bombing intensity in terms of sorties per day; and, second, the relevant variable is some measure of civilians killed in relation to such bombing intensity. Some prefer to speculate that "in post-modern war, it may be possible to achieve victory while largely sparing civilians." See Mike Moore, "A New Editor," *Bulletin of the Atomic Scientists* 56, 3 (2000), 2–3. Regarding civilian casualties in Kosovo, Fred Kaplan men-

tions the much more realistic figure of 1,200. "Bombs Killing More Civilians Than Expected," *Boston Globe*, May 30, 1999, A33.

38   A.P., "One Month In: How Three Different Wars Were Similar," *St. Petersburg Times* (Florida), November 4, 2001.

39   Details in Sandy Smith, "Rain of Terror: The Bombing of Civilians in El Salvador," *Health & Medicine: Journal of the Health and Medicine Policy Research Group* 3 (Winter 1985), 21–28.

40   Stephen Budiansky, "How U.S. Stretched the Limits of Air Power," *Washington Post*, December 23, 2001.

41   Julian Borger and Luke Harding, "Week of Bombing Leaves U.S. further from Peace, But No Nearer to Victory," *The Guardian*, October 15, 2001.

42   David Fulgham and Robert Wall, "U.S. Stalks Taliban with New Air Scheme," *Aviation Week & Space Technology*, October 15, 2001, 32–35.

43   George Lopez, "The Gulf War: Not So Clean," *Bulletin of Atomic Scientists* 47, 7 (1991), http://ics.leeds.ac.uk/papers/.

44   Kaplan, "Bombs Killing More Civilians Than Expected."

45   Kenneth Hewitt, "Place Annihilation: Area Bombing and the Fate of Urban Places," *Annals of the Association of American Geographers* 73, 2 (1983), 257–84.

46   On this matter of "errors" in U.S. bombing, see Edward S, Herman, "'Tragic Errors' in U.S. Military Policy," *Z Magazine* 15, 9 (2002), 27–32.

47   Quoted in Doug Struck, "Danger Looms in Collecting a War's Explosive Residue: U.S. Bombings Add to Task of Clearing Mines, Ordnance," *Washington Post*, February 3, 2002, www.banminesusa.org/.

48   This theme is pursued in my essay, "The Bombing of Afghanistan as Reflection of 9/11 and Different Valuations of Life," September 11, 2002, www.globalissues.org/. The monetary valuation of life literature is summarized and critiqued in Frank Ackerman and Lisa Heinzerling, "If It Exists, It's Getting Bigger: Revising the Value of a Statistical Life," *G-DAE Working Paper* no. 01–06 (October 2001).

49   John MacLachlan Gray, "The Terrible Downside of 'Working the Dark Side,'" *Globe & Mail* (Toronto), October 31, 2001, R3.

50   Nicholas J. Wheeler, "Protecting Afghan Civilians from the Hell of War," Social Science Research Center Viewpoint Essay no. 9, New York, December 2001, 5–6, www.ssrc.org/sept11/essays/wheeler.htm.

51   Michael Walzer, *Just and Unjust Wars: A Moral Argument with Historical Illustrations* (London: Allen Lane, 1977), 156.

52   Today, officials estimate that as many as 60 per cent of Kabul's buildings are damaged or destroyed, largely a legacy of the 1990s' civil war, though U.S. bombing damaged over a thousand buildings. See Dexter Filkins, "Brick by Brick, Afghans Recycle and Rebuild City," *New York Times*, April 16, 2002.

53   As for example on October 28, 2001, when a U.S. bomb destroyed a Mercedes city bus leaving Kandahar. See "Bus Wreckage Testament to Stray U.S. Attack," *Sunday Times*, October 28, 2001. See also Sayed Salahuddin, "U.S. Bombers Kill Kabul Family, Bus of Refugees," Reuters, October 28, 2001, www.commondreams.org/headlines01/1028-03.htm.

54   Martin Parry, "Mounting Concern over the Human Cost of War in Afghanistan," *Agence France-Presse*, November 16, 2001.

55   Charles J. Hanley, "A Generation of War Leaves Many Afghans with Mental Disorders," *Associated Press*, May 5, 2002, 9:02 p.m. E.T.

56   Juergen Todenhofer, former German Bundestag member, in "We Can't Simply

Bomb a Just World into Shape: It's a Lot Easier to Declare Victory than to Earn It," *Chicago Tribune*, June 30, 2002, www.converge.org.nz/pma/cra0599.htm

57 Craig Nelson, "Dubious Intelligence Leads to Death," *Sydney Morning Herald*, February 23, 2002.

58 These and countless other examples of bombing are described in the masterful volume by Sven Lindqvist, *A History of Bombing* (New York: The New Press, 2000).

59 Joseph B. Abboud, "Ignorance in America Is Alive and Well," *Dawn*, December 23, 2002, www.dawn.com/2002/12/23/int18.htm.

60 See my "Truth about Afghan Civilian Casualties Comes only through American Lenses for the U.S. Corporate Media [Our Modern-day Didymus]," in *Censored 2002: The Year's Top 25 Stories*, ed. Peter Phillips and Project Censored (New York: Seven Seas Publishing, 2002). See also Kurt Nimmo, " 'Yes, We Censored News about Afghanistan': The Lapdog Conversion of CNN," *Counterpunch*, August 23, 2002, www.counterpunch.com/nimmo0823.html.

61 Fairness & Accuracy in Reporting (FAIR), "Action Alert: CNN says Focus on Civilian Casualties Would Be 'Perverse,' " *FAIR Action Alert*, November 1, 2001, www.fair.org.

62 Anthony Lloyd, "Don't Believe All the Major Tells you," *The Times*, May 10, 2002. Lloyd is referring to the inane press briefings held at Bagram air base by U.S. military personnel.

63 Barry Bearak, "Escaping Afghanistan, Children Pay the Price," *New York Times*, October 31, 2001, www.pulitzer.org/archives/6588.

Natalie Zemon Davis

Conclusion

Violence done to non-combatants has accompanied war over the centuries, so these essays have shown, and sometimes has been at its heart. In both wars considered "just" by many of us (the American Civil War, the Second World War) and those "unjust" wars of conquest, unarmed men, women, and children have been starved, maimed, and slaughtered; women raped; dwellings and other essential buildings or equipment burned to the ground or bombed; crops and animals destroyed. The weapons have changed over time, and so have the excuses and boasts. But these historical studies give shape to the violence and demonstrate that it cannot be simply dismissed as inevitable in the chaos of any war or as the fault of the enemy for putting non-combatants in harm's way. Rather the violence occurs in characteristic situations, is primarily the result of human decision or permission, and is justified in order to relieve the guilt of the perpetrators.

Military assault on non-combatants took place regularly in war zones; that is, in the areas where, say, Catholic and Reformed soldiers were at battle during the French Wars of Religion, or where troops were marching from one engagement to the next, as in the Union Army movement in Georgia in the American Civil War and the Soviet army movement through the Ukraine toward the end of the Second World War. In the military encounters examined in this book, it was evident from the beginning that non-combatants would be harmed: besieged cities, as in Louis XIII's siege of Nègrepelisse and other Protestant towns in the 1620s; the carpet-bombed cities of Germany in the last years of the Second World War; the urban neighbourhoods of Afghanistan destroyed in the current war by "precision" bombing.

Violence against non-combatants has also occurred independently of actual military encounters and troop movements: in the pillaging for food and widespread looting by soldiers, accompanied by killing and rape; and in the systematic burning of farm houses and the destruction of agriculture.

Though the essays here characterize some violence connected with combat as "unintentional" or emerging from a "killing frenzy," much of the analysis stresses purposive actions and spells out the military intentions or hopes behind them. Thus, the marauding of the countryside by soldiers in the sixteenth to eighteenth centuries was permitted for food supply and reward, and furthermore to pacify and frighten the rural population. During the American Civil War, as Scott Nelson says, the extensive havoc wrought on southern plantations by the Union Army was intended to cut off supplies for the Confederate Army and to facilitate the escape of slaves. In fact, slaves had been able to escape and join the army on their own, and the main injury of the raids fell on those blacks uprooted from their plantations: "a horde of starving vagabonds, homeless, helpless and pitiable," as W.E.B. Du Bois described them.

The imperial wars of conquest in Africa yield dramatic examples of planned assaults on non-combatants. In their initial invasion of Zululand in 1879, the British were taken aback when the huge army they had assembled was defeated by Zulu warriors. Whereupon, as Jeff Guy tells us, the commander, Lord Chelmsford, decided to apply the full weight of his forces onto the entire Zulu nation with the aim of terrorizing the population and thus forcing a surrender. This meant a war against everyone living and working on the homesteads: the Zulu men who were also soldiers outside of the agricultural season, the women, the young, and the old. Homesteads were burned, herds driven off, some Zulus killed, others driven out to take refuge in the forests or hills. "This strategy weakened African resistance by undermining the social and economic structures on which the military depended," Guy concludes, and any account of the British conquest that confines itself to "armed confrontation between armed men" is off the mark.

Such destructive practices flowered between the two world wars in British efforts to control their colonies and protectorates by bombing rebellious villagers. Now they could burn farms and lands from the air, a rehearsal, according to Sven Lindqvist, for the strategic bombardment of German cities throughout the Second World War. Evaluating the dream to win the war from the air, Lindqvist sees the bombing of German cities in 1940–41 as at least militarily and politically necessary: Britain was standing alone against the Axis and bombing was its only means to attack Germany. From 1942 to 1945, however, choosing strategic bombing over precision bombing – choosing, for instance, to bomb Berlin street by street rather than attacking specific German oil fields – was neither militarily necessary nor moral. To be sure, Germany had to expend resources in defence of its cities against the bombing, but the air attack did not hasten surrender. The Bomber Dream – to target "German cities and their inhabitants as such," as Bomber Harris put it – thus becomes for Lindqvist a military passion, sustained by the production of heavy bombers and fuelled by the desire to teach Germany a lesson, to bomb militarism out of the Germans forever.

If non-combatants are central targets rather than collateral damage in the bombing of cities, Marlene Epp argues that the same is true of the mass raping of women during war. There is still much to discover here on the seizure of women as slaves and booty during war, on the one hand, and raping them, on the other. Are these alternative patterns linked to different sociocultural situations? Rape has a long history, not merely as satisfaction for soldierly appetite but as a weapon of war. (The rape of Catholic nuns by Protestant soldiers during the wars of religion, in special mockery of the vow of celibacy, is a case in point.) The evidence from the twentieth century and our own day suggests that rape is being encouraged as military strategy, to humiliate and harm enemy women and to shame the men who cannot protect them.

Are there certain forms of difference between populations that incite the most limitless and sweeping violence? Some of the horrendous examples of wartime rape given by Epp took place between people of different national or ethnic origins – as in the Japanese rape of Chinese women in Nanjing in 1937 and the rape by Soviet soldiers of ethnically German Mennonites and other German women at the end of the Second World War – but other assaults took place or are taking place between people of common background, as in the mass rapes and mutilation by Bantu men of Bantu women in the current civil war in the Democratic Republic of the Congo. During the Civil War, Americans of European stock were able to shower ever more violence on each other's non-combatants and property (as in the Lawrence massacre by the Missouri bushwhackers and the Union raids on Confederate plantations).

The more fruitful question, then, concerns the procedures soldiers use to intensify or create hateful qualities in non-combatants they attack, the stories they are told and repeat to themselves in order to dehumanize and/or demonize the unarmed victims they injure or kill and whose property they set aflame. (These stories may overlap with, but are not necessarily the same as, the more formal justifications for attacks on non-combatants elaborated by authorities, which we'll consider in a moment.) Brian Sandberg describes the grievances of Languedoc Catholics against the Protestants of Nègrepelisse, which fuelled the fury with which soldiers raped, burned, slaughtered, and destroyed during the siege of that town in 1622. Protestant soldiers in the region had already been disrupting rural trade and agriculture. Then the year before the siege, in the dark of night, the Nègrepelisse townsfolk cut the throats of the Catholic soldiers in the coercive royal troops who were garrisoned in the city, leading to an outcry in Catholic propaganda. Thus the image of Protestants embedded in the 1598 Edict of Nantes – of people permitted to practise a religion different from the king's and the kingdom's and with whom Catholics could coexist so long as the Protestants stayed in their allotted place – was replaced by an image of insupportable heretics and treacherous murderers against whom revenge must be taken.

Likewise, Scott Nelson suggests that the devaluation of the southern countryside by anti-slavery Republicans, who thought that the labour of slaves defaced even the look of farm lands, flowed over into the sentiments and fears of Union soldiers. "This grammar of Southern agricultural failure may have conditioned Union soldiers to consider the Southern landscape as empty and wasted and prepared them for the more regular destruction that would come," says Nelson. The soldiers found the region ugly and frightening, with "bushwhackers" concealed in the strange foliage waiting to spring upon them.

An especially interesting example of military attitudes toward subjected territories and their population are the African soldiers in the service of German officers who stopped at nothing to create a colonial state in East Africa: the Sudanese and Ngoni mercenaries who were part of the 1888 German landing, with its looting, raping, and indiscriminate killing of the Hehe; the Sudanese and Ngoni subsequently recruited to be *askari*, as the regular troops were called, using the Arabic word for soldier; and the *rugaruga*, men in the service of African chiefs and warlords and hired by the Germans for especially destructive missions. From the German point of view, as Michael Pesek explains it, these men would be quite ready to behave with the brutality thought necessary to establish the German state. "African warfare" was limitless in its cruelty, so German officers claimed (and continued to maintain even after one of their administrators showed in an ethnographic study that this was not the case); the Africans believed they were defeated only when villages were destroyed and all property seized. Pesek quotes one of the German officers: "The ruga-ruga are of use, if one likes to destroy whole regions. In that they are top-notch." How the African soldiers legitimated their conduct to themselves is another matter. What seems likely is that their sense of entitlement was reinforced by the leeway given them by the Germans – to loot as they wished, to own slaves even against German formal policy – and by their German uniforms, allowing them to become "an embodiment of colonial rule."

If German colonialists justified their attacks on non-combatants by arguing that this was the only kind of war Africans understood, other authorities discussed in these essays sought legal justification for such violence. In late-sixteenth- and early-seventeenth-century France, the legal and moral standards to which military actions would ideally comply were expressed in books such as the one published by Alberico Gentili in London in 1589, *On the Law of War (De iure belli)*, and that published by Hugo Grotius in Paris in 1625, *On the Law of War and Peace (De iure belli ac pacis)*. In both instances, moderation was urged upon commanders and rulers. "The right of killing enemies in just war [is] to be tempered with moderation and humanity," wrote Grotius; "the innocent" – women, children and the aged – should be "spared ... unless they have committed atrocious acts." Moderation should also be used in regard to "despoiling an enemy's country." Specific cases were considered, such as the law of the siege, in which (as Brian Sandberg tells us) it was allowable to sack a city and kill its inhabitants if they refused to surrender to a besieging army; after surrender they were to be spared. At best this meant that commanders conducted negotiations during a siege and instructed their soldiers to use restraint after surrender.

Nègrepelisse was one of the many towns where such injunctions were ignored. The town refused formal entry to the king's troops, who were preparing the way for the king himself; there were no further negotiations; the soldiers broke through and murdered almost all the inhabitants. Louis XIII fully approved the violence as just and exemplary punishment: "necessary justice to reprimand the insolent temerity of these mutinous rebels." A 1622 pamphlet on the taking of Nègrepelisse did not conceal the "streets ... so full of dead and of blood that it was difficult to walk there" because, as its title proclaimed, it involved "le chastiment des rebelles."

The rightful punishment of rebels has a long history, as we see in two essays that describe the emergence of guerrilla warfare during the American Civil War and the South African (or Second Boer) War. Once the Union Army had moved into the South with its own raids, the Confederate Congress authorized groups of armed men without uniforms to enter occupied territory, raid supply lines, and wreak whatever destruction they could. How to treat these men when they were captured? The definitive answer came in the code drawn up by lawyer Francis Lieber, with revisions by Union general Henry Halleck; in an innovative move by a government, the code was approved by President Lincoln in 1863 as formal instruction for the management of the army when in the field. All persons who are not uniformed regular soldiers and who "commit hostilities" of various kinds, from plunder to destruction and killing, are not, if captured, to be treated as prisoners of war. The same is true of "war rebels," that is, "persons within an occupied territory who rise in arms against the occupying or conquering army." Such men could be executed. Scott Nelson argues that this governmental order legitimized severe punishment for raiding activities by "rebels" and the like, while allowing officers to turn a blind eye to Union raids in which non-combatants and their property were harmed. (At the same time, to be sure, Confederate officers were ordering the execution of captured black Union soldiers in uniform.)

The South African War of 1899–1902 provides an even stronger example of legitimating attacks on non-combatants as part of a move against rebels. By mid-1899, Boer resistance to the British was conducted through guerrilla war, and by that date as well the Lieber Code had provided a major source of guidance for the British *Manual of Military Law*. Chris Madsen shows how British and Canadian troops looted and burned farms, destroyed crops, and finally removed all Boer non-combatants to concentration camps, where many died of illness and malnutrition. All this was represented as legitimate action; indeed, as Madsen reminds us and is famously known from the Morant trial, General Kitchener was a stickler for law and punished soldiers who shot prisoners of war.

Madsen mentions the outcry of Emily Hobhouse and other English critics at the British treatment of civilians during the South African War. Their voices were a needed challenge to the mainstream press. If the anti-war *Morning Leader* sent J.M. Robertson to South Africa to report on the scorched earth policy of the military, the widely read tabloids were celebrating British heroism, culminating for the public in the 1902 *Te deum* victory chorale of Sir Arthur Sullivan. The same imperial celebration was found in the more expensive London illustrated weeklies, examined for us with fine attention by Tom Gretton. In picture after picture from the conquest of the Zulu kingdom, the South African War, and other imperial moves of the late nineteenth century, the outrage that sparked British intervention was portrayed, officers were shown in all their courage and distinction, camp life and nurses in all their decency, retreats – when they happened – with appropriate heroism.

In only a handful of illustrations were attacks depicted on non-combatants and non-military targets: the 1895 destruction of an Ashanti forest shrine and its human skulls is shown as a surgical cleansing of superstition; the 1879 looting and burning of kraals in Zululand appears in the distance behind a battlefield in which the savagery of the Zulu victors several months before is made evident. A single artist, Melton Prior, managed to disrupt this complacency for an instant with a picture of himself setting fire to a Zulu homestead, to which he appended a text: "However needful it may be, the burning of huts and the driving away of cattle to inflict distress on a hostile population cannot be regarded as the most elegant and dignified of military operations in the present age."

With the South African War, some representations emerged of the scorched earth policy, always showing through their captions that the soldiers had been treacherously fired on first under cover of a white flag on the Boers' houses. But even then, as Gretton shows, the pictures contained unsettling elements and concealment was the safest policy: "Refusal to depict was the only effective way of dealing with the problem of how to picture collateral damage."

Concealment also took place, so Sven Lindqvist's essay suggests, with respect to the British strategic bombing during the Second World War. Here the government, the press, and the public seem to have collaborated in misrepresentation. Government spokesmen stated that the targets of bombing were military and industrial. Newspapers and radio commentators announced that cities had been hit, but evidently did not foreground the destruction of civilian lives and neighbourhoods. The public could not have missed the full implications of the bombing policy, one scholar of the media has said, but preferred to console itself with the industrial and military damage done to its enemies. The situation changed as the war ended and journalists' photographs brought the extensive devastation before the public eye.

In addition to the varieties of subterfuge and truth telling found in public representation of violence against non-combatants, these essays give us some insight into the ways in which participants described such events to themselves and to those near to them. Timothy Brook allows us to enter the baffled mind of the young civilian Takada, dispatched by the Japanese army to Danyang and the villages surrounding it in the Yangtze Delta to bring order, pacification, and prosperity to the region in the wake of the horrendous destruction of the Japanese invasion of 1937. Takada arrived there believing in Japan's "benevolent" imperial mission and unprepared for what he would see. His work diary, written for himself and his superiors during his six-month stint in 1938, juxtaposes flat descriptions of towns and villages emptied of inhabitants, houses gutted, and people bayonetted by his own army with accounts of meetings with local leaders willing to collaborate with the Japanese, or at least to see them long enough to get Takada and his entourage of soldiers to depart. Only once does Takada express suspicion of the Chinese: they put on "the outward appearance of friendliness." For those who fled rather than have an encounter with him, he explains their refusal in terms of misunderstanding: they do not realize the good intentions of the Japanese. His final word: "I believe that these three military tours improved the people's attitude toward the Japanese army and achieved really big results."

Brook characterizes Takada's situation aptly as a dilemma – "having to espouse an ideology of deliverance while enacting a reality of oppression" – and wonders to what extent Takada was aware of the contradictions in his position. Though what Takada "really" thought and felt cannot be known to us from these work diaries, they do at least suggest cognitive dissonance; the mind can scarce contain acknowledgment of all the damage one's countrymen have wrought along with the insistence that one has come under the destroyers' auspices to do good. As Brook says, most aggressors coming as deliverers simply deny the violence.

Apart from the sarcastic commentary of the kraal-burning artist Melton Prior, these essays carry little direct expression from on-the-ground perpetrators of violence against non-combatants in the nineteenth and twentieth centuries. The letters of the Union surgeon Dr. Milton Carey, written to his wife from the South in 1862–63, describe violence that he heard about or saw himself without a quiver of regret. From a boat on the Mississippi, Carey comments, "The sun shines with great force so much so that it is uncomfortable to be on the deck of the boat. The evenings are cool and pleasant. Wherever we have stopped the soldiers have burned everything that they could reach for miles around."

His only reservation is expressed in the language of polite and civilized irony:

> We stopped at a plantation belonging to Judge Griffin. . . . He has a very fine house and it was splendidly furnished. . . . The boys gave him a call, and took everything out of the house that they could carry off. He had a splendid library, a fine piano, but the boys acted very indiscreetly and destroyed things that could do no good in the world.

Scott Nelson notes the contrast between Carey's anaesthetized response to cruel and unwarranted violence that he observed and his shame at writing about a dream in which he was violent to his wife: "It is so bad that it would not do to write it out on paper for fear that it might fall into the hands of some one besides yourself." Displacement of concern? Another example of moral indifference? Or perhaps a bit of both?

And, from Marc Herold's essay, what are we to make of the feelings of the American pilot as he reminisced about the confusion he and his fellows were in high above the lands of Afghanistan in 2002:

> We couldn't find the target area. . . . My wingman dropped a bomb to mark a target area, but it wasn't the target area that the GFAC [ground-based person who locates target] wanted. An F-14 came through. We trailed it. He dropped and missed, too.

They finally decided to stop bombing when one of their bombs missed its target and almost hit "friendly lines."

"Can collateral damage speak?" asks Robert Gregg challengingly at the end of his essay. This book has been devoted to making it speak, defining it broadly to include multiple forms of military violence to non-combatants and in some instances giving voice to victims themselves. Smita Tewari Jassal stretches the concept very widely: she discusses the punitive economic policies of the British government toward certain river-faring castes, the Mallah, in the wake of the 1857 uprising in India as a form of damage, and argues further that the enduring British characterization of the Mallah as "criminals" robbed their martyred heroes of their rightful status in the twentieth-century struggles for Indian independence. To counter this cultural robbery, the Mallah have developed their own list of martyrs, days of commemoration, and stories about their courageous defiance.

With Marlene Epp's study of rape of Mennonite women during the Second World War, we are back to the centre of violence against civilians, but getting the victims to speak has been an especially strong challenge. In some instances, as in the rapes in Cambodia in the 1970s and in Bosnia in the 1990s, women put up a wall of silence rather than admitting to the shame of being raped. Shame and horror suffused the Mennonite letters Epp was able to read and the interviews she was able to conduct: "I cannot describe this time to you adequately, it was too terrible." Talking of rape by Soviet soldiers, Mennonite women slipped into the third person – "she" or "they," not "I" or "we" – and sometimes spoke as if death would have been preferable to a lifelong sense of shame. The Mennonite literature about these events also served to muffle the women's voices. The men's humiliation at their inability to protect their women was transmuted into an affirmation of German Mennonite identity and a demonizing of their attackers as "cruel Asiatic people." The suffering of individual women was lost along the way.

Meanwhile, in the current war in Afghanistan, Marc Herold has been preserving the stories of individual Afghan men and women who have had the misfortune to live in a crowded city neighbourhood near a military target and are thus fair game for an American smart bomb. He tells of a refugee woman who left Kabul, whose house was hit by a smart bomb, killing her mother-in-law:

> She is angry at America, and when told that the United States is trying to minimize civilian casualties, she answered with a list of neighborhoods where innocents have been killed. . . .
> "It is easier to understand if it is you being bombed."

The prevalence of violence against non-combatants in so many settings over the centuries makes tragic reading, but these essays should not leave us with a fatalistic sense of the inevitable "horrors," "miseries," and "disasters" of war. Indeed, the great series of etchings by Jacques Callot and Francisco de Goya on these themes had a critical intent and even included pictures of perpetrators being resisted or punished.

At least one hopeful insight can be drawn from these essays: it really makes a difference when reports about the conduct and impact of military actions are full, as honest as possible, and written with some understanding of contemporary international conventions of war and some openness to the possibilities in moral human action. The protests of Emily Hobhouse about concentration camps and the articles and speeches of J.M. Robertson about the scorched earth policy during the South African War made a difference, perhaps only a small difference to the lives of the incarcerated Boers, but a difference nonetheless. They made a large difference in the encouragement of anti-imperialist and anti-militarist movements in England.

Further, we can see the possibility of transformation in the storytelling of participants in violence against non-combatants. If the accounts of observers and soldiers from the nineteenth and twentieth centuries given here are scanty and with little evaluation beyond mild irony, we have heard in our own time American soldiers describing with frankness and regret unacceptable treatment of civilians and explaining how it came about. The initiative of feminists and activists has made it easier for rape victims to tell what happened to them. Wartime rape continues apace, but at least victims can participate in its disclosure.

To be sure, Epp's warning is relevant here. Collective memories that demonize attackers and erase the violence of one's own group direct attention away from the suffering of individual women and perpetuate feuds and national enmities. During the French Wars of Religion in the sixteenth century, every pacification edict opened with a royal command that "the recollection of everything done by one party or the other [in the immediate past] . . . and during all the preceding period of troubles, remain obliterated and forgotten as if no such things had ever happened." If that command is an impossible and unacceptable one to fulfil, still we may hope that the stories we tell will help to change norms for behaviour in many settings.

Contributors

Timothy Brook is Shaw Professor of Chinese at the University of Oxford and the Principal of St. John's College, University of British Columbia. He is the author of seven books on the social history of Ming China, the Japanese occupation of China, and China's place in world history.

Natalie Zemon Davis is Henry Charles Lea Professor of History Emerita at Princeton University and Adjunct Professor of History and Professor of Medieval Studies at the University of Toronto. Her most recent book is *Trickster Travels: A Sixteenth-Century Muslim Between Worlds* (2006). She has received numerous honourary degrees.

Marlene Epp is Associate Professor of History and Peace and Conflict Studies at Conrad Grebel University College, University of Waterloo. She is a specialist in Mennonite history and culture as well as gender, ethnicity, and immigration in Canada. She recently published *Mennonite Women in Canada: A History* (2008).

Robert Gregg is the Dean of Arts and Humanities at the Richard Stockton College of New Jersey. He has written extensively on African-American history, cultural and intellectual history in imperial contexts, and comparative history, most notably in *Inside Out, Outside in: Essays in Comparative History* (2000).

Tom Gretton is a Senior Lecturer in the Department of History of Art at University College London. His research examines the culture of printmaking, particularly "popular prints" in Mexico prior to the 1910 revolution, and the development of weekly illustrated magazines intended for bourgeois readers in nineteenth-century Europe.

Jeff Guy is Professor of History and a Research Fellow at the Killie Campbell Collection of the University of KwaZulu-Natal. He has written several books on the Zulu state and its people's struggles against imperialism, most recently *Remembering the Rebellion: The Zulu Uprising of 1906* (2006).

Rick Halpern is Bissell-Heyd Chair of American Studies and a Professor in the Department of History at the University of Toronto. He is currently the Dean at the University of Toronto Scarborough. He has written extensively about race and labour in a number of national and transnational contexts.

Marc W. Herold is Associate Professor of Economic Development and Women's Studies at the Whittemore School of Business and Economics, University of New Hampshire. His research on political economy and third-world economic development led him to study the sometimes deadly consequences of modern wars for civilians in such countries.

Smita Tewari Jassal was recently Madeleine Haas Russell Visiting Professor in the Department of Anthropology and the South Asian Studies Program at Brandeis University. Her research includes interdisciplinary studies of human rights violations and gender inequalities in Indian society.

Sven Lindqvist has published thirty books in Swedish, eight of which have been translated into English and other languages. He has received many literary prizes, the latest from the Swedish Academy in 2000. He has an honorary doctorate from Uppsala University (1979) and an honorary professorship from the Swedish government (1990).

Chris Madsen is a Professor at the Royal Military College of Canada and the Canadian Forces College in Toronto, where he teaches strategy and history. He is the author of *Military Law and Operations* and *Another Kind of Justice: Canadian Military Law from Confederation to Somalia* (1999).

Scott Reynolds Nelson is the Legum Professor of History at the College of William and Mary. His academic interests focus on nineteenth-century American history, especially the South, the Civil War, and labour. His book *Steel Drivin' Man* (2006), on African-American legend John Henry, won numerous awards.

Michael Pesek teaches in the African Studies program at Humboldt University, Berlin. He has published widely on the politics and culture of German imperialism and colonialism, especially in East Africa, most notably in *Koloniale Herrschaft in Deutsch-Ostafrika: Expeditionen, Militär und Verwaltung seit 1880* (2005).

Stephen J. Rockel is an Associate Professor of History at the University of Toronto. He specializes in eastern and southern African social history and in colonial and post-colonial conflicts in Africa and Asia. His book, *Carriers of Culture: Labor on the Road in Nineteenth-Century East Africa* (2006), was awarded the Joel Gregory Prize.

Brian Sandberg is an Assistant Professor in the Department of History at Northern Illinois University and previously held a Jean Monnet Fellowship at the European University Institute. His forthcoming book is *Warrior Pursuits: Noble Culture and Civil Conflict in Early Modern France*.

Index

Mennonite immigration to 268; military wives 267; National Defence Act 160; North-West Rebellion 155; Quebec 146; Strathcona's Horse 152–53; troops in South African War 145–60, 334
Canadian Criminal Code 160
Canadian Mounted Rifles 159
Cape Colony 153, 227
capitalism, "gentlemanly" 231n1
capitulation 147
caravan trade 172
Carey, Milton 116–19, 336
Carr Center for Human Rights Policy 64, 77n12
Casement, Sir Roger 66, 185, 186, 198–200
Castells, Manuel 52
caste puranas 248, 260–61
castes, Indian 248–61
Catholics vs. Protestants, in French wars of religion 97–108, 331
cattle raiding 32, 43, 131, 133, 136, 139–40, 152
CBU-87 cluster bombs 312–13
Cecil, Robert (Lord Salisbury) 22
censorship 214–15
Central America, war in 115
Central Asia, political situation in 323
Cetshwayo (Cetewayo/Cetywayo) 130, 137, 207 217–18, 232n9
Ceylon 157
Chain caste 252
Chakrabarty, Dipesh 81n62
Chaudhary, Shivprasad 251
Chechaouen, bombing of 323
Chechnya 4, 300, 311
Chelmsford, Lord (Frederic Augustus Thesiger) 31, 130–31, 136–38, 139, 141, 144n12, 330
chevauchées 104
Cheyenne people 26, 27, 47
Cheylus, seigneur de 105
children, war against women and 283–300
China 87n198, 189, 191–92; Anti-Japanese War 46; art and architecture of, 225 225–26; Boxer Rebellion 69; British attacks on 77n4; Ch'ing dynasty 46; claims for justice against Japan

244n4; communism 46, 69; Cultural Revolution 69; delivery of from Western imperialism 234, 241; Guomindang 46, 69; Japanese invasion of 2, 3, 44–47, 68–70, 73, 233–44, 267, 295, 335; Number Two Historical Archives 244n4; Opium Wars 38–40, 69; Taiping Rebellion 46, 69
Chivington, John Milton 26–27, 82n102
Chomsky, Noam 78n24
Christianity 16–17, 18, 197–98, 226
Churchill, Ward 27
Churchill, Winston 38, 286, 288, 291, 293
City of Alton 124n15
civilian casualties: in Afghanistan 303–23; in American Civil War 115–23; in British bombing of Germany 283–300; claims for damages 64–66; cost of empire and 23–47; in French wars of religion 97–108; in German East Africa 161–76; index of 303–4, 316; as inevitable 130; as justifiable 130; as regrettable 130; in South African War 145–60; as unacceptable 130; in Zululand 129–43
civilization 184, 186–88, 196–97, 205, 230; barbarism and 221, 223, 227–28
Clark, Charles 156
Clausewitz, Carl von 166
Clive of India 190
cluster bombs 48, 312–13, 319, 321
Cockburn, Patrick 183–84
Code noir 21–22
Code One 310
Cohen, Stanley 250
Cold War 42, 146
Cole, Joshua 72
Colenso, Harriette 66, 140
collateral damage: "abstract" 304; vs. coaxial 222, 227, 230; as concept 15, 98; criminality and 251–53; early modern 109n5; as euphemism 4, 5–17, 183; history of 1–93; invisibility of 205–31; martyrdom and 254–57; non-military 183–201; progress and 183–201; purpose of term 6
collective amnesia 66, 67, 69, 259
collective identity 260
collective memory 247, 257, 338

colonialism 3, 184–85, 194; civilizing mission of 175; collapse of 2; conquest of in German East Africa 161–76; cultures of 198–200; progressive 185, 193; theatre of cruelty 164–71. *See also* imperialism
colonial state, presence of 161–76
colonial stations, in German East Africa 163–64
colonial warfare, invention of 171–74
Colorado Volunteer Cavalry Regiment 26–27
combatants vs. non-combatants 16, 28, 38, 48, 59, 101, 145, 148, 166, 206
"combat exclusion" 65
communications network 48
Communism 297
"concealment warfare" 4, 54, 77n11
concentration camps: in Second World War 298; in South African War 157–59, 227–28
Condé, prince de 103
Condorcet, Nicolas de 20, 22, 25
Confederate Army (American Civil War) 115–23, 330–31, 333
Congo: Democratic Republic of 266, 267–68, 274, 331; Free State 33, 35, 41, 185, 198, 200
Connelly, Mark: *Reaching for the Stars* 283, 285, 287–88, 290, 293–95, 298
Connor, Patrick Edward 27, 70–71
conquistadores 26
co-prosperity, Sino-Japanese 234, 239
corporate media, American 303, 309, 315, 319, 323
cosmopolitanism 19
Côte-d'Ivoire 35, 51, 55
counter-imperialism 241
counter-insurgency 54, 145
counter-propaganda 43
Counter-Reformation 106
Coventry, bombing of 294–95
Cramer, Joseph 27
crimes against humanity 235, 244, 311
criminality, collateral damage and 251–53, 259, 261
criminalization 115, 121, 123
criminals, in Indian caste narratives 249–51, 254

crops, destruction of 32, 34–35, 38, 55, 57, 98, 100, 131, 147, 153, 156, 159, 329
Crusades 17, 18
Cuba 123
"cult of the weapon system" 80n46
cultural silence 248, 257, 260
cultural stereotypes 261
culture: anarchy and 189–93; "armament" 80n46; of colonialism 198–200; Ethiopian 43; extinction of 223–27, 230; German 68; of imperialism 22, 76; Indian 198; Irish 198; Italian 66; Mennonite 274; of militarism 267; of poverty 202n13
custom, decay of 194–98
Cyrenaica 33, 66

Dahlgren gun 124n11
Dakota Plains wars 115, 123
Damascus, bombing of 323
Danyang city/county (China) 234, 236–37, 239–44, 335; Peace Maintenance Committee (PMC) 236–37; Self-Government Committee (SGC) 237
Danzig 269
Dao, James 310
Daponte, Beth 304
Dar es Salaam 169–70
Darwin, Charles 22, 25–26
Darwinism, Social 25, 45, 197
D-Day 285
Declaration of the Rights of Man 82n84
"decolonization" 3, 44, 47–61, 63, 87n197
dehumanization 331
de Kock, Hendrik Markus 36
de las Casas, Bartolomé 16, 80n57
del Boca, Angelo 66
Deleuze, Gilles 175
Demerara 184
democracy 185
demonization 331
denial 28, 53, 69, 70, 250, 271
Denmark 200
Depelchin, Jacques: *Silences in African History* 63
depersonalization 271
depleted uranium (DU), radioactive 306–8, 319, 321–22
de Rosas, Juan Manuel 26

Fleischer, Kass 70–71
Foner, Eric 116
food supplies, destruction of 34, 42, 54, 57, 100, 103, 131, 147, 156
fortifications 102–3, 112n37
Fort Pillow Massacre 125n38
Foucault, Michel: *From the Light of War towards the Birth of History* 174–75
Fox, Beryl: *The Mills of the Gods: Vietnam* 11–14
France 87n198, 296; bombing by 296, 299, 323; civilian casualties in wars of religion 97–108; colonialism 3, 19, 35–36, 205–31; *Déclaration des droits de l'homme et du citoyen* 21; monarchy 100; war in Algeria 2, 50–51, 66, 67–68; wars of religion 97–108, 329, 338
Franco-Prussian War 147, 166
French West Africa 35–36
"friendly fire" 6, 183, 303–6
Frontier Post, The 311
Fuchs, Eduard 232n12
Fulbright, William 53
Fuller, John Frederick Charles 159
fundamentalism, religious 48

Galbally, Joe 74
Gall, Carlotta 319
Galton, Francis 22–23
Gandhi, Mohandas K. 187, 259
Ganges River 248
Garne, Mohamed 93n305
Garrett, Stephen: *Ethics and Air Power in World War II* 287
gas weapons 292
Gaza 311
Geiger, George 187
gender 17, 132, 135, 139, 140; imbalance 268; migration and 269; militarism and 266, 270; violence and 265–76
gender hierarchy 274
gender roles 273–75
Geneva Convention (1864) 147–49, 166
Geneva Conventions (1949) 3, 18, 48, 49, 50, 147, 184; Additional Protocols of (1977) 3, 48, 54, 145, 291, 300
Geneva Protocol (1925) 42
genocide 25, 70, 81n80; Armenian 42,

88n203; Rwandan 267, 269
Gentili, Alberico 106; *On the Law of War* (*De iure belli*) 332
George, Henry 185–93; *Progress and Poverty* 186–93
German East Africa 33–35, 161–76, 332; civilian casualties in 161–76; District Commissioners (DCOS) 164–65, 170; Maji Maji Rebellion 2, 33, 35, 163, 164, 169; as theatre of cruelty 164–71
German East Africa Company 162
German South West Africa. *See* Namibia
Germany: bombing of civilians in 283–300, 325nn36–37, 329–30; bombing of Guernica by 295; civilian deaths in 68, 283–300; Colonial Department 169; colonialism 33–35, 161–76, 332; Imperial Protection Bill 162; lack of strategic airforce 294; Mennonite refugees and 268–75; murder of Jews and *Untermenschen* by 297–98; occupation of Ukraine 268; Reichsmarineamt 169; Schutztruppe 42; support for Boers 41, 150
Gettysburg, Battle of 118
Ginestous, Charles de 105
Gingingdlovu, battle of 134
Gond caste 256
Gordon, Sir Arthur 194–95
Gordon, Charles 40
Götzen, Graf von 34
Goya, Francisco de 337
Graphic, The 206, 213, 221–22, 227, 230
gravity bombs 314
Graziani, Rodolfo 43, 66
Green, T.H. 193
Greg, William Rathbone 22
Grey, Sir Edward 199
Griffiths, Philip Jones 53
Grimsley, Mark 28, 70, 111n21, 114n68
Grotius, Hugo 290; *On the Law of War and Peace* (*De iure belli ac pacis*) 332–33
Guantanamo Bay 120, 185; British version of 157
Guernica, bombing of 295, 322
guerrilla warfare 4; American Civil War 119–20; South African War 145–60, 333
Guha, Ranajit 37
Gulf War, first 4, 6, 78n22, 90n244,

91n264, 303–4, 306, 310, 314–18. *See also* Iraq; Kuwait
Gulf War syndrome 307
Gurkhas, *209, 210*
Guy, Jeff 31–32
gypsies 297

Hagopian, Patrick 59
Hague Convention/Regulations: (1899/1900) 147–51, 160n2, 166, 168, *211*; draft rules against bombing of civilians (1922–23) 290–91; Fourth Convention (1907) 235, 245n5, 290, 291
Halleck, Henry 120–21, 333
Hamas 77n11
Hamburg (Germany) 284, 293, 294, 297
Hamilton, Andrew J. 125n34
Handcock, Peter 155
handicapped people 297
Haneke, Michael: *Caché* 68
Hanoi-Haiphong, bombing of 317
Hanson, Haldore 47
Hanson, Victor Davis 78n25; *Carnage and Culture* 6–7
Harris, Arthur "Bomber" 283–85, 291, 292–93, 296, 297, 330
Harris, Ruth 271
Harrison, Deborah 266–67
Hawkins, James 56
Hay, David 16–17
Hazrat, Ghulam and Rabia 311
health effects, of bombing 322
Hedges, Chris 65–66
Hegel, G.W.F. 25
Hehe people 163, 171–72, 178n20
Helvétius, Claude 22
Henningham, S. 258–59
Henry, Jamie 74
Herat, bombing of 312
Herbst, Jeffrey 161
Herero people 47, 83n117
heroes, in Indian caste narratives 249–51
Herold, Marc 4, 64
Hilder, Albert 152
high technology 4
Himmelfarb, Gertrude 188
Himmler, Heinrich 159
Hiroshima, bombing of 285, 298–99

Hispanic Americans 52
historical narratives 247–61
Hitler, Adolf 3, 286
HIV/AIDS 272
Hizbullah 4, 77n11
Hobhouse, Emily 41, 158, 334, 337–38
Hobsbawm, Eric 130, 234, 245n8
Hobson, J.A. 187
Holland. *See* Netherlands
Holland, Thomas 160n2
Holocaust 267, 298
Holy Roman Empire 177n11
homesteads, Zulu 131–33, 135, 136, 138–40, 330
homosexuals 297
houses, destruction of 73, 97, 99, 105, 117, 147, 153, 159, 218, 329
Huguenots. *See* Protestants
humanity, crimes against 235, 244, 311
human rights 271, 272
Human Rights Watch 78n22, 304
human sympathy, universalizing 215
humiliation 265, 274
Hundred Years' War 112n45
Hunt, Ira 59
Hussein, Qusay 14–15
Hussein, Saddam 14–15, 304
Hussein, Uday 14–15
Hutu people 267, 275
Hyndman, H.M. 187, 191
hypocrisy 7

ibutho/amabutho 132, 137, 139
iconoclasm 100–101; civilizing 223
identity formation 62
identity politics 259
ikhanda/amakhanda 132, 137
Iliffe, John 34–35, 42
Illustrated London News (ILN) 205, 206, 213, 218–22, 225, 226, 228–31
impact deaths 311
imperialism 3, 21, 22, 23, 25, 32, 37–38, 40, 45, 76, 143; assumptions of 205; British 3, 19, 29–32, 36–42, 49–50, 62, 67, 87n201, 129–43, 146, 190–93, 198–99, 205–31, 247–61, 297, 330, 333–34; in China 233–44; contradiction of 244; depiction of in magazines 205–31; Dutch 3, 36; French 3, 19,

35–36, 205–31; German 33–35, 332; in German East Africa 161–76; in India 247–61; Japanese 233–44; liberal 193; nostalgia of 129; racism and 47; in South Africa 145–60; Spanish 23; Union Army 115; in Zululand 129–43
Imperial South Africa Association 41
impis 218, 232n10
incarceration: American Civil War 122–23; South African War 157–69
"incorporation of America" 187
India 25, 36–38, 150, 187, 189–93, 198, 200, 296; All India Fisheries Act 252; caste groups 248–54, 257; caste-based solidarity 257; caste intelligentsia 249; colonial rule in 247–61; Criminal Tribes Act (1871) 252; Denotified Tribes 252; independence 247, 252, 259; Indian Forest Acts 252; Mineral and Metals Act 252; Most Backward Caste (MBC) status 249; Mutiny (1857) 37, 184, 248, 250, 251, 257, 260; Non-Cooperation Movement 249; Northern India Ferries Act (1874) 252, 253; river-faring castes 248, 252, 257, 336; Scheduled Tribe/Scheduled Caste (ST/SC) status 249, 252
Indian Frontier, *209, 210, 221*
Indian Mutiny 37, 184, 248, 250, 251, 257, 260
Indochina 33, 47, 213, 299, 315
Indonesia 25
industrialization 48, 187
industrial revolution 21
infrastructure, destruction of 320–22
Inquisition, Spanish 16
intercontinental ballistic missiles (ICBMS) 5
International Committee of the Red Cross (ICRC) 20
International Criminal Court 160, 321; Rome Statute (1998) 79n36, 235
international law 48, 50, 66, 160, 290–92, 294, 300, 311, 321
International Military Tribunal, Nuremberg 234–35
International Military Tribunal for the Far East 235, 244; Charter of 235; Count 55 of Charter 235, 245n7
International Red Cross 300

Iraq 185, 296, 306–8; bombing in 284; civilian casualties in 4, 61, 64–66, 78n22; invasion of Kuwait 267; twenty-first-century war in 2, 3, 4, 14–15, 23, 33, 49, 60, 64, 90n244, 115, 120, 142, 145, 176, 183–85, 265, 300, 304. *See also* Gulf War, first
Iraq Body Count 64, 90n260
Iraq Family Health Survey Group 64
Ireland 192, 198–200; potato famine 192, 202n13
Irish Land League 187, 192
Isaac, Jeffrey C. 325n24
Isaacson, Walter 323
Isandlwana battle 31, 32, 129, 130–31, 134, 136, 139, 144n12, *217* 217–18
Isike of Unyanyembe, Chief 167, 172
Israel 4, 77n11; bombing of Gaza 311; occupation of Palestine 66
Italy: colonialism 42–44, 66–67; partisans in 121

Jamaica 184
Jameson, Fredric 62
Janowski, Louis 59
Japan: claims for justice against 244n4; expansion by 3; invasion of China by 2, 3, 44–47, 68–70, 73, 233–44, 267, 295, 335; nuclear attacks on 69, 285, 298–99, 325nn36–37
Japanese Self-Defence Force 233
Java 36
jayhawkers 120
Jehovah's Witnesses 297
Jewish people 267; Eastern European 42; murder of by Germans 297–98
Jim Crow racism 28
Johns Hopkins Bloomberg School of Public Health 64
Johnson, Alexis 315
Johnson, Andrew 125n34
joint direct attack munition (JDAM) 312–13, 315, 318
jus gentium 18
jus in bello 106

kaMpande, Cetshwayo. *See* Cestshwayo
Kant, Immanuel 25
Kaplan, Fred 304, 316, 326n37

Kashmir 217, 221–22
Katha, Satyanarain 260
Keen, William 25
Kenya 4, 70, 299; Emergency in 59–61, 65, 74; Mau Mau revolt in 49–50, 51, 55, 67, 70, 72–75; "Pipeline" 50
Kenyatta, Jomo 70
Kewat, Mahadev 255
Kewat caste 252
Khalilzad, Zalmay 23
Khambula, battle of 134
Khoisan people 33
Kiboroboro 49
Kidd, John 22
Kiernan, Ben 324n4
Kiernan, V.G. 37
Kikuyu people 49–50, 67, 70, 72–73
kinship 149
Kitchener, Horatio Herbert, Lord 41, 146, 150–59, 334
Kol caste 256
Kommandos 227–28
Korean War 2, 10, 24–25, 42, 49, 115, 299–300; No Gun Ri massacre 24
Kosovo, war in 4, 90n244, 300, 304, 312, 314, 325n37
kraals, Zulu 218–22, 230, 334, 335
kriegraison 7–8
Kuwait 267, 304. See also Gulf War, first
KwaZulu-Natal 129, 135

Laconia Affair 79n32
Ladysmith, siege of 215, 227, 230
Lancet, The 61, 64
Landers, James 58
land mines 321
Langalibalele 135
"language of slaughter" 78n23
lansquenets 173
Laos 53, 315–17, 325n36
Lary, Diana 45–46, 68–70, 92n293
las Casas, Bartolomé de. See de las Casas
law: inhumanity and 145–60; international 48, 50, 66, 160, 290–92, 294, 300, 311, 321; of war 145–60, 292
"law of the siege" 106, 333
Lawrence massacre 331
Laxmibai, Maharani 259
Lazarevic, Vladimir 304

League of Nations 44
Lebanon 4, 160
Lees, Lynn Hollen 188
Lefkowitz, David 16
Left Hand 27
legitimate military targets 289
Leopold, King 41, 185
Lesotho 134, 135
Lessard, François-Louis 152
Lewis, Bernard 86n178
liberalism 188, 193, 196
Libya 66
Lieber, Francis 121, 149, 333
Lieber Code 120, 121–22, 148–49, 334
L'Illustration 206
Lincoln, Abraham 115, 125n34, 333; Amnesty Proclamation 122; Emancipation Proclamation 122
Lindqvist, Sven, viii 20, 21, 22–23, 68; A History of Bombing 283
L'Italia in Africa 66
livelihood, criminality, collateral damage and 251–53
livestock, destruction of 31, 42, 100, 103, 147, 152, 156, 159, 218, 321. See also cattle raiding
Lloyd, Anthony 323
Loch, Henry Brougham 40
Lodhi, Avantibai 255
Loeb, Vernon 309–10
logistics 48
London Charter 235
Lonsdale, John 70, 88n202
looting 156, 173, 218, 258–59
"lootpillageandrape" 268
Louis XIII (France) 97, 107, 108, 329, 333
Lübeck (Germany) 284
Lynn, John A. 100

Macaulay, Thomas 190
MacDonald, Callum 44, 47
Machemba, Chief 171
MacKinnon, Catharine 71
MacKinnon, Stephen 46, 68–70, 92n293
Madagascar 213, 299, 323
Madley, Benjamin 70
Mafeking, siege of 227, 230
magazines: depiction of imperialism in 205–31, 334; process of producing

images in 213–15; relationship between text and image in 213–15, 219

Mahabharata 260

Mahathir Mohamad 1–2, 5

Mahsud people 38

Majhi caste 252

Maji Maji Rebellion 2, 33, 35, 163, 164, 169

Makonde people 34

Makua people 34

Malakand Field Force 221–22

Malaya 49, 87n201, 299

Mali 48

Mallah, Bhima and Maiku 250, 260

Mallah caste 248–61, 336–37

Mallah martyrs 255, 337

Malthus, Thomas 188–89, 192–93, 202n13; *An Essay on Population* 188–89

Malthusianism 185–89, 202n13

Manamate, Chief 167

Manassas, Battle of 117, 118

Mandela, Nelson 50

Mannheim, bombing of 295

Manual of Military Law 148–49, 334

Maori people 32

Mao Zedong 69, 145

marginalization 247, 248, 257; economic 248, 252

Mark 83 bombs 312–13

Mark 84 bombs 312–13

martial law 154–55

martyrdom: collateral damage and 254–57; commemorations and days of observance for in India 256, 337

martyrs, in Indian caste narratives 249–51, 254–57, 337

Marx, Karl 174

masculinity 274–75

mass media 62, 308

Massenta, Chief 167

Massu, Jacques Emile 51

Matumbi people 33, 47

Mau Mau revolt 49–50, 51, 55, 67, 70, 72–75

Mauritius 37

Mayer, Chris 79n37

Mazar-e-Sherif (Afghanistan), ix

Mbunga people 34

McAdoo, William 194–95

media management 78n23

medieval jurisprudence 8

memory 62–75, 88n208, 250; collective 247, 257, 338; history and 62

Mendible, Myra 265

Mennonite refugees 268–75, 331, 337

mental disorders 322

mercantilism 185

metropolis vs. empire 20

mfecane 133

Michel, Sir John 136

Middle Ages 16–17, 177n11

militarism: gender and 266; potential for rape and 267

military budgets 48

military casualties, aversion to 60

military discipline 146, 1450, 155

military industrialism 48

"military kraals" 143n6

military necessity 7–8

"military objectives" 290–91

Mirambo (African warlord) 172

misinformation 6–7

missionary uplift 198

Mitchell, Billy 284

Mitterand, François 51

Mkwawa, Chief 168, 178n20

modernization regime, empire as 194–98

Mohamed, Saad 183–84

Monde Illustré, Le 206, 215

"mongrelization" 196

Montauban (France) 99, 105, 108

Montesquieu, Charles de Secondat, Baron de 22, 25

Montmorency, duc de 104–5

Moorhouse, Sean 318

morality 8–9, 16; sexual 197–98; vs. immorality 288

moral prohibitions 289

Morant, Harry 155, 334

Mormons 71

Morning Leader 334

Morocco, bombing of 296

Morozumi Shōichi 242–43

Morris, Madeline 267

Morrison, E.W.B. 153

Moynier, Gustave 20–21

Mozambique 4, 75, 173; RENAMO rebels 75

mujahideen 319

Mukarwego, Athanasie 269
Munda, Birsa 255, 256
Munda caste 256
Muslims 1, 17, 51; vs. Serbs in Bosnia 71
Mussolini, Benito 42
Mwera people 34
My Lai massacre 58–59

Nagasaki, bombing of 285, 298
Namibia 30, 83n117
Nanjing (Nanking), Rape of 44–46, 68, 73, 233, 245n7, 267, 331
Naoroji, Dadabhai 187; *Poverty and Un-British Rule in India* 187; "The Poverty of India" 187
narratives 247–61; structures and traditions of 260–61
Natal, Colony of 130–31, 135
nationalism 4, 21, 187, 198, 200, 249, 258, 267, 275
Native Americans 26–28, 33, 52, 70, 83n107
NATO: airstrikes 23, 300, 304, 312, 317; International Security Assistance Force (ISAF) 23
"natural immunity" 16
Nazism 285, 286, 298
Nègrepelisse (France) 97–98, 102, 105–8, 329, 331, 333
Nehru, Jawaharlal 258
Neillands, Robin: *The Bomber War* 283–92, 294–96, 298
Nelson, Craig 322
Nelson, Tony: "The Battle Hymn of Lieutenant Calley" 89n237
neo-liberalism 86n178
neo-Nazis 298
Netherlands 268; colonialism 3, 36
New Liberalism 186, 193
Newsinger, John 39–40
Newsweek 58, 59, 89n228
New Zealand 32, 40, 193
Ngindo people 33
Ngoni people 34, 162, 173, 332
Nicaragua, bombing of 296
Nightingale, Florence 191, 202n11
Nigmann, Ernst 172
Nîmes (France) 103–4
Nishad, Jawahar Lal 253

Nishad, Samadhan 255
Nishad, Tilakdhari 251
Nishad Jyoti 252, 255, 258
Nishad caste 248–49, 256, 257, 259
nomadic rule 164
Non-Aligned Movement 1, 3
non-combatants. *See* civilian casualties; combatants vs. non-combatants
non-governmental organizations (NGOs) 23–24
Nordstrom, Carolyn 75
Normandy, invasion of 285
North Africa, battles in 296
Northwest frontier 213
"nostalgia for the present" 62
nuclear conflict 4, 5, 15
nuclear weapons 292, 298–99
Nuremberg, International Military Tribunal 234–35, 292
Nyamwezi people 176
Nyungu ya Mawe (African warlord) 172

occupation, code of war and 121–22, 147–48
Odhiambo, E.S. Atieno 70
Official Records of the War of the Rebellion 118
Oliphant, Laurence 39, 76
Operation Speedy Express 58–59
Oppenheim, Lassa: *International Law* 291
Orange Free State (Orange River Colony) 150, 153, 154, 156, 227
Organization of the Islamic Conference 1
Orissa people 37
orphans, war 321
"othering" 44
Ottawa Conference on the Prohibition of the Use, Stockpiling, Production, and Transfer of Anti-Personnel Mines 48
overpopulation 189
Owens, Mackubin 303

pacification 115, 146, 219, 222, 338; Japanese teams 234, 238–43
Pakistan 85n145, 267
Palestine 1, 66, 296
Palumbo, Patrizia 66
Pampas Indians 47, 70
Paraguay, Mennonite immigration to 268

Parsons, L.B. 124n15
Partisan Ranger Act 120
partisans/partisanship 115, 120–22
"partisan war" 102
Pashtun (Pathan) people 38
Patel, Sardar (Vallabhbhai) 252, 262n11
patriotism 198
Peace Maintenance Committees (PMC)
  (Japan) 236–37, 241–42
peacemaking, gender and 266
Peace of God movement 16–17
peasants 111n25
Peires, Jeff 134–35
Perham, Marjorie 62–63
peripatetic rule 164, 177n11
"persistence of restraint" 114n68
Peru 71
Peters, Carl 162
Phelps, John S. 125n34
Philippine-American War 28, 115, 123
Philippines 25
Philips, Julie 71
Philosophic Radicalism 193
pillaging 167, 329. See also raiding warfare
piracy 266
plantation agriculture 115–16
Plymouth, bombing of 295
Pogoro people 34
poison gas 42, 43, 86n168
Poland 269, 298; murder of nationals of
  297
policing 194–95
populism 188
Portal, Charles 288, 293, 296
Portes, marquis de 101
Portsmouth, bombing of 295
Portugal 87n198
Portuguese Africa 42; assimilados 80n61
Portuguese East Africa 171, 173
positional warfare 102–3
positivism 3, 21, 22, 25, 40
postcolonial wars 47–61
postcolonial world 4
poverty 185, 187–90, 193, 259; culture of
  202n13
precision-guided munitions (PGMS)
  303–4, 314, 318
"precision weaponry" 309–10, 316,
  329–30

Preisendörfer, Bruno 177n11
presence, colonial 161–76; redoubling of
  164–71, 177n14
Pretoria (Transvaal) 150
Prior, Melton, 217 218–19, 220, 221 228,
  229 230–31, 334, 335
prisoners of war 147, 150–51, 154–55,
  297
Progressive Age 187, 188
progressivism 185, 193, 196
propaganda 6–7, 17, 43, 50, 107, 275–76,
  293, 298
proportionality rule 9, 16, 149
prostitution 266, 273
Protestants vs. Catholics, in French wars
  of religion 97–108, 331
Prussia 268, 269
puranic writings 248, 260–61
Putumayo 185, 199, 200

Quit India Movement 255, 259

race/racial difference 3, 44, 71–72, 197,
  199
racism 4, 21, 25, 28, 36–37, 47, 50, 52,
  166, 219, 229, 275; scientific 22, 44
raiding warfare: American Civil War
  117–19, 123; French wars of religion
  102–5; Zululand 131
Ranger, Terence 29
rape 70–75, 99, 106, 158, 162, 266–76, 329,
  331, 332, 337–38; as "common act of
  war" 267; as gendered form of wartime
  death 271; as pernicious weapon of war
  273; prostitution and 273
Rasool, Ghulam 322
Raynal, Guillaume 22
reason of war. See kriegraison; military
  necessity
reconstruction of history 248
Record, Jeffrey 59
Red Cross 24, 42–43; International 300;
  International Committee of the 20
refugees, plight of 46
Rejali, Darius 71–72
religion: Chinese 226; French wars of
  97–108, 329, 338
religious fundamentalism 48
remembrance. See memory

republicanism 187, 202n13
Republicans (American Civil War) 116, 332
requisitioning 155–56
resettlement 115
Reynolds, Jefferson D. 53–55, 57, 77n10, 78n22, 79n31, 91n264
Richelmann, Georg 165
Riel, Louis 155
risk-transfer 60–61
Roberts, Frederick Sleigh, Lord 146, 150, 152–56
Robertson, J.M. 334, 338
Rodgers, Daniel T.: *Atlantic Crossings* 186–87
Rogers, Clifford, J. 111n21
Rohan, duc de 101–2, 105
Roosevelt, Theodore 28
Rorke's Drift battle 32, 78n25, 129, 131, 134
Rostock (Germany) 284
Rotterdam, bombing of 294
Rousseau, Jean-Jacques 18–19, 22
Roy, Amrita Lal 187
Rufiji people 33
Rugaro, Battle of 163, 178n20
rugaruga (irregulars) 172–73, 332
rule of law 146
Rumsfeld, Donald 99, 308
Russia 3, 42, 296, 300, 311; murder of nationals of 297; partisans in 121
Rwanda 33, 267, 268, 269, 271, 275; villagization program 123

Sahni, Jubba 250, 255, 258–59
Saint Bartholomew's Day Massacre 98, 109n4
St. Helena 157
St. Petersburg Declaration 147–48, 290
Sala-Molins, Louis 81n62; *Dark Side of the Light* 21–22
Salbi, Zainab 268
Sallah, Michael 56, 59, 89n223
Sampson, Anthony 50
Sand Creek massacre 28, 82n100
Santal people 37–38
Santhal rebellions 256
savagery: African 129; civilization vs. 129
Sappa Creek massacre 82n100

Sbacchi, Alberto 43
Schelling, Thomas 5
Schmidt, Rochus 171
Schmitt, Eric 310
Schönberg, John, *225*
Scotland Yard 185, 194, 198, 199
Sebald, W.G.: *On the Natural History of Destruction* 68
second-degree intentionality 318
Second World War 2, 3, 42, 68, 92n293, 234, 235, 244, 268–75, 283–300, 325nn36–37, 329–31, 334, 337
segregation 5
Seifert, Ruth 274
self-censorship 214–15, 230
Self-Government Committees (SGC) (Japan) 237, 238–42
Senegal: *quatre communes* 80n61
Sepoy regiments 36–37
September 11 attacks 1, 185, 323
Serbia 42, 267, 284, 312, 315–17
sex: "instrumental" 273; as weapon of war 267
sexual violence 70–75, 265–76
Shambook 260
Shanghai: invasion of 233, 235, 236; Pacification Office 236, 241
Sharon, Ariel 159–60
Shaw, George Bernard 202n7
Shaw, Martin: *The New Western Way of War* 60–61, 80n46
Shepley, George F. 125n34
Sheridan, Philip, vii 121
Sherman, William: March to the Sea 117, 156
Shiloh, Battle of 116, 117
Shomali Plain, bombing of 318
Shona people 29
Shoshoni people 27, 70
Sidgwick, Henry 9
siege warfare 106–8
Sierra Leone 266
Sikhs 36
silence 62–75; cultural 248, 257, 260
Singh, Bhagat 259
Singh, K.S. 257
slavery 3, 19, 21–22, 25, 62, 81n78, 115, 118–19, 122, 191, 193, 330, 332
slave uprisings 184

Time 58
Timperley, Harold 46
Tokyo, bombing of 285, 306, 316
Toledo Blade 59, 89n223, 89n238
Tolstoy, Leo 187
Toner, Mike 310
Tonga 194
Tora Bora 322
Trachtenberg, Alan 187
Transvaal 150, 153, 156, 215, *216* 217, 227
Treitschke, Heinrich von 23
Trenchard, Hugh 284
Trevor-Roper, Hugh 63
Tuan, Yi-Fu 116
Tumulty, Joseph 204n53
Turner, Nat 184
Turse, Nicholas 58–59
Tutsi people 267, 275
Twain, Mark 183

Uganda 266
Ugogo (German East Africa) 167
Uhehe (German East Africa) 168, 170, 172
Ujiji (German East Africa) 170
Ukraine 268–69, 273–75, 298, 329; murder of nationals of 297
Ulundi, Battle of 32, 131, 134, 137, 139, 141–42
umuzi/imizi 131
Union Army (American Civil War) 115–23, 329–33; imperialism of 115; partisan interest in 115
United Kingdom 87n198; Army Act 148, 149; attacks on China 77n4; Blitz 284, 294–95; Bomber Command 286, 291, 293–95, 297; bombing of Germany 283–300, 330, 334; colonialism 3, 19, 29–32, 36–42, 49–50, 62, 67, 87n201, 129–43, 146, 190–93, 198–99, 205–31, 297, 330; Intelligence 200; policing 194–95; poor laws 188; Public Record Office 67; Royal Air Force 68; social policy 188; South African War 145–60, 334; War Cabinet 283
United Nations 4, 146; Declaration of Human Rights 50; Development Fund for Women (UNIFEM) 273

United States 48, 87n198, 288, 290–91, 300; Air Force 68; attacks on Japan 285, 298–99; Department of Defense Foreign Claims Commission 64; Irish in 200, 202n13; Japanese attack on 286; military 5, 14, 15, 24, 26, 34, 52, 53, 60, 64–66, 78n23, 176, 267, 303–23; military and state expansion 115; National Public Radio (NPR) 63–64; Native Americans and 26–28; Navy 312; recession 192; war in Afghanistan 303–23; war in Iraq 4, 14–15, 265; war in Vietnam 4, 6, 11–14, 42, 44, 49, 51–60, 66, 74, 75, 115, 123, 146
universalism 19–21, 81n78
Universal Races Congress 199
Untermenschen, murder of by Germans 297
Unyamwezi (German East Africa) 172, 175–76
Unyanyembe (German East Africa) 168
Upadhaya 253
"uplift": missionary 198; social 193, 196
uranium: contamination 307; radioactive depleted (DU) 306–8, 319, 321–22
Urban II, Pope 17
Urundi 164, 169
USAF Intelligence Targeting Guide 6
U.S. News & World Report 58
Usukuma (German East Africa) 168, 172
utilitarianism 188, 193

Valera, Eamon de. *See* de Valera
van Diemen, Antonie 36
Vattel, Emmerich de 20, 81n69, 148–49; *Law of Nations* 148
Vesey, Denmark 184
Viet Cong 53, 56–59
Vietnam: bombing of by France 296; National Liberation Front (NLF) 54–56, 59; newsmagazine reporting of 58; North Vietnam Army (NVA) 56; Rolling Thunder campaign 316–17; South Vietnamese Army (ARVN) 55; "strategic hamlets" 123; war in 4, 6, 11–14, 42, 44, 49, 51–60, 66, 74, 75, 115, 123, 146, 159, 267, 284, 299–300, 316, 325n37
Vietnam: American Holocaust 93n316
villages, destruction of 296

vita vya kwanza (First War) 162
violence 16, 33, 44, 46, 75–76, 98, 100,
   101, 106, 162, 165, 207; domestic 266;
   guerrilla 119–20; history of 63; politics
   by means of 162; sexual 70–75, 265–76
Voltaire 22
von Liebert, Eduard 170
von Prince, Tom 167, 170
von Trotha, Trutz 167

wage labour 37
Wallace, Alfred 22
Walzer, Michael 2, 5, 7–11, 79n44, 319;
   "due care" 319
war: American rules of 120–22; conduct
   of 147–48; laws of 145–60, 292; sociol-
   ogy of 60
war crimes 160, 173, 183, 244, 271,
   290–94, 297–98, 300, 311, 321
warfare, chemical and biological 288, 292
War on Terror 2, 48, 90n244
war rebels 333
Warsaw, bombing of 294
Washington, Booker T. 203n39
Washita massacre 82n100
Wazir people 38
weaponry 48, 129; conventional 77n16;
   used in Afghanistan 313. See also
   bombing
Weiskel, Timothy 35
Weiss, Mitch 56, 59, 89n223
Welch, Richard E. 28
Wells, H.L. 28
Werther, Waldemar 168
Westmoreland, William 56, 58, 159
Wheaton, Henry: Elements of Interna-
   tional Law 121
White Antelope 27
white flags. See flags of truce
"white man's burden" 193
widows, war 321
Wilhelm I, German emperor 162

Williams, Dai 306
Williamson, Murray 78n22
Wilson, Woodrow 200, 204n53
Winter Soldier Investigation 74
Wissmann, Hermann 162, 164, 167
Wolsely, Sir Garnet 141
women: agency of 111n24; in military
   266; sexual violence against 70–75,
   265–76; war against children and
   283–300
Women for Women International 268
Woodville, R. Caton, 209 228, 229
World Health Organization 64, 322
Wright, H.C. Seppings, 224
Wynkoop, Edward 27

xenophobia 226
Xhosa people 134–35
Xuzhou, Battle of 242

Yang Daqing 44
Yangtze Delta 233–34, 237, 244, 245n7
Young, Marilyn B. 24–25, 59–60
yperite gas 43
Yugoslavia (former) 146, 267, 269, 275,
   303–4, 315. See also Bosnia; Bosnia-
   Herzegovina; Serbia

Zanzibar 162
Zarambo people 33
Zimbabwe 29–31
Zululand: British invasion of 31–32,
   129–43, 207, 217 217–21, 220 222, 230,
   330, 334; civilian casualties in 129–43;
   essential features of 131–33; homesteads 131–33; monarchy 132; regiments 132
Zulu people 47, 66, 78n25, 330; as armed
   131–34; military strategy 133; non-
   combatants 129–43